Writing for Multimedia and the Web

Garrand's *Writing for Multimedia and the Web* is the best textbook I've found for examining the theory and practice of multimedia writing. The text is straightforward, and the case studies and tools facilitate student achievement. I've tried several other texts for my Writing for Multimedia course, but I always return to Garrand. His book sets the standard in the field.

—Michael Huntsberger, Ph.D., University of Oregon

Writing for Multimedia and the Web is really working well for a college course I teach titled, "Writing and Interactive Design." I have used the text for more than 5 years and it is the best book overall that I have seen that is a good balance of application and theory.

—Ken Loge, Oregon Research Institute. Applied Computer Simulations Lab

Writing for Multimedia and the Web is a book for rank beginners and experienced professionals alike, for the neophyte student or the traditional media writers who want to expand their skills. Teachers will find it invaluable as a text and scholars will appreciate the way Garrand integrates theory with application. How can he accomplish so much for such a varied audience? With a smart balance of interviews, explanation, and examples. The novice can work his way through from the beginning, where Garrand, patiently supplies a succinct overview of the field, replete with definitions and an easy to understand description of where the media writer fits into this dizzying process. The veteran writer, on the other hand, will enjoy the first hand accounts and insights about approaches and processes from the numerous writers that Garrand interviewed for his book.

Tim Garrand's *Writing for Multimedia and the Web* continues to be the "must have" book for any writer, aspiring or otherwise, student or teacher interested in this burgeoning field.

—Dr. Gregg Bachman, Chair, Department of Communication,
The University of Tampa

Writing for Multimedia and the Web

A Practical Guide to Content Development for Interactive Media

THIRD EDITION

Timothy Garrand

AMSTERDAM • BOSTON • HEIDELBERG • LONDON
NEW YORK • OXFORD • PARIS • SAN DIEGO
SAN FRANCISCO • SINGAPORE • SYDNEY • TOKYO

Focal Press is an imprint of Elsevier

ELSEVIER

Focal
Press

Acquisitions Editor: Amy Jollymore
Project Manager: Dawnmarie Simpson
Assistant Editor: Doug Shultz
Marketing Manager: Christine Degon Veroulis
Cover Design: Cate Barr

Focal Press is an imprint of Elsevier
30 Corporate Drive, Suite 400, Burlington, MA 01803, USA
Linacre House, Jordan Hill, Oxford OX2 8DP, UK

 Recognizing the importance of preserving what has been written, Elsevier prints its books on acid-free paper whenever possible.

Library of Congress Cataloging-in-Publication Data
Garrand, Timothy Paul.
   Writing for multimedia and the Web/Timothy Garrand.– 3rd ed.
        p. cm.
   Includes bibliographical references and index.
   ISBN-13: 978-0-240-80822-2 (pbk. : alk. paper)
   ISBN-10: 0-240-80822-3 (pbk. : alk. paper) 1. Interactive multimedia–Authorship. 2. World Wide Web. I. Title.
   QA76.76.I59G37 2006
   006.7'8–dc22
                                                        2006008399

British Library Cataloguing-in-Publication Data
A catalogue record for this book is available from the British Library.

ISBN 13: 978-0-240-80822-2
ISBN 10: 0-240-80822-3

For information on all Focal Press publications
visit our website at www.books.elsevier.com

09 10 11   10 9 8 7 6 5 4 3

Printed in the United States of America

To Teachers

In addition to being a popular book with professional writers, this book has also been successful in the classroom. One teacher who uses the book wrote:

> *I have used the text in my class for more than 5 years and it is the best book overall that I have seen that is a good balance of application and theory.*

> Ken Loge, Oregon Research Institute

Writing for Multimedia and the Web includes this book and CD-ROM, plus a web site and a Teaching Manual available on request. Please read below for details.

Courses Using This Book

This book has been used for several types of courses including:

- Writing for the web and multimedia
- Interactive design
- Interactive media production courses, as the content component paired with a more technical text
- Interactive media studies, providing a solid overview of many types of interactive media

Teaching Manual

To see sample syllabi, assignments, exercises, and other tips for using the book and CD-ROM in the classroom, instructors can access the free electronic teaching guide that accompanies this book by visiting:

http://textbooks.elsevier.com

Once on the web site, register as an instructor, then request access to the media technology subject area or search by author name or book title.

Instructors may also call (781) 313-4700 and ask for the textbook sales representative for Focal Press. For more general questions, you can call the general customer service number at (800) 545-2522.

Other Resources

See the book's web site, http://www.interwrite.com/book, for additional information and updates.

There are also complete case studies on the CD-ROM that are not in the book as well as extensive additional material supporting the book chapters.

If you have any questions or suggestions, please feel free to contact the author at tpg@interwrite.com.

To Users of the 2nd Edition Book

Some of the older but still valid case study chapters have been removed from the book and placed on the book's attached CD-ROM. Look at the CD-ROM's Chapters menu in the Case Studies: CD-ROM Only section. If you have a favorite older case study, you can still use it in your classes by having the students view it or print it out from the CD-ROM.

Writing for Multimedia and the Web
The Book at a Glance

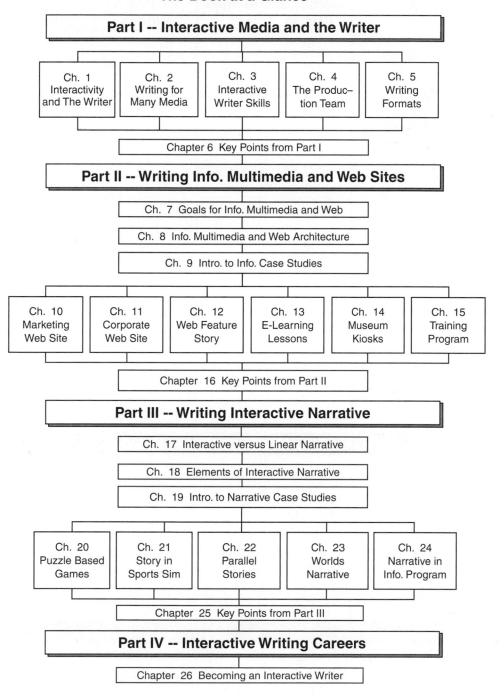

Part I -- Interactive Media and the Writer

Ch. 1 Interactivity and The Writer	Ch. 2 Writing for Many Media	Ch. 3 Interactive Writer Skills	Ch. 4 The Produc-tion Team	Ch. 5 Writing Formats

Chapter 6 Key Points from Part I

Part II -- Writing Info. Multimedia and Web Sites

Ch. 7 Goals for Info. Multimedia and Web

Ch. 8 Info. Multimedia and Web Architecture

Ch. 9 Intro. to Info. Case Studies

Ch. 10 Marketing Web Site	Ch. 11 Corporate Web Site	Ch. 12 Web Feature Story	Ch. 13 E-Learning Lessons	Ch. 14 Museum Kiosks	Ch. 15 Training Program

Chapter 16 Key Points from Part II

Part III -- Writing Interactive Narrative

Ch. 17 Interactive versus Linear Narrative

Ch. 18 Elements of Interactive Narrative

Ch. 19 Intro. to Narrative Case Studies

Ch. 20 Puzzle Based Games	Ch. 21 Story in Sports Sim	Ch. 22 Parallel Stories	Ch. 23 Worlds Narrative	Ch. 24 Narrative in Info. Program

Chapter 25 Key Points from Part III

Part IV -- Interactive Writing Careers

Chapter 26 Becoming an Interactive Writer

Writing for Multimedia and the Web
The CD-ROM at a Glance

Case Study Material Supporting Book Chapters				
Genre and Title	**Scripts & Charts**	**Images**	**Demos & Videos**	**WWW Links ***
Web Site *Prudential Verani Realty*	√	√		√
Web Site *T. Rowe Price Web Site*		√		√
Web Feature Story *The Harlem Renaissance*	√	√		√
Museum Kiosk Simulation *The Nauticus Shipbuilding Co.*		√		√
Multimedia Training *Vital Signs*	√	√		√
E-Learning Lessons *Interactive Math & Statistics*	√	√		√
Puzzle Based Mystery Game *Nancy Drew*	√	√	√	√
Story in a Sports Sim *Amped III*	√	√		√
Parallel Stories Narrative *The Pandora Directive*	√	√		√
Worlds Narrative *Dust*	√	√	√	√
The Immersive Experience *New England Econ. Adventure*	√	√		√
Worlds Narrative *Titanic*		√		√
Case Study on CD-ROM Plus Chapters from Previous Books				
Online Advertising *ZDU & Personal View*		√	√	√
Educational Multimedia *Sky High*	Included in Chapter			√
Multiplayer Narrative *Boy Scout Patrol Theater*	√	√		√
Puzzle-Based Game *The 11th Hour*	√	√	√	√
Cinematic Narrative *Voyeur*	√	√		√

Background	Reference
Playback/Delivery Systems	Glossaries of Media Terms
Production Systems and Software	Writers & Production Companies
Accessible Multimedia & Web Pages	Info. for the Teacher & Student
Multimedia & Web Legal Primer	Links To Writing Related Software

* Links to sites on the World Wide Web can be accessed if the reader has an Internet connection.

Book Contents

Interactive Media and the Writer

PART I

1

Interactivity and the Writer

3

2 Writing for Many Media   23

3 High-Level Design, Management, and Technical Skills Useful to the Interactive Writer   43

4 The Multimedia and Web Site Production Team 57

5 Script and Proposal Formatting 63

6 Key Points from Part I: Interactive Media and the Writer 85

Writing Informational Multimedia and Web Sites
PART II

7 Defining and Achieving Goals for Informational Multimedia and Web Sites 91

8 Informational Multimedia and Web Architecture   109

9 Introduction to the Informational Multimedia and Web Site Case Studies   125

Writing Interactive Narrative

PART III

18 The Elements of Interactive Multimedia Narrative   281

19 Introduction to the Narrative Multimedia Case Studies   299

Interactive Writing Careers

PART IV

26 Conclusion: Becoming a Professional Interactive Writer

CD-ROM Contents

How to: The Author's Tips on Getting the Most from This CD-ROM

- How to use this CD-ROM
- Highlights of the CD-ROM
- Link to the *Writing for Multimedia and the Web* web site
- How to contact the author

Chapters: Script Samples, Screen Shots, Game Demos, Articles, and Videos Arranged by Chapter

Chapter 10 Case Study—Writing a Marketing Web site from Proposal to Documentation: Prudential Verani Realty

- Color screen shots of web pages
- Complete interactive outline
- Complete production sitemap

Chapter 11 Case Study—Corporate Web Site: T. Rowe Price

- Types of web sites defined with screen shots and links
- Color screen shots from current site
- Dynamic flow of information and navigation from 2nd Generation web site:

  - The Watch List
  - The Interactive Tutorial—Online Investment Strategy Planner
  - Commission Calculator
  - 2-click navigation

- Comparing home pages of 3 site versions

Chapter 12 Case Study—Research Portal Web Site and the Online Feature Story: Britannica.Com and the Harlem Renaissance

- Color screen shots from the web site
- Production sitemap

Chapter 13 Case Study—E-Learning: *Interactive Math and Statistics Lessons*

- Color screen shots
- Complete Math Script
- Complete Statistics Script

Chapter 14 Case Study—Museum Kiosk: *The Nauticus Shipbuilding Company*

- Color screen shots
- The overhead plan for the 3-D shipyard
- Links to museums that use multimedia

Chapter 15 Case Study—Training: *Vital Signs*

- Script samples
- Color screen shots

Chapter 20 Case Study—Adapting Classic Books to a Computer Game for the Female Audience: *Nancy Drew: The Secret of the Old Clock*

- Excerpt of Production Flowchart and Chart Legend
- Character Screen Shots
- Game Play Screen Shots
- Video Introduction

Chapter 21 Case Study—Adding Story to a Simulation: *Amped 3*

- Color Screen Shots
- Story Development Documents
- Script: Introduction and Act I

Chapter 22 Case Study—Parallel Stories Narrative: *The Pandora Directive*

- *The Pandora Directive*
  - The complete walkthrough
  - The complete list of the character Louie Lamintz's responses
  - Attitudes, dialogue, and Ask Abouts
  - Color screen shots illustrating the walkthrough and the Louie Lamintz material
  - Dialogue flowcharts
- *Under A Killing Moon* (the prequel to *The Pandora Directive*)
  - Response attitudes and Ask Abouts
  - Dialogue flowcharts
  - Screen shots
  - Bio of writer and description of developer with links to their web page

Chapter 23 Case Study—Worlds Narrative: *Dust: A Tale of the Wired West*

- *Dust: A Tale of the Wired West*
  - The complete dialogue transcripts for one of *Dust*'s characters, Marie Macintosh
  - The storytelling techniques used in *Dust* illustrated with screen shots
  - Screen shots
  - A working demo
- *Titanic: Adventure Out of Time* (the next program by the writer of *Dust*)
  - Screen shots

Chapter 24 Case Study—Immersive Exhibit: *The New England Economic Adventure*

- Screen Shots
- Treatment

- Script Treatment
- Script

Chapter 26 Conclusion: Becoming a Successful Interactive Writer

Links to schools, professional associations, job web sites, interactive media recruiters, and other resources for getting writing work and marketing your own ideas.

Case Studies: CD-ROM Only (Chapters from earlier book editions)

Online Advertising Case Studies: ZDU and Personal View Campaigns (Ch. 13 2nd edition)

- Complete 2nd edition chapter
- Working animations and color screen shots of the ZDU campaign
- An article entitled "Persuasion Theory and Online Advertising"
- Links related to online advertising
- ZD Net Personal View (case study from first edition of book)
- Color images of all drafts of the banner advertisement and the middle page for the Personal View campaign

Educational Multimedia Case Study: *Sky High* (Ch. 15 2nd edition)

- Complete 2nd edition chapter
- Links to educational web sites
- Bios of writers and description of developer

Multiplayer Narrative Case Study: *Boy Scout Patrol Theater* (Ch. 14 1st edition)

- Complete 1st edition chapter
- The complete script of *Boy Scout Patrol Theater*
- Color screen shots illustrating the script
- Links to other multiplayer games and experiences
- Bio of writer and description of developer

Puzzle-Based Game Case Study: *The 11th Hour: The Sequel to the 7th Guest* (Ch. 21 2nd edition)

- Complete 2nd edition chapter
- *The 11th Hour: The Sequel to The 7th Guest*

  o Script samples

- ○ Color screen shots illustrating the script
- ○ The documentary video *The Making of The 11th Hour*, which includes scenes from the game and interviews with the creators

- *The 7th Guest*

  - ○ Script Samples
  - ○ Color screen shots illustrating the script

Cinematic Narrative Case Study: *Voyeur* (Ch. 22 2nd edition)

- Complete 2nd edition chapter
- Script Samples
- Color screen shots illustrating the script
- Other issues illustrated with screen shots

Background: Articles on Multimedia and Web Production and Playback, Access, and Media Law

- Introduction to Interactive Media (Multimedia and the Web)
- Playback/Delivery Systems
- Production Systems and Software Writing
- Accessible Multimedia and Web Sites
- Interactive Media Legal Primer

References: References, Bios. of Writers, a Glossary of Multimedia Terms, and Information on Multimedia Education

- Searchable Glossaries of Multimedia Terms
- Bios of Multimedia Writers and Descriptions of Production Companies
- References
- Information for the Teacher and the Student

Software

Links to software useful to the interactive writer including software for scriptwriting, flowcharting, and WYSIWYG web site editors

N.B. All sections of the CD-ROM will include links to pertinent sites on the World Wide Web that can be accessed if the reader has an Internet connection.

Acknowledgments

I'd first like to thank the editors and staff at Focal Press for their help and support writing and producing this book and CD-ROM, especially my editor Amy Jollymore and assistant editors Cara Anderson and Rachel Epstein.

This book could not have been written without the generous donation of script samples and images by the copyright holders and production companies. Many thanks to The Federal Reserve Bank of Boston, Her Interactive, InterWrite, Jeff Kennedy Associates, CyberFlix Inc., Indie Built, Trilobyte Inc., Chedd-Angier Production Company, T. Rowe Price Associates, Access Software Inc., National Scouting Museum of the Boy Scouts of America, Ziff-Davis, Houghton Mifflin Company, Harvard Pilgrim Health Care, Encyclopaedia Britannica, Philips Media, and Prudential Verani Realty.

Equally crucial was the time generously donated by the many writers and designers interviewed for this project. In the informational programs they include Shawn Hackshaw, Andrew Nelson, Kevin Oakes, Deborah Astudillo, Maria O'Meara, Steve Barney, John Cosner, Fred Bauer, Matt Lindley, John Hargrave, Peter Meyerhoff, Tom Michael, Emmett Higdon, and Peter Adams. The storytellers are Anne Collins-Ludwick, Madeleine Butler, Jane Jensen, Shannon Gilligan, Tony Sherman, Matt Costello, Dave Riordan, Lena Marie Pousette, Aaron Conners, and Andrew Nelson. A full list of all who contributed may be found in the Appendix at the back of the book.

I also want to thank the readers of the first draft: Annette Barbier, Glorianna Davenport, and Maria O'Meara. I owe a special debt to writer Maria O'Meara, who not only critiqued the first edition manuscript but also contributed interviews and material for case studies for several editions of this book.

Introduction

Third edition! I guess I must be doing something right in these pages. I have been gratified by e-mails and testimonials from writers and interactive media developers from all over the world, including Brazil, Finland, Malaysia, and the United States, who have written and told me how helpful my book was to them.

This new edition continues the same approach that has been useful to my readers in the past but adds four new case studies; new sections, such as writing for blogs and usability tips for writers; a glossary; and updates throughout.

This is the only current book that takes on developing content for the full range of interactive media, including computer games, training programs, web sites, museums exhibits, and e-learning courses. Having a broad understanding of all types of interactive content is essential for success as a writer of interactive media. You may think you just want to write web sites or computer games or educational programs, but there is such a blending of the different content types that you really have to know it all. Informational web sites can include games and instructional programs. Educational media is all over the web with online courses and other e-learning programs. The gaming business has an even greater online presence both for the games themselves and for marketing and promotion. Writers radically increase their value by learning to write for all types of interactive media. This book addresses that need. It is a book on writing for multimedia and the web—and much more.

To be effective, an interactive writer has to be more than just a great wordsmith. The interactive writer must also understand the architecture, tools, and capabilities of interactive multimedia. This book provides a detailed explanation of the process of conceptualizing multimedia and web sites that both the newcomer and media industry professional will find valuable.

Part I, "Interactive Media and the Writer," examines the particular demands that multimedia and the web make on the writer, including interactivity, writing for many media, organizational tools, and script formatting.

Part II, "Writing Informational Multimedia and Web Sites," and Part III, "Writing Interactive Narrative," are devoted to in-depth case studies of a wide variety of projects, ranging from web sites, to training, to games. Some of the top writers and designers for multimedia and the web reveal their secrets for creating powerful programs. Their ideas are documented with extensive script samples, flowcharts, and other writing material.

Part IV, "Interactive Writing Careers," outlines the challenges the interactive writer faces and provides tips for developing an interactive writing career and for marketing your own projects.

The Glossary at the back of the book provides clear definitions of terms for readers who are new to interactive media.

The attached CD-ROM includes script samples, screen shots, program demos, multimedia production information, links to software, a video on the creation of a multimedia program and other supplementary material.

Read this book and CD-ROM interactively; choose what is valuable to you. If you are a NEWCOMER, start at the beginning of the book and browse through the background material on the CD-ROM.

If you are an experienced INTERACTIVE MEDIA PROFESSIONAL, focus on the later chapters and the case studies to see how some of the top multimedia and web professionals work their magic.

If you are or want to become a WEB WRITER or DESIGNER, you will benefit from the chapters about web sites and from the multimedia case studies as well, because many of the multimedia techniques discussed are now regularly used on the web or soon will be.

If you are a GAMER, read Part III to learn how current and classic games were created.

If you are a MEDIA SCHOLAR, study the entire book for a solid grounding in the principles and practices of interactive media.

If you are a JOB SEEKER, check out Part IV, "Interactive Writing Careers," for suggestions on how to develop an interactive media writing career and to market your own writing projects.

So turn the page or pop in the *Writing for Multimedia and the Web* CD-ROM, browse the contents, and choose the material that suits your needs.

Tim Garrand
tpg@interwrite.com

Interactive Media and the Writer

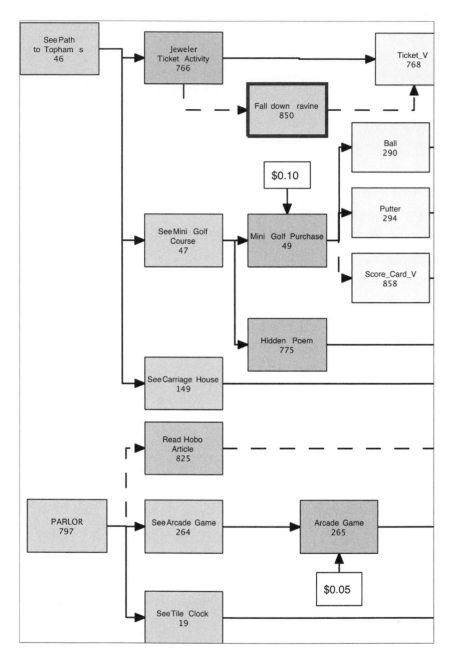

Figure I-1 *A portion of the writer's flowchart for Nancy Drew: Secret of the Old Clock computer game. Copyright Her Interactive, Inc.*

Interactivity and the Writer

Chapter Overview

This chapter defines important terms and explains the key concepts relating to interactivity, including:

- Interactivity versus control
- Thinking interactively
- Linking
- High-level design
- Interactive devices

Write It All!

Writing for multimedia and the web may be the most challenging work you will ever do.

- Writing great prose text is not enough!
- Creating engaging video scripts is not enough!
- Writing audio like a radio pro is not enough!
- Making characters come alive with snappy dialogue is not enough!

As a writer for interactive media, you have to do all these things and more.

To be truly effective in this field, you will have to do more than write great text. The most exciting programs today go beyond click-and-read. This includes the latest generation of web sites, as well as computer games, educational programs and other cutting edge interactive media.

To develop powerful interactive content, you will need to understand how to tame the complex structure of interactive media and write for video, audio, animation, and online applications. And, most of all, you will have to understand intimately each program's users and the impact of their interactions on your content.

Based on my experiences on nearly one hundred projects and on interviews with dozens of top experts in the interactive media field, I will describe how to master these skills and give examples from detailed case studies of successful programs. The case studies include professional interactive scripts, charts, and other documents that can serve as models for your own interactive writing assignments.

Defining Interactive Multimedia and the Interactive Writer

Defining a Few Terms

Why "Multimedia and the Web" in the title of this book? I know the word police will complain that this doesn't make sense, because multimedia is actually a common type of content on the web. The words "multimedia" and "web" are not mutually exclusive, I know. I agree, but many users still think of the web as a place of mainly static pictures and text, while multimedia is the more interactive and media rich world of computer games, edutainment programs, and the like. I wanted to make it clear that this book is addressing the broad spectrum of interactive media content development.

Before we go forward, I should define how we will use the terms "multimedia" and "interactive media" in this book.

Defining Multimedia

As used in this book, "multimedia" and "interactive multimedia" are defined by four basic characteristics:

- **Combination of many media into a single piece of work.**
  Combining several media or modes of expression into a single integrated program or piece of work is one aspect of multimedia. Video, text, audio, and still pictures are all examples of different media or modes of expression.
- **Computer mediated.**
  In multimedia, a computer is used to mediate or make possible the interaction between the users and the material or media being manipulated. "Computer" is used here in the broadest sense, including computers in cell phones, game consoles, and other devices, as well as traditional PCs. No computer involved = no multimedia. A book with pictures is not multimedia.
- **Media-Altering Interactivity.**
  User interactivity in multimedia is best defined as "the ability of the user to alter media he or she comes in contact with . . . Interactivity is an extension of our instinct to communicate, and to shape our environment through communication" (Jordan). Blowing up an alien in a computer game is altering the media. Customizing your broker's web page so that it presents only the financial information you want is altering the media, as is visually creating

your dream car on an automaker's site. Shopping on television does not qualify as interactivity under this definition.

- **Linking.**
  Linking allows links or connections to be made between different media elements. This can be the menu links connecting different sections of a web page, or the narrative links in a computer game that are triggered by the actions you choose for the character.

To sum it up, multimedia is a combination of many media into a single work where media-altering interactivity and linking are made possible to the user via the computer. This definition includes all the disc- and cartridge-based (CD, DVD, Xbox, etc.) programs and most of the web sites in this book.

Defining Interactive Media

"Interactive media" has traditionally been a much broader term than "multimedia." "Interactive media" is used to describe all media with interactivity. It usually refers to computer-delivered interactive media, including both multimedia programs and nonmultimedia interactive programs, such as click-and-read web sites that have limited interactivity and no animations, video, or sound. This is how the term interactive media will be used in this book.

In short, interactive media is computer-delivered media or modes of expression (text, graphics, video, etc.) that allows users to have some control over the manner and/or order of the media presentation.

"Multimedia" and "Interactive Media" in This Book

Based on the above definitions, I will generally use the terms "multimedia" or "interactive multimedia" in this book to indicate my major focus is on computer games, E-learning, training programs, web sites, and other projects that use a combination of computer mediated rich media, complex interactivity, and linking. I will use "interactive media" to refer to all types of computer-delivered media with interactivity, including multimedia, such as computer games, AND simpler interactive media, such as pictures-and-text web sites.

Types of Interactive Multimedia

The web is a growing platform for multimedia. Material is presented on sites through multiple media, including pictures, text, video, audio, and animation. The user controls the flow of information and/or performs complex tasks. Examples of Internet rich media applications include interactive animated presentations explaining a product; financial calculators with opportunities to input data and see visual presentation in charts and graphs; product searches with text, audio, and visual elements that allow the user to see how their search terms affect product choices; E-learning courses with exercises, examples, and student-teacher interactions; and online games of all types.

In addition to the World Wide Web, multimedia is presented on local networks, such as corporate intranets; computer hard drives, such as museum kiosks; interactive television, such as MSN TV; dedicated gaming systems, such as PlayStation and Xbox; mobile devices, such as PSPs (Play Station Portables), iPods, and phones; and discs, such as CD-ROMs and DVDs. Interactive multimedia has dozens of uses, with the most common being marketing, sales, product information, entertainment, education, training, and reference material. (See the Glossary at the back of the book for definitions of unfamiliar terms.)

 If you are completely new to multimedia and the web, and feel you need additional basic information on these subjects, you may want to review the Background section of this book's attached CD-ROM.

The Role of the Interactive Writer

The interactive writer may create:

- proposals,
- outlines,
- sitemaps,
- treatments,
- walkthroughs,
- design documents,
- scripts, and
- all the other written material that describes a multimedia or web site project.

This can include developing the information architecture, on-screen text, overall story structure, dialogue, characters, narration, interface, and more. The key difference between writing for linear media, such as television and movies, and writing for interactive media is interactivity, which allows the user of the program to have control over the flow of the information or story material.

Interactivity Versus Control

Potential Interactivity

Interactivity means that the user can control the presentation of information or story material on the computer. The potential interactivity of multimedia is awesome. It is possible to interact not merely by screen or page, but by controlling the presentation of individual objects within a screen, such as a single character's actions in a scene, the color of a part of an image, or the presentation of a line of text.

Limits to Interactivity

There are practical limits to the potential of a particular user's interactivity. The viewer's equipment has to be powerful enough to support the level of interactivity. And even if the viewer has the best system in the world, if the source material is a

CD-ROM, a DVD, or some other closed system, the player is working with a finite number of options. He or she can access only what the makers place on the disc. This limitation disappears when multimedia is delivered online, through the World Wide Web or an online service, which allow users to link instantly to thousands or perhaps millions of other sources throughout the world. However, for web surfers who still use a modem, the slow download speed can make the online multimedia experience sometimes frustrating.

 See the "Playback/Delivery Systems" article in the Background section of this book's CD-ROM for a detailed discussion of this issue.

Is unlimited interactivity the most effective way to communicate with multimedia, if technically possible for the user? It depends to a great degree on what your goals are. If, for example, you are trying to tell a story, such as the interactive narrative *Voyeur*, the degree of interactivity you can allow and still create believable characters, intriguing plot, and suspense will be far less than if you are simply creating a world for viewers to inhabit, such as *SimCity 3000*. Similarly, a web site with the focused goal of getting you to buy a car will have far less interactive options than an online encyclopedia that wants you to explore its information. *Voyeur* designer David Riordan echoes the feeling of many multimedia developers when he says that: "Infinite choice equals a database. Just because you can make a choice doesn't mean it's an interesting one." He says that the creators of multimedia must maintain some control for the experience to be effective.

Thinking Interactively

Thinking of All the Possibilities

The stumbling block for most new interactive writers is not limiting interactivity and maintaining control over the multimedia experience. Most new writers have the opposite problem of overly restricting interactivity and failing to give users adequate control over the flow of information or story material. This is because limiting options is what most linear writers have been trained to do. In a linear video, film, or book, it is essential to find just the right shot, scene, or sentence to express your meaning.

In writing for interactive media, "the hardest challenge for the writer is the interactivity—having a feel for all the options in a scene or story," says Jane Jensen, writer-designer of the *Gabriel Knight* series. Tony Sherman, writer-designer of *Dracula Unleashed* and *Club Dead* agrees. Unlike a linear piece in which it is crucial to pare away nonessentials, in interactive media, the writer must "think of all the possibilities."

Viewer Input

It is difficult to predict how the viewer will interact with all the possibilities in a piece. Jane Jensen warns that this can sometimes make multimedia "a frustrating and difficult medium . . . You have this great scene, but you have to write five times that much around it . . . to provide options. When your focus is on telling the story, that can feel like busy work and a waste of time."

For example, you have a telephone in one scene that your player must dial to call his or her uncle and find out who the murderer is. This is near the end of the game and getting the telephone number itself has been one of the game's goals. The writer needs to anticipate all the things players might try to do with that telephone. What if players get the telephone number from having played the game earlier, and they then jump ahead to the telephone scene? What should happen when they dial? Should they get a busy signal? What if they dial the number after they have gotten it legally in the game, but they don't have all the information they need, such as knowing that the one who answers is their uncle? Should the writer give them different information in the message? What if they dial the operator? What if they try dialing random numbers?

This can be equally complex in an informational multimedia piece where you must anticipate the related information that the viewers will want to access and all the different ways they may want to relate to the key information. *Compton's Interactive Encyclopedia*, for example, allows users to explore a particular piece of information through text, pictures, audio, videos, maps, definitions, a time line, and a topic tree. The design of the program allows all of these different approaches to be linked together if the viewer desires. This means that students studying Richard Nixon can mouse-click their way from an article about Nixon to his picture, to an audio of his "I Am Not a Crook" speech, to a video about Watergate and Nixon's resignation, and finally to a time line showing other events that happened during his presidency.

Knowing the User

A key way to anticipate users' input is to know as much about them as possible. This is also important in linear media, but it is even more crucial in interactive multimedia, because the interactive relationship is more intimate than the more passive linear one. Knowing the audience is absolutely essential. Knowing what the user considers appealing and/or what information they need will affect every element of a production, from types of links to interactive design.

On most multimedia and web projects, considerable effort is put into researching the user. Some sources for user information include customer support lines, customer surveys and interviews, bulletin boards, salespeople, user groups, trade shows, and bulletin boards. This information is usually put together into a document called a User Scenario or a Use Case. A Use Case first describes the user and his/her information and entertainment needs. Then the user's most common paths through the program to get information or complete a task are charted. This helps the designers understand how they need to present the content to meet the user's needs. Before a major project is released to the general public, it is tested with small groups of users in usability studies. The feedback from these studies allows the developers to refine their information design.

Linking

Links are the connections from one section of an interactive media program to another section of the same program or, if online, to a totally different program. When the information for a program or site is stored in a database, then the linked material can be even smaller or more granular. It is possible to link users' actions to single program elements, sentences, or even words. The simplest link is a text menu choice that the user clicks to bring up new information. When writers develop links, they must make a number of decisions:

- What information, program elements, pages, chapters, or scenes will connect with other sections of the program?
- How many choices will the user have?
- Which choices will be presented first?
- What will be the result of those choices?
- Will the links be direct, indirect, or delayed?

Immediate or Direct Links: An Action
In an immediate or direct link, the viewer makes a choice, and that choice produces a direct and immediate response that the viewer expects. For example, in the detail in Figure 1-1 from the T. Rowe Price investment company's web site, when the user clicks on the "Rolling Over Your 401(k)" link in the menu, they expect to and will get a page of information about 401(k)s.

Indirect Links: A Reaction
Indirect links, also called "if-then" links, are more complex. Users do not directly choose an item, as in the example above. Instead, they take a certain action that elicits a reaction they did not specifically select. The following example is taken from the walkthrough for the computer game *The Pandora Directive*. The walkthrough describes the program's story and the main interactive options for the user. At this point in the story, you, the user, are trying to escape with the woman Regan, but you have been cornered by the villains Fitzpatrick and Cross.

EXCERPT FROM THE PANDORA DIRECTIVE WALKTHROUGH

```
You get the choice of shooting Fitzpatrick, shooting Cross, or
dropping the gun. If you try to shoot Fitzpatrick, you get trapped
alongside Regan and Cross; then everybody dies, safely away from
Earth. If you try to shoot Cross, he kills you before you ever get
into the ship. If you drop the gun, you get to the spaceship.
```

How We Can Help

Personal Guides

Use these Guides to help you
select the right solutions for
your investment needs

> **Investing in T. Rowe Price
Funds**
Evaluate and choose the right
funds for you

> **Rolling Over Your 401(k)**
Find the right rollover for you

> **NEW: Transferring Assets
to T. Rowe Price**
Move assets held at other
financial institutions to
T. Rowe Price

Figure 1-1 *Detail from the T. Rowe Price home page showing direct links. Copyright T. Rowe Price Associates, Inc.*

An example of an indirect link in an informational piece is a student who fails a test in a certain subject area and is automatically routed to easier review material, instead of being advanced to the next level. The student did not make this direct choice. It is a consequence of his or her actions. Figure 1-2 shows how a student who could not answer an arithmetic question in a math tutorial is sent back to an arithmetic review module as opposed to being advanced to the more difficult material. A number of educational multimedia programs work this way.

Indirect links can also cause multiple things to happen when the user clicks one choice. This is most common in a program or web site where the information is dynamic because it is stored in a database. What this means is that the information is not static in large sections, like the pages and chapters of this book or a traditional HTML web page. If this book was a database-generated web site, every paragraph or sentence in it would be a separate piece of information. Depending on what actions the user took on the web site, these separate pieces of information could be sorted, organized, and displayed in the order requested by the user. For example,

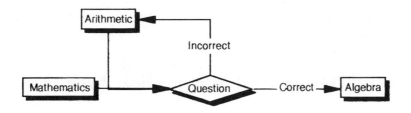

Figure 1-2 *Indirect links: A reaction to user input.*

on the T. Rowe Price web site, users can fill out a form and establish the list of mutual funds and stocks that they are most interested in. After they have done this once, when they log on to the site in the future, they are activating a program that searches out the most current data on their topics in the database, organizes this data, and presents it to them. Chapter 11 profiles this site and describes dynamic information flow and customization in more detail.

In the T. Rowe Price example, the multiple actions (sorting, organizing, etc.) are finally displayed in one location, but a single indirect link can also create multiple actions throughout a site or program. For example, on a well-designed web site for an auto dealer, when a salesperson sells a car and enters the final sales form into the system, the car is automatically removed from the display on the public web site and from the dealer's inventory list. The site might also automatically generate an e-mail message to the customers thanking them for their business.

Intelligent Links or Delayed Links: A Delayed Reaction

Intelligent links remember what choices the user made earlier in the program or on previous plays of the program and alter future responses accordingly. These links can be considered delayed "if-then" links. In a story, intelligent links create a realistic response to the character's action; in a training piece, they provide the most effective presentation of the material based on a student's earlier performance.

In *The Pandora Directive*, for example, you as the player are a detective who is trying to get in touch with Emily, a nightclub singer. You meet Emily's boss, Leach, well before you meet her. If you are rude to him, he mistrusts you. Later in the script when you try to rescue Emily, he will block your entrance to her room, and she will be strangled. If, however, you are nice when you first meet him, he lets you in, and you save her.

Certain web sites record every click you make and gradually define your preferences. This allows the sites to personalize their presentation to you so that they only show you information and products of interest to you. One example is Amazon.com's recommendation of new book titles to repeat users based on past purchases. The most sophisticated sites might also personalize the way the information is presented. For example, a user who always jumps right to the online videos would be presented with pages containing more multimedia.

Customization and personalization will be discussed in more detail later in this book in Chapter 7.

High-Level Design and Information Architecture

The complexity that interactivity and linking add to a multimedia project demands strong high-level design and/or information architecture for the program to be coherent and effective. High-level design determines the broad conceptual approach to the project, including the structure, interface, map, organizing metaphors, and even input devices. Information architecture or interactive architecture is the term usually applied to web sites for the overall grouping of the information, design of the navigation, and process flows of online applications.

Structure as an Interactive Device

The overall structure of a piece is one of the main ways interaction can be motivated in a narrative. In the computer game *Half-Life 2*, scientist Gordon Freeman is on an alien-infested Earth and he must rescue the world from the evil he unleashed in the first *Half Life*. The player's main interactions, which are motivated by this story, are exploring the barren futuristic world and (of course) blowing away bad guys. In another game, *Grand Theft Auto: San Andreas*, you play the role of Carl "CJ" Johnson who is returning home to find out why his mother has been killed. It's not long before you/Carl are rebuilding your street gang in order to get to the bottom of the problems and set things straight. In the narrative informational piece *A la rencontre de Philippe*, the player is motivated to learn about Paris through the role of helping Parisian friends find an apartment. In another narrative information piece *The Oregon Trail*, your task is to outfit a wagon, join a wagon train, and make the journey safely across the country. This basic premise inspires a whole series of user interactions with the program from buying supplies, choosing a team of animals for the wagon, and shooting deer for food on the trail.

The overall structure and navigation of a nonnarrative informational multimedia piece is called the information or interactive architecture. This is a large topic that will be dealt with in more detail in Chapter 3 and in the case studies, but it is worth mentioning here. Poorly structured information will cause the user either to fail to interact with the program at all, or to get confused and give up part way through. For example, good information architects knows what information to put on the top level of the interactive program, such as a web site's home page, to engage the user's interest. After hooking the user, this top-level information has to lead the user logically to the information that the user wants.

Interface Design

Another way to help users find their way through the complex structure of an interactive media production is through good interface design. The interface is simply the "face" or basic on-screen visualization of the information or story material in a program. The interface governs how we will interact with multimedia. An interface can be as simple as a list of words in a clickable menu that organizes the information into content categories, such as the T. Rowe Price menu in Figure 1-1. The interface can also be more graphical, such as the time clock and icons from the Harlem Renaissance site in Figure 1-3.

The interface can also be much more complex, such as the interface for the computer game *Nancy Drew: Secret of the Old Clock* computer game, which allows the user to interact with the story material in a variety of ways using items in the bottom tool bar and items in the main screen (Figure 1-4). From the bottom bar players can bring up the tools and clues they have found, consult their notebook, track their money, and get help. There are many more options in the main interface, including walking, driving the car, talking to people, solving puzzles, and using the telephone.

The amount of input the writer is allowed to give regarding the interface design depends on the designer and the project, but the writer must consider the overall interface design and information architecture when they are writing. Interface design is crucial in deciding how multimedia content will be organized. It affects the structure of the script for the writer and dictates how the viewer will interact with that content.

Figure 1-3 *Timeline and icons from the Harlem Renaissance web site. Copyright Encyclopaedia Britannica, Inc.*

Figure 1-4 *Interface for Nancy Drew: Secret of the Old Clock computer game. Copyright Her Interactive, Inc.*

The interface also affects the navigation of the piece—how the viewer can travel through the information or story and the order in which the information will be presented. The navigation is often demonstrated through flowcharts and diagrams. (See the flowchart which introduces Part I.) The U.S. White House web site (http://www.whitehouse.gov/) uses a simple hierarchical menu for navigation in which users can first choose from a number of global links in the top navigation bar. By clicking the link "First Lady," the user is taken down a level to the First Lady's page, on that page you have a number of options including "Press Releases and Speeches." Clicking that link will lead to a list of actual speeches, which you can click to read the speech "The First Lady's Remarks After the Christmas Day Lunch." So this is an example of a hierarchical menu where you had to drill down four levels to get to the First Lady's speech you were interested in: White House Home Page → First Lady Main Page → Press Releases and Speeches Menu → "The First Lady's Remarks After the Christmas Day Lunch."

Map or Sitemap

An element of good interactive design is a sitemap or map that represents the overall structure of a piece in a concrete manner. A sitemap illustrates how the player should interact with the interface and navigate through the program. It can be as simple as a text menu that lists all the key pages of a web site, broken down by categories. This type of sitemap is used on the Prudential Verani web site profiled in Chapter 10. Sometimes the map is a flowchart of the entire production, as in the Oakes Interactive training piece for Fidelity Investments retirement counselors. In this program, a student can bring up the flowchart of the whole program and access any area of it by clicking on one of the labeled boxes. The "Book at a Glance" at the beginning of this book uses a flowchart to provide an overview of book contents. The sitemap can even be a literal map, as in *Grand Theft Auto: San Andreas*, in which the player can consult a map of the cities that make up the island of San Andreas to get oriented and decide where to go next. (The actual interface of the game is a 3-D animation of the town's buildings and citizens, with whom the viewer can interact.)

Metaphors

For software developers, the metaphor is a concrete image or other element that represents an abstract concept, making it clear and comfortable to the user. Perhaps one of the best-known software metaphors is the desktop. Windows PCs and Macs present the abstract concepts of computer files, directories, and software as file folders and documents that users can arrange and work with on the desktop.

Metaphors are also used to design individual screens and navigational aids. According to designer Aaron Marcus, "consistency and clarity are two of the most important concerns in developing metaphors" (p. 98). Familiarity to the viewer is a third item that could be added. Consistency means that users should not use buttons as the main navigational tool on one screen and then suddenly have to switch to a different approach, such as clicking on pictures, in the next screen. Both of these are valid metaphors for linked information, but they are confusing when mixed. Consistent placement of the same types of information in the same place on the screen is also important.

Creating familiar metaphors ties into knowing your audience. A valid metaphor for the structure of an elementary school education CD-ROM or web site might be a street in a town. This is something students are familiar with. It makes sense for them to click on a library to get information or a movie theater to see a film. On a micro level, a common metaphor is a book that opens. Click a dog-ear to turn a page. Click the table of contents to go to a chapter. Sometimes a metaphor can add to the mood of a piece. The Harlem Renaissance web site, profiled in Chapter 12, uses a tourist metaphor to help make the user feel that they are visitors to another era. The metaphor is strengthened with items such as street maps, e-mail postcards, and evocative full-page visuals. A common metaphor on many web sites, including the latest version of the Prudential Verani site profiled in Chapter 10, is a stack of file folders with tabs that can be clicked on to access the content of another "file folder" of information; see Figure 1-5. All of these examples are concrete objects or concepts that help make accessing information more usable.

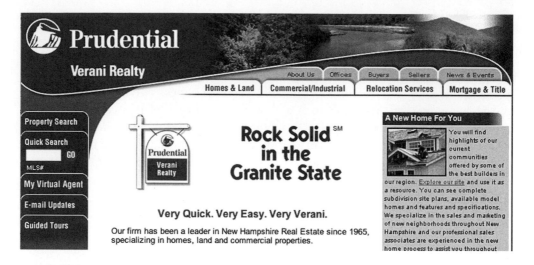

Figure 1-5 *Home page for Prudential Verani Realty, showing file folder tab navigation metaphor. Copyright Prudential Verani Realty.*

Familiar metaphors help orient viewers, but this certainly doesn't mean that metaphors have to be clichéd or boring. Certainly a designer who can push the envelope without losing the audience should by all means go for it. There is lots of room to be creative. It is important to make even the minor elements of a production work well. For example, one of the frustrating things in multimedia is the "wait-state" image. Many programs are content to give the standard clock or hourglass, but there is no rule that the wait-state image cannot be fun. *A.D.A.M. The Inside Story*, an anatomy program, shows a skeleton with a cup of coffee. Some children's programs have scurrying animals.

Input Devices

Writers might also consider how the users will input their responses to the program. Standard choices include the keyboard, mouse, game controller, guns, writing text on screen, and touch screen, but sometimes the input device can be integrated into the material. Instead of a mouse, the *Guitar Hero* game has a guitar you can play and become a rock star, complete with visual action at six different locations, from basement parties to sold out stadiums. *Redbeard's Pirate Quest* uses a model pirate ship loaded with electromagnetic sensors. Speech recognition is also finally coming of age, and this could have a major impact on interactive narratives. Even more exciting are the potential applications for multimodal interaction. "Multimodal systems process combined natural input modes—such as speech, pen, touch, hand gestures, eye gaze, and head and body movements—in a coordinated manner with multimedia output" (Oviatt, p. 74). For interacting with complex multimedia programs, such as virtual worlds populated with intelligent animated characters, a multimodal system will be far superior to the conventional Windows-Icons-Menus-Pointer (WIMP) interface.

Interactive Devices

In addition to the high-level design elements, the designer and writer must develop specific interactive devices that will make users aware of the interactive possibilities they have created. These devices include icons, on-screen menus, help screens, props, other characters, cues imbedded in the story or information, and more.

Icons

In computer usage, an icon is a symbol that represents a command or an ongoing action. For example, the floppy disc image in the toolbar of many software programs indicates the Save function. An hour glass icon indicates that the computer is doing a process and the user must wait. Various types of icons are used for interactive devices. In *Voyeur* they are used to inspire viewers to look into the rooms of the mansion that are visible from the voyeur's apartment. If the voyeur moves the camera over a room in which there is action to view, an eye icon appears. If there's something to hear, an ear appears. If there is evidence to examine, such as a letter, a magnifying glass appears. Clicking on the icons causes the material to be presented. The *Nancy Drew* games do something similar with the magnifying glass glowing when an item is clickable.

In Britannica.com's Harlem Renaissance web site, icons are used to efficiently indicate the main sections of the site in the web site's navigation bar; see Figure 1-3. The megaphone is for leadership, the page is for literature, the palette is for art, and so on. The meaning of the icons is clarified through the use of rollovers that show text labels when the mouse passes over one of the icons. In the *Oregon Trail*, icons on the bottom of the screen let the player/traveler check the status of supplies and health for the group. The supplies icon shows a bag of flower and some containers; the health icon has a medicine bag and medicine.

Be careful not to overuse icons or rely on obscure icons. Many icons benefit from a text label, and sometimes it's better to skip the icons altogether and rely on text alone.

Menus and Other Text

The text menu and the navigation bar are traditional and still effective ways to access material in informational multimedia. Figure 1-1 shows a menu from the T. Rowe Price web site. In addition to static text, menus can also be presented as popup or drop-down menus that take less screen space (Figure 1-6). They only appear when the user clicks on them. Text links can also be highlighted directly on

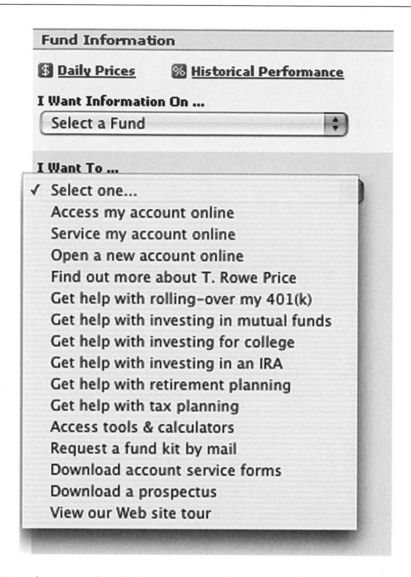

Figure 1-6 *Drop-down menu from the T. Rowe Price web site. Copyright T. Rowe Price Associates, Inc.*

a page within the body text, as in Figure 1-3, where the names of important figures of the era are links to additional information.

Although text menus can work well in an informational piece, they can disrupt the flow of a narrative. However, some designers are willing to accept that disruption to achieve a high degree of interactivity. In *Under a Killing Moon*, written by Aaron Conners, menus allow the player a wide variety of action options, including look, get, move, open, and talk. The player can even choose the tone of the lead character's dialogue by picking menu choices such as "Rugged Banter," "Indignant," and "Reeking of Confidence." (See Chapter 23, "Parallel Stories Narrative Case Study: The Pandora Directive," for a more detailed discussion of response attitudes.) *Grand Theft Auto: San Andreas* will also use text to indicate actions for the user. Text will appear on the screen at key moments with tips, such as "Ride the bike." or "Keep up with your buddy."

Sometimes words on the screen are optional. In *Under a Killing Moon*, players can pull down an optional hints window. This helps orient them in the game and tells them their interactive options. Sometimes written material is integrated into the story itself. Shannon Gilligan's *Who Killed Sam Rupert?* includes an investigator's notebook that keeps track of what the detective/player has done so far in the game. The *Nancy Drew* games use a similar device. Many online transactions, such as an online account opening for a bank, also have optional help text or product information that the user can decide to access or not.

Props

Props are a popular interactive device. In *Under a Killing Moon*, the character can click on objects in the room to get information. Depending on the object, a player might hear a voice-over wisecrack about a painting, or even see a full-motion video flashback that shows the detective's relationship with the object. In the educational CD-ROM *Sky High*, users can click on various props in a scene, such as toy helicopters and birds, to bring up additional information related to that aspect of flight.

Props that a character can actually use as they might be used in real life are particularly effective. In the educational game *Zoo Vet*, the player can use a wide variety of medical instruments to help sick zoo animals. The game *Half Life 2* has a wide variety of props that the user can manipulate, which encourages interaction. For example, in one scene, the character has to pile a group of boxes a certain way to climb out of a window.

Characters

Characters are another way to guide interactions. Sometimes this is the primary function of the character. In the *Nancy Drew* games, telephone calls from her friends and father nudge her in one direction or another and give additional clues. In the same games, talking with most of the main characters inspire additional actions. The investigators in *Who Killed Sam Rupert* and *Gabriel Knight* both have assistants who remind them of appointments, give them telephone messages, or suggest people to talk to. Other characters, who are not primarily information givers, might say things that suggest a location to visit or a person to interview. This is often used in *Half Life 2*.

A character can also be used as a guide to lead the viewer through the material. This can be successful in both narrative and nonnarrative pieces. For example, children's educational programs frequently have characters that suggest what actions to take and what information to explore. The veterinary assistants in *Zoo Vet* perform this function by telling the player/veterinarian when their diagnosis and treatment is off track. Many training e-learning programs will have an expert guide you can call upon for advice when you are trying to complete a task. This guide is usually represented as video, graphics, text, and/or audio of a specific person who can be called upon for help and advice as if they were a live consultant. In the narrative video game *Astronomica*, the daughter of the doctor who disappeared approaches you, the user, directly by banging on your bedroom window and asking you to help find her father. She leads you to her father's lab, where she works on the main computer, and sends you into the exploratorium to solve the problems there. She also appears now and again on a small communications monitor in the exploratorium to give you tips and encouragement.

Challenge of the Interactive Device

The challenge of the interactive device is to design something that will motivate interaction without radically disrupting the flow of information or story material. A well-designed interactive device will not pull us out of the dream state of story-telling or disrupt our train of thought as we pursue information. In short, interactive devices must be well integrated into the material.

Conclusion

This chapter has provided a broad overview of some of the key interactive issues the writer must consider when developing a multimedia informational or narrative program. Although the elements discussed above, such as interface design, are not always under the control of the writer, the writer must understand these concepts if he or she is to write effectively for interactive media. This chapter has discussed the "interactive" component of interactive multimedia. The next chapter will address the "multimedia" aspect of interactive multimedia. Writing for multimedia or many media is another key challenge for the writer.

References

Davenport, Glorianna. "Bridging Across Content and Tools." Computer Graphics 28 (February 1994), p. 31–32.

Halliday, Mark. "Digital Cinema: An Environment for Multi-threaded Stories." Master's thesis, Massachusetts Institute of Technology, 1993.

The Harlem Renaissance web site. http://www.britannica.com/harlem, 1999.

Jensen, Jane. Telephone interview with the author, July 1994.

Jordan, Ken. "Defining Multimedia." NOEMA web site. http://www.noemalab.org/sections/ideas/ideas_articles/jordan_multimedia.html

Marcus, Aaron. "Making Multimedia Usable: User Interface Design." New Media 5 (February 1995), p. 98–100.

Oviatt, Sharon. "Ten Myths of Multimodal Interaction". Communications of the ACM 42 (November 1999), p. 74–81.

Prudential Verani web site. http://www.pruverani.com, 1999.

Riordan, David. Telephone interview with the author, June 1994.

Sherman, Tony. Telephone interview with the author, July 1994.

T. Rowe Price web site. http://www.troweprice.com, 1999.

Writing for Many Media

Chapter Overview

The multimedia writer must be able to write effectively for a variety of media. This chapter outlines some of the basic principles for writing:

- Text
- Audio
- Video

The Skills of the Interactive Writer

The necessity of writing for many media in the same production is as demanding on the multimedia writer as is dealing with interactivity. Unlike a print writer who can focus on honing communication skills with the written word, or the screenwriter who can specialize in communicating with images, the writer of interactive multimedia must be expert in a variety of techniques: writing to be read (journalism, poetry, copywriting); writing to be heard (radio, narration); writing to be seen (presentations, film, video); plus writing for the special demands of the computer screen. This is because multimedia can easily incorporate many types of media in a single production or even on a single screen, and multimedia can manipulate these media in ways not previously possible. Depending on the project, a multimedia writer may write on-screen text, audio narration, video action and dialogue, and other material. Often writers also write ancillary material, such as hints files and help screens. There are basic style differences in each of these types of writing. Following are a few guidelines, but if there is an area where you feel you are particularly weak, consult some of the resources listed in the "References" section of this book's CD-ROM.

Text

The World Wide Web has brought a major resurgence in the writing and reading of text in multimedia programs. Even with the increased use of web video, audio, and animation, on-screen text still plays a major role on most web sites where the primary activity of most users is still reading.

The popularity of blogs (short for "weblogs"), which are composed mainly of text and links, has also increased online reading. A blog is a web site or portion of a web site that is set up to allow easy creation of additional content by multiple individuals. Information is posted on a regular basis, usually with the newest information coming first. Some blogs are restricted to one person or a set number of individuals, but many blogs are public so that anyone can add information and respond to earlier comments. Blogs are often used for noncommercial expression about a wide range of topics with current events, politics, and business among the most popular, but some commercial sites are starting to use blogs as a way to present news, PR information, and customer service. Blogs are also playing a larger role in political campaigns. Most of the writing tips below apply to blogs as well as to other online writing.

Another use of text is in disk-based multimedia, such as CD-ROMs and DVDs, where it is most common in informational, educational, and training pieces.

Clear, Concise, and Personal

An author writing blocks of text in an informational program or web site can take a few tips from print journalists:

- Be accurate, check your facts, and be sure you understand what you are writing.
- Keep sentences short and use simple sentence construction.
- Use the lead or first sentence to tell simply and clearly what the following text is about.
- Use the active voice—for example, "The dog bit the man," not, "The man was bitten by the dog."
- Use descriptive nouns and verbs; avoid adjectives and adverbs.
- Choose each word carefully, and avoid jargon or technical terms unless you are writing for a specialized audience.

Andrew Nelson, the writer of the Harlem Renaissance site profiled in Chapter 12, suggests that when writing for the web you should remember that most people view the web as one person sitting in front of a computer. To connect to your site users, it is important to "write as if you are talking to an individual, not a collective group of anonymous web surfers."

Web Writing Tips from Usability Experts

There are a number of text-writing techniques that are unique to writing for the computer screen. The main reason for using many of these techniques is that most people cannot read as quickly and as comfortably on a computer screen as they can from the printed page. Adding to the problem of writing for computer screens is that many readers use multimedia and the web to access information quickly. They do not want to sit down and read a six-page essay. They want to get the information quickly and then go about their business. The term "usability" describes how easy it is for users to perform tasks or get information on your web site or multimedia program. A number of usability experts have conducted tests with users and come up with conclusions about the most usable way to write and organize text for the web.

Write to Be Scanned

Several classic site usability studies by Dr. Jakob Nielsen, usability engineer and information architect, discovered that many users don't read web sites; rather, they scan them for the information they need. Later studies have confirmed that 80% of users scan web sites. (Koyani, Baile, Hall). To write effectively for these scanners, Nielsen suggests in *The Alertbox: How Users Read on the Web* that web writers use:

- highlighted keywords (hypertext links serve as one form of highlighting; typeface variations and color are others)
- meaningful subheadings (not "clever" ones)
- bulleted lists
- one idea per paragraph (users will skip over any additional ideas if they are not caught by the first few words in the paragraph)
- the inverted pyramid style, starting with the conclusion and most important information
- half the word count (or less) than in conventional writing

These concepts are particularly true on the first couple of levels of a web site or multimedia program where users are trying to find the information they want. Once they have located their information deeper in the site, users may be content to read longer text material.

Recent Usability Studies Related to Text and Online Writing

A more recent and more comprehensive study of web usability was organized by the U.S. Department of Health and Human Services and involved a large team of academics and practicing professionals who analyzed all the usability research currently available and came up with a number of conclusions that are useful to the web writer. (See http://www.usability.gov for additional information on this study.) The study confirmed Nielsen's earlier work, but added a number of additional suggestions that are listed below.

Know and Respond to All Your Users

- Writers must understand users' expectations of a site. These user expectations can be formed by prior knowledge and past experiences. This requires user research by the writer or other members of the production team. Some sources for user information include customers support lines, customers surveys and interviews, bulletin boards, salespeople, user groups, and trade shows.
- Present help for all users. This user assistance could be a help section, separate glossary, and/or being sure to define any unusual terms within the text.
- Have text or other alternatives for information that is communicated by color. About 8% of males and a smaller number of females have trouble distinguishing colors.
- Format information for multiple audiences. For example, if you have a medical web site, it might make sense to have differently written sections for doctors and patients.

Home Page, Navigation Pages, and Links

- Describe your web site's purpose clearly and simply on the home page. This can be done with a tag line or a brief piece of highlighted text high on the page. Don't make users dig through the site to determine that your site has research information on televisions and is not a place to buy televisions.
- Don't have a lot of prose text on a home page or a navigation page. When most users come to a home page, they scan quickly looking for links to the information they want. A lot of text will either slow down their information search, or they may skip your site altogether.
- For long pages that extend way below the fold, it helps users to have a clickable list of page topics at the top of the page. This allows them to quickly jump to the information on the page that they want.
- Write "glosses" to help navigation. "Glosses" are bits of explanatory text that appear when a user moves the cursor over a link. This helps the user understand where the link is going. "Glosses" are not, however, an excuse for poorly labeled links and tabs.
- Use a consistent clickability style. If your links are underlined and blue in one section, keep them the same throughout. Avoid using underlining for general, nonlink text because that suggests a link to most users. The top of the page and the left and right columns are common locations for link lists.
- Make links in the body of the text descriptive. If you need to make the links a few words long, that is better than having an unclear link. Users tend to ignore the text around an embedded link, so don't rely on that context to help. Avoid "Click Here." Instead use descriptive text that tells specifically where the link will take the user, such as "Reptile Food" on a pet products site.

Information Display

- Display quantitative information in a standard and easily understood format for your users. For example, presenting time in a 24-hour clock (e.g., 16:25) for an American audience is not appropriate because Americans use twelve-hour clocks and will have to translate the information to the time format they are used to (e.g., 4:25PM).
- Types of data with multiple information entries, such as statistics, is often better presented as a table, chart or other visual format.
- Keep information needed for comparison on the same page or available in a popup link. Users can only remember three or four items for a few seconds. If you ask them to read product information on one page and then make decisions about products on the next page, they will have difficulty. Tables are useful for comparing lots of information.
- Set appropriate page lengths: shorter for home pages and navigation pages; longer for pages that require uninterrupted reading of content.
- Place important information higher on the page so users can locate it quickly. Top center is the most prominent part of a page.
- Group information consistently. For example, if supplemental information is in a column on the right on one page, place it in the same location throughout the site to speed users' information search.
- Align items on a page. Bullets and menu items should be lined up along the left, such as the bullets in this list. This makes it much easier to scan information than if bullets are arranged in a diagonal or other artsy formation.
- Use appropriate line lengths. Users tend to prefer short line lengths, but they can actually read faster with longer line lengths. One study shows that line lengths as short as twenty characters consistently slowed reading speed. So home pages and navigation pages may want to use shorter line lengths to engage users, but pages with more text may want to use longer lines to speed reading.
- Limit page information only to what information is needed on that page. Do not add extraneous information unrelated to the page's purpose.
- Group related information and groups of links and give them meaningful headings.

Label

Label, Label, Label. A repeated result from a number of usability studies is the need to clearly and consistently label chunks of information or portions of a task. This includes:

- frame labels (frames divide a page in sections)
- input boxes on a form. Put the labels for input boxes close to the entry box that they define.

- navigation tabs and menu links. They should be descriptive of the content they are leading to and use language all your users can understand.
- category labels for groups of links and other information. If you have more than a few links on a page, group them and give each group a clear, descriptive heading.
- unique and descriptive headings of blocks of content. Don't use the same or similar labels for different content. Clear unique headings facilitate scanning.
- rows and column heading on tables. Don't use abbreviations unfamiliar to your user.
- push buttons and other widgets. Try to use standard meaningful labels, such as "Enter," "Cancel," etc.
- clickable images. Labels on clickable images makes it clear what information the image leads to and emphasizes that it is clickable.

Who Edits Interactive Media Text?

If you are a writer who is coming to interactive media from the print world of books, newspapers or magazines, you probably expect an editor to be as important a position in interactive media as it is in print media. Except for a few exceptions, this will not be the case.

Most interactive media projects will not have anyone on the team with the title of "editor." This does not mean you will not get feedback on your writing. A variety of other individuals take on this role including:

- The clients. They often know their business and message better than you do. The client will usually review your writing and offer detailed comments primarily on the accuracy of the content and the way certain products and business practices are described. But keep in mind that the client will probably not be a trained writer, as a book editor might be. The client will give feedback, but it is up to you to revise the writing so it accomplishes the client's goals.
- The instructional designer, information architect, or content strategist. If your project has one of these content experts onboard, it is likely that they might review your text to make sure it accomplishes their vision for the information presentation. People in this position are likely to have good writing skills and may be able to give some of the detailed comments you might expect from a print editor.
- The game designer or exhibit designer. If you are building a computer game or a museum exhibit, the high level designer will often look at your text and give comments.
- The development editor or subject matter expert. The place you are likely to see a traditional editor role is in e-learning and educational multimedia. In this case, it is not uncommon to have a subject matter expert editor, such as

a math editor. This person will review your text and suggest detailed text and content changes, as a book editor would.

- The copyeditor. Although most projects have some sort of copyeditor who will read through your text for typos and obvious grammatical errors, typically copyeditors do not offer substantial suggestions about your writing.

So a good first step when you take on an interactive writing assignment is to determine who will give you feedback and get some sense of their expectations. But as noted above, you are likely not to get the kind of detailed editing you would get on a print project. Instead, many interactive writers need to learn to be their own editor as well as the writer.

Style Guide

Although there may not be a human editor, most projects give editorial guidance through a writing style guide. This guide defines specific text usage for writers. Usually a project will have a custom style guide, but will also rely on a standard print style guide, such as *The Chicago Manual of Style*, for basic writing issues. Be sure to get a copy of the project style guide when you start a project. If there is no style guide, offer to write one. Without a project style guide, it is impossible to have writing consistency across the production.

How Editing Comments Are Presented

If you do get editing comments, they will be delivered in one or more of the following ways:

- Track changes. If you are not already aware of this feature of MSWord and other word processors, it is located in the Tools Menu. If "Track Changes" is clicked on, it allows an editor to enter and highlight changes. It then allows the writer to accept or reject changes and to compare multiple drafts of documents.
- Handwritten notes. Many client like to print out a screen of text and edit the old fashioned way, with handwritten notes. If this is the case, make sure you know the standard editing symbols, such as delete, replace, insert, and transpose. These are available in any manual of style and on the web (see the link "Proofreader's and Editor's Symbols" in the references at the end of this chapter).
- Comments in a second document. Clients also often simply write or list their comments in a separate document. The writer then has to integrate them into the final document. If we get this type of comments on a project, we will usually turn it into a table with the clients comments in one column and next to it in the next column—the resolution. The resolution describes how we addressed the comments or reason we did not address the comments if

Table 2-1 *A sample list of reviewer's comments.*

Number	Reviewers Initials	Location	Reviewer's Comment	Writer's Resolution
1.	D.G	Home Page	Line 2 of body text, should be "multiple" not "divide"	Fixed
2.	D.G	Addition Problem #1	Problem explanation is unclear. Clarify amounts of different types of fruit	Broken into bulleted list

we felt the suggestion was incorrect. See the sample above. It is good to capture the reviewer's initials in case you need further clarifications. It is also a good idea for each comment to have a unique number so you can easily refer to it in discussions with the client or development team.

Web Text Writing Example

The following excerpt from the T. Rowe Price web site illustrates many of the elements of good text writing for the computer screen described above, including the inverted pyramid, concrete statements, simple sentence construction, reduced amount of text, highlighted text, different fonts, bulleted lists, one idea per paragraph, and conversational style. Note that the underlined text in the sample below is shown as blue hyperlinks on the actual web site.

ONLINE COLLEGE PLANNER

This on-line College Planner can help you learn about meeting the costs of college. Our five-step College Planning Calculator calculates how much money you'll need to save, and suggests ways to invest your savings. Meanwhile, our College Planning Library gives you more information on other helpful resources, including:

- Tax Issues
- Education IRAs
- State Tuition Assistance Programs
- Sources of Financial Aid
- Ways that Grandparents Can Help

A wealth of additional college planning information is available on-line. See our Additional Sources of Information.

Blog Writing Example and Writing Tips

The following fragment of a blog is from Google' official blog (http://googleblog.blogspot.com/). Posting on this blog is limited to Google employees. It includes new product information, public relations information, and just plain goofy things that Google employees do. The goal is to connect with Google customers on a more personal basis than traditional corporate communications.

The blog below demonstrates most of the good online writing style techniques discussed earlier in this chapter:

- Descriptive heading.
- Clear, direct, short sentences.
- Gets right to the point.
- The tone is very personal and keeps its audience in mind. As public relations consultants Doug Hay and Sally Falkow point out, "a blog is not a corporate brochure. 'Corporate Speak' will not cut it. A good blog (i.e., one that gets a lot of attention) would be written in a conversational style, but must be well written. A sense of humor also helps to make it interesting."
- Links to other sites. This establishes a blogger as an expert because it shows you are knowledgeable about information resources pertaining to your subject. Linking also helps you get return links from other web sites.
- Uses keywords pertinent to the subject. This will help the search engine rating.
- It's not in the example below, but another common technique is to try to end with a question or something controversial to encourage reader response.

Searching for Music

Posted by David Alpert, Search Quality Product Manager

   It may come as no surprise, but I like to search for things on Google. Yep, when I'm looking for something, I always try it on Google first. And sometimes, that thing I'm looking for is music. Many of our users feel the same way, and we get a lot of search traffic on music terms like popular artists and albums.

   A few of us decided to try to make the information you get for these searches even better, so we created a music search feature. Now you can search for a popular artist name, like the Beatles or the Pixies, and often Google will show some information about that artist, like cover art, reviews, and links to stores where you can download the track or buy a CD via a link at the top of your web search results page.

Copyright Google. http://googleblog.blogspot.com/

Audio

Writing in which the audio carries the bulk of the meaning, as it does in radio, occurs fairly often in multimedia for three practical reasons:

- Audio is much cheaper to produce than video.
- Audio files are much smaller in size than video files. Because of this, it is much easier to include substantial audio material on a disc or to transmit audio files on web sites than it is to use video.
- The popularity of podcasts. A podcast is a type of web feed of audio files that a user can download and play on their computer or their mobile device, such as an Apple iPod or a Sony PSP. Initially used for music, podcasts are now used for a wide variety of content, including radio programs, education, politics, religion, and much more.

Writing where audio carries the primary meaning demands the skills of the radio writer, or the ability to write to be heard as opposed to being read. In addition to the print writer's skills of being accurate, simple, and clear, the radio writer must:

- Write conversationally, the way people talk. Radio is the most intimate medium. When most radio announcers talk through the mic to thousands of people, they imagine they are talking to just one person, because that is how most people experience radio: one person and a radio. This is the same intimate way most multimedia is experienced: one person and a computer.
- Write material to be understood on the first listening. Unless an instant replay is designed into the program, audio is more difficult to replay than text is to reread.
- Keep it simple. Be aware that the writing will be heard and not read. Avoid abbreviations, lots of numbers, unfamiliar names, parenthetical expressions and anything else that cannot be easily understood just by hearing it.
- Read all your work out loud when you are rewriting, or better yet, have someone read it out loud to you. You'll be amazed at how much of your perfectly acceptable written prose is unspeakable as dialogue or incomprehensible as narration.
- Write visually. A well-written audio-only piece can stimulate vivid images in the audience's minds. A famous radio ad once convincingly portrayed a ten-story-high hot fudge sundae being created in the middle of Lake Michigan. Create such pictures in the audience's mind by using:
  - Concrete visual words
  - Metaphors and other comparisons to images the viewer already knows
  - Sound effects

- ○ Different qualities of voices (sexy, accents, etc.)

- ○ Music

- ○ Words and phrases that appeal to other senses, such as touch, smell, and taste

Examples of audio-only or audio-dominant multimedia include web audio interviews and seminars; audio and image scenes in which narration carries the bulk of the meaning; and even streaming web video, which can easily degenerate to a series of still pictures with audio voice-over if the user has a slow connection or if the network is congested.

E-Learning Narration Example

The following example of narration is from the Houghton Mifflin Interactive Math and Statistics Lessons profiled in Chapter 13. This narration accompanies on screen text and graphics. So it does not really have to stand alone. Notice the short, uncomplicated sentences and clear straightforward language. The target audience is college statistics students.

```
    Bar graphs and pie charts are two common methods of representing
data graphically.

A bar graph is used to display quantitative or qualitative data.

Bar graphs have the following features in common.

    • The bars may be placed horizontally or vertically.
    • The bars are all the same width and are evenly spaced.
```

Narrative Audio-Only Example

Narrative scenes sometimes emphasize audio to save space or for dramatic effect, such as the following example from the interactive narrative Voyeur. In this scene the player is looking at closed window blinds and listening in. Notice the use of visual writing, sound effects, and different voices to create images in the audience's mind. (These items are in boldface type.)

```
CHLOE'S ROOM, LARA AND CHLOE. SLIGHT KNOCK ON DOOR.

                        LARA
                  (knock on door)
```

Chloe?

                    CHLOE
Yeah. Come on in Lara ...

                    LARA
                (embarrassed)
Oh, I'm sorry I didn't know you weren't **dressed**
...

                    CHLOE
No, no, no don't worry about it, man, don't worry
about it.

                    LARA
                (nervous **laughter**)
Maybe if I had a **tattoo** there, Zack would take a
closer look ...

                    CHLOE
Yeah? You like that? I'm not sure what hurt more,
the tattoo or the hangover ...

                    LARA
What am I doing wrong with him?

                    CHLOE
Oh, Lara would you stop it right now! Don't buy
into Zack's bullshit. You're a babe. You're
gorgeous. You've got a **terrific body**. You just
don't know how to package it.... I have got the
most terrific outfit for you. It's going to look
killer on you. I swear to God.

RIIING! She's interrupted by phone call.

                    CHLOE
Look,... Hold on a minute.

                (into phone)
Yeah?... Oh, hi.... Well, not exactly... Hey man
I'm working on it.... will you give me a fucking
break ... Hold a sec.

                        (to Lara)
         Lara, could you ... come back here tonight ...

                            LARA
         I don't want to be a pest ...

                           CHLOE
         Oh, come on, come on, it'll be fun ... please,
         come on, come by around eight.

                            LARA
         OK.... see you then ... **(door closes)**

                           CHLOE
                     (back to phone)
         Like I told you, give me a couple a more days ...
         I'll get you the damn money. Fine.

Copyright Philips Interactive Media.

Video

Writing for video is an important skill for the multimedia writer because DVDs can accommodate considerable full-motion video and animation. Likewise on the web, breakthroughs in compression, streaming tools, and faster user connections have made web video a reality.

In a video, the viewer is seeing the results of the writing, not just reading or hearing them as in print and radio. Writing for video is a complex subject about which many books have been written. Further complicating this topic are the very different demands on the scriptwriter of writing documentaries and fiction. It is difficult to reduce the specifics of scriptwriting to a few rules, but some of the scriptwriter's concerns include:

- Showing, not telling. Discover action to present the information. Don't have long-winded interviews about poverty in the ghetto; show scenes of poverty in the ghetto. Don't have your character tell us about how sad they are; have them do something that shows this.
- Structure. Have a clear grasp of how to structure a video. Academy Award-winning screenwriter Sheridan Gibney once said that scriptwriting has more in common with architecture than with writing. He said that screenplays are built, not written. Shots build scenes, scenes develop

sequences, and sequences create plots and subplots. Much of film and TV follows established structures that writers should be familiar with. (These structures are discussed in Part III, "Writing Interactive Narrative.")

- Interactivity and chunking. Keep in mind that your video is part of an interactive program. In most cases, you will have to chunk it or break it down into smaller units so that the user can access just the piece of video he needs, when he needs it.
- Setup. Exposition is one of the hardest elements to portray in video, and without proper exposition, characters are shallow, themes are undefined, and the setting is unclear. Exposition includes background information on the characters, setting, and the backstory (events in the story that happened before the beginning of the current narrative). An example of important backstory occurs in the classic film *Casablanca*. This film begins in Casablanca, a port city in Morocco, but essential backstory includes the lead characters' romance that occurred in Paris a year earlier.

    Setup is equally important in an informational video, where we need to understand the context of the material that is being presented. In the New England Economic Adventure profiled in Chapter 24, the program designers had to introduce users to economic history of New England before they could play the game.

    Unlike print, where it is fairly easy to "tell" the reader about background information, in video this material needs to be shown. In multimedia, novice video writers often either have the characters talking incessantly about things that happened years ago, or they dump the entire backstory into a separate background file and assume everyone has read it. Such a background file might be accessible from a program's help or hints menu.
- Characterization. There are a limited number of original stories but an unlimited number of unique characters. Finding and developing unique characters is essential in most fiction films and many documentaries. It is also important that you pick the right characters for your audience. An informational program aimed at high school students, such as The New England Economic Adventure has young, energetic characters. *Vital Signs* profiled in Chapter 15 is aimed at medical professionals, thus it has more mature characters who can relate to that audience.
- Conflict. Conflicts must be clearly defined. Most video focuses on conflict, whether it is a fictional battle between humans and aliens or a *60 Minutes*-type documentary on the concerned citizens of India versus their nuclear power industry.
- Cost. Unlike radio and print writing, video production is costly, and scriptwriters must be aware of this. Even though digital video cameras and desktop video editing software have brought costs down, a writer with a limited multimedia budget probably will have to forget about blowing up that rocket ship, do it as an animation, or use stock footage.

Informational Program Video Example

In the *New England Economic Adventure*, video, interactive games, and live hosts present information to high school students in an immersive museum exhibit in a theater. The excerpt below follows a short section that introduces the history of the times. Notice how they set up the background in this piece by making the main characters time travelers who can talk to us (the audience) directly.

Table 2-2 *Informational program video example. Script copyright Federal Reserve Bank of Boston.*

HOST	VOTE; PDA	VIDEO & LIGHTING	AUDIO, NARRATION & SFX	EFX
HOST Now let's begin the Decision Round. In this round, you'll have a chance to go back in time ... to the year 1813, ... where you'll decide how to invest your money ... and you'll see if you make a profit. Ready to make some more money? Let's begin our trip.		LOGO Decision Round	SFX Decision Round SFX	1813 gobo effect timed to movie Lights fade out.
		CHRIS and SARA on screen in modern-dress against plain background. They matrix out of the scene.	CHRIS Ready? SARA Ready.	
		TRANSITION TO PAST Lights dim as sound effects fill room. We enter a door, and then a dark, private office.	EFFECTS :5-:10 seconds Lighting and sound effects in room take visitors back to 1813 Boston.	
		MAIN SCREEN VIDEO ADVISORS matrix into an area outside of LOWELL'S office. CHRIS and SARA materialize in costumes of the day that would make them fit	CHRIS (looking at his outfit, brushing himself off, maybe little flecks of electronic time transport material fly off) (to audience)	

Continued

Table 2-2—*(Cont'd)*

HOST	VOTE; PDA	VIDEO & LIGHTING	AUDIO, NARRATION & SFX	EFX
		in with Lowell and his friends. The sounds of "aheming" and murmuring from inside the office. They open the door and enter the office.	Well, it looks like we all got here in one piece! SARA (brushing herself off) Let's fill you in quickly. We are all prosperous associates of a man named Francis Cabot Lowell. CHRIS We've made our money in trading, but Lowell has called us together to hear a startling new proposal. SARA C'mon. Let's go in.	
		LOWELL is presiding over a meeting. He sits at a functional office, or desk with ledgers, papers. There are two or three other men in the room. CHRIS and SARA enter the room, the camera following as if they are leading us to our seats. They slip into a couple of seats.	LOWELL (to the advisors/audience) Welcome, welcome. Come in. Sit down. Meet my associates. This is Patrick Jackson and Nathan Appleton. Sit down.	
		Props may hint at China trade, a porcelain tea service, a silk pillow or wall hanging of a Chinese scroll.	LOWELL I've called you here with a business proposition . . . After long hours of planning, I have devised a way by which we may avoid the catastrophic risks of the trading business . . . a new way to invest our money.	

Computer Game Video Example

The following video script example is by writer Matthew Costello from the opening of the video game *The 11th Hour*. Note how the characters, setting, background story, and key conflicts are set up quickly and visually through the use of the TV news show, the PDA, and Dennings reactions.

INTRO-1 INT / DENNING'S COUNTRY HOME-AFTERNOON*

CARL DENNING is watching television. His handsome face is grim and
determined, bathed in the flickering light of the TV's images. On
the TV screen, an anchorwoman is reading the evening news.

                         ANCHOR
               State Police have called off the intense search
               for producer Robin Morales of television's CASE
               UNSOLVED.

She continues to speak in voice-over as the screen is filled with
an image of an intelligent-looking woman with compelling beauty.
The words "ROBIN MORALES—CASE UNSOLVED PRODUCER" are superimposed
across the bottom of the screen.

                         ANCHOR (V/O)
               Morales was researching a story about the famed
               haunted house in the small town of Harley on
               Hudson—the abandoned mansion of Henry Stauf.

The anchorperson continues to talk over images of old newspaper
stories from the 1920s and mysterious photos of HENRY STAUF and
his ill-fated guests. The screen switches to current images of the
main street of Harley on Hudson.

                         ANCHOR (V/O)
               Police have expressed concern that Morales'
               disappearance may be connected to a series of
               killings that have plagued the Hudson Valley
               this year.

Another IMAGE, a BODY, lying in the grass. Signs of violence,
blood, the skin discolored, leaves and twigs stuck to the body.

                         ANCHOR (V/O)
               So far, four women and three men have been victims
               fitting a pattern of homicide, and several others
               are missing.

Another image of Robin comes onto the screen.

                         ANCHOR(V/O cont'd)
               Robin Morales has been missing for more than three
               weeks and seems to have vanished without a trace.

The anchorwoman again appears on the screen.

                         ANCHOR
          She is the producer for the very popular and
          flamboyant CASE UNSOLVED reporter Carl Denning.

An image of Denning fills the screen, smiling, confident.

                       ANCHOR (V/O)
          Denning is said to have been in seclusion in
          his country home in Connecticut since Morales'
          disappearance. It's rumored that the two were
          romantically involved before ...

Denning clicks off the TV with a remote switch. He slumps back
in his chair and massages his temples. He looks up at the sound
of a doorbell ringing, gets out of his chair and crosses the
room and opens the door. A UPS truck is pulling away and a
package is on the doorstep.
     Denning crouches down and picks it up and goes back inside.
He returns to his chair and opens the package, revealing a
small, portable computer of some kind. He switches it on, and
a game flickers to life on the machine ... "Funhouse From Hell"—
Cartoony images of mayhem, monsters ... Slowly, the computer game
changes to an image of Robin looking frightened in the basement
of an old house. She speaks to him from the small screen.

                          ROBIN
          Carl ... help me ... please! ... I can't get
          out ... I ...

The image of Robin fades away and the video screen goes blank as
if the game has shut itself off. Denning shakes the box and clicks
it on and off but it seems to have died.

                         DENNING
          What is this!...?

He sets the game computer on the arm of the chair, gets to his
feet and begins to pace. The game starts beeping. He grabs it
and switches it on. An image of the Stauf mansion appears
briefly and fades away and the game shuts down again.

                         DENNING
          Damn!

Then the screen comes alive for another brief moment: An image
of Robin appears. She mouths the word "Help" but there is no
sound and the picture quickly fades. Denning pulls on a leather
windbreaker and stuffs the game in his pocket as he crosses the
room and leaves in a rush.

————————————

Script copyright Trilobyte Inc.

Conclusion

A writer who is a master of all the types of writing described above will be an
asset on a multimedia production team, but additional skills will make you truly
invaluable. These are outlined in the next chapter.

References

Gibney, Sheridan. Lecture. University of Southern California, Los Angeles.
Google Official Blog. http://googleblog.blogspot.com/
Hay, Douglas and Falkow, Sally. "What Is a Blog Anyway?" http://www.falkowinc.
    com/inc/Blog.pdf
Koyani, Sanjay, and Bailey, Robert W., and Nall, Janice R. "Research-Based Web
    Design & Usability Guidelines." http://usability.gov/pdfs/guidelines.html
Nelson, Andrew. E-mail to the author, October 1999.
New Communications Blogzine http://www.newcommblogzine.com
Nielsen, Jakob. "The Alertbox: How Users Read on the Web." http://www.useit.
    com/alertbox/9710a.html.
O'Meara, Maria. Notes to the author, February 1996.
Proofreader's and Editor's Symbols. University of Colorado Style Guide.
    http://www.colorado.edu/Publications/styleguide/symbols.html
T. Rowe Price web site. http://www.troweprice.com, 1999, 2005.
webSite 101. Top 10 Blog Writing Tips. http://www.website101.com/RSS-Blogs-
    Blogging/blog-writing-tips.html
Yahoo Podcasts Directory. http://podcasts.yahoo.com/

High-Level Design, Management, and Technical Skills Useful to the Interactive Writer

3

Chapter Overview

Understanding interactivity and the ability to write well for many media are essential for the interactive writer, but writers who want to get more control over their material and expand their career options should consider developing additional skills. The skills this chapter discusses include:

- Information and interactive architecture
- High-level narrative design
- Project management
- Content expertise
- Content strategy
- Writing to the search engines
- Flowcharting and other techniques for organizing content
- Basic HTML skills

High-Level Design, Content, and Project Management

Information and Interactive Architecture

Information architecture is the overall structure and navigation of an informational multimedia piece. Structuring multimedia is far more challenging than structuring a linear piece, such as a book or a video, because multimedia is made up of many discreet units of information that can be connected in a myriad of ways, as was discussed in the last two chapters. Key issues for the information architect are:

- clearly identifying the project's communication and business goals.
- understanding the key needs of the targeted user, including what specific tasks they need to accomplish. These needs are usually incorporated in a narrative called a use case or a user scenario that tracks the users path through the site or program as they look for information or accomplish tasks.
- organizing the information into categories and subcategories.
- deciding how the different categories and pieces of information will be linked so that the user can easily navigate among them and interact with them.
- establishing the types of interaction and functionality that will be allowed and what technology (databases, simulations, etc.) will facilitate the needed interactions.

An information architect has to not only have a librarian's eye for organizing information, but the architect also needs a broad understanding of current technologies available for interactive multimedia. For example, the information architect should clearly understand how databases work and how dynamically-driven database information can be presented on a web site or multimedia program. This topic will be discussed in the case studies in Chapters 11. Some types of programs require information architects who specialize, such as instructional designers who focus on training and education programs. An instructional designer usually teaches a specific skill or body of content as opposed to the information architect whose job is usually to make it possible for a user to find the information they need in a larger body of information.

A well-designed information architecture not only helps users find the information they want, but it is also one of the most effective ways to initiate interaction with a program. For example, good information architects know how to hook the user by placing the most appropriate content on the top level of the interactive program, such as a web site's home page where most users first arrive. After hooking the user, this top-level information has to lead the user logically to the information that the user wants or that the designers want them to see, such as the purchasing section of the site. Structuring your site so that there are several ways to access information is also important because different users will approach the site differently. The main toy page on Buy.com (http://www.buy.com) is a good example. Click on Toys in the Home Page menu and you are taken to the main Toys page where you can choose to shop by search, age, price, gender, category, latest and greatest, and featured items. Not every type of site or program needs this many ways to access the program content, but some options should usually be presented.

An interactive architect performs most of the same duties as an information architect, but he or she is also expected to contribute more to the overall user experience on the project. This includes making suggestions about the interface, design, usability, and online applications. The last item, designing applications, is probably the biggest change for the interactive architect, who is no longer just organizing information, but must also help design user activities within a program. Examples of common activities include opening a bank account on a web site, purchasing a product, or completing an exercise on an e-learning program. The interactive architect must design how the user will complete each step of the activities and move through the entire program. The interactive architect works with other team members, particularly the technical architect, when designing applications, but it is one of the duties of the interactive architect to make sure all these elements work together effectively with the information architecture. In actual practice, the titles "interactive architect" and "information architect" may not be as clearly defined as I have suggested above. Sometimes an information architect's role will closely resemble what I have described above for the interactive architect.

Common deliverables for an information or interactive architect are:

- **use cases or user scenarios:** define how a user will use the site or program.
- **content outlines:** provide a hierarchical grouping and prioritizing of content in information programs.
- **process flows or sitemaps:** chart the information flow of an information product or the process flow of an activity primarily with the use of flowcharts. (See Figure 3-1.)
- **wireframes:** screen/page level illustrations showing the information arrangement on the page level. These are sometimes static illustrations. Other times they have simple interactivity, often designed in HTML.

Just as film writers become directors to gain more control of their work, interactive writers should consider moving up to the information or interactive architect role. In the case studies in Parts II and III of this book there is considerable discussion of the information architecture or structure of multimedia to give writers insight into this practice.

High-Level Narrative Design

Similar to the information architecture in an informational program, the high level-design of an interactive narrative defines the major elements and organization of the project, including:

- the story structure
- the characters
- the role of the player in the narrative and what they will be able to do
- the granularity of the interactions. For example, will the player be able to choose scenes, shots, or the dialogue of the characters?

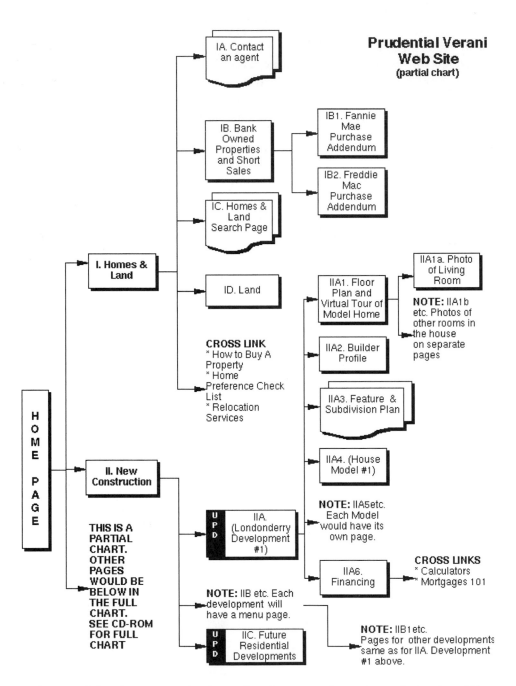

Figure 3-1 *Partial flowchart/sitemap for the Prudential Verani web site. Copyright Prudential Verani Realty.*

The writer's participation in the high-level design process of a narrative varies considerably from project to project. Sometimes the designer develops the story idea and the basic structure of the piece before the writer comes on the project. It is the designer who determines what the player will be able to do and how the interactions will work. Sometimes the writer's role is even more restricted; the designer may do much of the writing and bring in a writer to handle just a few scenes. But even in this diminished role, the writers need to be aware of how the scenes they are writing relate to the overall piece. Other designers bring the writers in early and encourage their contribution to the overall design. Many writers feel this is the best way to go, particularly when dealing with stories.

As writers gain experience in multimedia, many learn high-level story design and take more control of their material. This is actually a growing trend with the all-powerful designer disappearing on many projects and being replaced by a designer-writer. This was the case for the interactive narratives that are profiled in Chapters 22 and 23.

Project Management

Once a writer becomes responsible for the high-level story design or information architecture, he or she has an overall grasp of the project that is equal to or surpasses any other member of the team. Considering this, it is not a big leap from information architecture or high-level design to project manager, if the writer has organizational and people management skills. The project manager manages the budget, the personnel on the project, the client, and the coordination of all the elements.

Content Expertise

In informational multimedia, writers are more valuable if they have familiarity with certain types of content. It certainly doesn't hurt for a writer to have a specialty or several specialties, such as finance, medicine, mathematics, foreign languages or science. An important writing subcategory is localization. This involves the translation of multimedia and web content to other languages and cultures so that the program can have a wider audience. But unless the writer is assured of adequate work in one specialization, she should be careful to maintain enough flexibility so that she doesn't get pegged into just one type of work.

Content Strategy

Content strategy involves deciding the most effective way to present content for the user while also furthering the brand and business goals of the client. A content strategist must first clearly understand the content to be communicated, the needs and technical skills of the users, the business goals of the client, and budget constraints. Then the strategist can recommend the best approach for presenting the specific content. For example, would an explanation of erosion on a geology web site be best presented as text, text and graphics, video, animation or some combination of the above? A quite different example would be explaining banking products to a consumer. Would this best be done with text and graphics, a chart, or an online advisor (an interactive tool that asks a series of questions and gives advice). If information architects have content strategy skills, they are more valuable employees because they cannot only organize information but can also recommend the best way to present the information.

Web Site Marketing: Writing for Search Engines

If you write the most amazing web site and no one can find it, then you have failed. Most users find information on the web through major search engines, portals, and directories. On many search engines, link popularity and search results click through are equally if not more important than the site text. However, a web site writer needs to be able to write a site in such a way that within the limits of the search engine, the site text will improve the site's ranking on search engine results. This requires clever writing of site titles, site text, and to a lesser degree, meta tags. Meta tags are text on a web page that is hidden from the user but that can have some impact on how your site appears in search engine results. For a detailed discussion of writing for search engines see "Search Engines and Key Words" in Chapter 10.

Technical Skills

If the writer wants to expand his or her role beyond writer into information architect, project manager, and the other skill sets described above, learning a few technical tools can be quite helpful.

Flowcharting

One of the handiest tools for visualizing and organizing the branching structures of most multimedia programs and web sites is the flowchart (Figure 3-1). It is also a useful device to visualize online processes, such as the applying for a job or completing a series of exercises in an e-learning course. Fortunately, some of the software for creating flowcharts is inexpensive and easy to learn.

 Numerous examples of flowcharts as preproduction documents for multimedia productions and as illustrations appear in this book and in the "Chapters" section of the book's CD-ROM.

Flowchart Functions and Variations

A flowchart can have several functions and variations for the same multimedia production:

- **To design interactions.** Lines with arrows drawn between the labeled boxes on a chart make it possible to understand what links with what and in what way. For example, does the link work in both directions? Is it viewer-initiated or automatic?

- **To see the effects of revisions.** Continuity is a monstrous issue in interactive media. In linear media, changes in one scene may affect only the scenes immediately following it, but in interactive media, changes in one screen will affect all of the material that is linked to it. It is hard to determine these effects without a chart.
- **To chart character development.** Some writers create separate charts to track character development, particularly in parallel branching structures where the writers must be sure that the character change is properly set up and consistent in each plot line.
- **To present material to clients.** A complex interactive script can be inscrutable to a client, particularly one who has no interactive background. A one-page flowchart overview can do wonders to explain a project.
- **To communicate with the production team.** A production team chart is far more complicated than a client chart, especially a chart for the programmers, in which boxes are labeled with complicated programming code.
- **To track large productions.** Flowcharts combined with project management software can help chart the progress of a large production, keeping track of what has been accomplished and who is responsible for what lies ahead.
- **To form the basis for the user's sitemap.** Sometimes the chart itself is the user map, as in Fidelity Investments' retirement counselors' training program, where students can bring up the flowchart at any point and click on a labeled flowchart box to go to that section of the course.

Flowchart Symbols

A number of developers have suggested flowchart symbols to help make charts more useful. The symbols shown in Figure 3-2 include some commonly used symbols:

- **Decision Block:** A point where users have to make a choice that sends them to a different branch of the process or information.

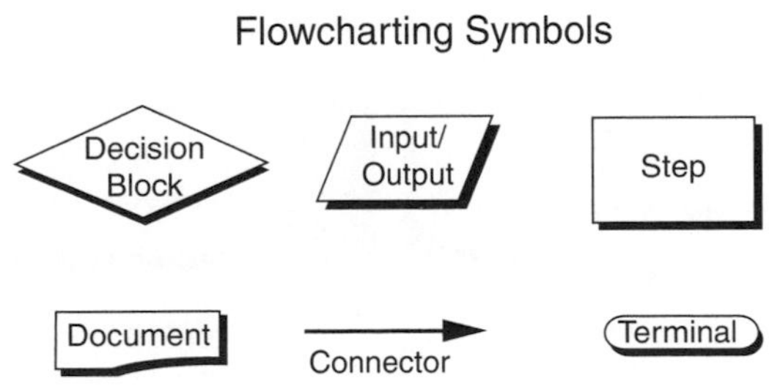

Figure 3-2 *Common flowcharting symbols.*

- **Input/Output:** User enters data of some kind, such as a test or a form.
- **Step:** A single step in a process (see also "Document" below).
- **Document or Page:** A single screen or web page, usually contains multiple elements. Particularly on web sites, the simple square is also commonly used for this.
- **Connector:** The link between symbols indicating process or information flow direction.
- **Terminal:** The beginning and ending points of a process.

Custom Symbols and Labels for a Project

The goal of using flowchart symbols or text labels is to increase clarity, but if there are too many complex symbols, they may add confusion. In my experience, a universal set of symbols has not been totally accepted. Instead, writers and developers seem to adopt symbols and labels that work well for them on a particular project. For example, Aaron Conners of Access Software uses shaded boxes to distinguish characters in his interactive dialogue. (See The Pandora Directive flowchart, Figure 22-2. For the Prudential Verani web site, the symbols illustrated in Figure 3-3 were used.)

Flowchart Design Tips

The goal is for the flowchart to be a clear visualization of the project structure. There are a number of techniques that help make it a more useful tool. The following points are illustrated in the Prudential Verani flowchart in Figure 3-1.

1. Give every page of the site a unique number and name. This makes communication with clients and production staff much clearer. Give pages in a specific section of the site the same first number with different second letters. In the flowchart example in Figure 3-1, standard outline conventions were used with numbers and different case letters. For example, the menu page for the Homes and Land section is Roman numeral "I." The Contact an Agent page, which is linked to that page, is page "IA," and so on.

KEY

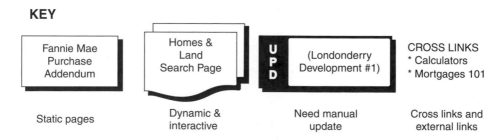

Figure 3-3 *Custom flowcharting symbols for a specific project.*

2. For ease of printing and presentation to a client or on a review web site, run the chart vertically, as in the sample in Figure 3-1, instead of horizontally. If this becomes a problem because your site is more than five levels deep, you may want to reexamine your information architecture and divide your material into more main categories. If a site has too many levels, it can cause navigation problems.

3. Simplify where you can. If there will be multiple sections that will be designed in the same way, it is OK to say that in a note. No need to draw out all the boxes for repetitive pages. There are several examples of this on the chart in the "New Construction" section where each housing development will be presented on the site the same way.

4. Make it easier to see the main sections by writing those pages in bold text. See "Homes and Land" and "New Construction" in Figure 3-1.

5. Indicate cross-links (links to pages within the site that are already on the chart) and external links (links to other web sites) as text only. This helps make the chart more readable and makes it clearer how many pages have to be produced for this project. If there are multiple cross-links or external links from the same page, use asterisks or bullets to separate them.

6. Visually indicate the pages that will have special functions, for example, pages that will have interactive elements or that will be generated dynamically from a database. Do not, however, make your chart confusing with too many different types of symbols. Three or four symbols with a simple key at the top are adequate. See the key sample in Figure 3-3.

Flowcharting Software

The key characteristics of a good writer's flowcharting program are that it can:

- Easily and quickly create and edit flowcharts.
- Export the chart in a standard image format, such as JPEG or GIF, and the outline as HTML for web publication. On almost every project that I have worked on, the client expects you to post work on a web site for review. A flowchart program that will automatically convert the charts and outline for web publishing saves a lot of time.
- Be used cross-platform. Ideally, there should be both Windows and Mac versions of the software. The files should also be cross-platform because your client or other members of your team may need to work with the outlines and flowcharts, and they may be on different platforms than you are. This condition will depend to a large degree on the platforms used by the production team and the client. If everyone is on Windows, then a Windows only software is acceptable. The most popular flowcharting software, Visio, is Windows only.

- Convert the chart into an outline and vice versa. This conversion is useful because:
  - some clients prefer outlines.
  - a chart can be converted into an outline, and then that outline can be used as the basis of a script for a program.
  - an outline can be imported from another program and then converted to a flowchart.

Software Recommendation

There are lots of tools that you can use to create flowcharts including word processors, draw programs, authoring programs, and presentation software, but like any dedicated task, you are going to be much better off getting software designed specifically for flowcharting.

There are many good flowcharting programs on the market. Depending on your situation, you many not be able to choose the software and will have to use whatever the client or the rest of the production team already uses. In most cases, this will probably be Microsoft Visio, which is one of the most popular flowcharting tools. This does not mean it is definitely the best tool or ideal for your situation. It is expensive, only works with Windows, and is loaded with features a writer may not need. If you do have the option of choosing your flowcharting software, you might consider Inspiration. This software is inexpensive, works on Macintosh and Windows, converts charts to outlines, and is very easy to use. All the demonstration charts in this book were drawn with Inspiration. Besides Visio and Inspiration, other major flowcharting software includes: SmartDraw (Windows only) and ConceptDraw (Windows and Mac).

Other Organizational Tools
Outlines

Some writers prefer to start their project with a simple hierarchical outline, as in a linear media writing project, such as a book or article. I find that an outline combined with a flowchart is a useful way to describe the content in a web site (see Chapter 10). Some storywriters find outlines one of the easiest ways to keep the story line and character development clear. Aaron Conners, whose interactive movies *Under a Killing Moon*, *The Pandora Directive*, and *Amped III* are among the most complex being written, uses an outline in the early stages of writing.

Storyboards or Wireframes

Storyboards or wireframes are an excellent organizing tool. A storyboard or wireframe is an illustration of the main screens of a program or web site combined with text explanations of the elements and how they will work together. Typically a storyboard screen is a more elaborate, finished product than a wireframe, but often these two terms are used synonymously. A storyboard or wireframe is a useful tool to plan out the information design at the page/screen level. They are also an effective way of presenting the information design to the production team and the client. Storyboards or wireframes can be very elaborate for complex programs, but often the client just needs a rough visualization of the proposed screens. There are dedicated storyboard programs, such as Boardmaster, but other multiuse programs will work equally as well for the writer. A WYSIWYG (pronounced "wiz-ee-wig," an acronym for "What You See Is What You Get") HTML editor, such as Macromedia's Dreamweaver, can create quick web pages that function like storyboards and even link the pages to give a simulation of the planned interactivity. Many information architects prefer a graphics program, such as Photoshop or Illustrator, to create static images of the proposed screens. Others use their flowcharting software to draw outlines of screen layouts. Sometimes just a rough sketch done in your word processor's draw program is adequate, such as the screen in Figure 3-4, which was done in Microsoft Word for a CD-ROM on careers.

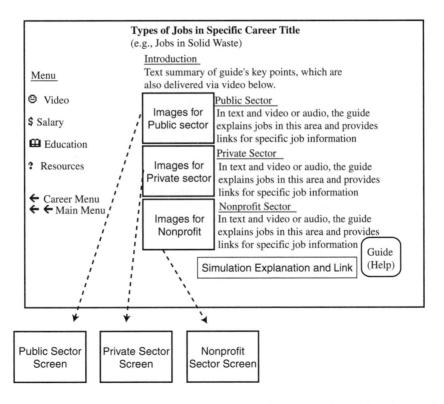

Figure 3-4 *Rough storyboard or wire frame for a CD-ROM done in Word. Storyboard copyright The Environmental Careers Organization.*

Database

Although the word "database" might strike fear in the hearts of many non-technical writers, database programs have become much easier to use. They can be a useful tool when writing, organizing, and managing large, complex projects. For example, my company InterWrite developed a geology web site and CD-ROM for the textbook company Houghton Mifflin. The project was large, had numerous assets (video, graphics, audio, animations), several content experts, and a number of editors. Developing a coherent script that would clearly describe and organize all these elements, plus allow all the content people and editors to add their comments to the script, was a challenge. The solution was to develop the script as a File-Maker Pro database that allowed us to have one master script as well as to sort and export various special versions of the script for different team members. See the end of Chapter 5 for a description of this solution and a sample page from the script. Don't feel that you have to learn to use a database to be an interactive writer. This was an unusual solution.

WYSIWYG HTML Editors

A WYSIWYG editor is a software program that allows the user to create web pages without knowing HTML, the markup language or programming code that is the basis of many web sites and browser based programs. A WYSIWYG editor's features include text formatting, image layout, linking, and much more. These editors are as easy to use as word processing software.

There are a couple of reasons why a writer should be able to create web pages. On almost every project that I work on, one of the first things that the client wants done is the creation of a review web site or extranet. This is a web site where I post scripts, flowcharts, images, and other production documents for the client to comment on. Sometimes it is also useful to rough out a complex section of a project in an HTML-based, interactive wireframe to help the client visualize it.

Basic WYSIWYG editors are inexpensive and adequate for most of a writer's tasks. If you are already skilled with a major word processor, such as Word or WordPerfect, then you may not have to spend any money at all. Most major word processors have converters that will convert your text into HTML. In most cases, however, these are not as versatile as a dedicated HTML editor. If you have the budget, my recommendation is to get Macromedia Dreamweaver, which is one of the easiest to use and most powerful HTML editors. If you are a student, there is usually a substantial student discount.

Conclusion

A multimedia writer does not have to learn all the skills described above to be successful. Many writers in large organizations are happy just writing content, but to increase your chances of success and your ability to handle any writing or organizational challenge, the more tools in your arsenal the better. On the other hand, don't forget to maintain your primary focus—presenting compelling information and exciting stories.

References

Inspiration Software. http://www.inspiration.com.
Iuppa, Nicholas V. *Interactive Video Design*. Boston, MA: Focal Press, 1982.
Macromedia Dreamweaver. http://www.macromedia.com/software/dreamweaver.
O'Meara, Maria. Notes to the author, February 1996.
Prudential Verani Realty Site. http://www.pruverani.com, 1999.

The Multimedia and Web Site Production Team

Chapter Overview

No matter how multiskilled a writer is, he or she will usually work as part of a production team. Understanding who these team members are and how to interact with them can add to the writer's success and ultimately that of the project. This chapter discusses the following members of the multimedia and web site production team:

- Writer
- Content Strategist
- Instructional Designer
- Information Architect or Interactive Architect
- Interface Designer
- Game Designer
- Usability Expert
- Subject Matter Expert
- Business Strategist
- Art Director/Creative Director/Graphic Artist
- Animator
- Project Manager
- Video/Audio Director/Developer
- Photographer/Videographer
- Voice Talent and Actors
- Programmer/Coder
- Product Manager

The Writer

The interactive writer may create: proposals, outlines, sitemaps, treatments, walk-throughs, design documents, scripts, and all the other written materials that describe a multimedia or web site project. This can include developing the information architecture, on-screen text, overall story structure, dialogue, characters, narration, interface, and more. Exactly which of these tasks the writer actually does on a specific project depends on the needs of the project, the size of the team, and the skill of the writer. Sometimes the writer simply writes text already outlined in detail by an information architect or an instructional designer. On smaller projects the writer might also play additional roles.

The Content Strategist

Content can be presented in a wide variety of ways: animation, video, text, graph-ics, exercises, etc. The content strategist determines the content strategy through analysis of the user's information needs, technical expertise, favored delivery media, and culture. He also researches the current format and organization of the client data and the client's business and branding goals for a specific type of content. Based on this research, the content strategist develops a strategy that suggests the most effective presentation for each type of content in the project. The content strate-gist will give clear direction to the writer. Sometimes the content strategist role is combined with the information architect of the instructional designer.

The Instructional Designer

This role occurs most commonly in educational multimedia, training, and e-learning programs where a specific skill or subject is being taught. Drawing from knowl-edge of the user, the content, and instructional design principals, the instructional designer carefully structures the information to teach the desired content to the user. Some of the tasks include breaking information into smaller units, sequenc-ing information units and determining the need for interactive elements, such as tests, exercises, and feedback. The key instructional design deliverables are process flowcharts and wireframes. Process flowcharts visually lay out the sequence and relationship of the information overall. Wireframes present the information design of individual screens in rough sketches or interactive prototypes.

The Information Architect or Interactive Architect

As described in the Chapter 3, the information architect is the person responsible for the overall structure and navigation of an informational multimedia and web project.

The information architect, sometimes also called an interactive architect, is a close cousin to the instructional designer. Sometimes the same person has both skill sets. Many of the same steps previously defined in the instructional design definition also hold true here, but the overall goal is somewhat different. A project requiring an information architect is not necessarily instructing the user, but instead is making a body of information easy to find and use, such as product information on an automaker's web site. An interactive architect might be designing the process flow for an online or offline application, such as a tool for doing your taxes. Similar to instructional design, the key deliverables for both interactive and information architecture are process flowcharts and wireframes. (See Chapter 3 for more information on wireframes and flowcharts.)

The Interface Designer

The interface designer position can vary from project to project. Sometimes it incorporates the information architect and instructional designer positions along with graphic design skills. Sometimes the position is primarily a graphic design position that works with a separate information architect or instructional designer. The job of the interface designer is to structure the layout and the visual look of a project's interface as presented to the user. The interface could be as simple as an information web site with menus and text or as complex as an elaborate computer game world with buildings, people you can talk to, and functional objects like telephones and cars. See Chapter 1 for more on interfaces.

The Game Designer

Related to the above skill sets is the game designer. On a large computer game, there may be several types of designers, but these categories are sometimes lumped into one title: "creative designer," "game designer," or just "designer." In most cases, a designer's responsibilities include the structure of the game play, the visual look of the project, and sometimes also the interface design.

The Usability Expert

Usability testing makes sure that the product functions effectively from the user's point of view, while achieving the client's goals. To refine usability, the usability expert gets user feedback on products in various ways, including questionnaires, interviews, blind testing, and site visits to the user's location. The usability expert also has knowledge of usability best practices and often has an advanced degree in a field, such as human computer interaction or communications. The usability expert provides usability test reports, analyzes questionnaire results, interview transcripts, and usability expert analyses. Reviewing some of this material can help the writer better understand the user. (See "Tips for Writers from Usability Experts" in Chapter 2.)

The Subject Matter Expert

Although the writer will often be in charge of doing his or her own research on a subject, if a subject is particularly complex or technical, there will also be a subject matter expert (SME) on a project. This person is crucial to the writer. The SME will often provide reference material, outlines, and will review the writer's script for accuracy. Sometimes the SME is simply a resource for the writer to interview.

The Business Strategist

This business strategist has some similarities with the subject matter expert in that the business strategist is an expert on business issues. Usually a business strategist has an MBA and some experience in business. This role is common on corporate e-commerce web sites and marketing web sites where it is important to understand the client's business goals and processes and come up with a way to achieve these goals in the interactive media project. The business strategist often writes the user scenarios, which describe typical users and how they might use the product. This is a great resource for the writer so that he/she can be sure to slant the writing toward the project's audience.

The Art Director/Creative Director/Graphic Artist

The art director, sometimes also called the creative director, oversees and sometimes creates visuals—backgrounds, interface screens, graphics, and animations. The art director supervises individual graphic artists. The writer should work closely with the art director/creative director, especially if considering more complex visuals, such as animations. He or she can make the writer aware of the communication potential of the graphic tools being used on the project. On a well-run project, the visual design serves the content. The creative director works closely with the information architects and instructional designers to visually engage the viewer, maximize a positive user experience, and support effective information presentation.

The Animator

On a complex project, a good animator is a real asset to the team. The writer should learn the capabilities of this individual because an animation is often the only clear way to explain certain subjects, such as scientific processes. Animation is also used for simpler uses, such as online tours of a complex web site or program. Macromedia Flash animation has become an important tool for web sites.

The Project Manager

On large projects, this is a separate position, but sometimes is combined with other positions, as described in Chapter 3. The project manager (PM) manages the budget, the schedule, the client, and the personnel on the project. If the writer needs resources or is unclear about deadlines or any other aspect of the project, the PM is usually the person to go to.

The Video/Audio Director/Developer

The video or film director is in charge of creating live-action video or audio. The director may also be in charge of developing the original audio for stock footage. The writer's relationship to the director varies with each individual, but in many cases it is a collaboration that starts with the director commenting on early drafts of the script, and extends into production with the writer performing last-minute rewrites. On projects with limited video, the director and the developer who actually produce the video and audio may be the same person. On larger projects, the director is in charge of a team of cameramen, editors, lighting technicians, sound artists, actors, etc.

The Photographer/Videographer

Another key person is the photographer or, if there is video, the videographer. On smaller projects, there will not be a separate video director. The writer has to be sure that the photographer or videographer can capture the images needed for the project. The writer must be able to adequately describe the project's visuals needs and to understand the capabilities of the photographer/videographer and the limitations of their equipment.

The Voice Talent and Actors

If a project has audio narration or on-screen actors, the voice talent or actors will be part of the team. It is useful for the writer to listen to the actors or voice talent speaking the lines the writer has written. This can help the writer tune the language so it is better suited for this particular speaker.

The Programmer/Coder

The programmer writes the code or uses the authoring program to make the dreams of the writer, designer, and other production members become reality on the computer screen. Establishing good rapport with the programmer is useful for the writer to understand what type of information or story element manipulations are possible with the tools available for this program. If a programmer's skills are limited to HTML and JavaScript for web sites, the team member is sometimes called a site developer. Site developers often also have graphic skills.

The Product Manager

On large projects, the product manager works with the client and deals with marketing issues if the program is aimed at the mass market. Sometimes the roles of product manager and project manager are combined. A writer who is brought in early can test ideas with the product manager, who often knows the client's needs or the intended market best. But writers should never completely abdicate their creative vision in favor of market research. If the marketing people could always predict what would be successful, then they would all be rich.

Conclusion

Not all of the individuals discussed above will be on every project. Many projects will have some of these duties combined. Very large projects will have even more positions. To get a sense of the types of positions evolving in multimedia and the web, go to the careers section on the web site of a big production company or recruiter and review their job listings.

The core creative team for most projects includes writers, designers, and programmers. Because of the complexity of multimedia, the writers must think of themselves as part of this team and learn all they can from their team members so that they push the communication potential of multimedia and the web to the limits needed for each project.

References

O'Meara, Maria. Notes to the author, 1996, 2005.

Script and Proposal Formatting

Chapter Overview

Multimedia and the web's use of many media and interactivity make script formatting difficult. Nevertheless, it is essential for writers to present their ideas effectively on paper so that clients and production team members can visualize their ideas. At this point in the industry, there is no one set format for all situations. The format chosen depends on the demands of the individual production. After discussing scriptwriting software, this chapter defines the following formats:

- Web site outlines
- Treatments
- Proposals and design documents
- Single-column scripts
- Multicolumn scripts

Scripting Software

There are number of software programs dedicated to script formatting and developing large writing projects, including:

- CopyWrite (Mac) is a project management tool for writers. It allows a writer to browse, organize, and manage the documents and information for a project.
- StoryView helps organize large writing projects. It is a visual outliner for writers that lets a writer brainstorm, create, structure, and organize ideas.
- WordMenu is an all-in-one dictionary, thesaurus, almanac, and more.
- Final Draft Screenplay and Movie Magic are two popular screenplay formatting and script development software programs.

Some writers swear by these programs and think that it makes the writing process much easier. The web sites for these programs are at the end of this chapter. Most of them have free demos so you can try them out and see if they work for you.

My own feeling, and that of many of the writers interviewed for this book, is that if you are competent with a major word processing program, such as MSWord, you don't really need a dedicated scriptwriting program. The key is in becoming skilled with tables and learning how to create macros. Macros allow you to automate certain formatting functions and make writing a script much easier. If you don't know how to use macros, go to the help section of your software, search for macros and follow the instructions.

Using your current word processor will not only save you money and the time it would take to learn a new program, it will also insure compatibility. Scripts and other documents are often shared with other members of the multimedia team. If you write in a major word processor, chances are that other members of the team will be able to open your files and edit your documents. If you use a specialized script formatting software, accessibility may not be the case, unless the software can export to a standard format, such as MSWord or RTF. This export feature should be a major consideration before buying one of these specialized scriptwriting tools.

Preliminary Documents: Outlines, Proposals, and Design Documents

A project's script or detailed design document includes every word of text, narration and dialogue; descriptions of all the images, videos, and animations; and explanations of the linking and functional elements. Fortunately, projects almost never start with a script. Usually some sort of preliminary written document is presented to the client and other members of the production team before the final script is written. This is useful for clients who may have difficulty understanding an interactive script. It also insures that the basic goals of the project are being achieved before the fine details are worked out in the script. Sometimes the preliminary form itself, such as a web site outline, is adequate to get the production green-lighted with the client. (One preliminary document, the use case, which defines the user's needs, is explained in Chapter 7.)

Outlines

Before writing a full text script of all the content on a web site or another information heavy program, such as an online course, it is useful to write a content outline and a flowchart to explain the content and navigation to the client and production team.

Flowcharts were discussed in detail under "Flowcharting" in Chapter 3. The flowchart illustrates the overall navigation, structure, and size of the site; the outline provides more details about the actual content and functionality of the individual pages. The outline sample that follows is most effectively used with an accompanying flowchart. The client consults the chart for overall structure, and then reads the outline for the details. The structure of each page on the outline below is fairly simple. The outline should be adjusted to match the specific project. The elements include:

- Title: The page title, which should be the same as what is on the flowchart
- Image: Describes possible images for the page, including animations or videos
- Text: Describes on-screen text
- Links: Includes all the links on this page from text within the page and from the navigation bar or menu
- Navigation: The specific buttons that will have to be created for the navigation bar or menu
- Functionality: This describes what the user can do on this page besides click and read. For example, if it is a real estate site, as in the example below, can the user search for properties or calculate a mortgage payment?

A useful feature of Inspiration software, which I use to create my outlines, is that it will convert the outline to HTML for publishing to a client's review site on the web. Part of this conversion creates a clickable menu at the top of the outline for every page in the site, so the client can quickly jump to the page they want.

 See the Chapter 10 section on this book's CD-ROM for a working example of this menu.

Partial Outline of the *Prudential Verani* Web Site

HOME PAGE

TITLE: PRUDENTIAL VERANI REALTY: The Real Estate and Relocation Resource for Southern NH

IMAGE: Images that demonstrate that Verani is a professional, friendly place. Possible images: Prudential logo, friendly Verani staff, Verani office, people enjoying a beautiful home. Might have other images on page to lead user to some of our key features, such as a calculator image for the tools and an e-mail icon for our custom e-mail notification service. Images will be small or designed in such a way that the page will load quickly.

TEXT: Explain that we are part of Prudential, one of the largest corporations in the world, but also a family-owned company with strong roots in Southern New Hampshire. We have the resources to sell your property effectively and/or make your home search efficient and successful. Also should introduce some of the key features of the site, such as our searches, custom e-mail notification tools, extensive information resources, and so on. Near the bottom of the page should be a short disclaimer stating that we have made every effort to make the information on this site accurate but are not liable for any errors or omissions; please see our Terms of Use Policy.

LINKS: Homes & Land, New Construction, Commercial & Industrial, Relocation Services, Verani Mortgage and Title, Real Estate Information & Resources, News & Special Events, Search/Site Map, About Us/Contact.

   Might also have a link from a calculator image to the tools and calculator section.

   In text on the bottom of the page and on every page will be links to Terms of Use, Privacy Statements and a webmaster e-mail link.

NAVIGATION BAR: Homes & Land, New Construction, Commercial & Industrial, Relocation Services, Verani Mortgage and Title, Real Estate Information & Resources, News & Special Events, Search/Site Map, About Us/Contact.

I. HOMES & LAND

TITLE: Homes & Land

IMAGE: Small image of attractive house. This could be the same picture all the time or a regularly changing featured house.

TEXT: Briefly explain the range of properties we offer and the area we cover. Direct the user to the search page and other services that will help with moving and home buying, such as Relocation Services, the How to Buy a Property Section, Home Preference Check List/Questionnaire, & New Construction.

LINKS: Home, Search, Contact, Relocation Services, the How to Buy a Property Section, Home Preference Check List/Questionnaire, & New Construction.

NAVIGATION BAR: Home, Search, Contact

IA. CONTACT AN AGENT

TITLE: Contact Us

IMAGE: Photo of friendly agent.

TEXT: Phone numbers, addresses, and e-mails for all offices. Plus a form that the user can fill out and submit so that we can contact them.

LINKS: Home Page, Search, Contact, Homes & Land.

NAVIGATION BAR: Home Page, Search, Contact, Homes & Land.

FUNCTIONALITY: Users can fill out form with their address and e-mail, click the type of information they want, write a short note and submit it to us. Message will go to different people at Prudential Verani depending on what type of information the user requests.

Copyright Prudential Verani Realty.

Treatments

Although a treatment could be used for a preliminary description of a web site, it is more commonly used for CD-ROM or DVD multimedia programs. The treatment, a form borrowed from linear film or TV writing, describes the structure and key elements of a project in a form similar to an essay or a short story. Guidelines for treatment writing include:

- Use the third person (e.g., "He shambles," not "I shamble" or "you shamble").
- Use the present tense ("he shambles," not "he shambled").
- Write visually. Be descriptive, but don't call shots.
- Capitalize:

   o Character names when they first appear.

   o Major sound effects.

   o Technical directions, such as ROLLOVER, LINK, etc. (but don't use unless necessary).

- Usually summarize on-screen text, dialogue, and narration, although a few bits of dialogue or narration are allowed if they help present the material.
- Usually double-space treatments, although sometimes they are single-spaced, with chapter or section headings in all capitals.

Multimedia Informational Treatment Sample

The following sample is from the conclusion of the treatment for *The Nauticus Shipbuilding Company*, a multimedia program about shipbuilding presented on a museum kiosk. (The entire treatment may be found under "The Proposal" in Chapter 14.)

```
Conclusion: After the last component has been selected, a 3-D
animation sequence depicts the launching of the vessel. If the
design is suitable for the mission, the visitor will see a
depiction of their design successfully carrying out the mission.
If the design is fundamentally flawed, the vessel will be shown
sinking. Some evaluation will be provided as to the ability of the
visitor's design to carry out the selected mission. Finally, the
visitor will be given the opportunity to print out his design and
evaluation.
```

Narrative Treatment Sample

A narrative interactive treatment is sometimes called a walkthrough. The following is a section of the walkthrough for *The Pandora Directive*. (See Chapter 22.)

```
In the introductory conversation with Gordon Fitzpatrick, you
learn that he is looking for a Dr. Thomas Malloy, who recently
stayed at the Ritz Hotel. Fitzpatrick and Malloy used to work
together (where, unspecified). Fitzpatrick then says he saw a
photograph of Malloy in the Bay City Mirror and found out that the
photograph had been taken at a local university (San Francisco
Tech). Fitzpatrick gives Tex a copy of the photo.
```

Proposals and Design Documents

A treatment is usually only one component of the first detailed description of an interactive project. This preliminary description is sometimes called a high-level design document proposal, a design proposal or just a proposal.

Format for an Informational Design Document Proposal

A proposal can be in many forms. There are several examples in the cases studies. One fairly standard approach includes the following elements. See Chapter 14 for a complete design document following this format.

- Design objective. This is a short description of what the program hopes to accomplish. It is sometimes no more than a paragraph, but it is important because it is the first chance to grab the reader.

- Creative treatment. This is a detailed description of the entire program. It will run for many pages, depending on the size of the project.
- Navigation. This is a description of the interface and how the user will navigate through the program. It often includes a navigation flowchart. The navigation is also described in the treatment.
- Production and marketing. Design documents often have sections dealing with the project schedule or, if it is a mass-market piece, ideas for marketing the program to the public. Biographies of the writer, designer, and other key personnel are sometimes included here.

Format for a Narrative Proposal

A proposal for a multimedia program that includes a story would follow much of the same format as above. It may, however, call the treatment a "story summary." There may also be sections describing the characters.

Storyboards, Scripts, and Final Documents

Unlike the preliminary documents discussed above that summarize the key features of a program, the script details every element of a piece. The examples that follow are only a few of the interactive script formats in use, but they present enough options that you should be able to find something that can be adapted for your production.

Be aware that many productions don't use traditional scripts at all and instead use combinations of flowcharts, dialogue lists, walkthroughs, and other types of written material. These materials and other script samples are documented in more detail in the case studies in Part II and Part III.

Linear Screenplay Format

Many approaches to formatting scripts for interactive multimedia use linear screenplay or teleplay format as their basis and then add variations, so it is useful to understand the specifics of the linear screenplay format.

Script format is important because the running time of a video is judged by the number of pages. One page, if it is typed in proper format, is roughly one minute of screen time. There are variations on the example below, such as greater use of double-spacing in television writing, but the example is a standard screenplay format that can readily be adapted to different situations. Note that margins and line spacing are distorted in the example below to allow space for the directions.

The format below includes some technical and camera directions. Be aware that if you are writing a script to hand off to a director or multimedia designer, they may not want such directions included. In that case, you can still use the same format below, but leave out the technical and shot material, such as "Camera Dollies Back."

DIRECTIONS

Top margin = 1". Number pages in upper right-hand corner. No number on page 1.

Slug lines are typed in CAPS at the beginning of each scene, telling whether scene is INT. or EXT. (interior or exterior), location of scene, and day or night.

Scene Description: Left margin 1.75", right margin 1" (7.5" if measured from left).

Break long descriptions into several short paragraphs. The first time a character's name appears in the scene description, type it in CAPS.

Single-space within scene description or dialogue. Add a blank line space between dialogue passages, scene description paragraphs, and slug lines.

Dialogue: left margin = 3.0", right margin = 2" (or 6.5" if measured from left).

THE MULTIMEDIA WRITER

FADE IN:

INT. ARNOLD'S BEDROOM DAY

The room is a wreck. The floor is covered with papers and trash, the bed is unmade and cigarette butts litter the desk and windowsills.

ARNOLD throws the door open and stumbles into the room. **CAMERA DOLLIES BACK** with him. Arnold is in his early twenties, thin and unkempt. His once handsome features are contorted in agony. He clutches what appears to be a multimedia manuscript in his hand.

He stumbles to the floor and falls to his knees, pulling the script to his bosom. He falls back with a scream and hits the floor in agony, dropping the script.

The title of the manuscript is revealed to be The Great American Computer Game.

                    ARNOLD (OS)*
                    (whispering)
          Why me?

DISSOLVE TO:

EXT. ARNOLD'S APARTMENT DAY LONG **SHOT**

The door of the apartment swings open and Arnold stumbles out clutching his script.

Name of person speaking dialogue is in CAPS and centered over the dialogue. No space between speaker's name and dialogue.

> **ARNOLD**
> I keep asking myself:
> What is the secret?
>
> The booming, powerful, authoritative
> voice from the unseen NARRATOR of our
> film is heard.

Dialogue direction is typed in small letters, centered under speaker and placed in parentheses.

> **NARRATOR (VO)****
> (booming)
> Arnold never did learn the secret.
> He should have read Tim Garrand's
> *Writing for Multimedia and the Web.*

Camera movements, such as tilt, pan, track, dolly, and zoom typed in CAPS in the scene description. On right side of page are placed: Fade out and Dissolve to. On left is Fade in.

> **THE CAMERA QUICKLY ZOOMS IN
> TO** Arnold. He tosses away his script
> in the trash and runs off.

Bottom margin = 1/2–1". It depends on how dialogue breaks. Don't break dialogue over 2 pages.

> His script sits on the top of the
> trashcan, its pages fluttering sadly
> in the breeze.
>
> **FADE OUT.**

*(OS) next to the speaker means off-screen. The character is part of the action, but we do not see him or her in this particular shot. A character yelling from the bathroom while the camera focuses on the bedroom is an example of an off-screen voice. Or, as in the example above, the camera could simply be focused on an object in the same room as the character, leaving the character nearby but off-screen.

**(VO) next to the speaker means voice-over. This indicates that the speaker is not a part of the film or video's action. A modern newscaster narrating a World War I documentary is an example of VO.

Single-Column, Simple If-Then Interactive Format

Use: Narrative or informational programs with limited interactivity, usually at the scene level. Because it is a single-column script, it would not be well suited to a program with extensive voice-over narration. That usually requires a multicolumn script, which is explained later in this chapter under "Double-Column Format" and "Triple-Column Format."

Description: This script is similar to the linear screenplay described above, except that at various points in the script the user is given two or three choices of different scenes. This type of script can be used when the interactivity is fairly simple. The following example is part of an interactive museum piece located at the National Scouting Museum in Irving, Texas. In this story, the characters have to choose whether to search the school, the farm or the neighborhood for a missing child. The situation is first outlined in a linear fashion, and then the options follow: first the school scene option, then the farm scene option. The neighborhood option is not included in this sample.

 The complete script is included in the "Boy Scout Patrol" area of the Chapters section of the book's CD-ROM.

BOY SCOUT PATROL THEATER
by Maria O'Meara

```
SCENE 2
TROOP HQ

2-1. WS GROUP


                        ALEX
        Okay. We all know why we're here. Bob has divided the
        map up into areas. We're going to use the buddy system
        to cover each one.


                        BOB
        Here's a map of the area we're searching.


2-2. MAP GRAPHIC


                     BOB (voice-over)
        This is where she was last seen—the school. Here's
        where she lives. Between the two is the old Wilson Farm.


WHICH PART DO YOU WANT TO SEARCH?
A. THE SCHOOL
B. THE FARM
C. THE GIRL'S NEIGHBORHOOD


IF A. THE SCHOOL
SCENE 2A
2A-1. CU ALEX


                        ALEX
        Chas and Don, you guys go see if she's not still hanging
        around the school.
```

```
M-1.
TRANSITION MONTAGE TO SCHOOL
1. POV HALLWAY
2. POV SCIENCE ROOM
3. POV POOL
4. POV STAIRS


SCENE 3
3-1.2 SHOT BOYS enter a classroom.
```

[Scenes have been deleted. The boys search the school and fail to find the girl. They return to scout headquarters and must choose again.]

```
WHICH PART DO YOU WANT TO SEARCH?
A. THE SCHOOL
B. THE FARM
C. THE GIRL'S NEIGHBORHOOD


[IF B. THE FARM]
2B-1. 2 SHOT ALEX AND BOB


                          ALEX

    Greg and Hal—search the farm.


M-2.
TRANSITION MONTAGE TO FARM AREA
1. POV WOODS


They happen upon their science teacher who is looking for mushrooms
in a field. He looks very scientific and has a sample bag, notebook,
magnifying glass, etc. He is humming a little song.
```

Single-Column, Complex If-Then Interactive Format

Use: The previous example had fairly simple if-then conditions. For example, if the scout decided to search the farm, then we cut to the farm scene. For many projects the interactivity is far more complex. In such projects, the questions users ask of characters in the program or what action users did previously will affect what new actions, characters or dialogue will appear on screen. This type of complex if-then interactivity requires a more complex format.

Description: The following sample is from the computer game, *Nancy Drew: The Secret of the Old Clock*. This is a highly interactive program where the player gradually accumulates clues and information to solve a mystery. The player gathers the information in a nonlinear sequence. So the game engine needs to keep track of what the player has already discovered in order to reveal the next pertinent bit of information.

For example, if the player has already asked a certain character about another character's middle name, he or she should get a different response than if he or she had not asked that question previously. In the first line of the sample below, there is an elaborate series of conditions that indicates what the player already knows: "If EV_Saw_Questions = True and EV_EC_Said_Lois = False and EV_JW_Said_Mid_Name = False." This indicated the player does not know the middle name is "Lois" and that the player has not asked this specific character JW about this before. When these conditions are met, the player will be able to click on (ask) the question that follows the conditions tagged with <>, and the character will respond with the line that's in square brackets ([ ]). However, if the conditions are different and JW_Said_Mid_Name = True (see the line below "Go to 1048"), that means the player has asked JW about this before and instead of Scene 1047, Scene 1048 will be used in which the player is sent to another character, Emily. This script format is used in conjunction with a flowchart. There is a more detailed discussion of this script format and this game in Chapter 20.

```
                    Scene 1047 Information Check
If EV_Saw_Questions = True and EV_EC_Said_Lois = False and
EV_JW_Said_Mid_Name = False

<What was Emily's mom's middle name, do you remember?><NJP47>

['Course I do. It was ... {frustrated} Oh, piffle! It's right on
the tip of my tongue. It was ... it was ...][JWP47]

                          Go to 1048
Flag Set: EV_JW_Said_Mid_Name = True
Info Check: No
Bye: No
===========


                          Scene 1048
[{with an exasperated sigh} It'll pop into this feeble brain of
mine one of these days. Why don't you just go ask Emily.][JWP48]
Flag Set: None
```

```
Info Check: Yes
Bye: Yes
===========
```

_____

Copyright Her Interactive Inc.

Single-Column, Screen-Based Informational Script with Element Labels

Use: This script is best suited to an informational program that has considerable interactivity and a variety of media, such as narration, text, and video. Screen elements are clearly defined in the script by labels.

Description: This script was used in the training program *Vital Signs*, which teaches medical technicians how to perform various tasks. Each script page is one screen of material. The script page has three parts divided by horizontal lines. The top part describes the lesson and topic. The middle part describes the actions. The bottom part describes the feedback (reaction to the actions) and linking.

VITAL SIGNS

Unit: u1
Lesson: Blood Pressure
Topic:
Title:
Screen: u1.4.13p
Type:
Graphic File:

_____

(GRAPHIC/VIDEO: Colette looking apprehensive)
Text:
Meet Colette, age 7.
You're going to take her blood pressure. You've explained the procedure to her. What do you use next?
(CAPTIONS)
   Cuff   Ball Pump   Valve on cuff Doll

(AUDIO: NARRATOR VO): Now it's your turn. Meet Colette, age 7. You're going to take her blood pressure. You've explained the procedure. What do you use next—the cuff, the ball pump, the valve on the cuff or the doll? SELECT your choice now.

_____

Feedback: (VO and text)
Cuff, Ball Pump, Valve = (SFX: Little Girl's Voice) **(VO audio ONLY):** No. I don't want that. It's going to hurt!

NARRATOR (VO): Apparently, Colette didn't buy your explanation. Try again.

Doll = **NARRATOR (VO):** You're good. That's right. From the look on her face, you can tell Colette didn't buy your explanation, so you demonstrate on a doll. (SELECT "GO AHEAD" to continue.)

Branching: u1.4.14p

Special Instructions:

Single-Column, Screen-Based Informational Script Written in a Database

Use: This type of script could be used for a narrative or information piece with substantial interactivity. It would only be needed for a complex program with many team members or where the final pages were dynamically generated from script segments in a database.

Description: My company InterWrite developed a geology web site and CD-ROM for the textbook company Houghton Mifflin. The project was quite large, had numerous assets (video, graphics, audio, animations), several content experts, and a number of editors. Developing a coherent script that would clearly describe all these elements and allow all the content people and editors to add their comments to the script was a challenge.

The solution was to develop the script as a FileMaker Pro database (see following for a sample page). Each of the elements below, such as screen text or visual layout, was separate fields or units of information in the database. This allowed us to have one master script with all the elements, but by using the databases sort and export functions, we were able to create multiple custom scripts and documents from that master script. These documents included: a list of scenes and a flowchart for the project manager; a table of assets needed for the media researcher; a script (free of internal comments) for an outside vendor; a detailed list of instructions for the animator; and so on. This database script could also be used as the basis of an asset database so that video, graphics, and other elements could be easily found for future projects.

GEOLOGY EXPLORER

Page Number. Title Date	VIII-2b Relative Ages
Screen Text	Now see if you can determine the year in which the car in the center was released. Write your answer

	in the space provided and then hit "Continue." If you have absolutely no idea, just hit "Continue."
Visual Layout	Layout 2 Text top, Graphic bottom. The graphic consists of the three cars in a row. A text input box labeled "Car Release Date" is above the 1955 Ford.
Screen Action	Input date; hit "Continue."
Feedback	
Links	Correct Answer + Continue. → VIII-2b1 Incorrect Answer + Continue. → VIII-2b2.
A: Graphic 1	D1) Model-T Ford
A: Graphic 2	D2) 1955 Ford
A: Graphic 3	D3) 1999 Lexus
A: Animation	
A: Audio	
A: Video	
A: Shockwave	Three pictures are arranged in a horizontal row with a text input box above D2)1955 Ford.
Assets Notes	
Notes Internal	No need to actually register whether the student is right. We can just give the correct answer.
Notes to Author	
Notes to Vendor	

Copyright Houghton Mifflin Company.

Double-Column Format

Use: Informational projects with substantial interactivity and voice-over narration.

Description: This format is similar to what is used for documentary video. It has two columns, with images on the left and audio and text on the right. An unusual aspect of this particular script is that it is illustrated, which works very well to present the feel of the completed project. Most double-column scripts do not include images.

This program is displayed in an interactive kiosk at the National Maritime Center in Norfolk, Virginia. This production teaches shipbuilding principles by having the player build a ship. In the following section, users can choose to get information on various hull types and then must pick one of these hulls for the ship they are building. Because there is only a small amount of material on each hull, all the choices are listed sequentially. See Chapter 14 for the full script.

THE NAUTICUS SHIPBUILDING COMPANY

```
         IMAGES                              AUDIO & TEXT
                                     "Press a number to learn about a
                                     hull"


                                              CHOICES:
                                     1) Air Cushion
                                     -Flat hull rides on cushion of
                                     air
                                     -Capable of high speeds
```

```
                                     -Needs flat water conditions
                                     -Flat, rectangular deck, easy to
                                     load
                                     2) Planing Hull
                                     -V-shaped hull capable of high
                                     speeds
```

```
                                     -Performs best in flat water
                                     conditions
                                     -High stress levels on hull
                                     3) Displacement Hull
                                     -Deep, rounded hull, very stable
                                     in all conditions
```

```
                                     -Very large cargo capacity
                                     -Stable platform for large
                                     propulsion systems
                                     -Needs very large propulsion
                                     system
                                     4) SWATH (Small Waterplane Area
                                     Twin Hull)
```

```
                                     -2 submerged hulls, very stable
                                     -Flat deck provides good work
                                     area
```

After selecting a hull to use, cut to Design Assembly screen, animation of hull rollout.	Loudspeaker VO: "Planing hull being moved into position."
Cut to POV animation moving to propulsion subassembly area.	Background sound of motors whirring and machinery clanging. "Next, you'll need to choose a propulsion system."

Three Column Format with Narration and Text Transcript

Use: Informational scripts with substantial interactivity and a variety of media including both audio narration and on-screen text transcripts of that narration.

Description: Often learning programs will have both audio narration and a text transcript of the on-screen narration. This helps learners who may prefer to read versus listen, do not have audio or who have a disability. The writer cannot just repeat the narration and the text transcript because there will be subtle differences in the narration, which must be listened to (and read aloud by the narrator) and the text transcript, which is read silently by the user. Note that the narration column is shaded to clearly identify it for the narrator who must read the text. This format also has a fourth column (not pictured here), which was used for production purposes, such as timing the narration. The animations and graphics are simply described by a file name, which is described in detail on a separate animation page of the script. See Chapter 13 in the book or CD-ROM for a more detailed example of this format.

Images, Text, Programming	Narration (Text Transcript)	Narration (Audio Transcript)
1)(Title) Creating Time Plots		
2)(Main Screen Text) When data are collected over a period of time, they can be represented by a **time plot.**	When data are collected over a period of time, they can be represented by a **time plot.**	When data are collected over a period of time, they can be represented by a **time plot.**
3)(Definition Box) A time plot is a graph showing data measurements in chronological order.	A time plot is a graph that shows data measurements in chronological order. It is important to	A time plot is a graph that shows data measurements in chronological order. It is important to note

	note that the interval of time between measurements should be the same. So, if you take a measurement once a week, it should be on the same day every week. Or, if you take a measurement every day, the same time period, such as one-half hour, should be used.	that the interval of time between measurements should be the same. So, if you take a measurement once a week, it should be on the same day every week. Or, if you take a measurement every day, the same time period, such as one-half hour, should be used.
4a)(Procedure Box)Making a Time Plot[il0262m02c01 anim01F1_IW.ai]	To make a time plot, use the following procedure.	To make a time plot, use the following procedure.

Copyright Houghton Mifflin Company.

Six Column Format with Live Host, Interactive Media, and Audience Interactivity

Use: Immersive exhibits in museums or complex presentations at major conferences and events that use a combination of live host and interactive media before live audiences.

Description: Script has six columns for the Host's dialogue, user interaction in this case through a PDA attached to each seat, video on big screen, audio and narration, lighting effects on the audience, and cues for the host who controls the program. See Table 5-1 for an example. A longer example of this script can be read in Chapter 24.

Conclusion

As you have seen in the variety of script and other document formats in this chapter, there is no one way to format for multimedia and web documents. The primary requirement is to make sure that whatever format you choose, it is clear to your client and everyone on your production team. And as with most things, keep it as simple as you can. Your format should be self-explanatory.

Table 5-1

HOST	VOTE; PDA	VIDEO & LIGHTING	AUDIO, NARRATION, & SFX	EFX	CUES
In our first game, we'll be visiting the year 1813 and exploring the beginnings of the textile industry here in New England. Look down at your screen to see how much you have to start with.		Graphic or animation Bank account icon from PDA.		1813 Gobo effect on queue with movie	Host – next at the word screen activates PDA info
HOST As you see, you each have $10,000 in your accounts. Remember, that's $10,000 in 1813 dollars. But in that time, just as today, you could *earn* money … so let's earn a little more money right now in our Lightning Round.	PDA GRAPHIC on system shows each person how much they have.	MAIN SCREEN Graphic Bank account shows amount of money each person has.			
HOST You'll have a chance to answer 3 questions. For each one you answer correctly, you'll earn $1,000! You'll have 10 seconds after the question to enter your answer. Anyone have any questions? … Let's start the lightning round.		GRAPHIC Lightning Roz und graphic or animation flashes on main screen. Possible lighting effects flash throughout room.	SFX Lightning round theme song plays.	Host spot and blue wash fade out. Gobo Lightning effects timed to main screen.	Host – Next on the words Lightning Round. Movie starts 30 frames after lights fade out.

Continued

Table 5-1 *Continued*

HOST	VOTE; PDA	VIDEO & LIGHTING	AUDIO, NARRATION, & SFX	EFX	CUES
	VISITORS have a pre-set amount of time to answer the questions	GRAPHIC & MAIN SCREEN TEXT BUILD, with graphics What was the relationship between Britain and the United States in 1813? a. They were at war. b. They were allies. c. The United States was a British colony. d. Europeans had not yet come to North America.	CHRIS (VO) First question. What was the relationship between Britain and the United States in 1813? a. They were at war. b. They were allies. c. The United States was a British colony. d. Europeans had not yet come to North America.		

References

Cockburn, Alistair. *Writing Effective Use Cases.* Addison-Wesley, 2000
Copywrite. http://www.bartastechnologies.com/products/copywrite/
Final Draft. http://www.finaldraft.com/
Loge, Ken. E-mail to Focal Press. January 28, 2005
Movie Magic. http://www.screenplay.com/products/mms/index.htm
StoryView. http://www.screenplay.com/products/sv/
WordMenu. http://www.wordmenu.com/

Key Points from Part I: Interactive Media and the Writer

Multimedia Defined (Chapter 1)

Interactive multimedia is a computer-delivered, communication medium that uses any combination of sound, pictures, video, animation, and text to communicate to the user interactively. Multimedia is presented on the World Wide Web; local networks, such as corporate intranets; computer hard drives, such as museum kiosks; interactive television, such as MSN TV; dedicated gaming systems, such as PlayStation and Xbox; mobile devices, such as PSPs (Play Station Portables) and iPods; and discs, such as CD-ROMs and DVDs. Interactive multimedia has dozens of uses, with the most common being marketing, sales, product information, entertainment, education, training, and reference material.

Thinking Interactively (Chapter 1)

Unlike linear media in which the writer must limit options, in multimedia and on the web, the writer must have a feel for all the possible interactions in a narrative scene or for all the different ways that information can be linked together in an informational program. Complicating the interactivity is the need to anticipate user input—the different ways that users will want to take advantage of the interactive options the writer has provided.

Linking (Chapter 1)

A link is the way that one element of a program is connected to another element in the same program or a completely different program. There are three basic types of links:

1. Immediate or direct links: An action.
2. Indirect links: A reaction.
3. Intelligent or delayed links: A delayed reaction.

High-Level Design and Information Architecture (Chapter 1)

The complexity that interactivity and linking add to a multimedia project demands strong high-level design and/or information architecture for the program to be coherent and effective. High-level design determines the broad conceptual approach to the project, including the structure, interface, map, organizing metaphors, and even input devices. Information architecture or interactive architecture is the term usually applied to web sites for the overall grouping of the information, design of the navigation, and process flows of online applications.

Interactive Devices (Chapter 1)

The designer and writer must develop specific interactive devices that will make users aware of the interactive possibilities they have created. These devices include on-screen menus, help screens, icons, props, characters, and cues embedded in the story or information.

Writing for Many Media (Chapter 2)

The interactive writer must be expert in a variety of techniques: writing to be read (journalism, copywriting); writing to be heard (radio, narration); writing to be seen (film, video); plus writing for the special demands of the computer screen. This is because multimedia can easily incorporate many types of media in a single production or even a single screen, and multimedia can manipulate these media in ways not before possible.

High-Level Design and Management Skills (Chapter 3)

Writers who want to get more control over their material and expand their career options should consider developing additional skills, such as:

• Information architecture or interactive architecture
• High-level narrative design

- Project management
- Content expertise

Flowcharting and Other Organizational Tools (Chapter 3)

To organize the complex elements of a multimedia or web production, the writer must learn organizational tools. Flowcharting is a particularly useful way to visualize an interactive program for clients and production team members. Other organizational and visualization tools commonly used by writers are outlines, storyboards, databases, and index cards.

Writing as Part of the Production Team (Chapter 4)

No matter how multiskilled the writer is, he or she will usually work as part of a production team. Understanding who these team members are and how to interact with them can add to the writer's success and ultimately that of the project. The size and complexity of the project dictates how large and varied the team will be. Some of the possible team members include: writer, content strategist, instructional designer, information architect or interactive architect, interface designer, game designer, usability expert, subject matter expert, business strategist, art director/creative director/graphic artist, animator, project manager, video/audio director/developer, photographer/videographer, actors/voice talent, programmer/coder, and product manager.

Script Formatting (Chapter 5)

The preliminary forms for many multimedia programs are proposals, design documents, and outlines. The elements of an informational design document include design objective, creative treatment, navigation, production, and marketing. A narrative proposal might also include a story summary and characters. There are a wide variety of script formats including single-column and multicolumn scripts.

Writing Informational Multimedia and Web Sites

PART II

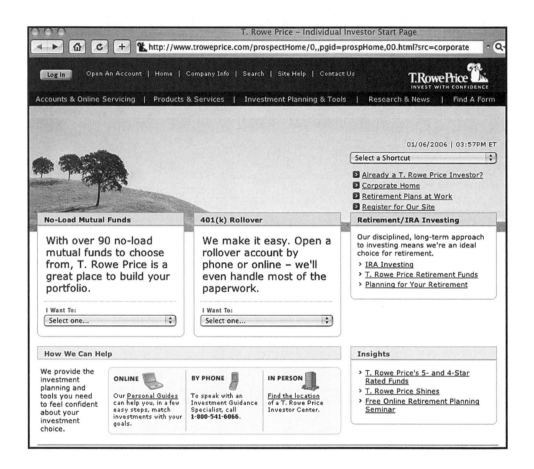

Figure II-1 *The start page for individual investors on the T. Rowe Price web site. Copyright T. Rowe Price*

Defining and Achieving Goals for Informational Multimedia and Web Sites

Chapter Overview

This chapter introduces multimedia and web sites that communicate information without using fictional storytelling techniques. The aspects of informational multimedia and web sites examined in this chapter include:

- Definitions of nonnarrative informational multimedia and web sites
- How to define your projects goal by considering business context, data, and users
- Techniques to achieve common informational multimedia and web site communication goals

Informational Multimedia and Web Sites Defined

Most multimedia and web sites are designed to communicate information or to allow users to perform information-based tasks. Multimedia informational titles include marketing and customer service web sites, e-learning online courses, educational and reference CDs and DVDs, corporate training programs, museum exhibits, some online advertising, and even extended edition movie DVDs that provide background on a film. If the information being presented is about something concrete, such as a person or a place, informational multimedia follows the documentary tradition of presenting its information through the actual locations and individuals studied. For example, *Compton's Interactive Encyclopedia* shows a video of Babe Ruth hitting a home run in Yankee Stadium, as opposed to having an actor portray Ruth in a studio. The Harlem Renaissance web site (see Chapter 12) has photos and video of Harlem in the 1920s.

If the information is more abstract, such as the process of buying a home, the material can be explained through text; visualizations, such as charts; and even interactive devices, such as calculators. See the case study in Chapter 10.

There would be nothing wrong with an informational program that used an actor to play Babe Ruth, and many informational programs are created using narrative fiction. Examples include character-driven training programs, in which an actor takes on the role of a typical employee, and dramatic re-creations of historical events, such as the videos of New England History in *The New England Economic Adventure*, profiled in Chapter 24. Narrative fiction and informational programs using narrative have special concerns of their own and will be dealt with later in Part III. The focus of Part II is on informational multimedia programs that do not use fictional storytelling techniques.

Defining the Goal: Business Context, Data, and Users

Before you can start building an informational multimedia program or web site, you need to clearly define your user and your goal for the project. Defining the user is actually one of the three components of defining the project's goals. These elements are listed in the table below.

Business Context

The business context includes the needs and resources of the client or the entity that is funding the project.

- **Corporate goals.** What does the client think that they need to get out of the project? For example, do they want to build a web site to sell more real estate, such as Prudential Verani Realty profiled in Chapter 10? Does the client also have secondary goals?

Components of Project Goal Definition		
Business Context	Data	Users
• Corporate goals • Resources • Brand	• Document types • Formats	• Information needs • Research modes • Expertise • Technology • Culture & language

Business Context + Data + Users = Project Goals

- **Resources.** Where are the resources that the client can commit to this project? These include the overall budget, development staff, subject matter experts, and staff to maintain project after it is completed.
- **Brand.** What is the company's brand? How is the company perceived by potential customers or how do they want to be perceived? For example, T. Rowe Price, whose web site is profiled in Chapter 11, is a financial investment company. Their brand is that they are knowledgeable, reliable, and serious about taking care of your money. There will be little that is light or funny on their site.

Data

- **Document types.** What type of information does the client already have? Is there adequate product information? Is there information about the company? What areas of information are lacking?
- **Formats.** What is the format of the data? Is it in databases, print brochures, videos, or just in the heads of key company personnel?

Users

Information programs are usually focused tightly to a specific group of potential users. For example, the Prudential Verani Real Estate site (Chapter 10) wants to serve people interested in buying homes, land, or commercial property in New Hampshire and northern Massachusetts. The training program *Vital Signs* wants to teach medical assistants how to take a patient's temperature, blood pressure, and other vital signs. Because users are so well defined for most informational programs, it is essential to understand the user before coming up with a program's goal.

- **Information needs.** What information or activities do the users want from your project? For example, on a real estate site, are they going to just want lists of houses for sale, or will they also want mortgage calculators and other tools? Will they need to perform any online transactions, such as buying a product?
- **Research modes.** How does your targeted user typically look for information? Do they like to search or browse? Do they need an online advisor tool that will allow the user to write answers to a series of questions and get advice? How will they want the information organized? What are their key information categories?
- **Expertise.** What does the typical user already know about the product or topic? Does there need to be a lot of background information, or can we move right into the main content?
- **Technology.** How will users generally access your information? Will they use a PDA, web phone, computer, etc? If a web site, will they use broadband or dialup? Are the users sophisticated enough with technology to allow advance features, or are they novices who will be easily confused?

- **Culture & language.** What is the dominant culture and language of your users? Is there a significant minority of users from another culture? If so, you may need to create separate programs for each, or at least create sections of your programs in another language. Adapting a project to another culture and language is called localization and is a complicated process usually handled by specialist localization companies, such as Lionbridge.

Use Cases and User Scenarios

One of the ways that interactive programs try to understand their users is in the writing of use cases. A use case is a way to capture the step-by-step information or action needs of a specific user of a software program or web site. A single use case will have a detailed description of a type of user and can have one or more user scenarios. Each user scenario describes the steps a user will take using the program and how the system should respond to meet user needs and achieve the client's business goals.

Use cases can be very detailed, include extensive research, and fill many pages answering all the questions posed in the previous section about users. There are also many formats for writing use cases. Some follow narrative prose similar to the treatment format outlined in Chapter 5, while others are in outline or table form, such as the sample below. To write an effective use case requires researching the users of a program. This can involve user questionnaires, interviews, blind testing, and site visits to the user's location. Often secondary sources that know the user, such as the sales team, are also helpful. Usually a business analyst, information architect or an instructional designer will write the use case. A writer should request these documents to help inform the writer about the user. Sometimes, particularly on smaller projects, the writer may be required to write the use cases. If you are on a project and there are no use cases, it is something you might suggest.

The sample below is a very simple user scenario for an online chemistry course. Notice the description of the user, the activity, and the step-by-step plotting of the user's actions. This use case attempts to put the writer in the head of the user and thus allows the writer to provide the content and functions that the user needs and expects.

A brief use case sample:

Chemistry Online Course Use Case Scenario 6: Instructor Reviews Grades

Description of User

- Instructor reviewing grades
- Viewing in office (broadband connection)
- Computer quality and speed ranges = very good
- Technically somewhat sophisticated

Activity

- Login to course already begun

- Navigates to grades

- Checks answers and grades

- Logout

Description of Steps/User Actions	Notes
• Each cell below = a screen • Popup screen text is in italics and separated from main text by lines	Explanation of screen view and user actions
1. Instructor logs on to Blackboard.	
2. This leads to Welcome page. Instructor clicks on course link on right under My Courses.	
3. This links to announcements page. Instructor clicks on control panel on announcements page in left menu.	
4. On control panel page, user clicks on Gradebook in Assessments area of control panel.	Other options in Assessment area of control panel: • Test Manager • Survey Manager • Pool Manager • Gradebook • Course Statistics
5. This leads to View Spreadsheet screen of Gradebook, which shows all students in course and a summary of their grades by exercise. The instructor clicks on a grade of a particular student.	Other Major options on View Spreadsheet page include • Add Item • Manage Items • Gradebook Settings • Weight Grades • Download Grades • Upload Grades

6. On the View Grades/Modify Grade page that results, instructor clicks on the View button at the right of the desired exercise listing that the instructor wishes to view.	[NOTE: The screen title of this page is View Grades, but the sequence menu at the top of the page calls it Modify Grade.]
7. The Modify Grade page shows the entire quiz with the question, the correct answer, and the student answer. The instructor also has the option of getting the Teacher Answer. Instructor reviews student work. Making notes offline.	• This screen will display student and correct answers to the questions, but not the answers to the hints. • The Teacher Answer consists of the worked-out solution and sometimes some additional notes to the instructor. When the Assignment is an algorithmic one, the solution should use the variables rather than a single numerical value. But the instructor also needs to see the numerical answer for a given instance of the algorithm. (Please note that this Teacher Answer does not include placing the algorithm used by the computer to determine the answer on the screen.) These requirements are not handled by Blackboard and will have to be met by the Interactive • In Blackboard, if desired, instructor can clear student attempt or change the weighting of each question in the exercise. • Instructor makes notes offline because there is no notes column in the Gradebook
8. Instructor logs out and returns to original login page.	

Example of Defining the Goal

Once you have answered all the questions listed in the previous section and have a clear understanding of business context, data, and users, you can define your informational project's goals. Goals should be clearly defined, measurable, and limited in number.

An example is probably the best way to understand how this process of goal definition works. Although the Prudential Verani Realty site will be discussed in more detail in Chapter 10, we will focus on the goal definition of this project here.

Prudential Verani Business Context

Prudential Verani Realty is a large regional company and was willing to commit significant resources to make their web site the dominant real estate site in their market. Because the Verani family has lived and worked in the New Hampshire real estate market for three generations, even though they are a fairly large organization, their brand is that of a friendly, local company. One of their slogans is "We're not just your realtor, we're your neighbor." They originally had multiple business goals for this Web site:

1. Better attract and serve customers (buyers)

2. Better attract and serve clients (sellers)

3. Sell properties more effectively

4. Help agents and staff make the most effective use of their time

Prudential Verani Data

Prudential Verani Realty main document types were descriptions of real estate listings. These were in a database that was not searchable online. They also had information in print material about the company, the real estate selling and buying process, mortgages, and other related information. Last, there was quite a bit of real estate knowledge in the heads of their top agents and managers.

Prudential Verani Users

The potential users of the Verani site were primarily English speaking and middle class New Englanders. Southern New Hampshire and Massachusetts is an area with lots of high-tech businesses, so many of the potential site visitors are sophisticated users of technology. Because buying a property is something most users do infrequently, their knowledge of current real estate practices is limited. The primary information need was to search for a property, but users also had significant secondary information needs about the real estate selling and buying process and related issues, such as radon, lead, and relocation assistance.

Prudential Verani Web Site Goals

The Prudential Verani web site goals were defined by analyzing the information described above on business context, data, and users. The main goal decided for the new site was to make it an information resource for sellers and buyers of real estate. Much of the information that was currently in print was made accessible online. This included school reports; town reports; lists of home inspectors; and tools, such as mortgage calculators, interactive check lists, and e-mail updates of current properties. This information greatly increased traffic to the site. Users came to the site for real estate information and tools. This well-presented online information helped the agents deliver information to clients more effectively and demonstrated that Verani is a well-run, knowledgeable, and friendly company. This encouraged users to consider them when they were buying or selling a property. To support this primary business goal, all properties were easily searchable by users, according to multiple criteria, and new homes had their own section with substantial graphics and virtual tours.

As much as possible, the information was presented in such a way that the user made a connection with the realtor. For example, after a site visitor used the mortgage calculator, he had the option of viewing Verani properties in that price range or of having the site connect him to an agent. The end result was a web site that achieved both the client's and the user's goals and made effective use of the existing data.

Techniques to Achieve Common Informational Goals

The goals for the Prudential Verani site as described above are the specific goals for just one type of informational program and audience. But as mentioned in the beginning of this chapter, informational multimedia programs and web sites cover a wide range of information including general reference, info-tainment, education, interactive magazines and newspapers, sales and marketing, training, public relations, customer support, and much more. The good news for the writer trying to grasp the techniques used to create this wide array of informational programming is that most of these productions have one or more of the following general goals, each of which have their own techniques for execution:

1. To persuade
2. To entertain
3. To enable transactions
4. To create a sense of community
5. To inform
6. To teach

Of the above goals, the two most fundamental to informational multimedia are the last two: to inform and to teach. (Informing users about real estate was one of the major goals of the Prudential Verani site.) Inform and teach are also the goals that are of the most concern for the writer and that are at the core of most other goals. Because of this, I will only briefly discuss goals 1 through 4 and devote the rest of the chapter to a detailed analysis of how to use interactive multimedia to achieve goals 5 and 6: to inform and to teach.

Goal #1: To Persuade

Persuasion is a meta-goal that most informational media share. Advertising sells products. Nonfiction book writers try to persuade us to accept their view of the world. And marketing web sites want to convince us that their company is the best. Because this is such a universal goal, extensive material has already been written about persuasion technique so this topic will not be discussed in detail here. Aristotle was the first to point out the three time tested modes of persuasion to change someone's heart and mind:

- **Ethical:** If your viewer believes the speaker, they will believe the speech. (*Ethos* means speaker in Greek.) This is the reason that we have to listen to all those highly trained athletes tell us that they love sugary soft drinks. A second meaning of ethical is to align your message with the beliefs or ethics of your audience. Many Americans are concerned about the environment. Hence the growth of "green" advertisements that seek to show that a product is as beloved by the little forest creatures as is Snow White.
- **Logical:** Logical simply means convincing us with facts. Show us why this is a better built toothbrush.
- **Emotional:** Connect to our emotions. "I am going to be one sexy dude if I wear those blue jeans." This is the approach most used by advertisers.

If you are not familiar with basic persuasion theory, please refer to the article "Persuasion Theory and Online Advertising" in the "Online Ads: ZDU & Personal View" area of the Chapters section of this book's CD-ROM.

Goal #2: To Entertain

Entertainment as a goal will be discussed in more detail in the book's Part III, but one point worth mentioning about entertaining the audience is that all programs must entertain or engage to some degree. Even if a program had the greatest information, it would have limited communication value if it was absolutely boring. A project can be viewed on a continuum, with a plain listing of information at one end, to a program that is pure entertainment at the other end. But most pieces do not exist at either end of this continuum; rather they fall somewhere along the line, embracing elements of both entertainment and information. Where a specific project sits on this continuum is an important consideration for the writer.

Goal #3: To Enable Transactions

The goal "to enable transactions" is important on web sites that allow users to perform an activity, such as to buy a book from Amazon.com or to open a bank account online at BankofAmerica.com. In transactional sites such as these, the writer is still teaching the user information. In this case, how to perform the transaction. Many of the principles we will discuss concerning the goal "to teach" will apply to writing for transactional sites. Online transactions and activities do, however, put special demands on the writer who must teach the user about the product and how to perform the transaction in the most efficient way possible. If it takes the user too long to get the information they need to perform the transaction, they simply won't do it. The actual designing of online applications that enable transactions is a topic worthy of detailed study but it is more the responsibility of the interactive architect and the technical architect than it is the job of the writer.

Goal #4: To Create a Sense of Community

Many informational web sites try to create a sense of community among their users. For example, many major software companies have online user forums on their web sites, where users of the same software tools can discuss tips and tricks with the software and get to know each other. At MySpace.com, tens of millions of mostly young users share their ideas, photos, and music. These types of techniques can make a user feel as if they belong to group of like-minded individuals. Physical communities, such as towns or cities, can use similar techniques on their web sites to get their citizens involved and make them feel a part of their community. Although this is a valid goal and useful techniques, they do not really demand the skill of the professional writer except to perhaps suggest such techniques be used as part of the larger information architecture of the site. Much of the information actually written for such sites involves informing the user about their community, its values, and common assumptions.

Goal #5: To Inform

A writer whose goal is to inform wants to provide users with access to a large body of information. This could be an online encyclopedia, a magazine site, or a comprehensive product information site, such as the web sites profiled in Chapters 10 and 11 of this book. The viewers need not and usually are not expected to access all of the information. Instead, they simply take what they need. The information is usually presented clearly and is structured into discreet units so users can find precise answers to their questions.

The database is the most common tool used in a program whose main goal is to provide access to a large body of information. General reference works, such as *Grolier's Multimedia Encyclopedia* and *Britannica Online*, and more focused references, such as *Microsoft Cinemania*, are based on databases. The multimedia database also has many uses in business. For example, real estate companies often have databases of homes for sale. Much of the Prudential Verani Realty web site profiled in Chapter 10 is based on their database of properties. The T. Rowe Price database of mutual fund information is the basis of many of the key features of their web site (Chapter 11).

Approaches to Inform

Creating access to loosely-related body of material, such as a database. The major challenge with a large body of loosely related data is to organize the information in a way that allows users to easily access the information that they want. There are a number of ways to do this.

Grouping by categories. The simplest way is to group by categories, that is, putting all the same types of items together. For example, *Cinemania* groups movie listings, biographies, awards, and media. The media category includes the subgroups of movie stills, portraits, dialogue, music, and film clips. A common developer's technique for grouping by category is the card sort method. Users first break the content into separate small units or chunks. Write this information on cards (paper or electronic) then sort the cards into the appropriate categories or bins.

Content categories are the most obvious grouping, but material can be organized according to numerous criteria, such as place, time, or theme. For example, *Cinemania* could have a feature that allows searching by place so a user could search for all the material that originated in New York. By time, a search could include all material before 1930. By theme, it could include all material involved with crime.

Even more useful is to combine categories into what is called a complex query. Combine the movie criterion with the place criterion and get all the movies made in New York. Add the time criterion and get all the movies made in New York before 1930. Add the crime theme criterion and get all the movies made in New York before 1930 that deal with crime.

The limitation of this category approach is that the categories that the writer comes up with may not be the ones that the user would come up with. The ideal program would help users create their own categories and customize the database to their use.

Concept maps. Concept maps are a way to visualize categories in a database or any body of loosely related content according to a visual image or map. A very simple concept map is the tabbed navigation used on many web sites that essentially try to make the web site look like a file drawer with tabbed file folders that can be sorted through (see Figure 1-5 for an example). The museum and journey approach are other common images. The museum approach allows users to enter a virtual museum, enter exhibit rooms in their area of interest, and view exhibits about a particular subject. The journey allows users to travel along a certain sequence.

A danger with concept maps is combining incompatible maps. An early draft of the program *Sky High* attempted to combine the temporal map of journeying along a time line with the spatial map of the stars and planets. These two different types of maps did not work smoothly together and had to be abandoned.

 See the book's CD-ROM Chapters section "Educational Multimedia Case Study: Sky High" for a full discussion of this incompatible maps issue.

Customized and personalized information. Another excellent approach is to presort the database and only present the user the information that they need or want. To do this, the web site or other multimedia program has to first collect the user's information preferences and/or needs. There are two basic ways this can be done: customization and personalization.

Customization involves the user consciously inputting their preferences into the computer program. This is usually done by filling out a form or clicking answers on a questionnaire. Once the user's preferences are noted, then just the information that interests them can be presented. For example, on the T. Rowe Price site (see Chapter 11), users can define what mutual funds they want data on. Next time they log onto the site, only those funds will be presented. Learning programs can also be customized by allowing the user to choose which sections they want to study and in what order.

Personalization's main difference from customization is that the user generally does not provide conscious input about their preferences. Instead, the computer program learns the user's preferences by previous activity on the program or web site. Personalization is most commonly used in transactional web sites that are trying to match their products with the user. The best known example is the online retailer Amazon.com, which tracks the books and other items you bought in the past and recommends new purchases based on your previous activity. Amazon.com will also try to guess your preferences by associating you with other customers. If you bought books about angels, and several other customers who bought books about angels also bought books about devils, then Amazon.com might suggest some devil books to you on your next visit. Personalization can also be used on learning programs that can track the user's progress through the program and adapt the type and difficulty of material it will present based on the user's previous performance. One popular math program for primary school children will offer review exercises of earlier material if the student gets several problems wrong.

Search. Search is one of the most useful tools when accessing a large body of loosely related or unrelated information. The World Wide Web itself fits that category, and tools such as Google and Yahoo! devise ever more sophisticated ways for the user to find exactly what they want. Any web site of any size usually has a search tool as part of it. Designing the search is not usually the writer's job, but a few things a writer can recommend are to make sure search results are in a usable form, design a search around the terms users commonly use, notify users when multiple search options exist and provide controlled vocabulary search templates for common searches' for example, to find information on "writing computer games," recommend that the searcher use "game designer," "interactive writing," "multimedia writing."

Guides and agents. One of the most promising approaches for making a database accessible is by creating guides or agents to lead users through the material. These guides could be software creations that are part of the program. For example, *The Mayo Clinic Family Health Book* CD-ROM includes an on-screen character who introduces material and helps to guide users in the direction that they want. This type of a guide is limited by the material that was written for the screen character to present, but there has been much research into how to create truly intelligent agents who could be told by the user what information he or she needed, and then the user could go get a cup of coffee while the helper searched the world and delivered the information to the user's desktop computer. From repeated interactions, such an agent could continue to refine their knowledge of the user's preferences. A common use of software agents on the web are those used on job sites, such as Monster.com and Dice.com. A job seeker enters the criteria for the type of job she is interested in on the site. The site will then e-mail the user when jobs that match her criteria appear in their database.

Avoiding Cognitive Overload by Controlling Complexity

Guides, agents, and customized information are some ways to keep users who are browsing a vast database or several databases from getting confused by the diversity and complexity of the unsequenced material they encounter, but cognitive overload is still a problem. Browsing a database is quite a different experience from reading a textbook, where the information is carefully explained and structured to build understanding of an overall topic gradually. In a database or any unstructured collection of material included the web, just the opposite can occur. Topics of varying degrees of difficulty can be encountered and only partially understood by the student. For example, search engines will often drop you into a middle page of a web site and you may have to backtrack to the home page to get your bearings. "A failure to control this complexity can lead to cognitive overload and failure to learn" (Ambron and Hooper, 127).

Cognitive load can be reduced in a number of ways, for example:

- Reduce the number of choices available on the screen at any one time: "seven plus or minus two" is optimal (Ambron and Hooper, 128).
- Reduce the level of difficulty available to the student at any different time. Students must have viewed crucial introductory material before they are allowed to access advanced concepts.
- Build a note-taking function into the program so students can track their progress and note partially understood concepts. (Note-taking can include text and pictures.)

- Give students the opportunity to "mark" a section of the program that they can return to later.
- Build in a clear orientation so students can understand where they are and that the various pieces of information are connected. Navigation maps and consistent interface design help with this.

Goal #6: To Teach

A database provides access to a wide body of information. Exactly what information the user accesses and learns is up to the individual. In a teaching program, however, the information may be more narrowly defined and the writer has a clearer goal of what information he or she wants the user to take away from the program.

The Integrated Media Group's *Video Producer* is a good example of a teaching program at the college level. Its goal is to teach the basics of video production. It is carefully structured to do this with mini-lectures, examples, reviews, and quizzes. Fidelity Investments' training program for retirement counselors is similarly focused on teaching a skill. Houghton Mifflin's *Geology Explorer* web site teaches key concepts about geology.

Instructional theory is a complicated subject that must be studied in depth if one is to become an instructional designer, but it is important to be at least familiar with some of the basic concepts of instructional design before writing educational or training programs.

Interactive Multimedia Instruction as Interpersonal Instruction

Some experts in interactive instruction claim that effective interactive instruction should include the characteristics of interpersonal instruction: immediacy of response, nonsequential access to information, adaptability, feedback, options, bidirectional communication, and interruptibility (Schwier and Misanchuk, 175–176).

Immediacy of response. In practical terms, this means that an action the learner takes should get a response immediately. It is psychologically important for the learner to feel connected. For example, when a student clicks on an answer in a quiz, he or she should get some sort of response even if it is just a sound. Similarly, if there is going to be a wait after a student clicks an icon to access a large file, something should be happening on the screen—preferably something more interesting and tied to the program than an hourglass or a watch. Wait-state and other responses should be in tune with the program. *Rodney's Wonder Window*, a humorous children's educational CD-ROM, has funny wait-state text messages, such as "Please wait, Rodney is putting on clean underwear," and visual images, such as the heads on the character icons spinning around or their hair curling.

Feedback. Immediacy of response does not mean complex feedback to every action. Deciding what kind of feedback to give and when to give it to the learner is a difficult question. There is no consensus on this subject. There is even disagreement on simple types of feedback. For example, some writers provide only a minimal response, such as "Correct," to correctly answered test questions, and reserve complex feedback for questions answered incorrectly. Others include detailed feedback for correct answers as well, to reinforce the message and to guard against students' guessing the right answers and not learning the material.

Bidirectional Communication. Clearly related to immediacy of response and feedback is bidirectional communication and interruptibility. A well-designed learning program gives the user ample opportunity to communicate with the program as well as for the program to communicate with the user. This includes letting the learner communicate through various methods, including typing text, manipulating images, and sound. This is essential if maximum learning is going to happen for the maximum number of students, because studies have proved that we all learn in different ways—some by watching, others by doing, and yet others by analyzing. Thus it is important to present the message in a variety of approaches.

Interruptibility. Students should be able to interrupt the program at any point and go in the direction that is useful for them. They should, for example, be able to return easily to earlier material for review. If they feel comfortable with the material, they should be able to jump ahead to a more advanced part of the program.

Programs that do not allow this movement can be frustrating. *Video Producer*, an otherwise excellent education program on video production, requires that students complete a series of quizzes on video production techniques before they are allowed to create a video in the program's studio. This defeats the purpose of interactive multimedia and incorporates the drawback of linear media and classroom instruction where all levels of students must progress through the material in the same way.

Inclusion of standard navigation tools can also improve interruptibility. Many programs respond to standard quit commands, such as "Command-Q" on the Macintosh. When users quit, they should be able to leave a bookmark at the spot they left and return to it when they start again without having to start at the beginning.

Help. Excellent help programs are now included in basic productivity programs, such as word processors, but a surprising number of educational programs or complex web sites do not provide a constant helping hand. Help features are particularly important with web applications, such as opening a bank account online. As in the case of wait-state messages, a writer who can make the access to help more interesting and in tune with the particular program than a help button will contribute to the program's effectiveness. It is important to build the help function into the interface design from the beginning as well as into the writer's schedule. Writing help pages can be extremely time-consuming.

Personalizing instruction: nonsequential access to information, adaptability, and options. Multimedia's ability to access information in the order that the user finds most useful allows a writer to personalize or customize a program and make it adaptable to the user. Many programs allow users to customize the program at the beginning by filling out a user profile based on such criteria as educational level, job, and familiarity with the subject. Once entered into the computer, this profile might cause the program to take the user down a completely different path, or just alter the text on certain screens, or offer different product suggestions.

Personalization can also occur without the user's conscious involvement. Transactional web sites, such as Amazon.com, track what products you have purchased and use this activity to determine what products to show you in the future. Whatever the approach, personalizing the program continues beyond the beginning by tracking the user's progress and adapting to his or her needs. For example, a learner who consistently has difficulties in a certain area might be directed to special remedial sections geared to that particular problem. The program might also alter the way it presents the instructional material in the rest of the lesson. If the student learned best from the video segments, the video might be increased and text minimized.

A simple way to customize a multimedia piece is to allow students to choose the level of difficulty and thus advance at their own rate. Another adaptation is the degree of control allowed the student over the learning material. Some studies have suggested that weaker students can benefit from more structure (Schwier and Misanchuk, 186).

The way subject matter is approached also customizes a program. Someone learning marketing should be able to choose various contexts designed into the program in which to practice their new skills, such as marketing a virtual baseball team, video store, or rock group.

Multimedia Games as Teaching Tools

The above discussion deals with all types of interactive media, but a specialized type of multimedia, the computer game, is also getting greater respect among educators. This is because at a closer look, it becomes clear that computer games exhibit many sound instructional design principles. The instructional principles embodied in games are outlined in an insightful article by Professors Douglas Gentile and J. Ronald Gentile.

- Most games have multiple levels of difficulty, allowing a user to first master easier tasks and information and then move on to more difficult tasks.
- Games usually offer multiple ways to solve the same problem, this allows students to better understand the solution and to transfer skills learned to a variety of settings.
- Even when students have learned a certain skill, the nature of the game experience makes them happy to continue to exercise that skill repeatedly in the game until it is absolutely mastered.
- The excitement generated by character identification, jeopardy, and the challenge and reward structure of games can make students almost addicted

to the experience and thus intently focused on the learning process built into a game.

- Students, who have been unsuccessful with traditional forms of instruction because of previous academic record or socioeconomic background can often do well with games. (Gentile)

Studies, such as the one quoted above, are pointing to new ways to use multimedia as an instructional tool and greatly increasing their legitimacy in the classroom.

Conclusion

By clearly defining your user and goals, you can then use the most effective techniques to achieve those goals. Likewise, poorly defined or contradictory goals are impossible to execute. The time spent in the early planning stages of a project will radically improve your chances of success.

References

Ambron, Sueann, and Kristina Hooper, eds. *Learning with Interactive Multimedia: Developing and Using Multimedia Tools in Education*. Redmond, WA: Microsoft Press, 1990.

Gentile, D.A., and Gentile, J.R. "Violent video games as exemplary teachers." Paper presented at the Biennial Meeting of the Society for Research in Child Development, 2005, Atlanta, GA.
http://www.mediafamily.org/research/Exemplary_Teachers_SRCD.pdf

Reddy, M. "The Conduit Metaphor: A Case of Frame Conflict in Our Language about Language." In *Metaphor and Thought*, Andrew Ortony, ed. Cambridge: Cambridge University Press, 1979.

Schwier, Richard A., and Earl R. Misanchuk. *Interactive Multimedia Instruction*. Englewood Cliffs, NJ: Educational Technology, 1993.

Informational Multimedia and Web Architecture

Chapter Overview

Multimedia programs and web sites have a wide variety of possible structures and navigation. Rarely do these approaches exist in a pure form. Most projects have some combination. A key question the writer must ask when developing a piece is which approach will best achieve the communication goals. As discussed in Chapter 3, information architecture is often planned with flowcharts and wireframes. Every possible interactive architecture is not listed here, merely those that are most commonly used by the writer and designer of nonnarrative, informational multimedia.

Linear Structure

Defined: Linear structure has no linking or interactivity. Linear structure can be compared to a desert highway with no crossroads. It is the structure of most motion pictures and television programs.

Use: Linear structure makes it possible to integrate into multimedia some of the standard linear informational structures, such as the problem-solution structure and the dialectical structure. The problem-solution structure is used by setting up a problem linearly and then asking the user to solve it interactively. Dialectical structure, a favorite of the TV news magazines, sets up a dialogue between two different points of view. First we hear from the Army general who wants to spend billions on a bomber, then we hear from the peace activist who doesn't want to spend any more money on new weapons. This A/B, love/hate pattern is repeated until a conclusion emerges or we can draw our own conclusion. A simpler use of linear structure in interactive media is the presentation of key information that should not be interrupted. This is often used for introductory material. For example, *The New England Economic Adventure* (Chapter 24) introduces each new section with a linear video on the historical background of the program.

Linear Structure with Scene or Section Branching

Defined: Linear structure with scene or section branching is basically a linear structure with a few limited choices as to how certain scenes will play out. This structure can be compared to the desert highway that has a few detours. (See Figure 8-1.) The detours, however, always return the traveler to the same highway.

Use: This is sometimes used in training pieces that are explaining a step-by-step concept by following a linear structure. There is often an option of detouring from the step-by-step instruction for a review of the concept or for additional material, but after the detour, the user is returned to the page that he or she had left. The Work-plus.com web site does this in the section of the site where it explains to the user how to use the company's product. The basic step-by-step instruction is brief, but users have the option to link to the help pages in each section for additional background material. Sometimes a program will actually force the user to link to different sections. In the marketing tutorial charted in Figure 8-1, the student who answers information incorrectly on radio or television advertising is

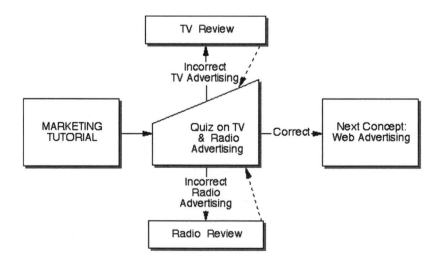

Figure 8-1 *Linear structure with scene or section branching for part of a marketing tutorial.*

sent back to the radio and television content to review before proceeding forward in the tutorial.

Hierarchical Branching

Defined: In hierarchical branching, information is organized according to categories and subcategories, so users can click an information category and then a subcategory to find the information that they want. This approach could be compared to going to a mall and searching for an Italian cookbook. At the first fork in the mall, you can choose left for the department store, straight ahead for the bookshop, or right for the electronic shop. You want a cookbook, so you choose straight and go to the bookshop. Now you must choose between nonfiction, fiction, and magazines. You choose nonfiction, which includes many choices, ranging from biography to cookbooks to zoology. You choose cookbooks. The cookbook section has French cookbooks, Indian cookbooks, and Italian cookbooks. You choose Italian and, phew, you are finally done.

Use: Hierarchical branching in a multimedia program works exactly this way with a hierarchy of ever-narrowing choices, except your finger does the clicking instead of your heels. See Figure 8-2 for a diagram of hierarchical structure for a program about shipbuilding. The user can click menus to drill down to the level that has the information that they want.

Although this is one of the most popular structures on the web, it has several potential pitfalls. One is branching explosion, which means creating too many user options. Too many options are created because increasing the number of decision points or the number of choices at each decision point means that the total number of possible branches increases exponentially. In Figure 8-2, the options quickly jump from three, to twelve, and, by adding one more level, to forty-eight. The amount of material quickly expands to a volume difficult for a writer to create and prohibitive to produce.

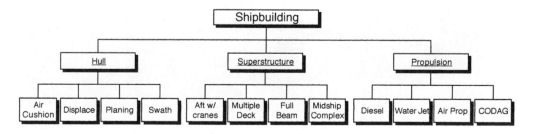

Figure 8-2 *Hierarchical structure for a web site on shipbuilding.*

Another danger with hierarchical branching is that if there are too many levels of information, the user can get lost and find it difficult to make connections with material on the same level, such as forty-eight subcategories on level four of a shipbuilding program. There is also a practical limitation to the number of choices at any one branching level. Some studies say that five to seven choices is the most people can easily comprehend.

Branching explosion is kept under control by limiting categories at a level, segmenting the audience at the top of the hierarchy, and by allowing alternate access to information on the site, such as search and sitemaps. See Figure 8-3 for an example of how T. Rowe Price segments their audience at the top level by key users, as opposed to using subject categories, such as mutual funds, that might apply to multiple user groups. This allows each major section to be less dense with information and categories because it focuses on the needs of just one group. In general, most effective web sites do not go very deep—not more than three or four subcategories.

Effectively done, hierarchical branching can be a useful and economical way to present information, which is why it is the dominant structure on most web sites. This does not necessarily mean it is the best structure for all types of information. Other alternatives are presented in this chapter.

Figure 8-3 *Segmenting audience to reduce branching explosion. Home page from the T. Rowe Price web site. Copyright T. Rowe Price Associates, Inc.*

Single-Level Linking

Defined: There is no hierarchy in this approach. Usually the user is presented with a problem and given a number of possible resources for solving the problem that can be accessed in any order. As opposed to hierarchical branching, which looks like a well-organized mall, single-level branching is like wandering into a chaotic flea market. At a flea market you can go any number of places and talk to anyone in any order.

Use: In the interactive documentary *A Right to Die: The Case of Dax Cowart*, Dax Cowart has a serious illness. He wants to refuse treatment and die. His doctors and others feel differently. The user of this program can access video interviews, text, and other material about this case in order to answer the question, does Cowart have the right to end his life? (The irony of this piece is that Dax was not allowed to die; the therapy was successful, and he went on to live a happy life.) Although single-level linking structure is useful, it is fairly rare on a complete program because it must be limited to a focused topic with limited options. If there are too many options, then a hierarchical structure or another approach has to be used to organize the material.

Single-level linking is more common in small parts of programs. An area of the *Geology Explorer* web site examines the formation of a cross-section of land. Within each part of the program, students have the option of looking at screens dealing with a description of a layer, an animation showing the process of layer formation, an explanation of the geologic event that caused the layer to be formed, or a quiz. Because it is useful for the student to compare all these elements, they have the option of accessing and reviewing this material in the order that makes most sense to them.

Parallel Path or Multipath Architecture

Defined: This approach is borrowed from interactive narrative where one of the main structures is parallel path stories. See Figure 18-4 in the middle of Chapter 18. In a parallel paths story, the writer lays out three or more possible versions of the same basic story. Depending on the players' choices as they move through the game, they move back and forth through the different story versions. This will be explained in more detail in the narrative section of the book. When applied to an informational program, this approach creates three or more distinct paths the user can travel through a specific body of information. In the physical world this could be compared to a traveler having three or more possible distinct routes that would lead towards the same destination or slightly different destinations.

Use: One of the most effective uses of this approach is with online transactions or other activities where the user is trying to accomplish a specific goal. One example would be users who wanted to open a bank account online at a bank web site. The challenge for the writer is that these users are a heterogeneous group. Some are web-savvy, others are newbies. Some know a lot about banking products, others need a lot of explanation. Some want certain accounts, others want totally different or less accounts.

To accommodate this variety of users, the writer can prepare multiple information paths through the online account opening application. One of the ways this can be achieved is through good interface design, such as putting the essential information and activities on the left side of the page and putting the secondary product information on the right side of page, perhaps in a box to indicate that it is secondary. Lastly, context sensitive help could be available from a drop down menu on every page. Another approach would be to allow users to customize the transaction by choosing their knowledge and skill level at the beginning of the process.

With designs, such as these, the web-savvy user who knows banking products can move quickly down one path performing only the essential activities. The web-savvy user who needs product information could take a slower path, moving first to the product information and then to the essential activities. The user most in need of help could move through the help feature, to the product information, and finally the essential transactional activities. This approach is different from a hierarchical structure because the user can easily move from one information path to the other and does not have to dig up or down through multiple subcategories.

Dynamically-Generated Database Driven Web Sites

Defined: Strictly speaking this is not a separate structure, but a technology by which web pages are assembled for the user. Many sites, particularly transactional, content-managed, and personalized sites, do not have static pages of information on their servers that are presented to the user. Instead they have a more or less blank framework page or template for different sections of the site. The actual content that fills that framework is drawn in small chunks from a database and then the pages are dynamically assembled to be viewed in your browser. What this means for writers is that they have to be particularly skilled in the technique we discussed earlier of being able to write small units of information that can stand alone, but also work in conjunction with other information if need be. In terms of actual structure, a dynamically generated web site will still appear to the user to be following one of the basic structures above. For example, if you drill down the category menus on Amazon.com, the structure is hierarchical.

Use. Most sophisticated transactional sites, sites that sell something or perform tasks, are dynamically generated from databases. For example, the amazon.com home page template is set up like the table below.

Amazon.com Header and Global Navigation: Your Store, Your Account, Cart, etc.		
Long Menu of Different Product Categories	Wide Center Content Area Listing Products and Special Offers Separated by Headers	Small Block Advertising Featured Product Small Block Advertising Featured Product More Small Blocks
Bottom Links: Customer, Support, International Sites, etc.		

What goes into each section of the template will change depending on your shopping habits and if you have been to Amazon.com before. If you have ordered toys before, the advertisements and products offered will show ads and links for toys. If you have never bought products before, then different, more general ads will be shown. This technique is called personalization. The web site is adjusted to you by the server software. These individual ads and bits of product information are in chunks on the server, and they are delivered to the template and displayed on your browser.

As mentioned above, the key point of this discussion for the writer is that many web pages are not "pages" at all, but rather snippets of information assembled on the fly to display in your browser as if they were a single page. Many if not most sophisticated web sites are closer to client-server applications than a collection of pages. (A client-server application involves client software on the user's computer, that requests data from the server on the company's computer.)

Passive Versus Active Information Delivery: Getting Beyond Click-and-Read with Simulations, Worlds, and Role Playing

Passive Information Delivery

Many interactive informational writers use the structures previously discussed in this chapter and deliver their content in a way that requires no user action beyond click-and-read. For example, users on a web site might click a series of menu items and read the linked content. This is a functional way to access information, but it keeps viewers at a distance by not making them use or think about the information. For example, Figure 8-2, in the discussion of hierarchical branching, shows the structure of a click-and-read approach to a project about shipbuilding. In this case, the writer simply organized the information according to categories and subcategories, so users can click an information category and view material about it. This information is presented in a clear manner, but it is not very engaging.

Active Information Delivery

Active or dynamic information delivery demands more of the user than simply click-and-read. For example, the same shipbuilding program charted in Figure 8-2 could easily be developed as a program that involves the user interactively. Figure 8-4 charts the structure of an actual program on this subject called *The Nauticus Ship-building Company*. In this program, the user plays the role of a shipbuilder. The user is first asked to choose between three different types of ships that need to be built: a transatlantic cargo ship, a cross-channel ferry, and an oceanographic research vessel. The user is then asked to assemble one of these ships by choosing from a variety of components for the hull, propulsion, and superstructure. At the end of the program, the completed ship is evaluated. As it leaves the dock, it floats or it sinks. This approach teaches the same information as the click-and-read hierarchical approach illustrated in Figure 8-2, but it does so in a much more engaging fashion. The answer to getting beyond click-and-read is to involve the user in some way. This is, after all, interactive multimedia.

Using Click-and-Read

Active information delivery is not appropriate for every type of project. Passive information delivery is actually much more common. For example if you want to present product information on a simple product or answers to customer support questions, click-and-read is perfectly fine. It is also generally less expensive than active information programs. But if your goal is to engage the user to fully experience and learn your topic, then active delivery should be considered.

Approaches to Getting Beyond Click-and-Read

The following approaches—simulations, worlds structure, and role-playing—are only a few of the many approaches and techniques that can fully engage the user and present information actively. The correct approach should emerge from understanding the information to be presented and the intended audience.

Simulation

Defined: In a simulation, an experience or activity is recreated virtually on screen. The activity can be driving a car, flying a plane, snowboarding (Chapter 21), or building an entire city. The structure is dictated by the activity.

Use 1, Problem Solver: Educational simulations that have extensive need of writers are usually more complex than simply flying a plane or driving a car. For educational programs, the simulations usually involve a problem for the user to solve or a task to accomplish. For example, the popular *Sim City* programs give the user the power to build a city by altering the landscape, adding parks, schools, railroads, power plants,

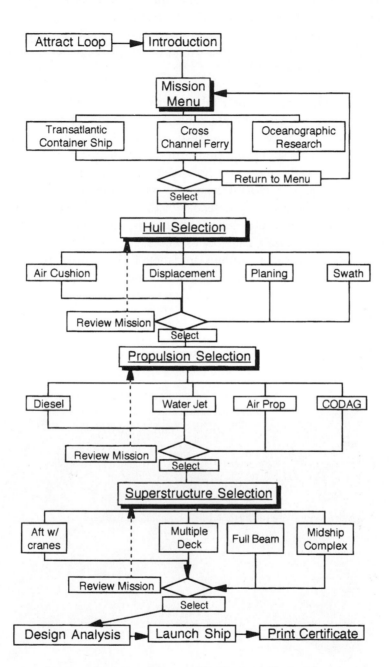

Figure 8-4 *Structure of active information delivery—The Nauticus Shipbuilding Company. Script sample copyright Chedd-Angier Production Company.*

and other components, but it must be done within budget and the user must cope with disasters, such as flood, fire, and alien invasion.

The Nauticus Shipbuilding Company, which was discussed earlier in this chapter and illustrated in Figure 8-4, is another example of a problem solver simulation. In this case the task is to build a ship.

Use 2, Gamer: In this case the user takes on the role of a player in a game. Not all games are simulations. For example, multimedia versions of crossword and word search are not. But if the player actively takes on the role of a character in the game, they generally are. This is somewhat similar to the problem-solver approach, except that it usually operates with more clearly defined game rules. For example Houghton Mifflin's *World Languages* CD-ROMs have a "Words in Space" game (Figure 8-5). The player takes on the role of a defender of the home planet. At the beginning of the game, it is announced that the planet is being attacked by spaceships from a planet whose name is a certain category of words, such as in Figure 8-5, "Numbers Greater Than Fifty." All the spaceships are labeled with words. Some have names of numbers greater than fifty in the foreign language. Others are friendly ships labeled with lower number words. The player has to translate the names of the

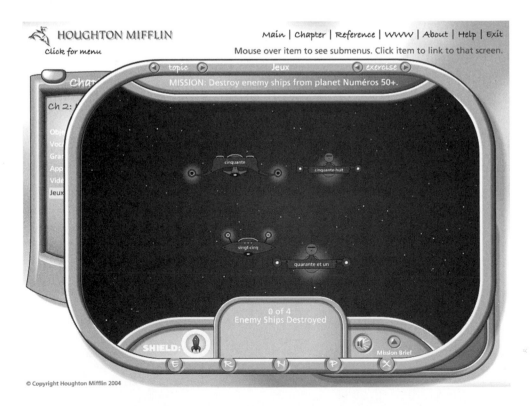

© Copyright Houghton Mifflin 2004

Figure 8-5 *"Words in Space" game in the CD-ROM for Mais Oui! Copyright Houghton Mifflin Company.*

ships and shoot them. If the player shoots the wrong ship, the player is shot by the enemy ships. Three enemy hits on the player, and it is game over and time to go back and study those vocabulary lists.

Use 3, Explorer, Worlds Structure: In this approach the user takes on the role of an explorer or traveler who explores an entire world of information. There is no set problem to be solved or sequence of actions to be accomplished as in the previous uses (gamer and problem solver). The worlds structure organizes the options available to the viewer not in a linear fashion or in a hierarchy but in a graphic spatial representation. This approach is most useful if there is a large body of information that can be incorporated in a location. It does not have to be a physical location that we normally visit. The museum interactive piece *Into the Cell* allows viewers to take a fantastic voyage into a living cell. A writer approaches a project like this by first deciding on a list of locations in the virtual world that he or she is creating, then determining what will happen in each location, and finally how the user will be able to discover these events. A flowchart is not very useful here. More useful is a graphical illustration of the world, a list of the locations, and descriptions of the events that will occur in each location. This is explained further in the following section.

Writing a Simulation

The writers Brian Sawyer and John Vourlis suggest that the best way to write a simulation is to start with the "most basic categories: 'Characters' and 'Locations,' then break these down into sub-categories, and so on . . . After laying out the categories, the next step is to fill in the details of each object: 1) its attributes and 2) its rules of behavior" (101).

For example, in *The Nauticus Shipbuilding Company*, the attributes of the air cushion hull are that it is capable of high speeds, needs flat-water conditions, and has a flat deck that is easy to load. Its behavior, if chosen for the oceanographic research vessel, is that it will sink because it can't withstand the rough seas off New England.

Attributes and Behavior of the Hulls in *The Nauticus Shipbuilding Company Simulation*

ATTRIBUTES	BEHAVIOR OF HULLS IF USED FOR OCEANOGRAPHIC RESEARCH VESSEL
Air Cushion: • Flat hull rides on cushion of air • Capable of high speeds • Needs flat water conditions • Flat, rectangular deck easy to load	Nonfunctional • Can't withstand rough seas

ATTRIBUTES	BEHAVIOR OF HULLS IF USED FOR OCEANOGRAPHIC RESEARCH VESSEL
Planing Hull: • V-shaped hull capable of high speeds • Performs best in flat water conditions • High stress levels on hull	Functional • Capable of high speeds • Not very stable in rough seas • Limited work and living space
Displacement Hull: • Deep, rounded hull very stable in all conditions • Very large cargo capacity • Stable platform for large propulsion systems • Needs very large propulsion system	Functional • Stable in rough seas • Plenty of work and living space • Deep draft limits access to shore areas
SWATH (Small Waterplane Area Twin Hull): • Two submerged hulls very stable • Flat deck provides good work area	Optimal • Very stable in rough seas • Plenty of protected work and living space • Shallower draft provides access to shore areas

Copyright Chedd-Angier Production.

Other Approaches to Active Information Delivery

Simulations, role-playing, and worlds structures are among the more popular techniques for active information delivery, but there are other options, ultimately only limited by your imagination.

- **Reporter.** A number of educational programs, including *Sky High*, allow users to report on their multimedia experience by using a virtual camera and a word processor to write a journal. This is probably not a true simulation because although you are playing a role, your actions don't affect what happens in the program. But being a reporter is at least more engaging than a simple click-and-read approach.

- **Tools.** Allowing the user to work with the information by giving them functioning tools in your program is another way to get users engaged. For example, the Prudential Verani Realty web site profiled in Chapters 10 has dynamic information elements such as calculators, rent versus buy estimators, and interactive checklists.
- **Virtual Advisors.** Virtual advisors are online forms that ask the user a series of questions. After the user has filled out the form, the online advisor suggests the proper product to buy or action to take. This is commonly used for more complex products, such as opening a bank account online. Many major banks have some sort of online advisor on their web sites to help users choose the type of account that is right for them.

Active Information Delivery as Part of Larger Passive Information Delivery Program

In the programs described above, *Sim City* and *The Nauticus Shipbuilding Company*, the complete programs are simulations. It is also perfectly good technique to add a simulation or other type of active information delivery to an otherwise click-and-read program. For example, in Houghton Mifflin's *Geology Explorer* web site, the users are asked to chart the location and magnitude of an earthquake using interactive animation tools. Another exercise in the same program allows users to date the geologic layers of a cross-section of land.

Benefits of Active Information Delivery: Learning to Learn

An additional benefit of an active information delivery, particularly a simulation, is that in addition to teaching a specific skill or subject matter, this type of multimedia is also very successful at teaching students how to learn. A generation ago, the standard structure for most elementary school classrooms was a teacher standing in front of a sea of students at desks and delivering knowledge from his or her information-packed brain to those of the empty-headed students.

A visitor to most classrooms today would find a different structure. The sea of desks is gone. Students are grouped in fours or fives around smaller tables and are engaged in activities. The teacher moves about the room, facilitating their learning. This different structure reflects current learning theory, which rejects the concept of empty heads waiting to be filled and replaces it with the goal of teaching students how to learn. Some theorists have used the metaphor of the toolmaker—that is, teaching students how to create the learning tools that will serve them throughout life (Reddy, 284–324).

A big reason for this major change is the rapid explosion in knowledge. A hundred years ago, the body of knowledge was relatively stable. Individuals could learn a trade and successfully perform that trade until retirement. Today, however, information is expanding so rapidly that education has become a lifelong pursuit. Students have no assurance that the information they are learning will be valid in a few years or even that the careers they are training for will exist after graduation. To thrive in this type of a world, students must be excellent learners and have a full bag of learning tools to take with them for the rest of their lives.

Teaching Toolmakers with Interactivity: Playing as If

One of the best ways to develop these tools—to learn how to learn—is through hands-on learning, an opportunity to interact with the subject under study. One way to do this is through interactive multimedia programs. However, as Edith Ackerman of the MIT Media Lab points out, "we should not assume that 'hands-on' activities alone will make for a meaningful experience of constructive learning.... Any activity remains essentially undirected and noncontrollable, blind, and meaningless, if it is just acted out without any evaluation of its consequences" (Ackerman 1–3).

Approaches to evaluating these consequences include soliciting reliable feedback and giving the learner the ability to reconstruct the experience. There should be some way to reconstruct and replay the learning experience in a safe environment, because the major way learners incorporate new material is not through the experience itself but through the ability to recreate the material in some fashion, thus making it their own. In short, "interactivity is important, not because it allows the direct manipulation of real objects, but because it fosters the construction of models or artifacts, in which an intriguing idea (thought and feeling) can be run or played out 'for good' in a make-believe world" (Ackerman, 6).

In an interactive multimedia program, this construction of models can range from trying out different marketing techniques in a practice case study in an e-learning course to building an entire city in one of the *SimCity* games. Such game elements allow the students to explore "what" will happen "if" they try various options. And as Ackerman points out, "Scientific inquiry, as much as other forms of cognitive investigation, indeed requires playing 'what if'" (Ackerman, 6).

Conclusion

Whether you use active or passive information delivery, it is important to pick the type of structure and approach to your material that will best fulfill your goals as discussed in the previous chapter. The user's needs, business context, and type of data will all have a major effect on your final decision. For example, creating a simulation will generally be more expensive than a click-and-read approach and may not be appropriate for a low budget web site project.

In general, when working on the World Wide Web, you need to also keep in mind that, unlike a CD-ROM or a museum kiosk, the web is an open system.

On the World Wide Web and other networks it is possible to link from words or images on one site to related information on other sites all over the world. The web allows the possibility of linking all of the structures described in this chapter in one unlimited search for information. A user might start at one site that is hierarchical, link to another site with a linear video, and yet another that involves her in a simulation. A graph of this would look like a mad combination of all of the examples in the chapter. With multisite branching such as this, the individual creator has the resources of the world to present his or her information, but the writer gives up much of the control in so doing. So if you add links from your web site to other sites, be aware of how the other sites are structured and whether this will impact the experience for your users. If the structure on the external site you are linking to is radically different, you may need to add an explanation before users take the jump to the other site.

This chapter concludes the introductory informational multimedia material. Beginning with the next chapter, major informational multimedia programs and web sites will be examined in depth to better understand how the principles we have been exploring so far are applied on actual projects.

References

Ackermann, Edith. *Tools for Constructive Learning: Rethinking Interactivity*. Cambridge, MA: MIT Media Lab, October 1993.
Sawyer, Brian, and John Vourlis. "Screenwriting Structures for New Media." *Creative Screenwriting* 2 (Summer 1995): 95–103.

Introduction to the Informational Multimedia and Web Site Case Studies

9

Description of Case Studies

The case studies in the chapters that follow demonstrate how various goals were achieved and challenges were met in specific multimedia programs and web sites:

- **Prudential Verani Realty web site:** A detailed profile of the writing of this site, from proposal to documentation. Prudential Verani is one of the largest realtors in New England.
- **T. Rowe Price web site:** The investment firm T. Rowe Price offers interactive information for new and seasoned investors. This chapter also includes a description of the different types of commercial web sites.
- **Britannica.com and The Harlem Renaissance:** An analysis of web site portals and writing the online feature story.
- **E-Learning: Interactive Math and Statistics Lessons:** Writing multimedia math and statistics lessons for the college audience.
- **The Nauticus Shipbuilding Company:** A museum kiosk shipbuilding simulation located at Nauticus, National Maritime Center, Norfolk, Virginia.
- **Clinical Support Staff Interactive Certification Program: Vital Signs:** An interactive multimedia training program for medical assistants at a health maintenance organization (HMO) on the process of taking vital signs—temperature, pulse, respiration, and blood pressure.

 Case Studies Note: *Informational multimedia case studies from previous edition chapters,* Sky High *and the ZDU Online Ad Campaign are now located in the Chapters section of the book's CD-ROM.*

Approach to Case Studies

An understanding of how the writers of these programs dealt with informational multimedia issues will give you insight into how to deal with similar issues when they arise in your work. Each case study answers the following questions:

- **Program Description and Background.** Is the program a typical example of its genre, or is it unusual? Who commissioned, developed, and wrote the program? What was the preproduction process?
- **Goals.** What were the writers and designers' goals in creating this project? What information or experience were they trying to communicate?
- **Challenges.** Which goals were particularly difficult to achieve? What approaches were successful in achieving these goals and which were discarded?
- **Response to the Project.** Did the program achieve its goals? Was it a critical and/or commercial success?

The case studies are documented with script examples, screen shots, and flowcharts.

 Additional script samples and other material are available for many of the programs on the Writing for Multimedia and the Web CD-ROM.

Note: Because all the case studies follow the above structure, the Chapter Overview section that has been appearing at the beginning of previous chapters will not appear on the case studies. It will be replaced by a descriptive summary of each case.

Case Study—Writing a Marketing Web Site from Proposal to Documentation: Prudential Verani Realty

10

Summary

Name of Production: Prudential Verani Realty Web Site,
    http://www.pruverani.com
Writer: Timothy Garrand
Developers: InterWrite
Audience: Commercial and Residential Real Estate Customers, General
    Public
Medium: World Wide Web
Location: Where web is viewed
Subject: Real Estate
Goals: Inform, teach
Architecture: Hierarchical branching, dynamic database generated

The text samples, flowcharts, and illustrations used in this chapter are copyright Prudential Verani
Realty.

Scope of This Chapter

This chapter studies all the different types of writing that can be required to develop a commercial web site, with an explanation of the goals of each document and some tips for achieving those goals. Although a writer's efforts are sometimes limited to the content of a site, the writer may be also called upon to write the initial proposals, planning documents, maintenance instructions, and online marketing writing, such as meta tags. The writer playing these roles needs to understand organizational tools, such as flowcharting software; how writing affects the site's online marketing efforts; and the capabilities of the latest web technology to communicate information effectively. This chapter is different from the later case studies that will focus primarily on writing the project's content.

Program Description and Background

Program Description
The Prudential Verani Realty web site is a marketing and content web site designed for Prudential Verani Realty, one of the largest real estate companies in New England. The goals of the site are to:

- Attract buyers of commercial and residential real estate
- Attract real estate sellers to list their properties with Prudential Verani
- Attract customers for other Verani services, such as relocation and mortgages
- Present a positive image for the Prudential Verani company
- Recruit new agents to join the company
- Present useful real estate information

The site includes extensive searchable information about Verani properties, descriptions of Verani services, general real estate information, and numerous interactive tools such as calculators, checklists, maps, and e-mail updates. The site consists of hundreds of HTML pages, many Active Server Pages and an extensive database of real estate properties. (Active Server Pages, or ASP, is a programming language that can be used to make web pages more interactive and functional.)

Production Background
Prudential Verani Realty approached my company, InterWrite, to develop the second generation of their web site. InterWrite is an interactive media developer that has been creating web sites and multimedia in the greater Boston area since 1996. The first, limited version of the Prudential Verani site had been done some years earlier and had to be completely redone with all new information architecture, graphics, content, and programming. None of the original site material was used. On the new site, I served as the writer, information architect, and project manager, Steve Street created graphics and HTML design, Ken Jones did the programming and technical development, and Laurie Strysko did the photographs. The Prudential Verani Realty executives on the project were Suzanne Burns and Giovanni Verani.

Some of the InterWrite developed site has since been revised with a different design and minor changes to the content. (It is usually a good idea to revise a site

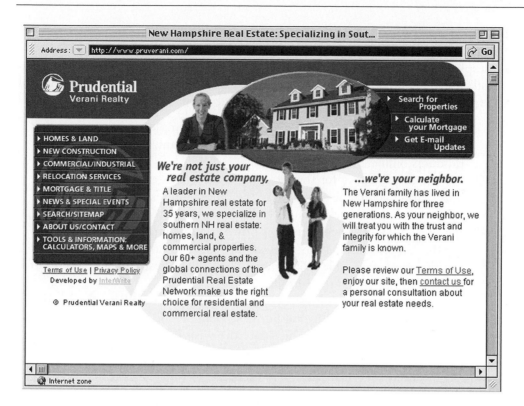

Figure 10-1 *The home page for Prudential Verani Realty.*

every few years to keep it fresh for users.) This chapter focuses on the creation of the InterWrite developed site because it gives us a rare opportunity to examine the complete site development process from concept to maintenance documentation, and the writer's role in each stage of the process. Take a look at the current site, compare it to the version described here, evaluate the changes, and discuss whether or not they have moved the site closer to its goals.

 The original color image for this screen shot and others is available on the Writing for Multimedia and the Web CD-ROM.

Planning the Prudential Verani Realty Web Site

One of the keys to a successful large-scale web site is adequate planning. Adequate planning insures that a web site achieves its goal and communicates its intended message for the least possible cost. A clear plan on paper allows a client to discuss options and make revisions for far less cost than it does to make revisions on a completed site.

Scoping a Project: Goals, Tools, and Price

The first stage of developing the site was to better define the project. This was accomplished through researching similar sites, meeting with the client, and digesting all of the client's existing marketing material. Some of the key questions that had to be answered and discussed with the client were:

1. What are the client's goals for this site? For example, is the primary purpose informational, marketing, content, or transactional—selling products online?
2. Who is the audience for this site? What are their demographics? What information about the product are they most interested in? What information do they already have? How sophisticated are they with using the web? How advanced are their browser and connection speed? What are the key use cases? (Use cases are the most common ways visitors will use the site.) If possible talk to users directly and test an early version of the site to determine their needs.
3. What is the client's wish list? What elements does the client think would be great for the site? Why would these elements be effective in achieving the client's goals? Can the client rate the wish list items in order of importance?
4. Who are the client's competitors? What are their web sites like? What techniques do they use?
5. Where will the site be hosted? What are the technical capabilities of the hosting service, or the client if they are doing the hosting? What platform will the hosting service be using?
6. What are the elements in existing company material that the client likes or that seem particularly effective? What resources already exist, such as pictures or a database of information? Is this material suitable for the web site?
7. What are the branding issues? Are there guidelines for a specific way material needs to be presented?
8. Is a web site the correct medium to present all the material, achieve the client's goals, and reach the intended audience? Would a disk-based interactive program, or even a video or a brochure, be more appropriate for some of the material?
9. What form does the intended information take? Is it numbers and statistics? Video? Graphics? Text?
10. How often and how extensively does this information need to be updated? Does the client have adequate staff to do updating, or will this require a maintenance contract?
11. Are there ways that we can present this information that are dynamic and customizable for the user?
12. Will this project need to pay for itself, for example by incorporating advertising?
13. What are the ways this site can be marketed to drive traffic to the site?

The Proposal for the Prudential Verani Web Site

Once the project has been defined by answering all the above questions, and a rough idea of costs has been established, then it is time to write the proposal. For the Prudential Verani site, the developer, InterWrite, created a proposal that outlined the goals of the site, two possible approaches to achieving those goals, and the approximate costs of each of these approaches. (Most proposals only present one approach to the client.)

The purpose of proposal writing is to present options to the client clearly, succinctly, and appealingly. This should not be a hard-sell document, but it should point out the advantages of the work being suggested. Note the modular approach in the proposal to the design and pricing of the project. This allowed the clients to delete or combine elements in a way that created the site and budget they desired. This is only one approach to proposal writing. There are many other approaches. Some major companies request so many specific topics to be addressed that proposals can be forty to fifty pages long. Note also that the stage listed below as "The First Step" is often called "Discovery" or "Requirements."

Section of Prudential Verani Web Site Proposal
Goals of an Improved Web Site

1. Better attract and serve customers (buyers)

2. Better attract and serve clients (sellers)

3. Sell properties more effectively

4. Help agents and staff make the most effective use of their time

5. Improve cooperation with business partners

The First Step: Requirements Gathering

The first step to revise the Verani site is to clearly define the message, content, functionality, and navigation. This material will be presented in outlines and flowcharts of the proposed site. Once this step is completed, we can develop a precise budget. Until then, the amounts below are estimates.

The cost to develop the outline, flowcharts, and budget would be: $XXXX-$XXXX.

Site Revision Options We've presented two approaches to revising your site in the document that follows.

• Option 1: Achieves the most important goals for your site at a moderate cost.

- Option 2: Achieves all the goals that we discussed for your site at a higher cost.

Both of these options have been broken into sections so we can delete and combine elements to achieve exactly the web site and budget you desire.

Option #1: Revision to Achieve Most Important Goals

Suggested Revision
   (To protect the client's privacy, all dollar amounts
   have been blocked out.)
	Estimated Cost

Expand Content: The Real Estate and Relocation Information Source for New Hampshire Your current site tells the user about your company and your properties. An alternative is also to make your site an information resources for sellers and buyers of real estate. This would greatly increase traffic to your site. Users would come to your site for information. This well-presented information would demonstrate that you are a well-run, knowledgeable company. This would encourage users to come to you when they are considering buying or selling a home. The site would also of course continue to fulfill its current functions of presenting your properties and company. Types of information that could be included are: • Mortgage calculator • School reports • Town reports • Relocation information • List of home inspectors • Interactive tutorials on how to buy a property This material would be presented in such a way that the user makes a positive connection with your agency. For example, after a site visitor uses our mortgage calculator to determine how much they could afford, then we would offer to show the visitor Verani properties in that price range.	$XXXX

Graphic and HTML Redesign of Site This includes a complete graphic redesign of the site, including redesigning the home page, secondary pages, headers, buttons, original graphics, and integration of graphics into HTML. The goal is to make the site a more upscale, friendly place, demonstrating that Prudential Verani: • has the resources to sell your property most effectively • has the knowledge and resources to make your home search efficient and successful • has a friendly, professional staff that would be a pleasure to work with	$XXXX

NOTE: This is only part of the proposal. In the full proposal, many additional elements are outlined in the table and the total budget is estimated. The proposal also includes a second, more expensive revision option and an approximate production schedule for completing the project. The actual budget numbers are crossed out on this proposal sample to protect the client's privacy.

Scope of Work/Revision Plan

The above proposal was discussed with key members of the Prudential Verani team and eventually options were eliminated and the scope of work of the project was clearly defined. This scope is an important document because it can be the basis of your contractual agreement with the client. The writing needs to be very clear and unambiguous. There is no need for salesmanship here. Do not promise anything you cannot deliver, and make it clear what work is not your responsibility. Many of the elements in the scope of work/revision plan have been refined and simplified from the original proposal.

REVISION PLAN/SCOPE OF WORK FOR THE PRUDENTIAL
VERANI WEB SITE

1. Production Planning and Content Definition

The first stage of designing the web site is to clearly define the site in an outline and flowchart. The flowchart will consist of a complete graphical plan of the site, illustrating every internal page in the site and each page's place in the overall site architecture. A first draft of the outline and flowchart will be presented to key Verani staff for comments. Based on these comments, a second draft will be created that will also be submitted for comments.

Once the tasks and content are clearly defined, then we can produce a detailed and final budget, production plan/time line, and payment schedule.

Production Planning Costs: $XXXX Payment for production planning will be in three stages:

- $XXXX to initiate the project
- $XXXX due at completion of first draft outline and chart
- Balance of costs for production planning due at sign-off for final draft chart, outline, budget, and production schedule. Costs for the outline/charts will be a minimum of $XXXX but no more than $XXXX.

2. Web Site Creation

Once the production planning is complete, the second stage of the process is to produce the web site. The tasks contracted for include the following:

Graphic and HTML Redesign of Site. This includes a complete graphic redesign of the site, including redesigning the home page, secondary pages, headers, buttons, original graphics, and integration of graphics into HTML. The goal is to make the site a more upscale, friendly place, demonstrating that Prudential Verani:

- has the resources to sell your property effectively
- has the knowledge and resources to make your home search efficient and successful
- has a friendly, professional staff that would be a pleasure to work with

Improve the Content about Your Company and Properties The current site presents your properties, company, and agents. We will create new material and build on the existing material to make this presentation more effective. For example, we will improve the graphic design of the results page for the properties database search. This page will also include links to other relevant information on the site. Another improvement would be to create custom templates for the New Construction section, making this section easily updateable.

In addition, we will add new material about the company that is not on the current site, such as a new mortgage and title section.

We will also increase the functionality of the site, such as adding
a site-wide search and an easily updateable Special Events page for
announcing open houses or special meetings.

NOTE: This is a fragment of the scope of work/revision plan. The complete
scope continues similarly to the above, clearly defining every element that will
be created for the site. The last part of the scope below defines the services and
production schedule.

3. Services Included

InterWrite or its subcontractors will complete all of the tasks agreed
upon in the final outline. All payment will be made to InterWrite,
who will be responsible for payment to all subcontractors and for
subcontractors completing their work. Prudential Verani agrees to
pay InterWrite within 30 days of the agreed upon dates in the payment
plan. Payment will be made at the completion of major stages of the
project. This payment plan will be developed after completion of
the production planning and outlines, described in Step 1 at the
beginning of this document.

   The final product will be a fully functioning and tested web site
placed on the server of your choice. The final web site will be
owned and copyrighted by Prudential Verani.

   After the web site is completed, Prudential Verani will be
responsible for the regular upkeep of the site unless additional
contracts are made with InterWrite Design.

4. Approximate Time Frame

- This time frame can be finalized after completing the final
  outlines. At this point, the following is a rough estimate,
  subject to change.
- Keeping this time frame requires a speedy turnaround
  (2-3 days) of drafts for comment from Prudential Verani.
  With longer turnaround times, InterWrite cannot keep this
  schedule.

Project Start	December 7
Final Outlines/Charts Completed	December 31
First Drafts of Content and Graphics	January 29
Complete First Draft of Site Launched	February 19
Final Site Launched	March 1
Online Marketing Completed	March 8

Gathering and Grouping Site Material

Once the scope of work is accepted by the client, the next step is for the web site developer and the writer to gather as much information as they can about the client's products and services. This information can come from existing information collateral, such as brochures, advertisements, older web sites, and even marketing videos if they exist. But the source for the most current information will be the client themselves. In the case of this site, a number of the top executives and agents at Prudential Verani Realty were interviewed.

It is also a good idea to examine the user scenarios. User scenarios describe exactly how users will use the site. User scenarios will discuss where each type of user might enter the site, what information they will be looking for, and step by step how they will move through the site to get to that information. For example, someone looking to buy a commercial warehouse and get a mortgage will need different information and travel a different sequence through the site than would someone buying their first home with cash. The developer's job is to make sure the information each user wants is where they expect it to be on the site and in the proper sequence.

In addition to grouping the content by following user scenarios, another common method is the card sort. Sometimes actual physical paper cards are used, but I prefer electronic "cards" that can be sorted on the computer. The first step is to determine the "bins" or main categories, such as "Homes and Land," and subcategories if the site is big enough, such as "New Construction." Then all the possible information on the site is broken down into discreet units or chunks, such as "Radon and Lead Information." Then, working with the client, these information units are sorted to the proper bins. A variation with a large group of stakeholders is to place the bin categories on the wall and give each user a sticky labeled with each content chunk. The stakeholders can then vote by placing a sticky under each bin category on the wall. If the majority of the "Radon and Lead" stickies are placed under the "Homes and Land" category, then that is probably where that information should be placed on the actual site.

If using the card sort method, it is important to make sure that the content arrangement supports the user scenarios. You may have to rearrange some content or create cross links to make sure that users can accomplish their goals. As with any major change, when you have settled on an initial site structure it is a good idea to verify it with potential site users.

Flowchart/Sitemap

Once the content groupings have been approved by the client, the next step is usually the development of a flowchart or sitemap of the site. The flowchart should indicate every page of the site. The goal is for the flowchart to be a clear visualization of site structure. See Chapter 3 for a detailed discussion of flowcharting and flowchart software. As discussed in Chapter 3, there are a number of techniques

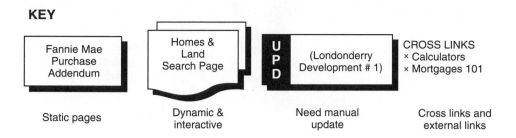

Figure 10-2 *Symbol key for Prudential Verani web site flowchart/sitemap.*

that help make the flowchart a more useful tool, including:

1. Give every page of the site a unique number and name.
2. For ease of printing and presentation, run the chart vertically instead of horizontally, as in Figure 10-3.
3. Simplify where you can. If there will be multiple sections that will be designed in the same way, it is OK to say that in a note. No need to draw out all the boxes for repetitive pages.
4. It can make it easier to see the main sections of the web site by writing those pages in bold with drop shadows.
5. Indicate cross-links (links to pages within the site that are already on the chart) and external links (links to other web sites) as text only.
6. Visually indicate pages that will have special functions. For example, pages that will have interactive elements or that will be generated dynamically from a database (see Figure 10-2).

Outline

As discussed in Chapter 3, the flowchart illustrates the overall navigation, structure, and size of the site; the outline provides more details about the actual content and functionality of the individual pages. The flowchart and outline that follow are most effective when used together. The client consults the chart for overall structure, then reads the outline for the details. Not all sites use outlines, but they are particularly useful for information heavy sites and to explain content groupings to nontechnical clients.

The structure of each page on the outline below is fairly simple. The outline should be adjusted to match the specific project. The elements include:

- **Title:** The page title, which should be the same as what is on the flowchart.
- **Image:** Describes possible images for the page.
- **Text:** Describes onscreen text.

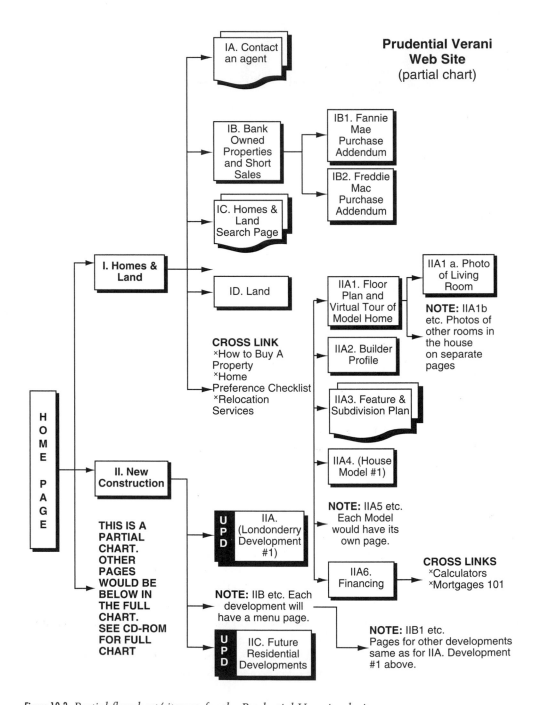

Figure 10-3 *Partial flowchart/sitemap for the Prudential Verani web site.*

- **Links:** Includes all the links on this page from text within the page and from the graphical navigation bar.
- **Navigation bar:** The specific buttons that will have to be created for the navigation bar.
- **Functionality:** This describes what the user can do on this page besides click-and-read. For example, can they search for properties or calculate their mortgage.

Partial Outline of the Prudential Verani Web Site

Home Page

Title: Prudential Verani Realty

The Real Estate and Relocation Resource for Southern NH

IMAGES: Images which demonstrate that Verani is a professional, friendly place. Possible images: Prudential logo, friendly Verani staff, Verani office, people enjoying a beautiful home. Might have other images on page to lead user to some of our key features, such as a calculator image for the tools and an e-mail icon for our custom e-mail notification service.

TEXT: Explain that we are part of Prudential, one of the largest corporations in the world, but also a family-owned company with strong roots in Southern NH. We have the resources to sell your property effectively and/or make your home search efficient and successful. Also should introduce some of the key features of the site, such as our searches, custom e-mail notification tools, extensive information resources, etc. Near the bottom of the page should be a short disclaimer stating that we have made every effort to make the information on this site accurate but are not liable for any errors or omissions; please see our Terms of Use Policy.

LINKS: Homes and Land, New Construction, Commercial and Industrial, Relocation Services, Verani Mortgage and Title, Real Estate Information and Resources, News and Special Events, Search/Site Map, About Us/Contact.

   Might also have a link from a calculator image to the tools and calculator section. In text on the bottom of the page and every page will be links to Terms of Use, Privacy Statements, and a webmaster e-mail link.

NAVIGATION BAR: Homes and Land, New Construction, Commercial and Industrial, Relocation Services, Verani Mortgage and Title, Real Estate Information and Resources, News and Special Events, Search/sitemap, About Us/Contact.

I. Homes and Land

TITLE: Homes and Land

IMAGE: Small image of attractive house. This could be the same picture all the time, or a regularly changing featured house.

TEXT: Briefly explain the range of properties we offer and the area we cover. Direct the user to the search page and other services that will help them in their moving and home buying, such as Relocation Services, the How to Buy a Property Section, Home Preference Checklist/Questionnaire, and New Construction.

LINKS: Home, Search, Contact, Relocation Services, the How to Buy a Property Section, Home Preference Checklist/Questionnaire, and New Construction.

NAVIGATION BAR: Home, Search, Contact.

IA. Contact an Agent

TITLE: Contact Us

IMAGE: Photo of friendly agent.

TEXT: Phone numbers, addresses, and e-mails for all offices, plus a form that user can fill out and submit so that we can contact them.

LINKS: Home Page, Search, Contact, Homes and Land.

NAVIGATION BAR: Home Page, Search, Contact, Homes and Land.

FUNCTIONALITY: Users can fill out a form with their address and e-mail, click the type of information they want, write a short note, and submit it to us. Message will go to different people at Prudential Verani, depending on what type of information the user requests.

NOTE: This is a partial outline. See the Chapter 10 area in the Chapters section of the Writing for Multimedia and the Web CD-ROM for a full outline.

Writing the Web Site

Once the outline and site flowchart have been thoroughly discussed with and approved by the client, a detailed budget and scope of work will be created. (Because this final scope of work is similar to the preliminary scope discussed earlier in this chapter, and because production budgeting is outside the parameters of this book, these documents will not be discussed here.) With an approved outline and final scope of work/revision plan, the content for the web site can now be written.

Online Writing Style Tips
As discussed in Chapter 2, strong writing for the web and multimedia follows many of the principals of good journalism, including:

- Strong lead sentences that summarize content
- Inverted pyramid style: put most important content first
- Simple sentence construction
- Concrete words: nouns and verbs, avoid adjectives and adverbs
- Active not passive voice verbs

As also discussed in Chapter 2, there are also a number of writing techniques that are specific to writing for the web and multimedia. Please refer to Chapter 2 for the full discussion; following are just a few of the main points.

- highlighted keywords
- meaningful subheadings (not "clever" ones)
- bulleted lists one idea per paragraph
- half the word count (or less) than conventional writing

Nielsen, The Alertbox: How Users Read on the Web

These concepts are particularly true on the first couple of levels of a web site or multimedia program where the user is trying to find the information they want. Once they have located their information deeper in the site, users may be willing to read longer text material.

These general style techniques apply to most online writing, but specific types of pages make unique demands on the writer. Examples of special types of pages on the Prudential Verani web site include:

- Home page
- Section menu/introduction pages
- Static content pages
- Interactive and dynamic content pages

Each of these page types will be discussed in detail in the remainder of this chapter, including how to write pages so that a site will show up well when users search for the site's topic in search engines and directories.

Search Engines and Keywords

A unique aspect of writing for the web is the need to consider search engines. In most cases, search engines such as Google, and directories such as Yahoo!, are a primary way that new users will find your site. When users go to Google and type in words related to your site, such as "New Hampshire real estate," you want your site to appear in the top ten to twenty search engine results. To achieve this, with many search engines, it can help to pay attention to keywords.

Keywords are simply the words that your potential customers and/or site visitors are likely to enter into a search engine to find your site. The challenge is to decide which keywords to use. For the first draft of your site, you can start by asking your clients what keywords they expect potential customers to use. They know their business better than you do. Ideally, you should also ask a number of users if you can. Many search engines also maintain web sites that list the most common search terms. Reviewing common terms in your category can help you to phrase your keywords correctly. A couple good sites for common search terms are:

- AOL Hot Searches: http://hot.aol.com/
- Google Zeitgeist: http://www.google.com/press/zeitgeist.html

Because repetition is an important factor in search-engine ranking, you need to focus on a few keywords and repeat them judiciously throughout the home page. For the Verani site, the primary keywords are: "New Hampshire real estate," "NH real estate," "Southern New Hampshire real estate," and "southern NH real estate." As in this example, it is usually wiser to use keyword phrases of two or more words. Single word keywords or even common short phrases, such as "real estate" are not specific enough to allow a user who is making a focused search to pull up your site on the first page or two of the search results.

Your work with keywords is not completed once you finish the site and submit it to search engines. Evaluating and modifying your choice of keywords is an ongoing process to better your search engine placement. Software tools can help with this process and allow you to better refine your keywords. After you have submitted your site to the search engines, and the site begins showing up in the search engine indexes, you can use site analysis software, such as WebTrends (http://www.webtrends.com/), to monitor who comes to your site and what search words they use. Once you have determined the most common search words being used to find your site, you can rewrite your site to include more of them.

Another useful tool in this process is search-engine position-analysis software, which will search specific keywords on the major search engines and report your ranking for that specific terms. For example, when searching Google for "New Hampshire real estate," the Prudential Verani site comes up fourth in the search results. You can do without the search position software by doing multiple searches of your keywords in the major search engines, but it will take a while.

Later in this chapter, we will have more discussion about how to write your web site to improve search engine placement, but adjusting the site's text is not the only way to improve search engine and directory rankings. For example, most search engines currently track link popularity. If your site has many links from high quality sites, your site will be higher in the rankings. Click-through measurement can also be important for search engines. If your site initially appears lower on the search results listings but gets lots of clicks by users, a search engine may give your site a higher ranking. Most search engines also accept paid rankings. For other nonwriting tips on marketing your web site, check out the reference material on Search Engine Watch (http://www.searchenginewatch.com). Also, if your client has sufficient resources, they might consider a search engine optimization company. These companies have special techniques to boost your search engine rankings. But because this is a book about writing, we will not address these nonwriting topics further here, but instead discuss how writing can enhance search engine ranking as one of our web writing considerations.

The Home Page

The home page is the most important page of a web site. (See Figure 10-1 for a screenshot of the home page.) If this page does not accomplish its goals, then the user may go no further and the site can fail. There is a heavy burden on the home page. It must:

1. Hook the user's interest.
2. Communicate the basic message and tone of the site.
3. Introduce key site elements and lure the user deeper into the site.
4. Provide the correct keywords and frequency of keywords to help search engine placement.
5. Address legal issues.

The writer shares some of the above duties with the graphic and interface designers, but good writing is a major component of the success of any home page. It is important for the writer to work with the graphic designer when creating the page so that the designer's images support and expand on the writer's content.

The Title

Word for word, the title is probably the most important text on your home page. The page title and the main heading are frequently confused. The page title is not the heading that appears immediately above the text. On the Prudential Verani home page (Figure 10-1), the main heading is "We're not just your real estate company . . . we're your neighbor." The title on the Verani page appears in the bar at the very top of the browser: "New Hampshire Real Estate: Specializing in Southern NH Homes, Land, and Commercial Properties."

The functions of the title are to:

1. Identify an open web page.
2. Provide key site information to search engines' spiders. (Spiders are software programs that search web sites and collect information for search engine ranking.)
3. Identify the site in search engine and directory lists.
4. Identify the site in bookmark lists.

Of these functions, the last three are by far the most important. For many search engines, the title is one of the most important elements for determining how your site will rank when someone searches for one of your keywords.

The title in the first draft of the home page,

```
"Welcome to Prudential Verani Realty"
```

identifies the business and is a common sort of title on the web. However, this title made a poor showing in search engine tests. The second draft title is much more descriptive of the Prudential Verani services. It also contains many keywords that will help determine search engine placement with search engines that track keywords. The second draft title is:

```
New Hampshire Real Estate: Specializing in Southern NH
Real Estate, Homes, Land, and Commercial Properties.
```

Longer titles, such as this, may not show in their entirety in all browsers and search engine results, but the entire title will be indexed for keywords, which can boost your search engine ranking on some search engines.

Do not write keywords in your title that do not relate to your site. Also, do not write a long list of keywords, especially repetitive words in the title. Search engine companies are getting better at determining keyword and link spam (attempts to fool the search engine) to gain good search engine placement. If a search engine detects spam, it may penalize your site by dropping it lower on the list or eliminating it from its index altogether. So make sure that your title makes sense grammatically and in terms of the content of your site. It takes clever writing to create a site that gets strong search engine placement and is still a good read for the user.

In addition to improving your search engine ranking, another key function of your title is to identify your web site in search engine and directory lists. Remember that, unlike the title of a newspaper story, a web site title often must stand-alone in a search engine or directory list. So be sure that your title is effective on its own. Don't use a teaser or trick title that has little independent meaning. Stick with something that is clear and descriptive of your site.

The Main Menu

The main menu on the home page is the clickable list of the main sections of the site. Its key functions are to:

1. Provide a brief outline of the site, giving the user a sense of what lies within.
2. Serve as a main navigational tool

The titles in the main menu should be descriptive and brief. Many designers also believe that they should be limited in number. Other designers, however, like to give their sites a portal look with dozens of links. This approach requires careful text design, but it can still overwhelm the user who is looking for quick information. The first draft menu titles on this site are:

- Residential
- New Construction
- Commercial/Industrial
- Relocation Services
- Mortgage and Title
- News and Special Events
- Search/Sitemap
- About Us/Contact
- Resources

The only change with the second draft was to use more descriptive language for two of the titles: "Residential" was changed to "Homes and Land;" "Resources" was changed to "Tools and Information: Calculators, Maps, and More."

If a menu is made up of text links, it can also provide a good source of keywords to boost search engine placement. Unfortunately, in many cases a graphic menu is more visually attractive. You can compensate for the use of a graphic menu by using alternate image tags in the HTML code that describe the content of the picture. But only a few search engines read these tags. Another alternative is to repeat your graphic menu links on the bottom of the page as text links. This not only helps search engine placement, but is also useful to the visually impaired who have special machines that can read text but not graphics. (See "Writing Accessible Multimedia" in the Background section of the *Writing for Multimedia and the Web* CD-ROM.)

Links to Exciting Elements

In addition to the main menu links on the home page, it is also a good idea to have links to any areas of your site that the user might find particularly exciting or interactive. The goal is to:

1. Lure the user deeper into your site.
2. Get the user interacting with your site. If you can get a user doing things on your site besides reading, you have taken a good first step to getting them to explore the site.

Some designers call this making the site "sticky." On this site the links to exciting elements include:

- `Search for Properties`
- `Calculate your Mortgage`
- `Get E-mail Updates`

As you can see, these links are brief, descriptive, and written in terms of actions. They address some of a user's key interests for visiting a real estate site, and they encourage the user to do something. There were no changes between the first and second drafts.

Slogans/Headings

A slogan can help express the tone of the site. If the slogan has keywords, is in text, and is written as a heading, it can also boost search engine placement. Some search engines give greater importance to words surrounded by HTML heading tags. (See the Background section of the *Writing for Multimedia and the Web* CD-ROM for an introduction to HTML.) As is the case with menus, as discussed above, a slogan or heading may look better as a graphic, and you may choose to forego the search engine advantage to improve the visual look of the page.

The slogan for this page is:

`We're not just your real estate company ... We're your neighbor.`

Each of the two parts of the slogan is centered over the paragraph that relates to it. There is not much text on this home page, but web pages that do have more text should break the text into sections and have clear, descriptive headings at the top of each section of text. This helps the user scan your information more quickly.

Body Text

The body text is the main text on the page. Its functions are to:

1. Hook the user by explaining why this is the site you want to explore for your real estate needs.
2. Introduce the type of material that is in the site.
3. Boost the search engine rating by including keywords.
4. Get the user to make contact.
5. Strengthen the legal protection for the company.

The first draft body text below satisfies many of our requirements for good web writing:

- Brief: The user can see the entire home page without scrolling.
- Strong lead sentence that summarizes content.
- Inverted pyramid style: put most important content first. The integrity of the Verani family is secondary to the size, experience, and capabilities of their company.
- Concrete words: uses nouns and verbs, avoiding adjectives and adverbs. There is little fluff here. The user is not told that Verani is the best company around. Instead, the company is described in very concrete terms: the number of agents, years of experience, sales figures, and affiliations. This information shows rather than tells the user that this is a hot company.
- The word "contact" in the last sentence is a link to a contact information page encouraging the user to get in touch.

```
FIRST DRAFT: More than 60 agents, 35 years of experience,
$100 million in sales, and the global connections of the
Prudential Real Estate Network make us the right choice to
help you buy or sell residential and commercial properties.
    The Verani family has lived in New Hampshire for three
generations. As your neighbor, we will treat you with the
trust and integrity for which the Verani family is known.
    Enjoy our site, then contact us for a personal consultation
about your real estate needs.
```

The problem with this first draft was that in tests with search engines, this text produced poor search engine rankings for the site. This is important because the body text is used by virtually all search engines to rank your site. The first paragraph was rewritten to include more keywords and keyword repetition. On a longer page it is also important to have keywords high on the page and as page and section titles. The challenge was to incorporate more keywords while continuing to make the site engaging to the user. The ideal page from a search engine's point of view is a page without tables or frames, limited graphics, and lots of text. Such a page may get a site a high ranking in a search engine, but once the user gets to this unattractive, text-heavy page, they will probably not click beyond the home page.

```
SECOND DRAFT: A leader in New Hampshire real estate for 35 years,
we specialize in southern NH real estate: homes, land, and
commercial properties. Our 60+ agents and the global connections
of the Prudential Real Estate Network make us the right choice for
residential and commercial real estate.
```

The one other change, which was on advice from the company lawyer, was to add a link to the terms of use statement in the body text:

```
SECOND DRAFT: Please review our Terms of Use, enjoy our site,
then contact us for a personal consultation about your real
estate needs.
```

The Terms of Use is an important legal document that can help reduce the site owner's liability. Every commercial site should have one. But don't worry, this is not one more job for the writer. A lawyer must write the Terms of Use. When you are on the web, click the "Terms of Use" link at the bottom of the Prudential Verani home page to see what such a document looks like.

Bottom Text Links

Text links at the bottom of the home page are typically used for legal and business purposes, such as links to Terms of Use or the webmaster. It is also the place where you will often place the name of the site developer.

For the second draft, the writer added a text menu of key site links to aid navigation and to incorporate additional keywords for search engine placement. Do not just put a list of keywords in tiny or invisible text at the bottom of the page or the search engine will punish you for trying to spam them. A text menu at the bottom of the page is, however, a legitimate addition to your home page.

Complete First and Second Draft Home Page Text

After the previous discussion about writing the home page, review the first and second drafts of the home page text to get an overall understanding of the impact of the changes. Changes are in bold.

First Draft Home Page Text	Second Draft Home Page Text (Changes are in bold)
TITLE: Welcome to Prudential Verani Realty SECTION MENU: Residential New construction	TITLE: **New Hampshire Real Estate: Specializing in Southern NH Real Estate, Homes, Land, and Commercial Properties**

Commercial/industrial
Relocation Services
Mortgage and Title
News and Special Events
Search/sitemap
About Us/Contact
Resources
LINKS TO EXCITING ELEMENTS:
• Search for Properties
• Calculate your mortgage
• Get E-mail updates
SLOGANS/HEADINGS: We're not
just your real estate
company ... we're your
neighbor.
BODY TEXT: More than 60 agents,
35 years of experience,
$100 million in sales, and
the global connections of
the Prudential
Real Estate Network make us
the right choice to help you
buy or sell residential and
commercial properties.
The Verani family has lived
in New Hampshire for three
generations. As your neighbor,
we will treat you with
the trust and integrity for
which the Verani family is
known.
Enjoy our site, then contact
us for a personal
consultation about your
real estate needs.
BOTTOM TEXT LINKS:
• Terms of Use
• Privacy Policy
• Developed by InterWrite

SECTION MENU:
Homes and Land
New construction
Commercial/industrial
Relocation Services
Mortgage and Title
News and Special Events
Search/Sitemap
About Us/Contact
Tools and Information:
Calculators, Maps, and More
LINKS TO EXCITING ELEMENTS:
• Search for Properties
• Calculate your Mortgage
• Get E-mail updates
SLOGANS/HEADINGS: We're not
just your real estate
company...
we're your neighbor.
BODY TEXT: **A leader in New**
Hampshire real estate for
35 years, we specialize in
southern NH real estate:
homes, land, and commercial
properties. Our 60+ agents
and the global connections
of the Prudential Real
Estate Network make us the
right choice for
residential and commercial
real estate.
The Verani family has lived
in New Hampshire for three
generations. As your
neighbor, we will treat you
with the trust and
integrity for which the
Verani family is known.
Please review our Terms of
Use, enjoy our site, then
contact us for a personal
consultation about your
real estate needs.

```
BOTTOM TEXT LINKS:
• Terms of Use
• Private Policy
• Developed by InterWrite
• New Hampshire Homes and Land
• New Hampshire New
  Construction
• New Hampshire
  Commercial/Industrial Real
  Estate
• Relocation Services
• Mortgage and Title
• Real Estate Tools and
  Information: Maps,
  Calculators, and more
• Contact
```

Home Page Meta Tags

Meta tags are HTML tags that enclose special text at the top of your web page. Unlike the page title, the text between meta tags never appears on the web page that is displayed on your user's computer screen. As with the page title, either you or (more likely) the production team need to access the HTML code of your page to write meta tags. You can view the meta tags and the HTML source code for a web page simply by opening the View menu of your browser and clicking "Source" and looking for the word "meta" near the top of the page. In the past, the meta tags could be helpful to search engine ranking, but in recent years their impact has diminished. Nevertheless they are still worth at least a brief discussion.

The meta tags of key concern to the writer are the Keyword and the Description meta tags. These tags can affect the way some search engines:

1. Rank your site for specific keyword searches
2. Describe your site in search results

It is important to note that most major search engines no longer index Keyword meta tags but many do use the Description meta tag. For the search engines that do use them, however, well-written meta tags can still make a difference.

Description Meta Tag: The description meta tag describes your site. This tag is indexed by some search engines for keywords that will affect your search engine ranking, and some search engines also use this meta tag as the description of your site that will appear in the list of search engine results when a user searches for one of your keywords.

It is important to have a strong first sentence that summarizes your site and convinces the user to click on your link in the search engine results. One reason for this is that the amount of text search engines will display for a description range from approximately 130 to 400 characters. So in many search engines, the first sentence may be all that is displayed for the description. Another reason for the importance of the first sentence is that users are in a rush. They are quickly scanning the search engine results to find the information that they want. So be sure to quickly and clearly tell them who you are and why you are worth clicking on. Stay away from meaningless marketing hype.

The following example clearly states that Prudential Verani is a successful real estate agency. This statement is backed up by the concrete figure of their annual sales. The second sentence explains what type of real estate they sell. Additional paragraphs are also added because they add additional material for the search engine to index, and the longer description may show up in some search engine results, although it will not in most.

```
<meta name="Description"
   content="Prudential Verani is one of the largest and most
successful real estate agencies in New Hampshire with $100 million
in annual sales. We can help you buy and sell homes, land, and
commercial property.
   We have served the real estate needs of New Hampshire and
northern Massachusetts for more than 35 years under the ownership
of the Verani family. We know the area, and as your neighbor, we
will treat you with the trust and integrity for which the Verani
family is known.
   Our emphasis on customer service, commitment to employee
training, affiliation with the Prudential Real Estate network,
and utilization of the latest technological resources give us
a competitive edge in all our real estate dealings.
   We are the real estate information resource for New Hampshire.
Our Relocation Services division can supply school reports, town
reports, and free moving publications. Our 300+ page web site is
packed with interactive tools and information to help you make
informed real estate decisions."
```

Keyword Meta Tag: The keyword meta tag lists keywords that a user might type in a search box to find your site. This tag is no longer indexed by any major search engines, but is still indexed by some speciality search engines for keywords that will affect your search engine ranking. See the discussion about choosing your keywords under "Search Engines and Keywords" earlier in this chapter.

Some keyword tips:

1. You may list up to a thousand characters in your keyword meta tag.
2. Put your most important keywords first.
3. Concentrate on two or more word phrases.
4. Enter your keywords all in lowercase, because in most search engines, even if the user searches in uppercase, the search engine will match that search with lowercase keywords.
5. As was discussed earlier with titles, do not list the same word multiple times or you may trigger the search engine's spam detector and your keywords—and maybe even your site—will not be indexed. It is, however, OK to list different phrases that include some of the same words, such as "new hampshire real estate" and "southern new hampshire real estate."
6. Think of as many synonyms and variations on your keyword as you can so you can catch as many searches as possible, such as using "new hampshire" and "n.h."
7. If there are common misspelling of your most important keywords, it is also not a bad idea to include a few of them.
8. Put commas between each of your keywords.
9. Review your keyword choices with your client. They know their business better than you do.

```
<meta name="KEYWORDS"
    content="new hampshire real estate, nh real estate, southern
new hampshire real estate, southern nh real estate, southern nh
realtors, relocation services, nh homes for sale, new hampshire,
nh, southern new hampshire, southern n.h., property listings, new
construction, real estate financing, land development, manchester
new hampshire, commercial locations, n.h., massachusetts, homes,
houses, residential, commercial, realty, prudential, prudential
verani realty, relocation, nh realtors, verani, mortgage, property,
properties, housing, mortgage calculators, mortgages, land, real
estate careers, manchester nh, londonderry, salem, nashua, kingston,
derry, interstate 93, i-93, bank owned, reo, short sale,
subdivisions, rural, lease, school reports, town reports, agents,
real estate agents, real estate maps, radon, lead, windham, raymond,
bedford, pelham, exeter, plaistow, skiing, employee assistance,
portsmouth, municipal permitting, bank-owned, pru review"
```

Alt Tags

Alt tags are similar to meta tags in that they are part of the HTML of your site that the user does not see on the web page. The alt tags describe the images on your site in text. The following example shows the alt tag for the first navigation button on the home page. The alt tag is located immediately after the image source tag, which tells the browser where to find the image that will be displayed on your page.

```
img src="homepix/navhomes.gif"
alt="New Hampshire Homes and Land"
```

The function of the alt tag is to:

1. Boost search engine rankings on the few search engines that index them.
2. Describe your images for surfers who have their images turned off.
3. Describe your images for the visually impaired, who use text readers to access your site.

Alt tags should provide a clear, succinct description of your images. This includes navigation buttons. Because a few search engines still use alt tags to boost your search engine rankings, it is advisable to work keywords into your alt tags if you can do so without distorting the content. In the example above, the actual navigation button says "Homes and Land," but the alt tag is "New Hampshire Homes and Land" to create a more effective keyword.

Another reason for descriptive alt tags is that some search engines create the description of your site that appears on the search engine results from all the text on your page, including the alt tags. If you are using an HTML editor to create your site, it may automatically enter alt tags for every image. Be sure to edit them and delete the ones that have no relevance to the content. For example, if you have a decorative bar on top of your menu, your editor might give this bar the alt tag of "Navbar top." A search engine might use this text in the description of your site, which will be useless for the user.

Main Section Menu/Introduction Pages

If you have a large site with sections of unique content, then you will need to write an introductory page for each section of the site. The primary function of these pages is to:

1. Explain what is in the section
2. Lure the user to click deeper into the site
3. Provide local navigation to complement the global navigation for the entire site
4. Improve search engine rankings

There are three main parts of a well-written section introduction page:

1. The body text
2. Local navigation
3. Global navigation

Figure 10-4 is the introduction page for the Homes and Land section of the web site. This example shows the global navigation on the top of the page (a graphic "navbar" on the actual site), the local navigation in a text menu on the left, and the body text on the right. Global navigation links relate to the site as a whole. Local navigation links relate primarily to this section. Underlined text indicates a link.

Homes and Land Section Introduction Page

Navigation

A surprisingly large number of web sites make the error of using global navigation throughout the site to the exclusion of local navigation. This error loses an excellent

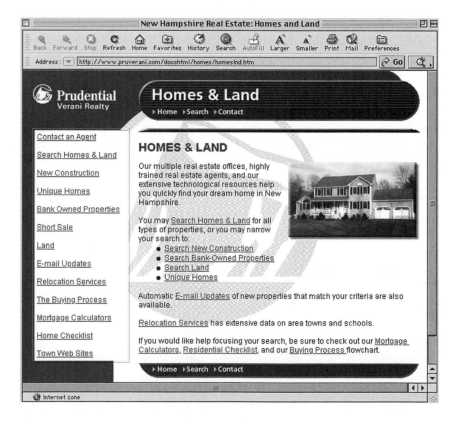

Figure 10-4 *Homes and Land Section introduction page.*

opportunity to encourage a user to explore deeper into the site. In the Homes and Land example, global navigation allows the user to go to the home page and from there access the menu for the main sections of the site. Global navigation also allows the user to go to a search page that has a site-wide search and a sitemap.

With global navigation dealt with simply and cleanly in a navigation bar at the top of the page, the main menu area on the left can be used for local navigation. This menu concentrates on listing the main pages and activities of the site related to homes and land. It introduces the elements of this section and hopefully lures the user deeper into the site. The writing challenge here is the same as it was writing the main menu on the home page. The menu items need to be succinct, descriptive, and engaging.

Body Text

The body text of the section introduction page serves many of the same functions as the menu. The body text is peppered with links to other sections of the site, but it also includes brief explanations of why the user might be interested in these links. This provides redundant navigation to accommodate different users. Some users of a site never read the body text. They just jump to the menu to find what they want. Other users want a little more help and read the body text for guidance. A writer needs to accommodate as many types of users as possible.

The body text also has unique functions not shared by the menu. The introductory sentence explains in concrete terms why Prudential Verani can serve your Homes and Land needs. The text also directs the user to the personalized search service. If site visitors want to, they may focus their search to specific types of properties: new construction, bank-owned, or land. The style of the text follows the guidelines established at the beginning of this chapter under "Online Writing Style Tips": clear, concrete, simple construction, bullets, and highlighting key terms.

Meta Tags and Title

Like the actual home page, you should pay attention to the section introduction page's title and meta tags. The reason is that most search engines will index all the main pages of your site, and some search engines will display multiple pages from the same site in search engine results. Just as with the Home Page title, the section page titles should also be clear and descriptive. You should focus your meta tags for these section introductory pages to their specific content. For example, for the Homes and Land section main page, the meta tags focused on homes, land, residences, and so on. As noted earlier, the most important meta tag is the Description tag, which is often used by search engines and the title in search results. It is also the title that appears in site user's bookmarks.

Static Print Content Pages

If the writer and designers have correctly written the home page and the main section introduction page, then the user will be drawn to the primary content pages of the site. The content pages contain the major information that the site has to offer. For a commercial site such as the Prudential Verani site, the primary function of these pages is to:

1. Present information
2. Lure the user into other parts of the site
3. Get the user to explore the client's products and/or contact the client

The content pages have a local and global navigation system similar to that described for the section introduction pages, except the local navigation links on the content page are of course focused on that particular content. The concept of local navigation was discussed extensively earlier in this chapter in the Main Section Menu/Introduction Pages discussion, so it will not be repeated here.

Content Page Example

The main challenges presenting complex content on a web site are to write succinctly and to chunk the content down into bite-sized bits with meaningful headings. (Chunking is a web term meaning to divide large amounts of content into subcategories and if necessary display these subcategories on separate pages.) Nothing sends web site visitors running more than a long uninterrupted page of text. The following example is an explanation of mortgages, a topic that could easily fill a book. Notice how the material is broken down into short paragraphs with meaningful subheadings. There are also abundant links to some of the more interactive elements in the site. Lastly, there is a link to the agents' directory to encourage the user to get in touch.

This page does not directly connect to the client's product, in this case real estate, but the pages to which it links do. For example, after users use the mortgage calculator to determine how much property they can afford, there is a line of text on the calculator results page that asks them if they want to search for properties in that price range. This takes them to the search page and the client's product.

MORTGAGES 101

How Much House Can You Afford

Before starting serious house-hunting, it is a good idea to get an estimate of how much house you can afford. Review some of the basic concepts below, then try out our **How Much House Can You Afford** and our **Renting vs. Buying Calculators**.

The Down Payment Most mortgages require a minimum down payment of 5% of the house purchase price ($10,000 dollars on a $200,000 home).

If you are a military veteran or a first-time buyer and qualify for a VA or FHA loan, it is possible to pay 3% or no down payment at all.

Debt to Salary Ratio Generally, your housing payment should not exceed 25% to 35% of your gross monthly income, and your total long-term debt should not exceed 38% of your gross monthly income. Long-term debt include school loans, car loans, credit cards, etc.

Total Monthly Payment (PITI) It is important to keep in mind that your monthly housing payment includes more than the loan for the property. It includes principle, interest, taxes, and insurance. In New Hampshire, property taxes can be a large percentage of your costs. Use our *Mortgage Calculator* to determine your monthly payment.

Closing Costs In addition to the down payment, there are a number of other expenses when you finalize or close the purchase on your property. These other costs may include: points (fees paid to the lender for lower interest rates), taxes, title insurance, private mortgage insurance (PMI), property appraisal, credit report, homeowners insurance, and real estate taxes. Use our *Closing Costs Calculator* to get an estimate of your closing costs.

Types of Mortgage

There are various types of mortgages available:

- Fixed rate mortgages maintain the same interest rate over the life of the loan.
- Adjustable rate mortgages (ARM) adjust their rate according to fluctuations of interest rates in the market.
- FHA and VA mortgages are guaranteed or insured by the federal government. These mortgages often have lower down payments and lower interest rates than standard mortgages. VA loans require the borrower to be a military veteran.

Preapproved and Prequalified

Visiting your mortgage lender early in the house-hunting process is a good idea. After looking at your financial materials, the lender can prequalify you, which means that they give you an estimate of how much house you may be able to afford. Preapproval takes this one step forward by actually submitting your full loan application. Once this is accepted you know for sure how much you

can spend on a house. Preapproval also speeds up the house-buying
process when you finally make a decision.

See an Expert

The calculators on this site and the above material are meant to
give you general information about mortgages, but you should see
a qualified mortgage lender before making any final decisions.
There is a **_list of mortgage lenders_** in the directory section of
our site. Your **_Prudential Verani agent_** also has other resources
for mortgage information, such as the free "Easy Moves" magazine.

Blogs

Another type of text content that is not used on the Prudential Verani site,
but is used on many sites is the weblog or blog. A blog is a web site or portion
of a web site that is set up to allow easy creation of additional text by multiple
individuals. Many blogs are public so that anyone can add information and respond
to early comments. Although blogs can include video, pictures, and audio, most
blogs are text with links. Blogs are more often used for personal expression, but some
commercial sites like Prudential Verani are using blogs as a way to present news, PR
information, and customer service. Blogs can also help a site's search engine ranking
by increasing keyword count, freshness of information, and linking. Most of the web
writing techniques mentioned earlier in this chapter still apply to blogs. It is still
reading online and not to be confused with the comfort of the printed page. Check
out the New Communications Blogzine (http://www.newcommblogzine.com) for
discussions of blogs, including their commmercial uses.

Graphical Content

The writer should examine the content to be communicated and determine if there
is a way to present it that would be more effective than straight text. Depending
on the capacity of the site, video, audio, or even a graphic chart might be an
option.

The example that follows is a portion of a chart that explains all the steps
that occur in the buying process. For reasons of space, only the last half of the
chart is presented here. Because of the various directions the buying process can
follow, this chart provides a more effective way of visualizing this information than
would a list or an essay. The writing challenge here is to break the information into
smaller units, chart the process, and write brief, clear symbol titles.

Interactive, Personalized Content

Whenever an interactive media project can get the user to interact with the content beyond clicking and reading, and thereby customize the content for that

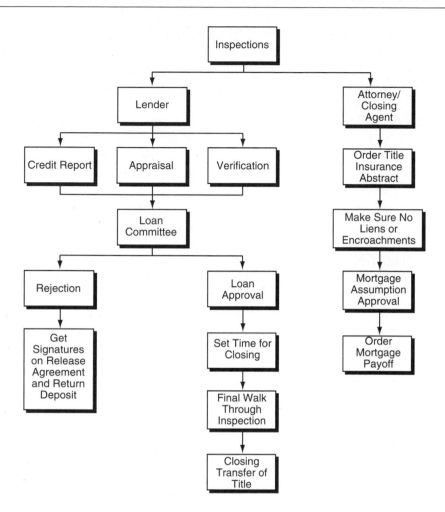

Figure 10-5 *A portion of the real estate buying process illustrated with a flowchart. An earlier version of this chart was created by Prudential Verani Realty for their print material.*

particular user, the user is more likely to feel connected and dig further into the information.

The Prudential Verani site has a number of examples of interactive content. Calculators allow the user to compute how much house they can afford, renting versus buying options, closing costs, and mortgages. The Homes and Land search can be customized to the user's needs through multiple criteria. E-mail updates allow the user to get e-mail notification of houses that meet their criteria as soon as they come on the market. The interactive checklist creates a customized list of user preferences.

The execution of these tools and others owe much of their success to the skills of the site's programmer, Ken Jones. But the writer's skills are still required to explain how these tools work and to write the interactive content.

Interactive Content Writing Example 1: Checklists

The custom checklist allows the user to define their dream house by clicking a series of options. When they push "submit" a custom checklist with only their criteria is produced. They can then take this checklist with them as they visit properties for sale.

On the site, this custom checklist has the Prudential Verani name and contact information at the top to encourage the user to get in touch with them. This list also gives the user the option of e-mailing the completed checklist to Prudential Verani and/or getting e-mail updates that match the criteria that they have defined in the checklist.

Writing something like this checklist makes the writer realize that one of the major jobs of the writer is selecting, sorting, and organizing information. Once that is done, then this information needs to be expressed as clearly as possible. This is only a section of the complete checklist.

CUSTOM CHECKLIST FOR YOUR NEW HOME	
DEFINE YOUR IDEAL HOME Create a custom checklist using the form below to: • Focus your priorities for your new home for you and your realtor • Evaluate and track the properties you visit	DIRECTIONS • Select your choices below • Push the "Create Custom Checklist" button at the bottom of the page • Print out one copy of the resulting Custom Checklist for each property you will visit
CRITERIA Type of home What type of home are you looking for?	CHOICE o Single family o Multifamily o Condo/Condex o Mobile Home
Price range What is your price range?	o Under $100,000 o $100,000–$125,000 o $125,000–$175,000 o $175,000–$225,000 o $225,000+
Neighborhood What type of neighborhood are you looking for?	o Urban o Subdivision o Rural

After the Site Is Finished

Maintenance Instructions

The last type of writing which is much appreciated by clients is a "how to" manual for the site. In many cases, clients expect to do a certain amount of site maintenance themselves. Written instructions can help them stay on track and keep them feeling positive toward the developer. The best designed maintenance system can sometimes be overwhelming without some instruction. A key part of these instructions should be design specifications—describing fonts, colors, and other design elements used on the site. This is usually called a Style Guide.

Outstanding Issues

At the completion of a large project there is often the urge to exit as quickly as possible, but the smart developer writes up an outstanding issues proposal similar to the proposal at the beginning of this chapter. This is your chance to remind the client of all the bells and whistles that they could not afford or did not have the time to produce this time around. This memo can also point out additional enhancements to the site that might be needed as the business grows. Be careful not to write this proposal in such a way that you are saying the site you just built is inadequate. Written and presented correctly, this memo can sometime result in additional contracts from the same client.

Conclusion

The goal of this chapter was to outline all the different types of writing that goes into the development of an interactive media project from the first proposal to the final exit memo. The example used here was for a medium-sized web site, but the suggestions above hold true for many types of interactive media projects as well, with larger projects being much more complex.

References

Inspiration Flowcharting Software's web site. http://www.inspiration.com

New Communications Blogzine. http://www.newcommblogzine.com

Nielsen, Jakob. "The Alertbox: Current Issues in Web Usability." http://www. useit.com/alertbox

Nielsen, Jakob. "The Alertbox: How Users Read on the Web." http://www. useit.com/alertbox/9710a.html

Prudential Verani Realty web site. http://www.pruverani.com

Search Engine watch web site. http://www.searchenginewatch.com

WebTrends Site Analysis Software web site. http://www.webtrends.com

Case Study—Corporate Web Site: T. Rowe Price

Summary

Name of production: T. Rowe Price Web Site
Writers: Members of the Shareholder Communications Group
Developer: T. Rowe Price Internet Services
Subject: Mutual funds, investment, and retirement planning
Audience: Personal investors, institutional investors, financial intermediaries
Medium: World Wide Web
Goals: Inform, teach, transact
Architecture: Hierarchical branching

The images used in this chapter are copyright T. Rowe Price Associates, Inc.

Program Description and Background

Program Description

The T. Rowe Price web site is the online home of T. Rowe Price, an investment management firm headquartered in Baltimore, Maryland. This site offers extensive information to help investors learn about and invest in mutual funds, as well as information about other financial products, such as 401(k)s, IRAs, and Tax-Advantaged College Savings Plans. The strength of this site is that much of the information is dynamic; the information is either updated frequently or can be customized for each user.

The site navigation makes effective use of audience segmentation. This allows users to quickly get to the content that interests them.

In addition, there are a variety of effective tools and tutorials. The interactive tutorials called Personal Guides explain investment topics, such as "Investing in T. Rowe Price Funds" which helps the user define their investment strategy. The site's tools include calculators, sophisticated portfolio analysis tools, and other applications that help investors make informed investment decisions. (See the Chapter 11 section of the *Writing for Multimedia and the Web* CD-ROM for links to the T. Rowe Price site and other sites mentioned in this chapter.)

T. Rowe Price and the Commercial Web Site

There are five basic categories of web sites:

1. **Personal.** Created by individuals to share material about themselves and their interests. Blogs are probably the most popular type of personal web site at the time of this writing.
2. **Educational.** This includes sites created by schools, museums, and other educational institutions to provide information as well as online e-learning courses and educational multimedia.
3. **Governmental.** Created by government agencies or elected officials as a service to their constituents.
4. **Entertainment.** Created by publishers, movie studios, TV production companies, computer game companies, and others to provide online entertainment. Online magazines, soap operas, travel sites, and computer games (usually multiplayer), are examples of this category.
5. **Commercial.** Created by businesses to promote and/or sell their company's products or services. T. Rowe Price is a commercial site.

Types of Commercial Web Sites

According to Poppe Tyson agency's Peter Adams, the designer of T. Rowe Price's first-generation web site, companies create sites for various purposes.

- **Transactional site.** The primary purpose is to perform transactions, such as ordering merchandise. All the content in the site revolves around that function. Example: Amazon.com (www.amazon.com) sells books, videos, and much more from their site.
- **Consumer site.** This type of site is promotional. It's fun and highly visible but does not usually offer much information. Example: The Absolut Vodka site (absolut.com) has various games and graphics with limited hard data about vodka.
- **Marcom (marketing communications) site.** This approach has lots of information about the company, including material on the company's products and how to contact the company. Example: The Daimler-Chrysler site (www.daimlerchrysler.com) has extensive information on corporate

developments as well as links to subsites with information on Chrysler and Mercedes vehicles.

- **Content site.** A content site offers extensive information on the general type of product or service that the company is involved in, such as investment information on the T. Rowe Price site, or real estate information on the Prudential Verani site, which was profiled in Chapter 10. The goal of a content site is to draw users to the site because of the strong content and then to get them interested in the company's products. Excellent content on a site also demonstrates to users that this company is expert in its field.

A content site differs from a Marcom site in that a content site is generally bigger, has much more content on the general topic (e.g., investment information) offered to users, and has less emphasis on marketing and more on information. This is not to say it can't be used for marketing purposes. It is also possible to transform a content site into a transactional site, such as one for buying or selling mutual funds. A content site is financially supported by transforming part of it into a transactional site or through online advertising.

Sites have successfully blended elements of the above categories, but one key to a successful site is to be clear about your site's primary focus: transactional, consumer, marketing communications, or content site.

Production Background

The first generation T. Rowe Price site was launched in the early days of the World Wide Web, in 1996. In recent years, the site has been substantially revised. For the first generation site, T. Rowe Price commissioned the Poppe Tyson agency to create its web presence through the online subsidiary poppe.com. The site was created in-house at poppe.com under creative director Peter Adams. Adams, Ken Godfrey and Matt Freeman wrote some of the material for it, but the members of T. Rowe Price's Shareholder Communications Group primarily wrote the content. Poppe Tyson has since merged with Modem Media to create a major digital marketing communications company that was first called Poppe Tyson Modem Media, and then just Modem Media. More recently Modem Media joined with Digitas under the parent company, Digitas Inc., combining two of the leading direct and digital marketing agencies into one corporate unit.

The second generation of the T. Rowe Price site was created in-house by T. Rowe Price Internet Services, with additional content created by members of T. Rowe Price's Shareholder Communications Group. Many elements of the first-generation site were retained. Emmett Higdon, T. Rowe Price Assistant Vice President of Internet Services, said that it is important not to change a site that deals with the general public too quickly and too often. Users don't want to have to completely relearn how a site works every six months. One of the challenges of developing a large site is to make changes without losing a large portion of your audience. The changes on the T. Rowe Price site are driven largely by the needs of customers.

These needs are tracked through site usage and through special audience focus groups. The latest generation of the site furthers this tradition of user centered design. This third version of the T. Rowe Price site is the primary focus of this chapter.

 Please see the CD-ROM for comparisons of the different versions of the T. Rowe Price site.

Preproduction Process

Poppe.com's process for writing and designing the first-generation T. Rowe Price site is worth looking at as an approach for developing content sites. A key part of the approach is to work from the beginning with the entire production team: writers, programmers, art directors, and designers. At poppe.com, developing a web site was a collaborative process with several stages:

1. **Gathering content.** The team engages in lengthy talks with clients to understand their business and digest existing material on the subject. The goal of this first stage is to understand and identify all the content that will be involved in the site, business goals, and user needs.

2. **Defining categories and placement of content.** The gathered content is spread out on a table before the entire production team, who ask a variety of questions: How would users make sense of all this content? What do they need to know when they get to the home page? What general category of information does this site offer? What is the main focus within this category?
   Once the above questions are answered, then the team needs to:

   - Group content into categories

   - Determine the importance of each category

   - Decide on accessibility of categories. How quickly do users need to get this information? Should it be on the home page? What information is going to change regularly and what is going to remain static?

3. Organize information below the main categories and decide on the interactive structure. For example, how will categories and subcategories be linked? The team evaluates whether a tree structure, branching, or dynamic flow will be best, and then they flowchart this interactive structure. They start at the home page, then the level 2 pages, then the level 3 pages, and continue to the bottom level. The final form at this stage is flowchart boxes with legends indicating the type of content and whether it is dynamic or static. This flowchart is attached to a marketing creative brief that explains the goal of the site in detail.

4. Writing and designing the content. When the flowchart is approved, the team writes and designs the actual pages, starting from the top down and building section by section.

Meeting the Challenges of Writing and Developing the T. Rowe Price Web Site

The main challenge with this site was to write and organize it intelligently from the user's perspective so that it would be easy to navigate and understand. This was not an easy task because of the breadth and difficulty of the content.

User Centric Design and Audience Segmentation

It is illuminating to compare the second generation T. Rowe Price home page (Figure 11-1) with the current site home page (Figure 11-2). The second-generation site is more product specific. When user enters the site, he must pick from a wide array of products. Some of these products interest certain users, such as individual investors, and others might be of more interest to other types of users, such as institutional investors. Because the content is organized by product instead of by user, it is up to the user to determine which content is right for him. There is also quite a bit of content, some of it of limited interest to specific users, on a single page.

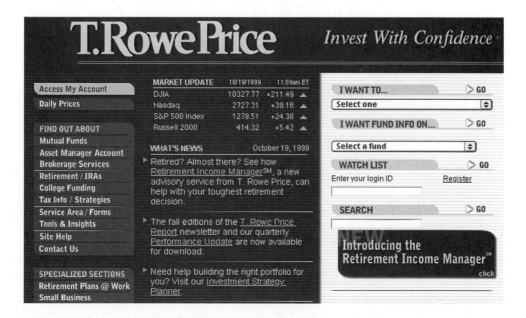

Figure 11-1 *Second generation home page for the T. Rowe Price Web site (see the* Writing for Multimedia and the Web *CD-ROM for the color image).*

Figure 11-2 *Current corporate gateway/home page for T. Rowe Price Site. Segmenting audience to reduce branching explosion.*

The latest generation of the site takes a considerably different approach. The first page a user sees on the T. Rowe Price site is the page illustrated in Figure 11-2. Unlike the earlier site, shown in Figure 11-1, which breaks the site content down by products, the current generation of the site breaks the content down by users segments, the main links offered are: "Individual Investors," "Institutional Investors," "Financial Intermediaries," and "Non-U.S. Individual Investors." Clicking on "Individual Investors" breaks the site content down further by additional subuser groups: "New to T. Rowe Price" and "Already an Investor."

The effect of this user-centered design is that the content is clearly grouped according to the user's needs. Once we have clicked the "New to T. Rowe Price" link in the "Individual Investors" menu, we have narrowed the content down considerably. When we arrive at the next page, the home page for new individual investors, the content is focused on our specific needs and there is no extraneous content to sort through. This is an excellent example of how user-centered versus product-centered design can radically improve the usability of a site.

Because the audience segmentation is fairly precise, the writer will have to be very aware of this specific user's needs and slant the writing style and content to meet those needs. This is quite different than a general discussion of mutual funds that could be acceptable in the previous product centered design approach.

Customization

A major element that was retained from the earlier generation site and expanded upon is the use of customization. This approach makes the program easy to navigate and understand. As discussed in a previous chapter, customization is often confused with personalization, but they do not mean the same thing. Personalization involves a software program creating unique content for a user on a web site or application based on the user's previous site activity. The user doesn't choose the unique content; the personalization software program does it automatically. The best example is amazon.com, which will track what types of products you are looking at and offer similar products to you the next time you visit the site or even during the same shopping trip.

Like personalization, customization also creates unique content on a page for a user, but in this case the user not a software program specifically chooses what content they want displayed. In customization, the user controls what content will be displayed on future visits. The current generation of the T. Rowe Price site allows customization in many ways both big and small. A small way is that when you choose the individual investor link from the initial home page (Figure 11-2), you are asked in a popup if you want to make the individual investor page your default page the next time you login. This way you get to start next time on a page focused on your audience segment, as opposed to going through the general home page (Figure 11-2).

Custom Portfolio View

A more complex example of customization is the Custom Portfolio View. Using the Create View tools you can create your custom portfolio page on the site. Next time you login, you will only see the investments in your accounts and the information you want about those accounts. You can also change your view with up to five customer portfolio views for different purposes. Please see Figure 11-3.

This Custom View approach is obviously superior than making users dig through long lists of mutual funds to see how their investments are doing, and then dig through equally long lists of tools to perform the desired investment analysis.

Personal Guides: Investing in T. Rowe Price Funds

The site's Personal Guides are another way of focusing content for users. These guides help the users define their information needs by asking them a series of questions in an interactive online advisor tool. The user clicks through several screens, with each one asking them a question or two to help define their investment needs. The questions deal with account time, investment time horizon, risk tolerance, investment amount, tax bracket, and tax sensitivity. At the end of the tutorial, the users are presented with an analysis in the form of a graph that recommends their basic investment decision. See Figure 11-4. Notice the answers to the questions in the right column and the white dot in the Stability section of the graph. This white dot indicates the investment strategy for this user based on her answers to

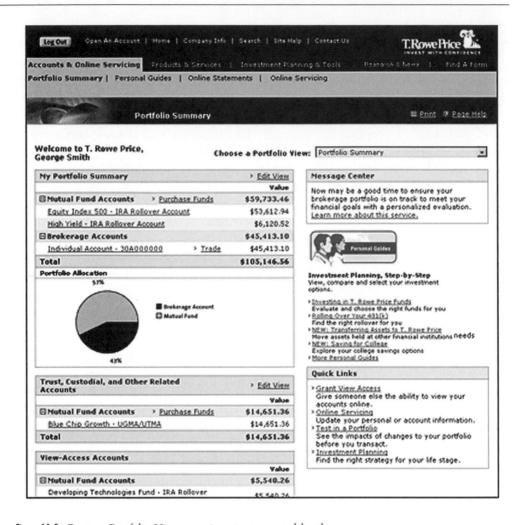

Figure 11-3 *Custom Portfolio View, a unique page created by the user.*

the question in the tutorial. If the user continues one step further, then the tutorial will suggest mutual funds that might suit her investment approach, along with tools to evaluate them, such as comparing funds and testing them in a portfolio.

Navigation

One element users did not like in the first generation site was the hierarchical navigation that required three or four clicks to get to desired information. In response to user demand, navigation was completely redesigned for the second-generation and later sites.

The goal of the navigation redesign was to make important information on the site no more than two clicks away. The designers wanted to achieve this goal

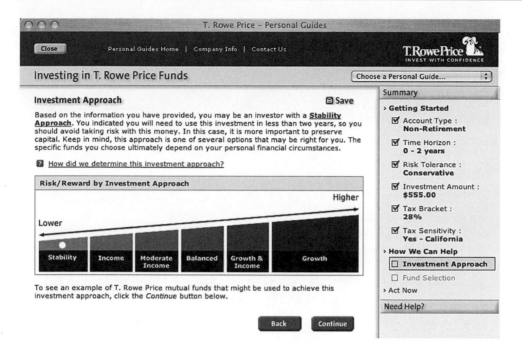

Figure 11-4 *Recommendations at end of investment tutorial.*

without confusing new users. Focus group studies had told the designers that new users prefer static menus, whereas the more experienced users are comfortable with search functions and more dynamic navigation features.

Drop-Down Menus and Global Navigation

A change on the current site to improve navigation is the use of global navigation tabs on every page. Global navigation is site-wide navigation to all the important areas of a site. A common error on web sites is to lose global navigation as the user digs deeper into the site. When this error occurs, users typically have to navigate back to the home page or some other main page to find a main menu. The alternative, which is used effectively on the T. Rowe Price site, can be seen at the top of Figure 11-5. The section of the site users are on is highlighted at the top of the page in tan. But navigation to all other major sections of the site stay in the navbar. This allows a user to easily move around main sections of the site. For example, a user could quickly jump from deep in the Accounts & Online Servicing section of the site to the Product & Services section.

There is also effective use of local navigation, which deals with a particular section of a site. Once the user arrives at the chosen section of the site, there are local navigation menus on the left-hand side of the page to find the information that he or she wants in that section. Every major information page of the site has a static menu on the left-hand side.

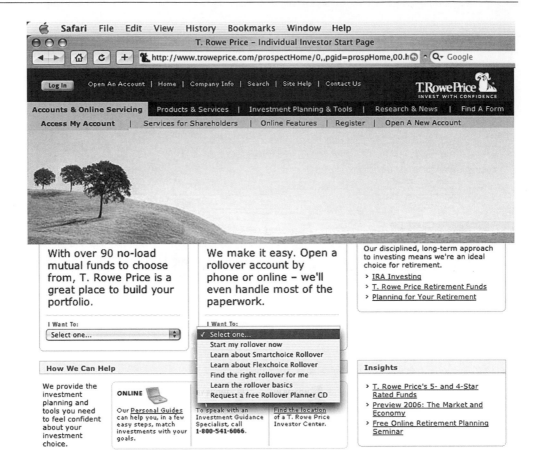

Figure 11-5 *Global navigation and drop-down menus.*

Drop-down menus are another part of T. Rowe Price's navigation strategy. A drop-down menu is revealed when a link is clicked. Before that, it is not visible. Drop-down menus are used as part of the global navigation, as pictured in Figure 11-5. When "Accounts & Online Servicing" is clicked, the additional links "Access My Account," "Services for Shareholders," "Online Features," and others appear.

There is also effective use of drop-down menus in the "I Want To..." feature pictured in the middle of Figure 11-5. When the user clicks "I Want To..." a menu drops. The "I Want To..." drop-down menu allows the experienced user to jump immediately to the desired sections of the site. User centric drop-down menus speed navigation and eliminate mouse clicks. (In Figure 11-5, this menu has already been clicked to drop down.)

Other Navigational Aids and Tools

Another navigational feature on every page is a link to the search box. Users can enter a term and search the site for whatever information they want. It is important to have a search feature on a site because this is the first place that many experienced users go on a new site.

Also included on every page is a login button so users with accounts can easily access their investment information.

Information Grouping

The other major area where users requested a change from earlier sites was in better information grouping, particularly in the areas of Mutual Funds and Tools and Services. In the site revision, T. Rowe Price responded by gathering all the mutual fund information into one location. Now the user can easily access information on price, performance, management and top holdings, and download a prospectus or annual report, all from one screen.

The tools and services on the site were similarly grouped into one area. From a main "Investment Planning & Tools" link, users can now access all the tools and special services on the site. These include interactive calculators, worksheets, retirement planning software, special forms to open a new account and sophisticated portfolio analysis tools, including interactive charts and current investment information.

Managing Content on a Content Site

One of the challenges of a content site is figuring out how to update a site with lots of dynamic content without the cost of having a whole team of web experts on staff. Even on the earliest site, poppe.com solved this problem by creating content interfaces that allow the user to change the content without programming. Content management has only improved in later site variations. For example, anyone can add new press releases to the site simply by cutting and pasting copy. An old release can also be put into an accessible archive for future use. A content management system and easy updating is a feature most clients request for web sites.

Conclusion: Response to the Project

The site has been very popular. Thousands of users have registered and the site saved T. Rowe Price tens of thousands of dollars over traditional ways of presenting the information (direct mail, salespeople, etc.). This web site also creates immeasurable value, such as developing awareness of the T. Rowe Price brand.

References

Adams, Peter. Telephone interview with the author, March 1996.
Higdon, Emmett. Telephone interview with the author, July 1999.
Modem Media.Poppe Tyson web site. http://www.modemmedia.poppetyson.com
T. Rowe Price web site. http://www.troweprice.com

Case Study—Research Portal Web Site and the Online Feature Story: Britannica.com and the *Harlem Renaissance*

Summary

Name of production: The Harlem Renaissance spotlight on Britannica.com (later Encyclopaedia Britannica Online)
Writers for the *Harlem Renaissance*: Andrew Nelson, Tom Michael
Developer: Encyclopaedia Britannica Harlem Renaissance
Subject: Black history and culture in the 1920s Harlem neighborhood of New York City
Audience: Students, general audience
Medium: World Wide Web
Goals: Inform, teach
Architecture: Hierarchical branching

The images used in this chapter are reprinted with permission from the *Encyclopaedia Britannica*.

Program Description and Background

Program Description

The Harlem Renaissance feature story was created for Britannica.com, a web site created by Encyclopaedia Britannica, the company that has been known for their book encyclopedias for generations. Britannica.com is currently called Encyclopaedia Britannica Online so we will use that name unless we are talking about the past when the Britannica.com name was still in use. Encyclopaedia Britannica Online presents a synthesis of recommended links to other web sites, articles from Encyclopaedia Britannica's own massive database, and new material, such as a news digest and multimedia features called spotlights. The spotlights are special sections of the Encyclopaedia Britannica Online site that focus on a specific topic, such as women's history, D-Day, or black history. The purpose of these spotlights is to engage the user by presenting information in a highly visual and interactive manner, as opposed to the more text and still picture based encyclopedia articles. There is a link to a featured spotlight and spotlight archives on the Encyclopaedia Britannica Online home page (Figure 12-1).

The *Harlem Renaissance* is a spotlight multimedia feature story. This spotlight was designed to encourage interest in black history. Rather than presenting a broad overview of this subject, Britannica Editor Tom Michael and writer Andrew Nelson decided to focus on telling the story of a key moment in black history—the Harlem Renaissance. The Harlem Renaissance took place in Harlem, New York in the 1920s. It was a period of astounding black cultural and political activity.

Figure 12-1 *Home page of Encyclopaedia Britannica Online.*

The spotlight uses powerful writing, period graphics, and multimedia elements to evoke an era and engage users in the broader study of black history.

 See the Chapter 12 section of this book's CD-ROM for a link to the sites mentioned in this chapter.

The Web Site Portal and Britannica.com (Encyclopaedia Britannica Online)

Britannica.com was conceived as a type of portal web site. The goal of a portal web site is to be the user's entrance or doorway to the web. A portal's designers want it to be the page that you use as your start page whenever you go online. The portal organizes links to other web sites into key categories and provides tools to search those sites. The best portals also review all or most of their sites before including them in their database so that you have some guarantee of quality. Some portals, such as realtor.com and ZDNet, review sites and organize links to other sites on a narrow subject, in these cases real estate and high-tech, respectively. Other portals, such as Yahoo! and Excite, attempt to cover a broad range of content.

In addition to directories of links, major portals also include basic information and tools, such as news, stock quotes, sports scores, chat, e-mail, games, entertainment guides, product reviews, and shopping. A number of portals also have customization features, such as My Yahoo!, that allow the user to custom design the portal page so that it presents the information that they are most interested in.

The major portals attract millions of page views a day. Because of this heavy traffic, portals are one of the most sought after sites for advertising and e-commerce. This success has made the portal approach common designs for sites attempting to attract mass users. With sites such as Yahoo! already well established in the broad information portal category, new portals have had to come up with fresh angles to make themselves appealing to users.

When Britannica.com later named Encyclopaedia Britannica Online launched, Executive Director of New Product Development, Peter Meyerhoff, said that Britannica.com filled a niche somewhere between Yahoo.com and Discovery Channel Online. He labeled Britannica's approach to portals as a research or knowledge portal. Britannica.com and later Encyclopaedia Britannica Online covers a broad range of content, similar to Yahoo!, but Britannica also creates and presents it own content. Because of its huge archive of material from years of creating encyclopedias and other publications, Encyclopaedia Britannica is uniquely qualified to create such a site. For example, a search on Yahoo! for the Harlem Renaissance will produce a list of sites and categories on this topic. You'll also have the option of clicking a link for related news stories. A similar search on Britannica will provide more substantial results, including:

- Articles from Encyclopaedia Britannica
- Reviewed and rated web sites

- Full text magazine articles
- Related books with options for ordering them
- Access to definitions and pronunciation guides for every word in the Merriam-Webster's Collegiate Dictionary (separate search)
- A multimedia and a multimedia feature story related to the topic called a Spotlight. Spotlights are one of the ways that Britannica.com (Encyclopaedia Britannica Online) distinguishes itself from the other portals.

When Britannica.com originally launched, it was conceived as a free site. On this site, the full text of the Encyclopaedia Britannica was available online in a searchable database. The business plan was for the site to earn money from online advertising and from on-site sales of ancillary products, such as Encyclopaedia Britannica books, videos, and CD-ROMs. This model worked for a while, but when the Internet bubble crashed and advertising dollars dried up, Britannica had to rethink its revenue plan. The site was renamed Encyclopaedia Britannica Online. The full text of the Encyclopaedia Britannica was no longer available. Instead a user gets a brief summary of the Encyclopaedia Britannica articles and has to become a paying member of the site to view the entire article. This is the model that Encyclopaedia Britannica currently follows instead of the free portal approach originally conceived for Britannica.com. The story of Britannica.com is useful to study for anyone trying to figure out how to make money from a content site.

The current Encyclopaedia Britannica online still creates feature stories called spotlights that can be accessed from the home page. The writing and information design of these spotlights, particularly the *Harlem Renaissance*, will be the primary focus of the rest of this chapter.

Production Background for the Harlem Renaissance

The *Harlem Renaissance* was conceived as a spotlight for Encyclopaedia Britannica Online. The *Harlem Renaissance* was initiated by Peter Meyerhoff and developed by Tom Michael and Andrew Nelson. The *Harlem Renaissance* site was created to promote Britannica's encyclopedias and as a service to customers in schools. Black History Month is important in middle and high schools.

Unfortunately, the *Harlem Renaissance* is no longer available on Britannica sites. However similar spotlights can be still be viewed from the Spotlights home page link on Encyclopaedia Britannica Online.

 The Chapters section of this book's CD-ROM has color pictures of the Harlem Renaissance *spotlight.*

Preproduction Development Process for the Harlem Renaissance Spotlight

Britannica had previously created The Encyclopaedia Britannica Guide to Black History, a popular spotlight that presented an overview of black history. The goal with the *Harlem Renaissance* site was to do something very different: to present a large body of information by focusing on a specific story, similar to a feature story in print journalism. According to online editor Tom Michael, after the *Harlem Renaissance* topic was chosen, the site was developed according to the following steps. This is a useful model for organizing a site that draws from a large database of information.

1. Research the topic. Get an understanding of the history and the mood of the period, looking at books and other available material.
2. Create a master list of articles on the topic. Search the database of articles Britannica already has as well as obtain needed outside essays. Because of the encyclopedic tone of the existing articles, an overarching essay was needed to bring it all together.
3. Divide articles into categories. Work with the writer to organize all these articles and link them to the master essay and other navigational devices. Organize these categories and links into a sitemap, presented with a flowchart (Figure 12-2). Check if any articles need to be updated or rewritten, and decide if new articles are needed, including introductions to the major sections.
4. Identify and locate images. Identify what images are needed for the site.
5. Finalize the navigation and interface. This included creating a hot spots map of Harlem and a time line.

Challenges Writing and Developing the *Harlem Renaissance*

Harlem in the 1920s was the site of a major flowering of black culture, but it is a period that many members of the potential audience know nothing about. One of the goals of the site was to create an immersive experience to give users the feeling that they are in Harlem, seeing the sites and hearing the voices of the era. Writer Andrew Nelson said that he tried to create the project as if the user were a tourist visiting Harlem. One of the ways that Nelson and the designers wanted to achieve the feeling of being there was to create a mood that is celebratory and upbeat. Another important part of creating this immersive experience was to develop clear navigation that allowed the users to access the material from a variety of approaches.

Meeting the Challenges

Creating an Immersive Experience
Graphical Pages

Perhaps the most unusual element of this site's design is the rendering of the text and graphics for every page into full-page images (Figure 12-3). This allowed the

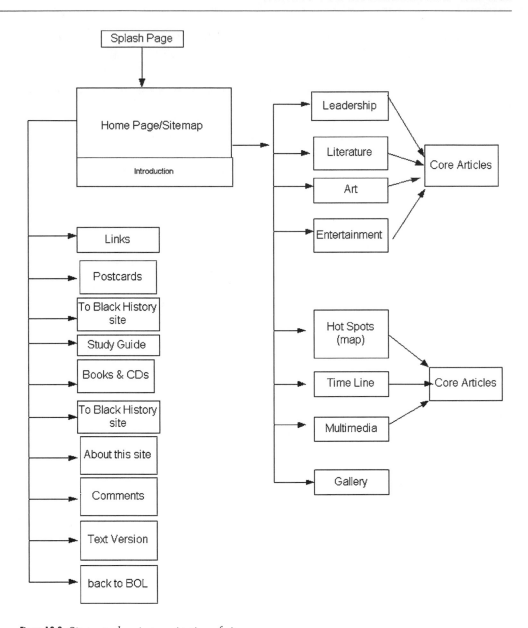

Figure 12-2 *Sitemap showing navigation of site.*

close integration of the site's text with images of major figures of the era, Harlem locations, and graphics from period books and artwork. The entire page/image was then sepia-toned to add to the period mood. Each main section (Leadership, Literature, Art, and Entertainment) was then subtly tinted a different color for variations on the mood. The effect is to create the feeling that visitors to the site are entering a different era.

Figure 12-3 *Introduction to the Literature section of the site, with cover of The Weary Blues by Langston Hughes.*

Although this approach of making each page into one large graphic achieved its goals of bringing the user into the experience, according to Tom Michael, it created production challenges. The major problem was that it limited the editing of the site. HTML text is easy to change, and small pictures are easy to move about or delete, but because every page was one or two large images, even minor text changes required the entire image do be redone. An additional problem for users on slow modem connections is that the large images load slower than a text and small image page.

Video and Audio

Extensive graphics, video, and audio on the site are another way the designers tried to make the era come to life. A few examples include:

- Fats Waller (on piano) performs the song "The Joint is Jumpin'."
- Tap dancer Bill "Bojangles" Robinson performs his trademark "stair dance," 1932.
- Bessie Smith sings with a backup choir in the film *Saint Louis Blues*, 1929.
- Langston Hughes reads his poem "The Negro Speaks of Rivers," 1921.

There is also an extensive photo gallery of Harlem Renaissance figures and locations.

Hot Spots Map

Some of the navigational devices contributed to Nelson's goal of making the user feel like a tourist to the era. The "Hot Spots" map (Figure 12-4) not only allows the user to get an overview of the location, but it is also a clickable menu. When the name of a location, such as the Cotton Club, is clicked, a picture and description of the nightclub appears.

Writing Style

The visual style of the writing on the site also plays a key role in getting the audience involved. The Entertainment section's first paragraph is a good example:

> *The Roaring '20s produced a deafening prosperity. Across the nation saxophones wailed, factories thrummed, Wall Street crowed, and Tommy guns spat in Prohibition inspired firefights . . . For many, the decade was a party, and it was African American entertainers who set the tone and tempo.* (Harlem Renaissance *Spotlight*)

Figure 12-4 Harlem Renaissance *site's clickable Hot Spots Map.*

In addition to visualizing the scene, parts of the paragraph, such as "the decade was a party, and it was African American entertainers who set the tone and tempo," lure users deeper into the site by creating questions in their minds. How was this a party? What did people do? How did African Americans have this much impact?

The site's writer Nelson suggested that another way to get users to click deeper into the site is to use small "ads" on the Home Page or upper-level pages, advertising or hinting at content deeper in the site. "Whatever you do, make the link to the advertised section clear and easy. I favor hot linking the graphic itself. People look at that and want to click immediately."

He also pointed out that to connect with your site users it is important to "write as if you are talking to an individual, not a collective group of anonymous Web surfers. Ask direct questions of them: 'What do you think?,' 'Do you agree?'"

Navigation: Multiple Approaches to Content

A strength of the navigation on the *Harlem Renaissance* site is that it allows the user to access the information from at least four different perspectives. This is important, because every user approaches the search for information in a different way. A site that relies on just one navigational approach will have many frustrated users. The navigational approaches include the following.

1. **Hierarchical Menus**

    (a) **Main Categories.** From the home page and any page of the introduction, the user can go to the main menu with one click. On the main menu, the site categories are listed: Leadership, Literature, Art, and Entertainment. Links to these categories are also repeated as icons on the top of every page (see Figure 12-3). Clicking on one of the main menu links or one of the icons, such as Literature, leads to an introductory article that describes the category (see Figure 12-3). From this article, the user can click to the next level of information—specific people and events.

    (b) **Bibliographies.** Users can also jump directly to a list of the core site articles by clicking a "TO ARTICLES" link in the upper right of each introductory essay. From every page of an article, you can click a "TO BIBLIOGRAPHY" link that leads to a descriptive bibliography of key books on the era. Clicking the title of one of these books leads to barnesandnoble.com, where you can purchase the book. A portion of these book sales are returned to Britannica. Thus, this bibliography not only adds depth and convenience to the site for the user, but also adds important revenue to support the site. Writer Andrew Nelson said that online retailing, such as this, will play a much bigger role in the future.

2. **By Location**

In addition to the hierarchical menus described above, users can also access information by location. The Hotspots map (see Figure 12-4) allows spatially oriented users to chose a location, such as The Cotton Club, and click on it to get a description and image.

3. **By Time**

The Timeline (Figure 12-5) allows users to click on a specific year and get a list of key events for that year. Key people and events in the list can be clicked on to access detailed articles.

4. **In Context**

All of the articles (see Figure 12-3) also provide links within the text through highlighted words. For example, clicking the highlighted words "Jean Toomer" in the first paragraph of the text on Figure 12-3 leads to an article on that writer.

Other Site Elements
Send a Postcard

The "Send a Postcard" link at the bottom of every site page leads to a section that allows the user to e-mail picture postcards about the site to friends.

Figure 12-5 Harlem Renaissance *clickable Timeline.*

This element helps support the tourist-to-the-era approach that the designers were trying to achieve. It is also a free marketing device for the site.

Study Guide

This section of the site (reachable from a link at the bottom of every page) provides activities related to the site. Among other activities, the guide asks students to:

> *Imagine that you are staging a 1920s variety show in a Harlem club at which African Americans will be welcomed. Your show will feature writers reading from their books, an art installation, and performances of music, theater, and dance.* (Harlem Renaissance Spotlight)

Conclusion: Response to the Project

The launch of Britannica.com was, if anything, too successful. The site was shut down for a week because of the high volume of users. Since getting back online, it has become a very popular site on the web. It has currently changed from a free portal site to a subscription-based site called Encyclopaedia Britannica Online.

The *Harlem Renaissance* also gained equally strong response from its users, with comments peppered with adjectives such as superb, magnificent, thorough, and riveting. As noted earlier, unfortunately, the *Harlem Renaissance* is no longer available on Britannica sites.

References

Encyclopaedia Britannica Online web site. http://www.britannica.com

The *Harlem Renaissance* web site. No longer available online. To see similar "Spotlights," go to Encyclopaedia Britannica Online and look for the Featured Spotlight link on the home page.

Meyerhoff, Peter. Telephone interview with the author, September 1999.

Michael, Thomas. Telephone interview with the author, September 1999.

Nelson, Andrew. E-mail to the author, October 1999.

Nelson, Andrew. Telephone interview with the author, September 1999.

Case Study—E-Learning: *Interactive Math and Statistics Lessons*

Summary

Name of production: Interactive Math and Statistics Lessons
Writer: Shawn Hackshaw
Developers: Houghton Mifflin Company; Dolphin MultiMedia, Inc; Larson Texts, Inc; InterWrite
Audience: College Students
Medium: Online (web, network) and CD-ROM
Presentation location: College labs, student computers
Subject: Math and statistics
Goal: Teach
Structures: Linear with section branching

Materials used with special permission of Houghton Mifflin Company. All Rights Reserved.

Program Description and Background

Program Description

In the United States alone, more than twenty billion dollars is spent annually on course materials for schools and colleges (Education Market Research). Billions more are spent for government and corporate training. Because of students' exposure to the web and multimedia, there is an ever-greater demand for digital course material. This material can take a variety of forms, including digital textbooks, online courses, and supplementary or ancillary material that supports print textbooks.

The supplementary material delivered online or on a disk includes background material, drill and skill exercises, interactive lessons explaining key concepts, and more. Publisher Houghton Mifflin's *Interactive Math and Statistics Lessons* is an example of supplementary material that explains key concepts.

The Interactive Math and Statistics lessons were developed to teach math and statistics to a college audience. Each lesson takes a key math or statistic concept and uses audio, animation, video, text, and graphics to present this concept in an engaging way. The goal of these lessons is to reduce each concept to a format easily understood by students who may not have had great success in math. Most lessons can be completed in less than ten minutes. The lessons are primarily used to support and extend traditional print textbooks.

Each lesson has up to eight modules or sections:

- Prepare for the Tutorial (includes Prep Tests)
- Study the Concept
- Try an Example
- View a Video Example
- Practice Exercises
- Apply the Concepts to Real Life
- Explore the Concept
- Mastery Test

The lesson structure listed above follows a traditional but effective instructional design: introduction, pretests, concept explanation, example, apply/explore concept, and post test to verify mastery. A closer look at each of the lesson modules explains their function.

Prepare for the Tutorial

A brief summary of the lesson in a bulleted list, a photograph describing a real life application of the concept, a summary of the basic preskills needed to do the lesson, and links to pretests (Prep Tests) on these skills.

Study the Concept

A detailed explanation of the concept including animation, static images, text, and audio narration. The student has the option of listening to audio narration, reading text, or both. The text appears section by section with corresponding images and narration. For example, in Figure 13-1, the animated time plot appears step by step as it is explained in the text. The student can move the lesson back, forward, or replay the entire lesson if they wish.

Try an Example

The "Try an Example" screen uses animation, static images, text, and audio narration to present an example of the concept explained in the previous screen.

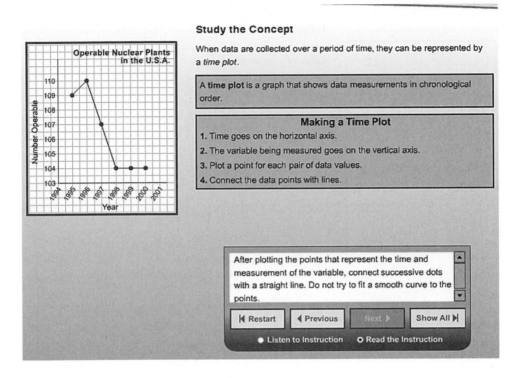

Figure 13-1 *Study the Concept screen.*

Usually at least two examples are presented, one without user input, and the other requiring students to input data to complete the example as pictured in Figure 13-2.

View a Video Example

This screen includes a short video of a classroom lecture explaining the concept.

Practice Exercises

These exercises provide a chance for the student to work with the concepts they have just learned in previous screens.

Apply the Concepts to Real Life

In an attempt to make the concept more meaningful to students, this module gives them a chance to solve a real life problem using the concept. Elements included on this screen are animation, static images, text, and audio narration.

Explore the Concept

This is a highly interactive exploration of the concept. This is custom made for the concept, and is the most challenging module for the writer to create.

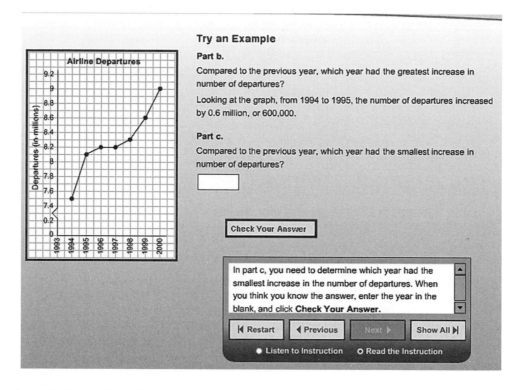

Figure 13-2 *Try an Example Screen.*

Mastery Tests

These are the posttests that demonstrate that the student has learned the material.

Hundreds of these lessons have been produced. They support most of Houghton Mifflin's Math and Statistics college textbooks. Material that can support more than one textbook is an important criterion when designing ancillary material. It is too expensive to create unique ancillary material for a single book unless the textbook is very popular. Instead, the approach is either to create generic material in the subject, such as the math lesson, or to create a software shell/engine that can be customized for each book with additional unique content. A software shell/engine is a piece of software that has certain capabilities, such as presenting various types of exercises, video, audio, etc. Different information can be added to the shell without rebuilding it.

Production Background

The math editors of the Houghton Mifflin Company College Division conceived the idea for the Interactive Math and Statistics Lessons. The idea was refined and the Interactive Lessons software engine created by Dolphin MultiMedia, Inc. Initially, math content development and lesson production was by Larson Texts, Inc.

Later, InterWrite was also brought into the project to help develop and create additional math and statistics content.

Headquartered in Boston, Houghton Mifflin is one of the top educational publishers in the United States. It publishes textbooks, instructional technology, assessments, and other educational materials for teachers and students of every age. The company also publishes reference works and fiction and nonfiction for adults and young readers. The company was founded in 1832.

Dolphin MultiMedia provides strategic consulting to help their clients communicate their messages to their audiences. They create interactive CDs, video, web, and computer-based demos or presentations for sales, marketing, education, and executive briefings. The media may include graphics, interactivity, web links, and video or animation. Dolphin was founded in 1972 and is based in Sunnyvale, California. Dolphin created the software engine and integrated the produced lesson components for the Interactive Math Lessons.

Larson Texts, Inc. has several divisions. Larson Texts produces math textbooks for sixth grade through calculus. Larson Learning, Inc. offers interactive educational math software, print materials, and staff development workshops. TDLC.COM publishes online math course materials. Larson is located in Erie, Pennsylvania. For the Interactive Math Lessons, Larson developed math content and created lesson elements, including creating animations, graphics, and audio narration.

InterWrite is an interactive media consulting and development company located north of Boston. They create teaching, training, and customer information projects for the web, CD-ROM, DVD, and other interactive media. Their primary clients are educational publishers, educators, trainers, and anyone who needs to present sophisticated information to their customers, students, or employees. InterWrite performed a similar function as Larson Texts on the Interactive Math Lessons project, developing math and statistics content and creating the lesson elements.

There were numerous math writers on this project working for both InterWrite and Larson Texts. Some of the writers are math teachers by trade. Others are professional math content developers. The writer interviewed for this case study was Shawn Hackshaw, who worked for InterWrite. Shawn has taught high school pre-algebra and algebra and currently teaches developmental math at New England College and Hesser College, both in New Hampshire. He has a Master's degree in math education at the secondary level and is a certified math teacher in the State of New Hampshire. Shawn wrote fifteen Interactive Math lessons and provided storyboards for the graphics and animations.

Goals and Challenges Writing the *Interactive Math and Statistics Lessons*

Goals

One of the writers on the project, Shawn Hackshaw, outlined his primary goals in creating the lessons in the quote below. Note that the lessons need to support a variety of textbooks. The authors of the lessons draw their basic content from these texts.

> *My goals with each lesson were to summarize and simplify materials in a given text or series of texts without compromising the integrity of the material. The multimedia presentation had to be accurate and brief...*
>
> *I needed to be able to describe and illustrate a process in clear and precise steps that any user could follow, regardless of their mathematical background. Each individual lesson had goals that were outlined in the texts that the lessons were being created to support, and I needed to be cognizant of the [book] authors' intentions as well as understanding of the attention span and learning needs of the average student user.*

Challenges

The challenges to these straightforward goals were numerous. Some challenges relate to the content. Others to the production process itself.

Production Challenges

- Master the required software and technical skills to write the lessons.
- Help come up with a script format that will satisfy the needs of the client's nontechnical math content reviewers, the production team's programmers and animators, and the narrator who will read the audio narration.

Content Challenges

- Understand the specific restriction, format, and style of the Interactive Lessons.
- Ensure that the concepts could support all twelve textbooks and five different authors.
- Reduce sometimes vast amounts of content in the books to smaller amounts that could be effectively presented in an interactive, online format, keeping in mind the needs of the audience, particularly their short attention span with math subject matter.
- Find ways to explain, visualize, and make interactive the complex math and statistics concepts.

Writing the *Interactive Math and Statistics Lessons*: Meeting the Production Challenges

Software and Technical Skills

Writing for most technical subjects, such as math and science, requires more software and technical skills than writing nontechnical material, such as English and history. For example, chemistry writers often know modeling and visualization tools for creating images of molecules and other scientific elements. The writer is not responsible for creating the final production graphics, but the clearer he can be in sketching out the illustrations, the easier it is for the project's graphic designers and programmers to create accurate models and interactions. When a writer can create very clear preliminary models, it also saves the production team time and money. So it is definitely a plus for the writer to have some graphic and technical skills related to his subject matter.

On the math and statistics interactive lessons, writer Hackshaw used several tools to write math symbols and present illustrations. MathType by Design Science is a professional equation editor that makes it much easier to write out complex mathematical symbols and formulas. A limited version of MathType is included with Microsoft Office, AppleWorks, and other products, but the professional version is much more powerful. MathType easily integrates with most word processing software and has handy features, such as an ability to export equations from MathType to MathML, an XML-based language used to present math in interactive media, such as web sites. MathML was the standard for this project, so this export feature saved considerable time for the XML programmers.

For the Interactive Lessons, it was also useful for the author to have some basic graphic skills. There were many images and animations that had to be created to explain math and statistics concepts. Because the author could provide clear preliminary illustrations, it was a great help to the designers and programmers. The software that Hackshaw used on this project for charts, graphs, and illustrations included Graphsight, Excel, and TI Connect (to capture screen shots directly from the TI-83 graphing calculator). The web sites for these applications are listed at the end of this chapter and on the CD-ROM. So in general if you are interested in writing for the educational market, you will not only need writing skills and a knowledge of the subject matter, but you may also need some basic technical and graphic skills, such as those described above.

Developing a Script Format

Designing the right script format for a project is essential. The script format helps the writer present on paper a complex interactive multimedia program. Developing a script format for a project is not usually the exclusive responsibility of the writer, although sometimes it is. Often the production team and/or the client will have an approach that they prefer, particularly if the content is being developed for an existing software engine. In this project, the production team, InterWrite, revised the client's suggested format with significant input from the writer Shawn Hackshaw.

The challenges designing a script format for this project are shared with many technical, multimedia projects. The script format has to present the content for a variety of audiences that have different needs:

- **Client**: Needs to have a clear, uncluttered visual representation of how the screens will look so that they can evaluate and comment.

- **Production Team**: Animators, programmers, and other team members need very specific technical details so they can execute the author's vision. Hackshaw said that explaining his vision clearly for the development team was one of his biggest challenges on the project.
- **Narrator**: Copy that can be easily read out loud.

After some experimentation, a multipart script format was used by InterWrite for this project. A detailed explanation of the script format follows.

The Storyboard

As mentioned earlier, each lesson is divided into several modules, including "Prepare for the Tutorial," "Study the Concept," "Try an Example," "Explore the Concept," "Apply the Concepts to Real Life," and others. Except for the tests and the video screen, all of the screens are represented visually by a storyboard. A storyboard attempts to represent how the screen layout will actually look by showing placement of illustrations and screen text. A storyboard is a commonly used tool in developing content for both interactive media and linear media such as film and TV. Some storyboards, particularly in the advertising industry, can be very detailed and well crafted productions. For this project, however, a much simpler storyboard was adequate. The storyboard was created using Microsoft Word tables. A graphic designer created the art based on the rough illustrations of the writer.

The storyboard below is the storyboard from which the final lesson pictured in Figure 13-1 was created. This was a storyboard for a simple module. Others were more complex. (See the Chapters section of the CD-ROM for more complex storyboards.) Note the following in the storyboard below:

- Title bar clearly indicates the concept title and the unique concept tag: m02c01. It is important in a complex project for each element to have a unique tag. This is essential in production, but also helps the development team and client refer to a specific module without confusion. In this case, "m02" means the second concept within this lesson, and c01 lets us know it is the Study the Concept module within this second concept. You can create whatever tagging system makes sense to you and your team, but the important thing is to use it consistently throughout the script.
- In the produced lesson, the screen text and animation appears gradually. But on the storyboards, all the text is presented at once along with the final frame of the animation. This is because the storyboard is supported with a more detailed script (discussed later in this chapter). If the storyboard were the only production document, there would need to be multiple storyboards, showing exactly how the text and animation elements appear.
- The grayed-in boxes indicate that these are process boxes or definition boxes and should also be grayed boxes in the final lesson. Process boxes list the

steps of a procedure. Definition boxes define a term. See Figure 13-1 to see how these boxes look on the final screen.

Study the Concept *(Storyboard)*

Concept: Creating Time Plots	m02c01
	Creating Time Plots When data are collected over a period of time, they can be represented by a *time plot*.
	A **time plot** is a graph that shows data measurements in chronological order.
	Making a Time Plot 1. Time goes on the horizontal axis. 2. The variable being measured goes on the vertical axis. 3. Plot a point for each pair of data values. 4. Connect the data points with lines.

Script Animation Page

In the storyboard shown previously, the animation is shown as a static image in order to illustrate the approximate layout of the page, but it was also necessary for both content review and production development to have a precise idea of how the animation would unfold. This is handled on a separate animation page, which follows the storyboard. The animation page has the file name of the animation frame on the left, an image of the frame in the middle, and the corresponding text that triggers that frame appearing on the right.

Study the Concept *(Animation Page)*

Concept: Creating Time Plots		m02c01
File # il0262m02c01anim01.swf **Frame #**	**Animation Frame Image**	**Corresponding Text**
il0262m02c01anim01F1_IW.ai		To make a time plot, use the following procedure.
il0262m02c01anim01F2_IW.ai		After you draw your horizontal and vertical axes, time should be placed on the horizontal axis.
il0262m02c01anim01F3_IW.ai		The variable being measured goes on the vertical axis.

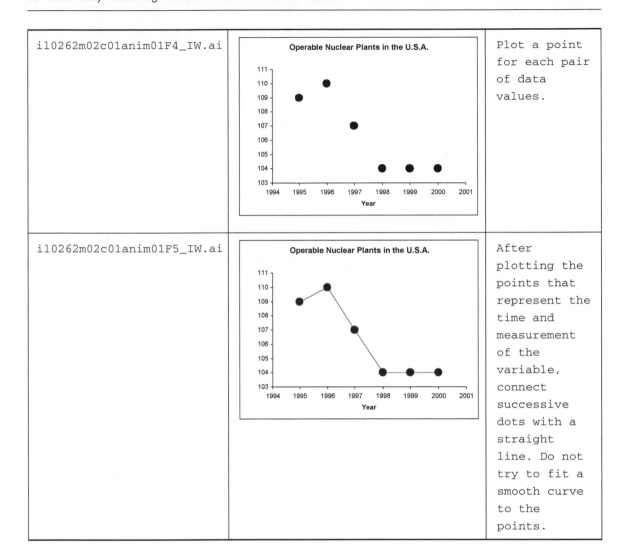

i10262m02c01anim01F4_IW.ai		Plot a point for each pair of data values.

i10262m02c01anim01F5_IW.ai		After plotting the points that represent the time and measurement of the variable, connect successive dots with a straight line. Do not try to fit a smooth curve to the points.

Programming, Text, and Narration Script

The final written script section for each module is the Programming, Text, and Narration Script. This script has all the details necessary for the production team, including the narrator, to create the actual lesson.

The script on a complex project becomes the bible for the development team. All elements must be spelled out clearly. In the sample script that follows, all the file names for this module are listed at the top of the page. This allows the graphic designer to give a name to files and the programmer and animators to create links to those file names correctly. The file names follow a standard project naming convention. Writers should be aware of that convention if they are going to be listing file names, such as in this script.

Below the file names are multiple rows and four columns. All the content in a row appears on the screen at one time, followed by the next row, etc. The four columns each describe different content:

- **Images, Text, Programming**: This column lists the file names of the images, on screen text, and any programming, such as indicating a Definition Box.
- **Narration (Text Transcript)**: The next column over is the text transcript, which appears in the box at the bottom of the screen for the student to read. See Figure 13-1. This is an accurate text rendition of the audio narration.
- **Narration (Audio Transcript)**: The audio transcript is what the narrator will say. Even though the Text Transcript and Audio Transcript are identical in content, they are written somewhat differently to make it easier for the listener and reader. In the sample below, there are no differences, but examples of what appears in other scripts are numbers written out in narration but appearing as numerals in text and difficult words written out phonetically in the narration.
- **Project Note**: This is used by the production team for a variety of purposes, including timing narration for developing the lesson and tracking bug fixes. (Bugs are errors discovered during review.)

The real script is created in landscape format to allow the columns to be wider. It is restructured here in portrait format for easier display in the book. (See the Chapters section of the CD-ROM for the complete script in original format.)

Concept: Creating Time Plots	m02c01

Study the Concept *(Programming and Text Script)*

File Names This Module (Study the Concept)

ID: m02c01
Audio: il0262m02c01.mp3

Animation:

il0262m02c01anim01.swf
il0262m02c01anim01F1_IW.ai
il0262m02c01anim01F2_IW.ai
il0262m02c01anim01F3_IW.ai
il0262m02c01anim01F4_IW.ai
il0262m02c01anim01F5_IW.ai

Images, Text, Programming	Narration (Text Transcript)	Narration (Audio Transcript)	Project Note
1)(Title) Creating Time Plots			
2)(Main Screen Text) When data	When data are collected over a	When data are collected over a	

are collected over a period of time, they can be represented by a **time plot**.	period of time, they can be represented by a **time plot**.	period of time, they can be represented by a **time plot**.	
3)(Definition Box) A time plot is a graph showing data measurements in chronological order.	A time plot is a graph that shows data measurements in chronological order. It is important to note that the interval of time between measurements should be the same. So, if you take a measurement once a week, it should be on the same day every week. Or, if you take a measurement every day, the same time period, such as one-half hour, should be used.	A time plot is a graph that shows data measurements in chronological order. It is important to note that the interval of time between measurements should be the same. So, if you take a measurement once a week, it should be on the same day every week. Or, if you take a measurement every day, the same time period, such as one-half hour, should be used.	
4a)(Procedure Box) Making a Time Plot [il0262m02c01anim 01F1_IW.ai]	To make a time plot, use the following procedure.	To make a time plot, use the following procedure.	
4b)(Procedure Box) 1. Time goes on the horizontal axis. [il0262m02c01anim 01F2_IW.ai]	After you draw your horizontal and vertical axes, time should be placed on the horizontal axis.	After you draw your horizontal and vertical axes, time should be placed on the horizontal axis.	
4c)(Procedure Box) 2. The variable being measured goes on the vertical axis. [il0262m02c01anim 01F3_IW.ai]	The variable being measured is placed on the vertical axis.	The variable being measured is placed on the vertical axis.	

4d)(Procedure Box)
3. Plot a point
   for each pair
   of data values.
[il0262m02c01anim
01F4_IW.ai]
	Plot a point for
	each pair of data
	values.
		Plot a point for
		each pair of data
		values.	

4e)(Procedure Box)
4. Connect the
   data points
   with lines.
[il0262m02c01anim
01F5_IW.ai]
	After plotting the
	points that
	represent the time
	and measurement of
	the variable,
	connect successive
	dots with a straight
	line. Do not try to
	fit a smooth curve
	to the points.
		After plotting the
		points that
		represent the time
		and measurement of
		the variable,
		connect successive
		dots with a straight
		line. Do not try to
		fit a smooth curve
		to the points.	

With the production challenges solved, the writer next must face the content challenges.

Writing the *Interactive Math and Statistics Lessons*: Meeting the Content Challenges

Understanding the Requirements for This Project

Any complex multimedia or web project will have a series of rules that will affect the writer. If you are writing for a unique product that will be built from the ground up according to your script, you will have fewer restrictions. But if you are writing for an existing software engine, which is often the case, you must know what the engine can and cannot do. As mentioned previously, the interactive math lessons were written for an existing software engine. Be sure to ask for the project guidelines before you start a project. They are usually included in a document called a "style guide" or "project specifications." Sometimes no style guide exists, and it is part of the writer's job to create a style guide to ensure consistency in content development. Some of the things you need to know before writing a complex project include the following.

Screen Layout

You need to know what kinds of media or text can go where in the interface. Can the screen scroll? Is the amount of text limited in certain areas? Figure 13-3

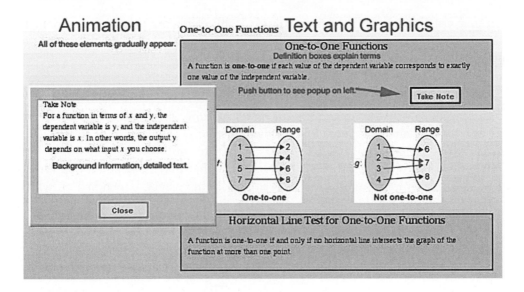

Figure 13-3 *Illustration from style guide explaining layout for writers.*

is part of the Interactive Lessons style guide that tries to answer some of these questions.

Engine Capability

You also need to know what this software engine can do. What kind of media can it present, such as video and animation? What kind of exercises is it capable of, such as multiple choice, true and false, etc.? Does it have any other tools or functions, such as note-taking tools or tracking student progress?

Unique Project Elements

If there are unique elements in the project that require special terms and layout, you need to be sure you understand them. These unique elements are often related to production issues.

Dividing Content into Various Display Areas

Once the writer understands the screen layout and engine capability, then he/she is better able to make effective use of all the display elements in a project and not just put all the content in one location. For example, in the Interactive Lessons, it is usually best to limit the amount of text on the screen because reading lots of text on screen is uncomfortable for most users. On screen text should just cover key points. Concepts should be visualized as much as possible in diagrams and animations. If details need to be discussed, leave them off the main screen text, and cover them instead in the audio and other special elements, such as Definition Boxes and Hints. This allows a more sophisticated user to move through the main screen text and visuals to finish the lesson quickly, while allowing an average student to get additional help by referring to other lesson elements. This is an example of multipath information flow discussed earlier.

Writing Style Guide

Important information for the writer is the writing style guide. This guide lays out exactly how elements should be handled in text. This will include how to write certain types of technical material, such as math formulas, style of items such as bulleted lists, and consistent use of certain words that may be handled in a variety of ways. For example, website and web site are both correct, depending on which dictionary you consult, but within a project, a specific word should only be spelled one way.

Writing style guides are used even in print projects, but the added complication for a multimedia project is that depending on where the text appears in the program it might be handled differently. For example in this project, there were different style rules for the narration and the text script. The goal was to make one easier to be read by the student and another easier to read out loud by the narrator. A sample from the style guide follows.

1. Math Symbols are spelled out and numbers are represented in Arabic.

Audio Transcript (A)	Text Transcript (T)
negative nine over six	negative 9 over 6

2. Superscripts and subscripts are written as symbols. Subscripts are always written "variable" "sub" "number."

Audio Transcript (A)	Text Transcript (T)
x squared	x^2
x sub one	x_1

Reducing and Structuring Content for Interactive Media

Once all the project rules as discussed above are understood, the author can finally begin the actual writing. The first challenge for most interactive writers is to chunk the content. This means taking the large amount of continuous content that can be covered in a book or even a chapter of a book and breaking that content into smaller units that can be portrayed interactively. In the case of this project, math and statistics concepts needed to be broken down to fit into the module structures of the Interactive Lessons. Also, keeping in mind the needs and attention span of the student audience, the amount of content covered by a particularly concept must be reduced as much as possible to make it bite-sized, and easily digestible by the audience.

The writer also had to keep in mind that the one concept that he was working on was part of a much larger body of concepts that explained other issues. This meant that the author did not have to include background material on his concept because that background material would be covered in a different lesson. It is important for an interactive writer to understand the big picture of a project and how all the elements fit together. This helps avoid repeating material that is presented elsewhere in the project.

The Outline

The client's math editors help with this process of chunking by presenting the writer an outline of the concepts for a particular math or statistics concept, such as this outline for the time plots (second concept below) presented earlier in this chapter in script samples and screen shots. In general, an outline can be a good starting point to chunk content.

```
Prepare for the Tutorial
View a Video Example
Explore the Concept
Concept: Creating Bar Graphs and Circle Graphs

    • Study the Concept
    • Try an Example
    • Practice Exercises

Concept: Creating Time Plots

    • Study the Concept
    • Try an Example
    • Practice Exercises

Concept: Creating Histograms and Relative-Frequency Histograms

    • Study the Concept
    • Try an Example
    • Practice Exercises

Concept: Creating Stem-and-Leaf Displays

    • Study the Concept
    • Try an Example
    • Practice Exercises

Mastery Test
```

The first job of the writer is to analyze this outline and determine if the concept is too large to be handled in one lesson and should be broken down into multiple lessons. In the outline above, the elements in each module are pretty straightforward, with each of them including "Study the Concept," "Try an Example," and a "Practice Exercises." The writer could suggest adding more elements to better explain the concept. For example, he may think that a certain concept needs multiple examples, a video, or a real life application.

Continued Refinement: The Writing and Review Process

To effectively present the information, the writer should be involved in as much of the content development process as possible. The outline discussed above is the beginning, but once the outline was refined, the author next had to study the various textbooks that these lessons needed to support. For this project, there were twelve textbooks written by five authors. Writer Hackshaw's process was to sit at a large table with all the textbooks open in front of him. Each textbook would be turned to the section covering the concept being written. Hackshaw then marked up the textbooks with numbers, underlines etc. to highlight the points he wanted to cover. Then he began writing his first draft storyboard and script.

The finished first draft would be reviewed by InterWrite and then more extensively by the Houghton Mifflin math editors. They would return suggested changes to the author. The author had the option of arguing for his approach instead of the client's suggestions. It is not a good idea to rubber stamp a client's changes if you strongly oppose them. If later they prove to be bad choices, it is the writer who will sometimes carry the blame for the client's suggestions, because the writer is responsible for the script. Of course, when arguing any point with the client, the client will have the final word, and the writer should learn how to give in gracefully if she has not been able to persuade the client to adopt the writer's point of view.

With the Interactive Lessons, once the client approved the script, the developer produced it. In the case of the time plots lesson described earlier, the developer was InterWrite. Because the writer on a project, such as this, is also the subject matter expert, he was also responsible for reviewing the first draft of the produced lesson. If a writer can be involved in this way, it is often helpful. Sometimes ideas that looked great on the script do not come off as well in the final production. Sometimes explanations are not clear and need additional text or illustrations. Lastly, the author must make sure that no errors were introduced in production. A single deleted math symbol can make an entire calculation incorrect. Unless there is some issue that needs to be resolved later in the production, usually this ends the writer's involvement with a particular concept. Being involved from outline to production is important to guarantee accuracy and a consistent presentation of the content.

Explain and Visualize Concepts in an Engaging Way

One of the biggest challenges for the writer was to find ways to clearly explain the concept and engage the student interactively. Hackshaw found a few techniques that were particularly helpful.

Step-by-Step Instruction and Reinforcement

Hackshaw said that one of the most important techniques in explaining technical subjects is careful step-by-step instruction. For example, when graphing a line, such as in the lesson pictured in Figure 13-1,

> *students need to understand how points on that line are found. If you don't take the time to show how to find the points, and just plot them on the graph, students won't make the connection. That line just showed up without an explanation.... Students need to be constantly reminded in systematic step-by-step process of how the concept works.*

The structure of the Interactive Lessons encourages this step-by-step process and reinforcement with multiple media. Hackshaw said that when you teach a concept, first explain what is it, then visually represent it in numerals or a formula, then present it in audio, then develop a picture or animation that illustrates it.

Allow Multiple Ways to Interact with a Concept

Allowing multiple ways to interact with content is an effective use of interactive multimedia as a teaching tool. Hackshaw tried to foster this type of interaction within the lessons he wrote.

In Figure 13-4 that follows, the top image has no data entered. The student has the option of entering his or her own number or clicking the "Random Data" button. Clicking the Random Data button enters numbers in the left column of the table located on the right of the screen. Then by clicking the "Calculate" button, the numbers are sorted in the column on far right, a whisker plot is created in the middle, and a range is shown under the buttons. (See the bottom image.) This setup allows students to see all the elements of a concept on one screen and to view them interactively. Students can change a number or two and click "Calculate" to see the changes in the three main screen elements (sort, plot, and range). The Random Data button is also a recommended feature for an exercise like this. It allows students to experience the exercise without having to spend several minutes inputting data. Once they understand how the exercise works, then they are often tempted to enter their own data for further exploration of a concept.

Another example occurs in a lesson dealing with confidence intervals. See Figure 13-5. In this exercise, instead of being asked to input numbers, students are given sliders to input a wide range of numbers. As they slide the dark bars, the numbers next to the bar change. When they slide the bottom bar, the bottom four numbers change. Students can experiment with sliding this bar to see how an entire range of numbers changes the calculation. This is far more flexible and interactive than having students simply input single numbers.

Figure 13-6 shows another effective way to manipulate data. In this module, pushing one of the arrows moves the parabola on the graph and changes the corresponding formula over the arrows. This is one more way to avoid making students

Explore the Concept

In this exploration, you will be able to enter a short list of data or have the computer choose random data for you. The computer will then calculate the quartiles and create a box-and-whisker plot of your data. Through this exploration, you will discover how box-and-whisker plots display your data.

Explore

1. Enter up to 19 data values in the table. Be sure to use only positive values between 1 and 100. To enter the data value, click on an empty box in the data column. To have the computer automatically fill in the data values, click **Random Data**.

2. Click **Calculate**.

To try again, click **Clear** and start over.

Try this with several data sets before you continue to the questions. When you are ready to answer some questions, click **Continue**.

| Calculate | Random Data | Clear |

Low:
Q1:
Median:
Q3:
High:

| Continue |

Data	Sorted

100
90
80
70
60
50
40
30
20
10
0

Explore the Concept

In this exploration, you will be able to enter a short list of data or have the computer choose random data for you. The computer will then calculate the quartiles and create a box-and-whisker plot of your data. Through this exploration, you will discover how box-and-whisker plots display your data.

Explore

1. Enter up to 19 data values in the table. Be sure to use only positive values between 1 and 100. To enter the data value, click on an empty box in the data column. To have the computer automatically fill in the data values, click **Random Data**.

2. Click **Calculate**.

To try again, click **Clear** and start over.

Try this with several data sets before you continue to the questions. When you are ready to answer some questions, click **Continue**.

| Calculate | Random Data | Clear |

Low: 3
Q1: 24.5
Median: 68
Q3: 86
High: 95

| Continue |

Data	Sorted
67	95
10	91
26	90
91	86
86	86
95	76
73	73
4	71
3	69
23	67
76	55
69	41
90	26
22	23
86	22
71	10
55	4
41	3

100
90 — 95
80 — 86
70
60 — 68
50
40
30
20 — 24.5
10
0 — 3

Figure 13-4 *Box and Whisker Plot showing empty screen on top and after data has been inputted at bottom.*

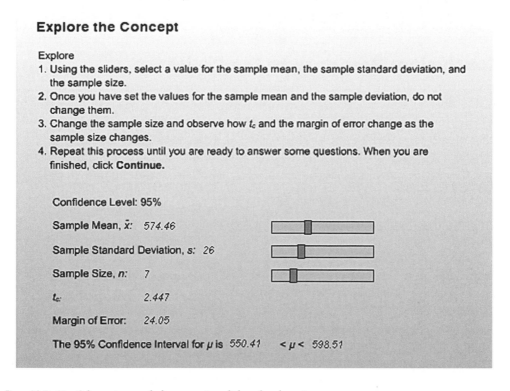

Explore the Concept

Explore
1. Using the sliders, select a value for the sample mean, the sample standard deviation, and the sample size.
2. Once you have set the values for the sample mean and the sample deviation, do not change them.
3. Change the sample size and observe how t_c and the margin of error change as the sample size changes.
4. Repeat this process until you are ready to answer some questions. When you are finished, click **Continue.**

Confidence Level: 95%

Sample Mean, $\bar{x}$:   574.46

Sample Standard Deviation, s: 26

Sample Size, n: 7

t_c: 2.447

Margin of Error: 24.05

The 95% Confidence Interval for μ is 550.41 $< \mu <$ 598.51

Figure 13-5 *Confidence intervals lesson using sliders for data input.*

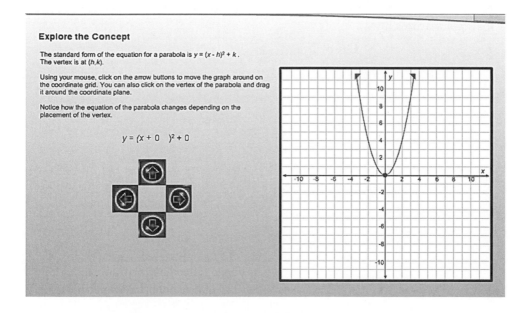

Explore the Concept

The standard form of the equation for a parabola is $y = (x - h)^2 + k$.
The vertex is at (h, k).

Using your mouse, click on the arrow buttons to move the graph around on the coordinate grid. You can also click on the vertex of the parabola and drag it around the coordinate plane.

Notice how the equation of the parabola changes depending on the placement of the vertex.

$$y = (x + 0\ )^2 + 0$$

Figure 13-6 *Graphing parabolas using arrows to shift graph.*

enter lots of data and it gives users a different way to experience the information and engage them in the learning process.

Conclusion: Response to the Project

Several hundred interactive math and statistics lessons have been produced. They have had a positive response with both students and teachers who have found the approach to be a major help in understanding math concepts.

References

Dolphin MultiMedia, Inc. web site. http://www.dolphinmm.com

Education Market Research web site. http://www.ed-market.com/r_c_archives/display_article.php?article_id=46

Graphsight web site. http://www.cradlefields.com/gs/graphsight.html

InterWrite web site. http://www.interwrite.com

Hackshaw, Shawn. Phone Interview with the Author, 2006.

Hackshaw, Shawn. E-mail to the Author, 2006.

Houghton Mifflin Company web site. http://www.hmco.com

Larson Texts, Inc. web site. http://www.larsontexts.com

MathType web site. http://www.dessci.com/en/products/mathtype

National Association of College Stores web site. http://www.nacs.org/public/research/higher_ed_retail.asp

TI Connect web site. http://education.ti.com/us/product/accessory/connectivity/features/features.html

Case Study—Museum Kiosk: The Nauticus Shipbuilding Company

Summary

Name of Production: *The Nauticus Shipbuilding Company*
Writer: Steven Barney
Developers: Tarragon Interactive, Chedd-Angier Production Co.
Audience: General
Medium: Computer hard drive in kiosk setting
Location: Nauticus: National Maritime Center, Norfolk, Virginia
Subject: Shipbuilding
Goals: Entertain, teach
Architecture: Simulation, hierarchical branching

The script samples and illustrations used in this chapter are copyright Chedd-Angier Production Company and the National Maritime Center.

Program Description and Background

Program Description

The Nauticus Shipbuilding Company is an interactive museum kiosk program that introduces users to basic concepts of shipbuilding. It is located at Nauticus: National Maritime Center in Norfolk, Virginia. The program is run on a computer's hard drive accessed by users touching images or menu items on the touch screen monitor. The computer and monitor are housed in a stand-alone kiosk in the museum's main exhibit hall. Near the kiosk is a wall of graphic and text information on shipbuilding

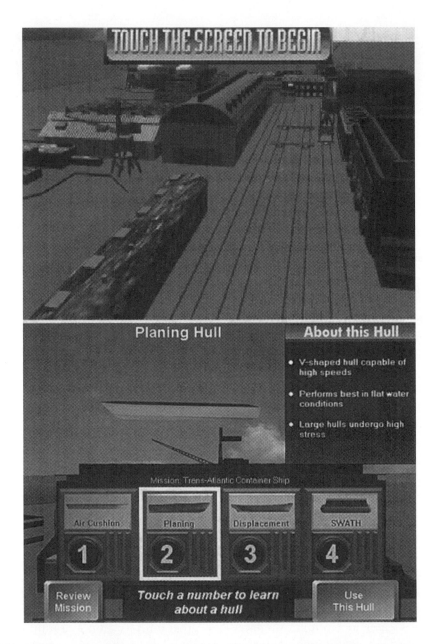

Figure 14-1 *Top screen: From the attract program for* The Nauticus Shipbuilding Company. *Bottom screen: Where the user chooses hulls.*

that supports the kiosk program. *The Nauticus Shipbuilding Company* is also being used in classrooms as part of the museum's curricular outreach.

 The original color images for these screen shots and others are available on this book's CD-ROM in the Chapter 14 area of the Chapters section.

Multimedia in Museums

A single-user kiosk presentation such as *Nauticus* is a common way to present multimedia in a museum or other public site. Because of the need to accommodate large groups, multimedia in museums is also presented in a group format, where a number of people control the action on the screen. An example is the National Scouting Museum's Boy Scout Patrol Theater, which allows eight users to take on the role of the individual Boy Scouts portrayed in the multimedia program.

 See the Boy Scout Patrol area of the Chapters section of this book's CD-ROM.

A growing trend in museums, conventions, and other public events is the immersive exhibit, which in addition to multimedia elements also includes live performers, audience participation, and actual objects. See Chapter 24 for more on this type of program.

In addition to exhibits, many museums also have learning centers, which house a variety of multimedia "edutainment" programs for groups or individuals. Larger museums are active in educational outreach, providing curricular support for schools. The old fossils-on-wheels programs, which brought artifacts to schools, is now being supplemented by multimedia programs such as *Nauticus*, and by online programs from museums, such as the Museum of Science in Boston, the Exploratorium in San Francisco, and the Franklin Institute Science Museum in Philadelphia.

See the Chapter 14 area of this book's CD-ROM for links to these sites.

Production Background

The Nauticus Shipbuilding Company was jointly developed by Chedd-Angier Production Company and Tarragon Interactive for Nauticus: National Maritime Center. The National Maritime Center, located on the Norfolk, Virginia waterfront, offers exhibits, films, and multimedia programs dealing with shipping, the Navy, and the sea.

The Chedd-Angier Production Company is a Boston-based media production company that Nauticus hired to develop a number of the media productions for the museum. Chedd-Angier in turn recruited Tarragon Interactive to develop The Nauticus Shipbuilding Company project. At the time of production, Tarragon was a custom developer of multimedia titles for marketing and sales, training, and "info-tainment" (museum and CD-ROM) titles. Tarragon has since been sold and no longer exists as a separate entity. The writer of this program is Steven Barney,

Figure 14-2 *Exterior of the National Maritime Center with the shipbuilding exhibit room in smaller image.*

who was president of Tarragon Interactive. He is a designer-programmer with a background in instructional design.

Writing and Developing *The Nauticus Shipbuilding Company*

The Development Process
On this project, the writer's primary involvement occurs during the first two stages of development, project definition and design/preproduction, but the writer is also often called in during production to make last-minute changes.

The project definition identifies:

- Design objective
- Target audience
- Delivery platform/location

Design/preproduction documents include:

- Proposals. Outlining the program's approach.
- High-level design document. A text-based content treatment and a program navigation flow diagram.
- Scripts. Program navigation flow plus narration, dialogue, screen text, and full description of visuals.

Development Challenges

Many of the challenges facing the developers of *The Nauticus Shipbuilding Company* are common to media development for museums and other public sites. These challenges are discussed below.

Design Objective

The design objective of *Nauticus* is to provide museum visitors with an interactive environment in which to explore how ships are built for specific missions. This piece uses technical information that must be precisely accurate. The project was reviewed for accuracy by the faculty of MIT's Department of Naval Engineering and members of the National Board of the Society of Naval Architecture and Marine Engineering. The entertainment aspect of this piece was tested through focus groups and by placing a test exhibit at a museum and evaluating viewers' reactions.

Another objective of this program is that users will go through the game and return to play it again. This means that diversity and depth must be designed into the experience, but because of run time, size limitations, and turnaround time (the amount of time it takes someone to complete the program and a new user to begin), this diversity cannot create a huge program. Long turnaround time would mean long lines and frustrated museum visitors.

Target Audience

Developing a program like this for the typical museum audience poses a number of challenges:

- **Diversity.** Museum audiences include people of all ages, backgrounds, education, and levels of interest in the subject. An exhibit has to have a little something for everyone.
- **Short attention spans.** Because there are so many exhibits competing for their attention, museum goers generally will not play a program for more than two minutes (sixty to ninety seconds is the typical experience time). A program has about five seconds to capture a user, but even when captured, many leave after thirty seconds. A complex subject puts demands on the developer to present the material succinctly or to create a piece, such as Nauticus, that is so appealing it can lure users into longer than typical play times.

Delivery Platform and Locations

The nature of the delivery platform and its location has a significant impact on what is creatively possible. A kiosk program running off a fast hard drive allows the use of video, 3-D graphics, and other features that would be difficult to deliver on media with slower access time. But because most museums are nonprofit organizations, money is often tight, and complex challenges must be met by the writer inexpensively. New museums or new wings of museums tend to be better funded than renovations of existing exhibits.

Meeting the Challenges

The program's objectives and the challenges must be met by the writer-designer's proposals, high-level design documents, and scripts. There were many revisions of the written material. Here are a few of them.

The Proposal

The initial proposal is the earliest stage of a project. Compare the proposal with the treatment that follows it and consider what changes were made before reading the analysis.

```
                 INTERACTIVE MODULE—#5,7
                    SHIP-BUILDING:
```

Objective

To simulate modular ship construction at work.

Treatment

Visitors will use a stylus to draw any kind of ship on a pressure-sensitive platen. Children might sketch out a simple shape. Others can create more sophisticated designs. When the drawing is complete, the user will push a button. The ship will disappear from the platen and will then be "built" on the video screen.

To do this, the program will divide the ship drawing into modular sections (based on the platen's grid and predetermined guidelines). These modules will then be "constructed" on screen, to the accompaniment of appropriate sound effects, such as hammering, riveting, and perhaps even the shouts of work crews. When all the modular sections are complete, they will be united, forming a replica of the visitor's original design.

The video game will be, in effect, a simulation of the CAD/CAM process, whereby ships are designed on screen and then built with the aid of computers—in separate modules.

If feasible, the computers can be linked to a printer, and visitors can take home sketches of their creations.

Technique/Method

Visitor-activated platen with video monitor.

High-Level Design Document

After the initial proposal was revised several times and the basic concept refined, the high-level design document, which includes a design objective, creative treatment, and a navigation flowchart, was prepared:

1.0 Design Objective

The objective of the program is to provide museum visitors with a
fun, interactive environment to explore how ships are built to
accomplish specific missions. Visitors will be able to experiment
by building custom ships from a variety of components. Through this
experience, visitors will learn to apply the principle of "form
follows function" to the process of building ships. Visitors will
learn about the major design components of a ship: hull, hold, engine,
and special equipment. Visitors will learn how variations in these
design components affect a ship's ability to carry out a specific
mission.

2.0 Creative Treatment

ATTRACT ROUTINE: When no one is using the program, an attract routine
will invite visitors to come explore the program. The attract routine
will contain a brief glimpse of one of the mission introductions,
picked randomly. This will be followed by a series of snapshots of
components being selected, and a ship being built by the program.
Text overlays will repeat continuously. Sample text: "Build a Ship
to Accomplish a Mission"; "Touch the Screen to Begin."

INTRODUCTION: Immediately upon touching the screen during the attract
routine, the visitor is greeted with a brief sequence introducing
the program with audio and text. Sample text: "Pick one of the five
missions; then go to the shipyard to build your own custom-designed
boat. When you are done, see if your boat succeeds in accomplishing
the mission." "Let's go to the briefing room to choose a mission."

BRIEFING ROOM: The metaphor of a briefing room will be used to allow
the visitor to select from a menu of missions, and then to review
each mission. Upon selecting a mission from the menu, the visitor
is briefed. Each briefing will consist of a full-screen graphic with
text. A one-quarter screen video clip with a talking head keyed over
stock footage will introduce the mission. Design criteria for the
mission will appear on a checklist. At the conclusion of the
briefing, the visitor can either select this mission or return to
the mission menu.

Mission 1. North Sea Fire Fighter The North Sea is full of gigantic
oil-drilling platforms that use mile-long pipes to drain oil from
under the sea floor, then store it in tanks until tankers come to
take it to the mainland for processing and distribution to the

general public. Sometimes these platforms catch on fire. Your job is to design a ship that will be able to put out these fires.

The ship must be stable enough to remain near the platform until the fire is put out, and must have pumps powerful enough to drive large amounts of water through its hoses. It must also be able to withstand the rough seas and weather of the North Sea.

Mission 2. Alligator Census Many years ago, the Everglades were viewed as a wasteland, home to millions of potentially disease-spreading mosquitoes. Because of such concerns, the Everglades were drained to create farmland. People now recognize that the Everglades is a beautiful, but fragile ecosystem that was greatly disrupted by the drainage and dredging projects. Many birds and other creatures died as a result. These species are believed to be making a comeback, but the only way to know for sure is to go into the Everglades by boat and count them. The ideal boat for this mission must be quiet so as not to disturb the wildlife, and it should be able to navigate shallow waters and swamp.

Mission 3. Coast Guard Drug Interdiction Undercover police and FBI investigators routinely attempt to infiltrate suspected drug rings and break up shipments of drugs from South America and various countries. They have just ordered a ship from your shipyard that will be able to intercept shipments of drugs coming into Miami, Florida. It must have a high top speed, be able to travel at or near that speed for long distances, and be outfitted with weapons sufficient to threaten and subdue vessels operated by suspected criminals. It should also have a low profile, making it difficult to spot from a distance.

Mission 4. Trans-Pacific Freighter Exports account for an increasingly large portion of our country's economy. Trade with the Far East is expected to double in the near future. Efficient freighters are needed to transport the large flow of goods to and from this important economic region. The design should be cost-efficient, have enough range to travel to Korea, Japan, Singapore, and Taiwan, and be able to carry large quantities of cargo. Speed is a secondary design consideration.

Mission 5. Arctic Ice Breaker The "Land of the Midnight Sun" is an accurate name for the Arctic. Due to the Earth's orbit and tilt, the region experiences six straight months of darkness, followed by six straight months of light. This prolonged darkness contributes to temperatures as low as negative 70 degrees

Fahrenheit, more than sufficient to freeze Hudson Bay and the rest of the Arctic Ocean. Ice breakers are needed to clear shipping channels otherwise blocked for months. You must design such an ice breaker to clear a path from Churchill, Canada, to Barrow, Alaska. It must be heavy, as indestructible as possible, and be able to remain at sea for months.

 After the user selects a mission, he or she is told: "You have selected a difficult mission. Now let's go to the shipyard where you can design and build your own custom boat to accomplish the mission."

The Shipyard

OPENING ANIMATION: A 3-D animation sequence will give an overview of the shipyard, then zoom in to the point of view of a shipbuilder entering the gates.

 After the opening animation, the visitor selects components from a series of menus. The design features for each component are summarized upon selection. After selecting each component, the partially completed boat moves along a track to the next component selection area.

Components

Hulls

Single V:
Efficient, stable, with a large amount of room for supplies, cargo, fuel, and passengers, they make an excellent choice for almost any ship. Single V-shaped hulls are by far the most common.

Double V:
Double V-shaped hulls are far less common than single V's, but they also make a good choice for ships where the main hull not being penetrated is of the utmost importance, such as oil tankers.

Single Flatbottom:
Single flatbottom hulls are used mainly for riverboats and other craft where a shallow draft is important. They are less efficient and stable than other designs, but sometimes a shallow draft is the top consideration.

Hydrofoil:
Hydrofoils are radically different than the other three designs. The boat is fitted with several projections with angled metal plates on the bottom. They lift the boat out of the water when it runs at high speed. This design works only for small boats.

Hold

Cargo:
Cargo holds are used for holding large amounts of goods while on the ship. These range from weapons to cars to food, frequently packaged in the railroad cars, which transported them to the harbor.

Passengers:
Passenger space usually consists of many small rooms, of which the interior varies according to type of ship. Cruise lines commonly have rooms to rival the best hotels, where military ships often just have four hammocks.

Ballast:
Ballast is used as a stabilizer for ships with little weight in their hulls. It is usually just a room that has sea water pumped into it.

None:
Small boats infrequently have ballast, as there is not a huge need for it.

Engine

Nuclear:
Nuclear power plants in ships work much like their electricity-generating counterparts on land. Steam is heated passing next to radioactive material, usually U 235. It is then used to push turbines connected to the propellers, giving the ship its power. The shielding around nuclear plants is very heavy, making them efficient only for large ships.

Gas:
Gas power plants are much the same as jet engines, just on a larger scale. Their advantages are high speed and short start-up times, but they are noisy, inefficient for large ships, and require many people to run.

Diesel:
Diesel engines have many of the same characteristics as their counterparts in vans and trucks. They are efficient, low-maintenance engines with an ability to run at low revolutions per minute (RPMs). They are ideal for moving large ships at moderate to low speeds.

Steam:
Steam engines burn oil or gasoline to heat water until it is steam, and then use that to drive turbines.

Special Equipment

Weapons Mounts:
Turrets and mounts with machine guns and small cannon, from
.50 caliber to 5 inches.

Cranes, Booms, and Winches:
Equipment for lifting cargo from the decks and holds of ships.

Pumps and Hoses:
Used for spraying water on burning vessels, docks, and other objects
in or near the water. Water is drawn from the ocean or river that
the boat is in.

Reinforced Hull:
An extra layer of reinforcements to increase hull integrity in certain
areas. Useful for ships with a high potential of running into reefs
and other obstacles.

Grappling Hooks:
Lines and hooks for latching onto other ships or objects while
at sea.

CONCLUSION:
After the last component has been selected, a 3-D animation sequence
depicts the launching of the vessel. If the design is suitable for
the mission, the visitor will see a depiction of the design
successfully carrying out the mission. If the design is fundamentally
flawed, the vessel will be shown sinking. Some evaluation will be
provided as to the ability of the visitor's design to carry out the
selected mission. Finally, the visitor will be given the opportunity
to print out the design and evaluation.

3.0 Project Schedule

High-Level Design	completed
Research/Scripting	September 1–October 1
Detailed Design Approved	October 1
Prototyping/Initial Graphics Development	October 1–October 31
Initial Graphic Design Approved	November 1
Graphics and Program Production	November 1–December 15
Final Graphics Approved	December 15
Programming/Integration Completed	January 15
Final Delivery	February 1

4.0 Budget

High-Level Design	1 week @	$XXX
Research	2 weeks @	$XXX
	2 weeks @	$XXX

```
Scripting                    2 weeks @        $XXX
Video                        1 week @         $XXX
                             2 weeks @        $XXX
Graphics                    12 weeks @        $XXX
Programming/Integration      6 weeks @        $XXX
QA/Revisions                 2 weeks @        $XXX
Total Budget:                                 $XXXX
(Budget dollar amount deleted for this book.)
```

Proposal and Design Document Compared

Comparing the design document's treatment to the proposal shows some striking changes in the evolution of this project. The proposal's initial idea, to have a computer "build" a ship based on a user's rough sketch, was replaced in the treatment by the more structured approach of having the viewer build a ship to achieve a specific mission based on defined ship components. Another key aspect of the treatment is that the user's design is evaluated at the end of the process, and the user is encouraged to play the game again to improve the design.

Although the initial proposal is fun, it illustrates the importance of balancing interactivity with control to teach a specific subject. The proposal provides a rough demonstration of CAD/CAM, but the more controlled approach in the treatment accomplishes much more. It allows users to utilize well-defined principles concerning hulls, engines, and other components to build a ship. The evaluation function suggested in the treatment allows users to learn from their efforts and build on them in repeat plays. With no evaluation function in the proposal, the user does not even know if his or her ship would float.

There are also some practical concerns here. It is important to give the general museum audience a positive experience. The treatment approach of assembling parts means that even a young child can piece together an impressive boat. This may not be true with the proposal approach. What will the CAD/CAM process be able to do with the rough squiggles of a seven year old? There could be a few default ships automatically rendered from unintelligible sketches, but this would not be the ship the user drew, and on repeated plays, he or she could be disappointed if the same ship was produced from different drawings.

Navigation Program/Flow

The creative treatment of the design document lays out the basic content of the production; the navigation/program flowchart defines how that content will be accessed interactively. Compare the flowcharts on the next pages, Figures 14-3 and 14-4, and consider the changes that were made before reading the analysis that follows.

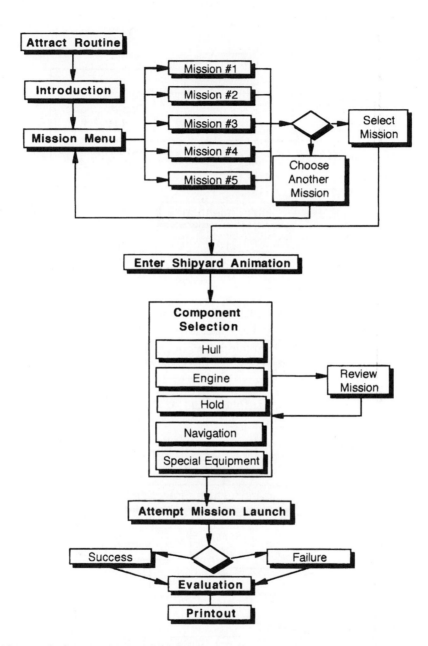

Figure 14-3 *First draft navigation/program flow.*

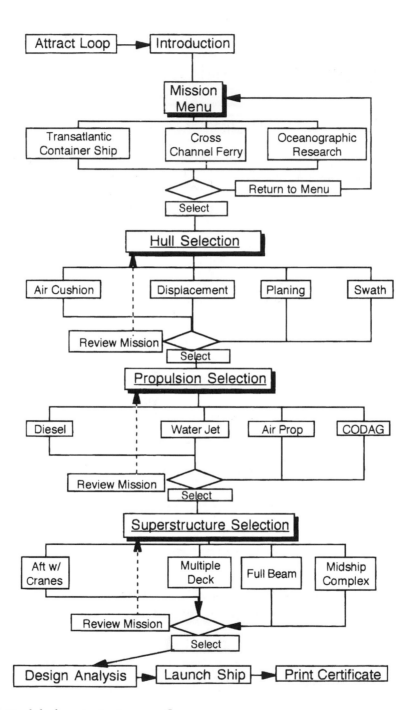

Figure 14-4 *Final draft navigation/program flow.*

Changes in Navigation/Program Flow

Different flowcharts serve different functions. Some, such as the one shown in Figure 14-3, lay out the possible navigation flow early in a project. Because this chart will be read by clients who may not be sophisticated in multimedia navigation, there is an advantage to keeping it as simple as possible. Detail is limited, particularly in the component section, where the multiple choices under each component are reduced to one broad category.

The second chart comes when the program is more defined. At this point, it is possible to chart all the paths in the project. A chart like this is useful to a sophisticated client and can also be the basis of a planning document for the production team.

Both of these charts are designed very simply, but there are a few conventions in the second chart worth noting. The diamond symbol suggests that this is a point where the user can make a choice. The text in main categories is underlined. The first program flow uses arrows and lines to suggest directions. Some designers also use arrows to suggest a link where the viewer has no choice, such as the Attract Routine to the Introduction. No arrows indicate a place where the viewer has multiple choices, such as in the Missions.

The Final Script

The script is the complete and detailed description of the program on paper. A well-written script also communicates the look and feel of the project. This is usually done with formatting and descriptive writing, but the writer of this script took a novel approach to achieve this goal. He included small illustrations of the ship components, which help present the visual experience to the viewer.

After reading the script, consider what changes were made from the design document before reading the analysis.

SCENE	NARRATION
ATTRACT ROUTINE	(Note: The following text banners are repeated throughout the attract routine:)
When no one is using the program, an attract routine will invite visitors to come explore the program.	1. "The Nauticus Shipbuilding Company" 2. "Urgent: Naval Architect Needed" 3. "Touch the Screen to Begin"
Attract Routine steps 1. Flyover of shipyard in 3-D.	
2. Cut to rotation of planing hull.	"The Nauticus Shipbuilding Company—the most highly advanced shipbuilding facility in the world." "Touch the Screen to Begin"
3. Cut to assembly area with planing hull rolling in.	"Urgent: Naval Architect Needed." "Touch the Screen to Begin"
4. Cut to launch area, showing ship launch.	

INTRODUCTION

Immediately upon touching the
screen in the attract routine.
Flyover of shipyard in 3-D.

Background sound of helicopter rotors.

Cut to helicopter descending
and landing on heliport.

"Welcome to the Nauticus Shipbuilding
Company. Thanks for being our visiting naval
architect on such short notice. The Nauticus
Shipbuilding Company is the most highly
advanced shipbuilding facility in the world.
We can custom-build many different types of
ships. Each ship we build is unique and is
designed to efficiently meet our client's
nautical mission requirements."
"Let's go to our Design Center to see what
ships are on order."

Cut to POV [point-of-view]
animation leaving the heliport,
past office building to Design
Center.

Loudspeaker VO: "Naval architect on
premises. Ready production facilities."

DESIGN CENTER

Doors of Design Center open,
wipe to view of the briefing
room.

"We currently have a backlog of orders for
3 ships":
1. "a trans-Atlantic container ship which
   will sail out of Norfolk."
2. "a ferry that will transport passengers
   and cars between England and France."
3. "an oceanographic research vessel that
   will operate off the coast of New
   England."
"Touch an order to learn more about its
mission and design requirements."

TRANS-ATLANTIC CONTAINER SHIP:

Map animating the route between
Norfolk and several European
ports.

"A large shipping company has asked us to
design and build a ship which can safely
and economically transport large amounts of
cargo between their home port, right here
in Norfolk, Virginia, and several European
ports. The ship:
— must be able to withstand the rough seas
  of the Atlantic

	— have a very large cargo hold with container-handling facilities
	— be moderately fast
	— have a long cruising range."
Dynamically build mission checklist.	Container Ship Checklist
	1. Ability to withstand rough seas of Atlantic
	2. Large cargo hold with container-handling facilities
	3. Moderately fast
	4. Long cruising range
Visitor is prompted to build the ship or review another mission.	"Press the flashing panel to build a ship for this mission or select another order."

PASSENGER AND CAR FERRY:

Map animating the route between Dover and Calais	"An English ferry operator has asked us to design and build a ship which can quickly cross the English Channel between Dover, England, and Calais, France. The ideal design:
	— will be very fast, have a cargo capacity for 200 passengers and 50 cars
	— be easy to load
	— be able to navigate shallow, crowded harbors."
Dynamically build mission checklist.	Ferry Requirements:
	1. Very fast
	2. Cargo capacity for 200 passengers and 50 cars
	3. Easy to load
	4. Able to navigate shallow, crowded harbors
Visitor is prompted to build the ship or review another mission.	"Press the flashing panel to build a ship for this mission or select another order."

OCEANOGRAPHIC RESEARCH VESSEL:

Show map animating area of research.	"A marine research institute requires a new flagship for its exploration of the

ocean floor. The ship should:
— be a safe platform for working with complex equipment
— be able to withstand rough seas
— have good performance at all speeds
— have accommodations for extended research work at sea

Dynamically build mission checklist.

Research Ship Requirements:
1. Safe platform for working with complex equipment
2. Able to withstand rough seas
3. Good performance at all speeds
4. Accommodations for extended research work at sea

Visitor is prompted to build the ship or review another mission.

"Press the flashing panel to build a ship for this mission, or select another order."

ORDER SELECTED

After selecting an order to build, scene cuts to POV animation leaving the Design Center, past building to hull subassembly area.

"You'll need to make 3 major design decisions to build the ship, all affecting the ship's performance and ability to carry out its mission. You must choose:
— a hull shape
— a propulsion system, and
— a superstructure."

CHOOSE A HULL SHAPE

Hull subassembly area, 4 compartments are shown.

Loudspeaker VO: "Hull type being selected."

After a compartment is selected, 3-D hull appears above the subassembly area and rotates around 360 degrees in y-axis, then 360 degrees in x-axis. As hull is rotated, text describing characteristics appears on data screen.

"Touch a number to learn about a hull."

After learning about the characteristics for a particular hull, the visitor is prompted to use this hull or examine one of the others.

After selecting a hull to use, cut to Design Assembly screen, animation of hull rollout.

Cut to POV animation moving to propulsion subassembly area.

PICK A PROPULSION SYSTEM
Propulsion subassembly area, 4 compartments are shown.

After a compartment is selected, 3-D propulsion system appears above the subassembly area and rotates around

"Use this hull or press another number."

Air Cushion:
— flat hull rides on cushion of air
— capable of high speeds
— needs flat water conditions
— flat, rectangular deck easy to load

Planing Hull:
— V-shaped hull capable of high speeds
— performs best in flat water conditions
— high stress levels on hull

Displacement Hull:
— deep, rounded hull very stable in all conditions
— very large cargo capacity
— stable platform for large propulsion systems
— needs very large propulsion system

SWATH (Small Waterplane Area Twin Hull)
— 2 submerged hulls very stable
— flat deck provides good work area

Loudspeaker VO: "Planing hull being moved into position."

Background sound of motors whirring and machinery clanging.
"Next, you'll need to choose a propulsion system.

Loudspeaker VO:
"Propulsion system being selected."
"Touch a number to learn about a propulsion system."

360 degrees in y-axis. As
propulsion system is rotated,
text describing characteristics
appears on data screen.

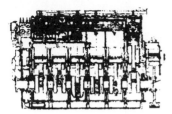

Diesel
— best performance at lower speeds
— fuel efficient
— infrequent maintenance

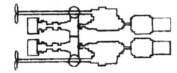

CODAG (Combination Diesel and Gas)
— good performance at all speeds
— improves maneuverability
— frequent maintenance

Water Jet
— low to moderate power
— high speed for right hull
— few underwater projections

Air Prop
— low to moderate power
— high speed for right hull
— no underwater projections
— affected by bad wind conditions

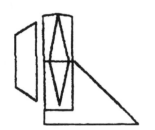

After learning about the
characteristics for a
particular propulsion system,
the visitor is prompted to use
this propulsion system or
examine one of the others.

"Use this propulsion system or press another
number."

After selecting a propulsion
system to use, cut to Design
Assembly screen, animation of
propulsion system being dropped
into selected hull.

Loudspeaker VO: "Air Prop propulsion system
being moved into position."

Cut to POV animation moving to
superstructure subassembly
area.

Background sound of motors whirring and
machinery clanging. "Next, you'll need to
choose a superstructure."

CHOOSE A SUPERSTRUCTURE

Superstructure subassembly area,
4 compartments are shown.

Loudspeaker VO:
"Superstructure being selected."
"Touch a number to learn about a
superstructure."

After a compartment is selected,
a 3-D superstructure appears above
the subassembly area and rotates
around 360 degrees in y-axis. As
superstructure is rotated, text
describing characteristics appears
on data screen.

After learning about the
characteristics for a particular
superstructure, the visitor is
prompted to use this superstructure
or examine one of the others.

"Use this superstructure or press another
number."

After selecting a superstructure to
use, cut to Design Assembly screen,
animation of superstructure being
lowered onto selected hull.

Loudspeaker VO: "Multiple Deck
superstructure being moved into position."

Bridge with Cranes
— shipboard crane system for container
  handling
— high bridge provides good visibility

Multiple Deck
— forward bridge provides excellent
  visibility
— sleek structure reduces wind drag

Full-Beam Bridge
— very high bridge house provides
  excellent visibility
— work spaces and accommodations close
  together

Complex Amidships
— compact and integrated work area
— good deck space fore and aft

DESIGN ANALYSIS

Animation of completed designs rotating 360 degrees in y-axis.

"Completed design ready for inspection and evaluation."
1 of 3 possible completed design outcomes:
"Very good! You have chosen an optimal design!"
"You have chosen a functional design."
"You have chosen a nonfunctional design."

Animation of hull choice rotationg 360 degrees in y-axis.

1 of 3 possible hull outcomes:
"Hull Choice: Optimal"
"Hull Choce: Functional"
"Hull Choice: Nonfunctional"
Followed by mission-specific feedback for chosen component (see Feedback below).

Animation of propulsion system choice rotation 360 degrees in y-axis.

1 of 3 possible propulsion system outcomes:
"Propulsion System Choice: Optimal"
"Propulsion System Choice: Functional"
"Propulsion System Choice: Nonfunctional"
This is followed by mission-specific feedback for chosen component (see Feedback below).

Animation of superstructure choice rotating 360 degrees in y-axis.

1 of 3 possile superstructure outcomes:
"Superstructure Choice: Optimal"
"Superstructure Choice: Functional"
"Superstructure Choice: Nonfunctional"
Followed by mission-specific feedback for chosen component (see Feedback below).

User is prompted to touch graphic of champagne bottle.
After button press or 5 seconds, animation of completed design being launched.

"Press the champagne bottle to launch your ship."
"Ship being launched."

If design was optimal, user is prompted to touch graphic of certificate to receive his/her printout of Optimal Design Certificate.

"Press the button to print your Optimal Design Certificate!"

DESIGN ANALYSIS FEEDBACK

Selected Mission:
Trans-Atlantic Container Ship

Hulls:

Air Cusion

"Hull Choice: Nonfunctional
— Can't withstand rough seas of Atlantic
— Can't support heavy bridge and crane
  system
— Cargo capacity too small"

Planning

"Hull Choice: Nonfunctional
— Can't support heavy bridge and crane
  system
— Cargo capacity too small"

Displacement

"Hull Choice: Optimal
— Very stable in rough seas
— Very large cargo capacity"

SWATH

"Hull Choice: Nonfunctional
— Cargo capacity too small"

Propulsion System:

Diesel

"Propulsion System Choice: Optimal
— Fuel efficient
— Performs well at low to moderate speeds"

Air Prop

"Propulsion System Choice: Nonfunctional
— Not powerful enough
— Needs flat water conditions"

Water Jet

"Propulsion System Choice: Nonfunctional
— Not powerful enough
— Needs flat water conditions"

CODAG

"Propulsion System Choice: Functional
— Performs well at many speeds
— High maintenance
— Gas turbine features not necessary"

Superstructure:

Bridge with Cranes

"Superstructure Choice: Optimal
— Cranes allow easy handling of containers
— High bridge provides excellent
  visibility"

Multiple Deck	"Superstructure Choice: Nonfunctional — No way to handle containers"
Complex Amidships	"Superstructure Choice: Nonfunctional — No way to handle containers"

Selected Mission
Cross-Channel Ferry

Hulls:

Air Cushion	"Hull Choice: Optimal — Capable of high speeds — Shallow draft allows easy access to harbors — Rectangular deck perfect for loading cars"
SWATH	"Hull Choice: Nonfunctional — Requires large propulsion system for speed — Deck shape makes car loading difficult"
Displacement	"Hull Choice: Nonfunctional — Requires very large propulsion system for speed — Deep draft limits access to harbors"
Planing	"Hull Choice: Nonfunctional — Requires very large propulsion system for speed"

Propulsion System:

Diesel	"Propulsion System Choice: Nonfunctional — Performs best at lower speeds — Hull projections increase draft"
Air Prop	"Propulsion System Choice: Functional — Needs large power plant — Affected by bad wind conditions"
Water Jet	"Propulsion System Choice: Optimal — Good for high speeds — No hull projections keep draft shallow"
CODAG	"Propulsion System Choice: Nonfunctional — Hull projections increase draft — Diesel features not necessary"

Superstructure:

Bridge with Cranes

"Superstructure Choice: Nonfunctional
— Cranes not necessary for cars and
  passengers
— Reduces deck space for cars"

Multiple Deck

"Superstructure Choice: Optimal
— Multiple levels perfect for cars and
  passengers
— Forward bridge good for high speeds"

Full-Beam Bridge

"Superstructure Choice: Nonfunctional
— Can't handle lots of passengers
  comfortably"

Complex Amidships

"Superstructure Choice: Nonfunctional
— Can't handle lots of passengers
— Reduces deck space for cars"

Selected Mission:

Oceanographic Research Vessel

Hulls:

Air Cushion

"Hull Choice: Nonfunctional
— Can't withstand rough seas"

Planing

"Hull Choice: Functional
— Capable of high speeds
— Not very stable in rough seas
— Limited work and living space"

Displacement

"Hull Choice: Functional
— Stable in rough seas
— Plenty of work and living space
— Deep draft limits access to shore
  areas"

SWATH

"Hull Choice: Optimal
— Very stable in rough seas
— Plenty of protected work and living
  space
— Shallower draft provides access to
  shore areas

Propulsion System:

Diesel   "Propulsion System Choice: Functional
                                        — Fuel efficient
                                        — Infrequent maintenance
                                        — Performs best at low speeds"

Air Prop   "Propulsion System Choice: Nonfunctional
                                        — Not powerful enough
                                        — Needs flat water conditions
                                        — Affected by bad wind conditions"

Water Jet   "Propulsion System Choice: Nonfunctional
                                        — Not powerful enough
                                        — Needs flat water conditions"

CODAG   "Propulsion System Choice: Optimal
                                        — Good performance at all speeds
                                        — Makes hull more maneuverable"

Superstructure:

Bridge with Cranes   "Superstructure Choice: Nonfunctional
                                        — Container handling system not necessary"

Multiple Deck   "Superstructure Choice: Nonfunctional
                                        — No work space on deck"

Full-Beam Bridge   "Superstructure Choice: Nonfunctional
                                        — Too big for appropriate hull
                                        — Too far aft"

Complex Amidships   "Superstructure Choice: Optimal
                                        — Good work space on deck
                                        — Well-integrated space for labs"

Script sample copyright Chedd-Angier Production Company.

Script and Design Document Treatment Compared

There were a number of substantial elements changed from the design document's creative treatment to the final script. These changes illustrate solid interactive writing principles.

Attract Routine Attract routines play when no one is using the kiosk. Clearly they are very important as bait to lure or attract the players. Without a strong attract routine, a kiosk program is ineffective because no one will play it.

Treatment: The attract routine in the treatment suggests showing one of the program's ships being built and the text: "Build a Ship to Accomplish a Mission."

Script: The script starts with a 3-D animation flyover of the shipyard and the text: "The Nauticus Shipbuilding Company—the most highly advanced shipbuilding facility in the world. Urgent: Naval Architect Needed."

The script changes give a much better introduction to the program by using the shipyard flyover, a standard cinematic establishing shot of the location. The location is extensive and impressive (see Figure 14-1). The script's text also helps build the simulation and the excitement of the program. We are now dealing with the most advanced shipbuilding company in the world. Players are also asked to assume the role of architect and become a part of The Nauticus Shipbuilding Company—and they are needed urgently!

Briefing Room Treatment: The treatment includes a video clip of a talking head of the shipyard president keyed over stock footage to explain the mission.

Script: The script eliminates the video talking head and the stock footage, replacing this material with more graphic elements, such as maps showing where the ship would travel.

There are several good reasons for this change. One is that the video talking head and documentary footage in a world of 3-D animation creates a conflict in style, one of the effects of which is to point out the artificiality of the animation. By eliminating this conflict, the program has stylistic consistency, and it is raised up one level of abstraction. The user can now more easily enter this fantasy world where he or she is the only real person.

The graphic elements, such as the maps, also ground the user visually in the mission, as opposed to being told about it by the talking head. Finally, the talking head video expanded the number of elements on screen, creating clutter and confusion for the viewer.

Missions Treatment: The treatment has five missions, ranging from North Sea Fire Fighter to Arctic Ice Breaker.

Script: The script has three missions: Transatlantic Container Ship, Cross-Channel Ferry, and Oceanographic Research Vessel.

The script reduces the number and changes the types of missions. Three factors motivated these changes:

1. The budget and running time of the program.
2. The particular missions that best presented a wide view of naval architecture.
3. The missions that best suited the game design. The ideal missions had to present shipbuilding problems where the answers weren't obvious but not impossible. The information had to allow clues that could be subtle.

Components Treatment: The treatment's ship components include hulls, hold, engine, and special equipment.

Script: The script's ship components include hulls, propulsion, and super-structure.

The special equipment was combined into the superstructure, and the hold was eliminated to reduce one variable in building the ship. It is important that the overall experience be as short as possible and still be effective. This has an impact on production cost and the time that the user would have to interact with the program.

Evaluation of Design The script increased the amount of evaluation of the ship design at the end of the program. The goal here was to encourage the user to go back and try the process again. This is ultimately a more successful learning approach than a one-shot deal where the user gets it right or wrong. The chance to try, fail, and redo something without penalty is an important learning feature of interactive multimedia.

Conclusion: Response to the Project

The response to *The Nauticus Shipbuilding Company* has been positive in both the museum and in classroom use. It makes strong use of the simulation model and hierarchical structure to accomplish its goals of teaching a subject to a general audience in an entertaining fashion.

References

Barney, Steven. Interview with the author, September 1995.

Case Study—Training: *Vital Signs*

15

Summary

Name of production: *Clinical Support Staff Interactive Certification Program: Vital Signs*

Writers: Instructional designer, John Cosner; writer, Fred Bauer

Developer: MediaViz Productions

Audience: Trainee medical assistants at a health maintenance organization

Medium: Interactive video disc

Presentation location: Place of employment

Subject: The process of taking medical vital signs: temperature, pulse, respiration, and blood pressure

Goals: Teach

Architecture: Linear, hierarchical branching, simulations

The script samples and images used in this chapter are copyright Harvard Community Health Plan.

Program Description and Background

Clinical Support Staff Interactive Certification Program: Vital Signs is a training program designed to teach trainee medical assistants at Harvard Community Health Plan (HCHP), a Boston-based health maintenance organization, how to take vital signs—temperature, pulse, respiration, blood pressure—and, for the OB/GYN assistants, urine analysis. Figure 15-1 shows the program's interface. The main image

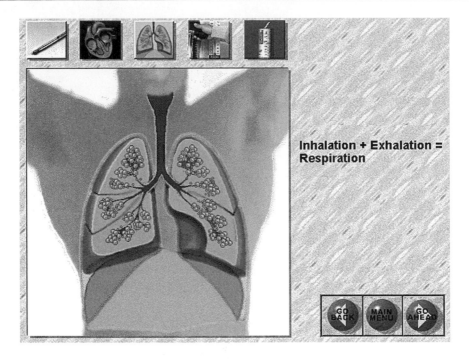

Figure 15-1 *The main interface for Vital Signs.*

area is in the center frame, text to the right, and buttons on top of the page that take the student to each section of the program: thermometer = temperature; heart = pulse; lungs = respiration; manometer = blood pressure; and dip stick = urine analysis.

Vital Signs presents a classic example of straightforward, effective, computer-based training. One of the ways it differs from the two previous case studies is that its goal is to teach a specific skill to a clearly defined audience. Properly learning this skill has life-and-death importance. Because of this, entertainment value is stressed far less than it is in the kiosk for the general public, *The Nauticus Shipbuilding Company*. *Vital Signs* is also different from the case study, *Interactive Math Lessons*, because the Math Lessons are offered on the Internet. *Vital Signs* is a disk-based program offered on individual computers.

Interactive Media Training Programs

Training programs are the bread and butter of many production companies. Training is a multibillion-dollar business, because in order to stay competitive, employers must constantly train and retrain employees. Training includes the traditional classroom, print material, and linear media, such as film and video. However, computer-based training and online training is becoming an increasingly popular part of this mix because it has been proven to be faster, cheaper, and more effective in many cases than other types of training.

Electronic Learning Terms Defined

Although the definitions of the various terms related to electronic learning keep evolving, it is probably worthwhile to make an attempt to define them.

- Computer Based Training usually refers to training delivered via a single computer or several nonnetworked computers.
- E-Learning is sometimes used to refer to any training or education delivered electronically or digitally, including web courses, video, CBT, interactive TV, and more. But generally, e-learning suggests computer mediated training that also includes a network or communications component, such as training delivered via the Internet, intranets, PDAs, and cell phones. We will use the second definition in this book.
- Online Learning generally refers to training or education delivered through computer networks, primarily the web, but it can also include intranets and other computer networks. Online learning is a subset of e-learning. This approach to delivery has become increasingly popular because of its cross-platform flexibility, ease of update, inexpensive distribution, and user familiarity with the web.

Types of E-Learning and Computer-Based Training Programs

Vital Signs was developed in traditional CBT (computer-based training) tutorial style: present the topic, test, and retest. This is a highly effective and common approach in CBT. Some CBT can, however, use more elaborate metaphors and simulations, such as creating a story or a game that the user plays to learn the material, or a discovery program where learners explore their environment.

Vital Signs is a disk-based, self-paced training program that teaches a specific topic to all students the same way. This means that students watch this program on their own at the speed that is appropriate to their learning style.

Some general characteristics of electronic training programs include:

- Live Versus Self Paced

  - Live Training. Scheduled sessions are presented by an instructor in real-time over the Internet, intranet, or some other means. The student can participate from his or her own computer if it is connected to the network. Unlike self-paced training, like *Vital Signs*, students must take the training at the same time and move at the same pace as the rest of the students just as they would in a classroom session. Live training often involves contact with the teacher via chat rooms, e-mail, or even telephone for questions and answers.

- o Self Paced. A self-paced training program can be viewed by the student when they want and at the speed that they want. There is not a live instructor in a self-paced program.

- Standardization or Customization/Personalization

  - o Standardization. In a standard program. Each student views exactly the same content. It does not change from student to student.

  - o Customization/Personalization. This type of training is focused more precisely to individual user's needs. With personalization this is accomplished by smart programs that adjust based on the user's learning pattern and/or by requiring more information about the user at the start of the program, either through registration or pretest. With customization the students themselves, as opposed to the program, can design how the content will be presented by making certain choices at different points in the program.

- Comprehensive Training or Just-in-Time Training

  - o Comprehensive Training. This type of training will present a comprehensive body of information on a relatively complex subject, such as presenting how to take vital signs.

  - o Just-in-Time Training. The formal name for JIT training is employee performance support system (EPSS). Instead of presenting entire programs, just-in-time (JIT) training presents small snippets of information when they are needed. With this approach, an employee with a question about a particular process can jump on the computer and get immediate help. This is similar to help programs in some applications.

- Traditional E-Learning Versus Rapid E-Learning

  - o Traditional E-Learning. This type of program deals with complex material and will take many weeks to produce and will involve a full production team.

  - o Rapid E-Learning. This approach is used for time sensitive, relatively simple, and often short shelf-life projects. For example, a new pricing structure may need to get quickly to salesmen. These programs are often done in-house using simple tools, such as PowerPoint, Breeze, or Captivate. There is usually no production team. Often one writer or developer will create the programs in as little as a few days. A writer who is interested in e-learning could strengthen his skill set by learning some of these rapid e-learning tools.

Based on the above definitions. *Vital Signs* is a self-paced, standardized, comprehensive, traditional, computer based training program.

Production Background

Why the Client Produced This Program in Multimedia

Vital Signs was commissioned by Harvard Community Health Plan, a New England-based staff model HMO. A staff model HMO has its own health centers staffed by its own medical personnel, who see only patients who belong to that HMO. Since the production of *Vital Signs*, Harvard Community Health Plan merged and has been renamed as Harvard Pilgrim Health Care, but because HCHP was the original producer of the program that name will be used in this chapter.

The *Vital Signs* training program was aimed toward HCHP medical assistants, who help the physicians and other clinicians by greeting patients, bringing them into the examining room, taking vital signs, and generally assisting with any other work that the physician needs to have done. In order to improve the training of the medical assistants, HCHP instituted an in-house certification program, of which the *Vital Signs* project is one component.

HCHP decided to teach these skills through interactive media for many of the same reasons that many companies choose multimedia for training:

- Students are dispersed. It was difficult to gather students together for a traditional group class, because they worked in many different departments all over the area, and they were usually hired only a few at a time. With a multimedia program, individual students could view the program as they needed it and did not have to wait for a group and a teacher.
- Students have varied backgrounds. The backgrounds of trainee medical assistants range from high school graduates to individuals with master's degrees. For some of the trainees, English was their second language. This wide mix of educational levels would make a traditional class nearly impossible to pace without either confusing the slow learners or boring the more advanced students. With multimedia, each student can learn at his or her own pace. Some can skip material; others may want to replay certain sections several times.
- Importance of keeping information consistent. Taking vital signs is an essential skill in all medical departments. It was important that all medical assistants perform this service in the same way and with the latest techniques. If all assistants watch the same multimedia program, this is ensured.
- Cutting training time. It was difficult to take a large group of medical assistants out of their jobs at any one time. It was much easier if they could come individually at slow times in their departments. In addition, for skills

such as these, independent studies have documented that students complete multimedia courses more than 30% faster than covering the same material in a traditional course. (Bank Technology News 25)

- Cutting expenses. Once the program is completed, major training costs are over until the program has to be updated. This is far cheaper than hiring teachers for every new group of students. Studies have documented that "multimedia cost an average of 64 percent less to develop, maintain, and deliver than traditional training" ("Multimedia Sights and Sounds," 25).

Program Development

This piece was developed by MediaViz productions, a production company specializing in the design and production of multimedia training programs for corporate clients. This project was designed by instructional designer John Cosner of MediaViz and written by Fred Bauer. Cosner also functioned as the project manager, along with HCHP's Comma Williams, who served as client contact and in-house project manager.

The development of this project followed a standard training model. The information in the program was based on several print training documents that HCHP had already produced. Using this material and additional research, the designer developed a design document. This document included a content outline, which laid out the structure of the course in standard hierarchical outline form. There was no flowchart for this project, although more complicated training programs commonly use flowcharts.

The design document was refined in several design meetings with the writer, the client, the instructional designer-project manager, and eventually the graphic artist. The writer developed several drafts of the treatment based on these meetings and, when the final treatment was approved, wrote several drafts of the script.

The Instructional Designer

The instructional designer is an important figure in multimedia training. According to John Cosner, the instructional designer on this project, there are different conceptions of what an instructional designer is. Many instructional designers have an advanced degree in instructional design and/or a teaching background. Other instructional designers have not been formally trained in the field.

On some projects, instructional designers do not write the script but instead deal with high-level instructional design, such as audience analysis, needs, and goals. In these cases, once the treatment and outline are taken care of, the project is handed over to the writer, with the instructional designer editing the material after it is completed. The role of the instructional designer depends on the attitude of the developer, the type of content, and the complexity of the project. Sometimes, there is no formal instructional designer, and the writer assumes the duties normally assigned to that position.

Goals and Challenges Writing and Developing *Vital Signs*

Challenges

The key challenges developing this project arose from the type of content, the time limitation on the program, and the nature of the students.

Content

The content involved teaching a specific process: taking vital signs. This process is an essential part of health care and the first thing the physician wants to know about the patient. This information had to be delivered precisely. A general or partial understanding of the topic would not be sufficient.

Time Limit

The client wanted the students to be able to complete this program in less than an hour. This was the amount of time that the stand-up class in the same subject took, so if the interactive program took longer, it would defeat the purpose of limiting the amount of time training takes from work. This time limit restricted the amount of material that could be placed into a program and meant that students wouldn't have time to learn the rules of an elaborate game or simulation. The program would have to be simple and clear.

Audience Issues

A number of issues affected the design of this project:

- Some students had English as a second language.
- For many of them, this was their first introduction to this kind of material.
- Most were not college graduates.
- There were three different types of students: internal medicine, pediatrics, and OB/GYN. After the introductory material, each student needed specialized information for his or her department. This meant a greater variety of information in the program, and a need to identify and track each individual student clearly.

Writer and Instructional Designer's Goals
Instructional Designer

Although the writer and the instructional designer shared many concerns, the instructional designer's primary focus was the overall content and design of the program. The instructional designer, John Cosner, had the following concerns on this project:

- **Content driven.** The serious nature of the content set the tone of this piece, and the process of taking vital signs set the sequencing of information.

The importance of a precise understanding of the information dictated that the same material be presented in a number of ways.

- **Clear navigation.** A primary goal for any training piece is to make the navigation clear and easy to use for the student. If the program feels complicated to a user, then it has failed. In a good training program, the students should be learning the material, not the program.
- **Humanize.** In a piece dealing with human interaction, such as this, it's a good idea to put a human face to most of the procedures. For example, the pediatrics section uses the same young girl through several scenes.

The Writer

The writer, Fred Bauer, had input into the overall design of the program. For example, he agreed with the instructional designer that clear navigation was a primary concern; students cannot learn if they are lost. His major concern, however, was with successfully realizing the overall design by achieving the following goals:

- **Pace.** A key to interactive multimedia is to pace the program in a way that keeps people involved. Users should not passively watch the screen for longer than 25 to 30 seconds before they are asked to interact with the program in some way. It's also important to vary the length and tempo of scenes and the length of time between actions required of the user.
- **Humor.** In education, humor can be effective in a number of ways: as a reward for a successful performance, as a memory aid, and as a way to help people relax. The opening of this piece is a good example. (See the humorous Introduction script sample later in this chapter.)
- **Emotion.** It is essential not only to present information but also to present feelings and to elicit an emotional response. In *Vital Signs*, it was important for the students to feel that, as medical assistants, they are a crucial part of the medical service provider team. Another goal was to make the students aware of the feelings that the patient has and to help the students look at the patient as a human being and not just part of the job. The pediatric section of this piece was particularly effective in achieving this.
- **Aligning program's voice with viewer.** The writer thought that users would feel more comfortable if he could match the program's voice with the users' emotions and expectations. The voice of a program is basically who seems to be talking to you through the program. A voice can be neutral, simply presenting the information without attempting direct contact with the viewer. A neutral voice is fine for an informational program, but in a training piece, it helps the user if the voice can be separated from the content and align itself with the user. For example, in this project, text on the screen frequently questions what was said in the dialogue or the narration.

Sometimes the screen text will even attempt to sympathize with a student's confusion if the student gets a question wrong. Actual tone of voice also helps here; the narrator should never talk down to or lecture the student.

- **Style of presentation.** A multimedia program is usually experienced as up close and personal. A student sits inches away from a screen and is connected via keyboard or other input device. It is also usually a one-on-one experience. Because of this, the writer said that multimedia programs should be more intimate. They should not be developed in the same style as a film or a TV program that will be viewed in a group from a much greater distance. Ways to increase this intimacy include adding more close-ups and using the screen as a window on the world rather than an artificial stage. With a window, characters' entrances and exits are framed in such a way that the users get a sense that there is a larger world beyond the borders of the screen. This is the same experience as looking out a of window of a house. Some critics call this "open form framing." Intimacy is also increased through the quality of the program's voice.

Meeting the Challenges and Achieving the Goals

Overall Design

As you read the descriptions and script samples that follow, be aware of the overall design. One of the strongest aspects of this piece is how the same information is introduced numerous times, but each time the information is presented, it is demonstrated in a more challenging manner. The program builds from simple linear demonstrations and definitions to highly interactive simulations and testing, as described in the following outline of the program.

There are also additional script samples included in the Chapter 15 area of the Chapters section of this book's CD-ROM.

1. Registration
2. Pretest
3. Humorous Introduction
4. Overview
5. Basic Terms
6. Detailed Instruction
7. Practice
8. Case Study Experience
9. Posttest

Registration, Pretest, and Humorous Introduction

Students register for the program with their employee number and department. This information helps to focus the material to their needs. For the purposes of demonstration, you, the reader, will register in the pediatric department. This means that after the general instruction, the program will link you to pediatric information.

After registration, students take a multiple-choice pretest on vital signs. The purpose of this test is to get them thinking about the subject. This test is not numerically graded. Instead the subjects are listed with a bright bulb or dim bulb next to the topic, depending on how well the students know that specific material. This feedback makes them aware of their strengths and weaknesses.

The pretest is followed by a humorous introduction in which users monitor the vital signs of Norman. (Light lines divide sections; heavy lines divide pages.)

Humorous Introduction Script Sample

Unit: *Vital Signs* Introduction (Video)
Lesson:
Topic:
Title:
Screen: I1.1
Type:
Graphic File:

(**GRAPHIC/VIDEO**: Photograph of a young man, mid-twenties, asleep. A panel opens in the upper right of the frame. It contains four running graph lines labeled: "Temperature," "Pulse," "Respiration," "Blood Pressure." All are moving, but quiescent. Temperature and pulse are steady, respirations peak with each inhalation, blood pressure shows almost no variation.) (NOTE: In general, 4 heartbeats per 1 respiration. Pulse is usually constant during sleep.)

Text:

NORMAL VITAL SIGNS: SLEEPING

If we wake Norman, will his vital signs ...
  Remain the same
  All show an increase
  Some remain the same, and some increase

AUDIO: NARRATOR (VO): (SOFTLY, SO AS NOT TO WAKEN NORMAN) Shhh—Norman is sleeping. His normal vital signs—temperature ... blood pressure ... pulse ... and respiration—are flowing along in that panel to the upper right. These values reflect body changes you can't always see just by looking at a patient. We take vital signs to spot early warnings, like high blood pressure—often, these warnings allow us to give preventative care. Norman's vital signs are normal for sleeping. What do you suppose will happen to them when we wake Norman up? Will his vital signs remain the same, all show an increase, or some remain the same and some increase? SELECT your choice, and we'll see.

Feedback: (AUDIO + Text) **NARRATOR (VO):**

Same = Close but not quite. Watch. All = A good guess, but not quite. Watch. Some = Very good. Watch. After all answers = (CALLING) Wake up, Norman! (SFX: snorts and grunts from Norman.)
Branching:
I1.2
Special Instructions:

Unit: *Vital Signs* Introduction (Video)
Lesson:
Topic:
Title:

Screen: I1.2
Type:
Graphic File:

(GRAPHIC/VIDEO: Photograph of young man sitting up in bed and yawning. Vital signs show waking norms.)

Text:

NORMAL VITAL SIGNS AWAKE

Button = "Breakfast, Norman!"

AUDIO: (SFX: Music assumes a more upbeat tempo.)

NARRATOR (VO): (IN REGULAR SPEAKING VOICE) In the morning, our temperature is at the lowest point of the day. Norman's waking pulse, respiration, and blood pressure are higher than when he's asleep. No surprises there. Well, time for breakfast. SELECT the breakfast button and we'll see what happens to Norman next.

Feedback:

Button = **NARRATOR (VO):** Breakfast, Norman! (SFX: clanging triangle, as in Western movies chuck wagon call.)

Branching:

Button = 11.3
Special Instructions:

In the next scenes in the script, which are not shown here, Norman's temperature rises as he drinks hot coffee. When Norman suddenly realizes he's late for work, his blood pressure goes up and his pulse increases. When he gets a flat tire, his vital signs go crazy.

Analysis of Humorous Introduction

The major function of this sequence is to introduce the topic in a light manner to initiate users' interest and get them relaxed and ready to learn. This sequence also gives students a chance to concentrate on learning how the program operates without having to learn complex course information. This makes program navigation clear to the students.

In the audio on the first page, the writer quickly sets up a friendly voice for the program and connects directly to the user. By creating the character Norman, whose vital signs the user monitors, the writer puts a human face on the information.

Under the feedback section on the same page, the user is asked to guess what will happen next, adding interactivity and greater audience involvement to what is essentially a linear sequence. The breakfast button on the next page works the same way and helps to maintain the pace.

Overview

After the humorous introduction, the piece turns more serious, outlining the importance of the topic and the objectives of the program. This is followed by a video overview showing an experienced medical assistant taking a patient's vital signs.

The overview puts a human face on the experience by creating characters for the patient and medical assistant. It also gives the students a general view of what they will be learning in a nonthreatening environment in which little is being asked of them in terms of answering questions and providing information. It is, however, more serious and fact-filled than the humorous introduction. This is part of the slow and careful buildup of the information presentation.

Basic Terms

After the overview, it is time for users to roll up their sleeves and start learning the nuts and bolts of taking vital signs. The lessons are first listed in the following interactive menu, which gives users an option of what to study first:

- Temperature
- Pulse
- Respiration
- Blood pressure

If the user clicks on "Blood Pressure," a series of screens that define this topic's basic concepts appear.

Basic Terms Script Sample

(GRAPHIC/VIDEO: Repeat animated diagram of heart showing flow of blood.)

Text: Blood Pressure Lesson (small heart symbol) (CALL OUTS)

Right Atrium   Left Atrium
Right Ventricle   Left Ventricle
  The pressure of blood—
    at height of wave from ventricles
    as heart relaxes between beats

AUDIO: NARRATOR (VO): While pulse and respiration are taken directly, blood pressure is measured indirectly using a device called a manometer. It is actually two values. Blood pressure is the measurement of the highest force of the blood on the walls of the blood vessels, at the height of the wave from the ventricles, and the lowest force of the blood on the walls of the blood vessels, as the heart relaxes between beats.

Feedback:

Branching:

u1.4.2

Special Instructions:

Unit: u1
Lesson: Blood Pressure
Topic:
Title:

Screen: u1.4.2
Type:
Graphic File:

GRAPHIC/VIDEO: (Animated diagram of artery with red dots flowing left to right, and vein, with blue dots flowing right to left.)

Text:

Blood Pressure Measurements:
Systolic and Diastolic
    Artery
     (Muscle)
    Vein
     (Valves)

AUDIO: NARRATOR (VO): Blood flows from the heart in arteries, which have muscles to help keep it moving. Blood returns to the heart through veins, which don't have muscles, but do contain valves that prevent blood from flowing backwards. Blood pressure consists of two measurements—systolic and diastolic. SELECT each to learn more. (When you've finished, SELECT "GO AHEAD" to continue.)

Feedback: (AUDIO + Text)
Highlight term when chosen.

Systolic = **NARRATOR (VO):** (ARTERY AND VEIN FREEZE AT HEIGHT
OF FLOW) Systolic values measure the pressure at the height
of the pulse wave.
Diastolic = **NARRATOR (VO):** (ARTERY AND VEIN FREEZE DURING PAUSE)
Diastolic readings measure the pressure during the relaxation
period between beats.

Branching:

u1.4.3

Special Instructions:

Analysis of Definition of Basic Terms
Because of the audience for this program, no scientific knowledge is assumed.
Basic terms are explained clearly and simply. The interactive animation on the
second page of the example is a good use of instructional multimedia.

Detailed Instruction
Once basic terms and processes are explained, the program moves to the next level
of complexity, which focuses on the medical assistant's specialty, such as pediatrics
or OB/GYN. For example, a user who registered from the Pediatric Department
would receive detailed instructions on how to take vital signs from a child.

Practice
Immediately following the detailed instruction is a highly interactive sequence in
which the user takes a little girl's blood pressure. It starts off with the challenge:
"Now it's your turn." Enough sitting around watching, it's time to do it.

Practice Script Sample

Unit: u1
Lesson: Blood Pressure
Topic:
Title:

Screen: u1.4.13p
Type:
Graphic File:

(GRAPHIC/VIDEO: Colette looking apprehensive)

Text:
Meet Colette, age 7.
You're going to take her blood pressure. You've explained
the procedure to her. What do you use next?

(CAPTIONS)
  Cuff   Ball Pump   Valve on Cuff   Doll

(AUDIO: NARRATOR VO): Now it's your turn. Meet Colette, age 7.
You're going to take her blood pressure. You've explained the
procedure. What do you use next—the cuff, the ball pump, the
valve on the cuff, or the doll? SELECT your choice now.

Feedback: (VO and text)

Cuff, Ball Pump, Valve = (SFX: Little Girl's Voice) **(VO audio
ONLY):** No. I don't want that. It's going to hurt! **NARRATOR (VO):**
Apparently, Colette didn't buy your explanation. Try again.
Doll = **NARRATOR (VO):** You're good. That's right. From the look
on her face, you can tell Colette didn't buy your explanation,
so you demonstrate on a doll. (SELECT "GO AHEAD" to continue.)

Branching:

u1.4.14p

Special Instructions:

Unit: u1
Lesson: Blood Pressure
Topic:
Title:

Screen: u1.4.14p
Type:
Graphic File:

(GRAPHIC/VIDEO: Animated graphic of manometer column at 110mm)

Text:
SELECT the valve, listen to the heart sounds, watch the mercury,
and read Colette's blood pressure. SELECT O.K. when you have it.
O.K.

AUDIO: (SFX: 7-year-old heart sounds.) **NARRATOR (VO):** SELECT the
valve, listen to the heart sounds, watch the mercury and read
Colette's blood pressure. SELECT O.K. when you've got it.

Feedback:

Branching:

ul.4.15p

Special Instructions:

Unit: ul
Lesson: Blood Pressure
Topic:
Title:

Screen: ul.4.15p
Type:
Graphic File:

(GRAPHIC/VIDEO: Animated graphic of manometer column at 110mm)

Text:
What is Colette's blood pressure?

94/68
92/66
92/68

(AUDIO: NARRATOR VO): What is Colette's blood pressure—94/68, 92/66, or 92/68? SELECT your answer now.

Feedback: (AUDIO + Text)

NARRATOR (VO):
94/68 = That's not right. Try again.
92/66 = That's not right. Try again.
92/68 = That's right (SELECT "GO AHEAD" to continue.)

Branching:

u1.4.14 (Orthostatic)

Special Instructions:

Analysis of Practice

This piece allows you as the student to practice what you've just learned by choosing the right approach to the child. It makes you aware of the feelings of the patient and helps you to see her as a human being and not just part of the job. It also lets you actually "take" her blood pressure with an ingenious, interactive animation. If you get the pressure wrong, you can try again.

Case Study Experience

The case studies present the information in yet another way. This time the student watches videos of a medical assistant taking the vital signs. The challenge is to catch the medical assistant's errors.

Case Studies Script Sample

Unit: u2
Lesson: Case History—Pediatric
Topic:
Title:

Screen: u2.4.1
Type:
Graphic File:

(GRAPHIC/VIDEO: CLOSE-UP SHOWS RUTH PROPERLY FEELING FOR PULSE AND FINDING IT. 1) DISSOLVE TO MEDIUM SHOT OF RUTH. SHE NOTES

HER WATCH, THEN LOOKS AWAY, CONCENTRATING ON THE HEARTBEAT.
2) DISSOLVE TO MEDIUM SHOT. SILENTLY, SHE BEGINS TO CONCENTRATE ON
THE RISE AND FALL OF COLETTE'S CHEST. 3) CAMERA CUTS TO
COLETTE'S CHEST. 4) DISSOLVE TO CLOSE-UP OF RUTH'S HAND AS SHE
WRITES PULSE AND RESPIRATION ON ENCOUNTER FORM. DISSOLVE TO SHOT
OF RUTH REACHING FOR MANOMETER CUFF.)

Text:

(AFTER RUTH FASTENS CUFF. ACTION FREEZE.)
Error

AUDIO: SFX: NORMAL, REGULAR CHILD'S HEARTBEAT OVER PULSE.
NORMAL, REGULAR CHILD'S BREATHING MATCHES RISE AND FALL OF
COLETTE'S CHEST. RUTH SPEAKS AS SHE TRIES TO WRAP TOO LARGE
A CUFF AROUND COLETTE'S ARM, FINALLY FASTENING IT LOOSE, AND
REACHING ALMOST TO THE CHILD'S ARMPIT.)
RUTH (ON CAMERA): I'm going to take your blood pressure now,
Colette. What's going to happen is, I'll put this cuff around
your arm, and pump it up. You'll feel a little squeezing, like
when your mommy gives you a big hug. Just nod if you're ready.
(COLETTE NODS "YES." RUTH PLACES CUFF ON ARM AND FASTENS.)

Feedback: [Selection before Ruth fastens cuff] **NARRATOR (VO):**
(Track 2) Sorry, no error yet but stay alert. (SELECT "GO AHEAD"
to continue.)
(Selection when Ruth fastens cuff) **NARRATOR (VO):** (Track 2) Good
work. You've helped Ruth become a better medical assistant.
(SELECT "GO AHEAD" to continue.) [MISS] **NARRATOR (VO):** (Track 2)
You missed an error. We've stopped the time so that you can step
in and help Ruth. If you think you know what that error is, you
can choose to continue. If you'd like to see it again, choose
replay.
Branching:
HIT, OR CONTINUE = u2.4.1q
REPLAY = u2.41
Special Instructions:

Unit: u2
Lesson: Case History—Pediatric
Topic:
Title:

Screen: u2.4.1q
Type:
Graphic File:

(GRAPHIC/VIDEO: FREEZE FRAME OF ERROR)

Text:

What error did you spot?
Using wrong size blood pressure cuff
Unprofessional attitude
Failure to tell patient she's counting respiration

AUDIO:

Feedback:
Unprofessional, or Failure = Not correct. Try again.
Using = That's right. What would you do to correct this error?

Note on Encounter form that cuff is wrong size.
Get proper size cuff.
Wait until it's time to remove thermometer, then get proper cuff.

Note, or wait = Not quite. Try again.
Get = That's right.

Branching: u2.4.2

Special Instructions:

Unit: u2
Lesson: Case History—Pediatric
Topic:
Title:

Screen: u2.4.2
Type:
Graphic File:

(GRAPHIC/VIDEO: HOLD FROZEN ACTION)

Text:

Using wrong size blood pressure cuff. Ruth has applied a cuff
that's too wide and too long. This will lower the patient's
blood pressure. SELECT "GO AHEAD" to help her get it right.

(AUDIO:)

_____

Feedback:

Branching: u2.5. 1
Special Instructions:

Unit: u2
Lesson: Case History—Pediatric
Topic:
Title:

Screen: u2.5.1
Type:
Graphic File:

GRAPHIC/VIDEO: REPEAT ACTION AS RUTH TRIES CUFF.

Text:

(WHEN RUTH PLACES CUFF ON ARM. FREEZE ACTION)
ERROR

(AUDIO: Just nod if you're ready. (COLETTE NODS "YES." RUTH
TRIES CUFF, REALIZES IT'S TOO BIG.) Colette, somebody must have
been taking the blood pressure of a giant—look how big this is.
I'm going to get a nice new cuff for you—one that fits. I'll be
right back. (DISSOLVE or WIPE TO RUTH RETURNING WITH PROPER CUFF,
PLACING IT ON COLETTE'S ARM.) That's better.

_____

Feedback:

[Selection before Ruth places cuff on arm] **NARRATOR**
(VO): (Track 2) Sorry, no error yet but stay alert.
(SELECT "GO AHEAD" to continue.)
[Selection when Ruth places cuff on arm] **NARRATOR (VO):**
(Track 2) Good work. You've helped Ruth become a better medical
assistant. (SELECT "GO AHEAD" to continue.)
[MISS] **NARRATOR (VO):** (Track 2) You missed an error. We've
stopped the time so that you can step in and help Ruth. If you
think you know what that error is, you can choose to continue.
If you'd like to see it again, choose replay.

Branching:

HIT, OR CONTINUE = u2.5.1q
REPLAY = u2.5.1

Analysis of Case Study

This section has a number of branching possibilities, which increases student involvement, but perhaps the best feature is that the students have the power to stop the disk and replay it. The chance to replay the material helps the students focus on the material and provides a sense of accomplishment when they finally find the error. Without the possibility of replaying the material, the students would simply miss the information and experience failure. This approach is mirrored in the feedback answers that suggest "try again" or "choose replay." This section of the program also continues the emotional quality of the previous segment by using the same little girl as a patient.

Posttest

The program ends with a multiple-choice posttest. This is the same test students took as a pretest, but the questions are rearranged. Like the pretest, the posttest is not numerically graded in order to reduce test anxiety and increase learning. Instead of grades, the subjects are again listed with a bright bulb or a dim bulb next to the topic, depending on how well the students knew that specific material. This device makes them aware of their strengths and weaknesses and gives them a chance to return to specific topics for additional study. The supervisors can, however, get a numerical grade for their workers if they want. Final certification of this skill, though, must occur in practice.

Conclusion: Response to the Project

Written and verbal responses from the medical assistants who have used it are very positive. They like going through it at their own pace. They like the privacy. Students who speak English as a second language enjoy the opportunity to replay difficult sections. Other students said that the interactive visualization helped them learn the material. Based on this initial response, the program has been made available in all of the HMO's facilities.

References

Bauer, Fred. Telephone interview with the author, November 1995.

Cosner, John. Telephone interviews with the author, November 1995.

Learning Circuits: ASTD's (American Society for Training and Development) Source for E-Learning. http://www.learningcircuits.org/

Macromedia Rapid E-Learning. http://www.macromedia.com/resources/elearning/?promoid=BINE

"Multimedia Sights and Sounds Bombard Banks." *Bank Technology News* 7 (February 1994).

Williams, Comma. Telephone interview with author, November 1995.

Key Points from Part II: How to Write Nonnarrative Informational Multimedia

Gathering Information

As in any other information-based project, the first thing to do when writing an informational multimedia program or web site is to gather as much information as possible on the subject and the audience. Study that information, and let your approach emerge from the material. If you are writing for a client, you also need to learn as much as you can about their expectations of the project.

Defining the Goal: Business Context, Data, and Users (Chapter 7)

Before you can start building an informational multimedia program or web site, you need to clearly define your users and your goal for the project. Because users are so well defined for most informational programs, it is essential to understand the users before coming up with a program's goal. One of the ways that interactive programs try to understand their users is in the writing of use cases. A use case is a way to capture the step-by-step information or action needs of a specific user of a software program or web site.

Defining the user is actually just one of the three main components of defining the project's goals. These elements are listed in the table below.

Components of Project Goal Definition		
Business Context	Data	Users
• Corporate Goals • Resources • Brand	• Document types • Formats	• Information needs • Research modes • Expertise • Technology • Culture & Language
Business Context + Data + Users = Project Goals		

Techniques to Achieve Common Informational Goals (Chapter 7)

Informational multimedia programs and web sites cover a wide range of information including general reference, info-tainment, education, interactive magazines and newspapers, sales and marketing, training, public relations, customer support, and much more. The good news for the writer trying to grasp the techniques used to create this wide array of informational programming is that most of these productions have one or more of the following general goals, each of which have their own techniques for execution:

1. To persuade
2. To entertain
3. To enable transactions
4. To create a sense of community
5. To inform
6. To teach

Discovering an Approach

If it suits your goals and your type of information, attempt to find an approach that goes beyond click-and-read to utilize the full power of multimedia to engage the audience. (See Chapter 8.)

Content Web Site (Chapter 11)

If your product or service is information-intensive and the information needs to be constantly updated, consider going online, such as the T. Rowe Price web site, which offers daily updates on stock information and other financial news.

Attempt to present your information dynamically, allowing the user to customize the presentation of information. For example, instead of offering a general list of stocks, the T. Rowe Price site allows users to customize the information they receive by choosing the degree of investment risks and the number of years that they want to invest.

Web Site Feature Story (Chapter 12)

If you want to discuss a specific topic in depth and reach a large audience, consider a multimedia feature story on the web. This is the approach that the *Harlem Renaissance* web site took to present material about black history. Instead of a broad overview this site presented a large topic, black history, by telling a detailed story about a key event in that history, the Harlem Renaissance.

E-Learning (Chapter 13)

If your subject can be broken into repeatable modules and potential users are spread over a wide area and have ready access to the Internet, you might consider creating an online tutorial, such as the *Interactive Math and Statistics Lessons* in Chapter 13. You might consider a module structure similar to the one used for this program:

- Prepare for the Tutorial
- Study the Concept
- Try an Example
- Explore the Concept
- View a Video Example
- Practice Exercises
- Apply the Concepts to Real Life
- Mastery Test

Simulation (Chapter 14)

If your information is focused on a process, consider a simulation, such as *The Nauticus Shipbuilding Company*. In a simulation, you first assign a role and a task to the user, such as a naval architect building ships. You then define all the elements of the task and describe the attributes and behaviors of each element. For example, the elements of the shipbuilding process include choosing hulls, propulsion systems, and superstructures. An attribute of an air cushion hull is that it is has shallow draft; a behavior is that it will sink in rough seas. Once the attributes and behaviors are defined, the user can perform the simulated task and receive realistic feedback.

Database

If your information is on a broad, loosely related subject, the key concern is organizing information into discreet units or categories and making this information accessible to the user. One way to do this is to organize the information around a concept map, such as the journey through time in the educational multimedia program *Sky High*. Another way is to use a guide or agent to lead the user through the material. It also helps the user's comprehension to present information with a variety of media (video, text, graphics, audio) and in a variety of ways, such as games, quizzes, and explorable spaces.

See Sky High on this book's CD-ROM in the Chapters Section.

Training (Chapter 15)

If the information is narrowly focused and is on a subject the audience needs to learn precisely, consider a training model, such as that demonstrated in *Vital Signs*. A classic approach to training is to present the material in a variety of ways, starting at the simple and moving to the complex. This is the structure of *Vital Signs*. Its sequences are: (1) Registration, (2) Pretest, (3) Humorous Introduction, (4) Overview, (5) Basic Terms, (6) Detailed Instruction, (7) Practice, (8) Case Study Experience, and (9) Posttest. You also need to present information in a variety of ways to accommodate each user's learning pattern.

It might serve students well to make the multimedia education process resemble the interpersonal education process by giving your program characteristics, such as immediacy of response, nonsequential access of information, adaptability, feedback, options, and interruptibility (Chapter 7).

Online Advertising

If the primary purpose is to present information to customers and get them interested in your product, consider online advertising. In this case be aware of the standard structure of the banner and the web site. Try to use the many advantages of online advertising to present your information in the best way possible. These advantages include measurability, rotation, direct contact with customers, interactivity, reduced cost, and unlimited space.

See "Online Advertising" on this book's CD-ROM in the Chapters Section.

Architecture (Chapter 8)

Once your basic approach is determined, then you need to decide what type of structure and navigation will work best for your material. Several different types of structure and navigation are often combined in one piece. Some possible structures and navigation include linear, linear with scene branching, hierarchical branching, multipath navigation, single-level linking, worlds structure, and simulation.

Writing the Program (Chapters 10 and 14)

The writing formats for information programs vary, but a fairly standard approach for multimedia programs is demonstrated in *The Nauticus Shipbuilding Company* (Chapter 14). After an initial proposal is approved, writers produce a design document. This document often includes the design objective, creative treatment, project schedule, and a navigation/program flowchart. The final stage is usually a complete script, which includes all the dialogue, narration, and descriptions of the images and actions. There are a number of script format options (see Chapter 5), depending on the type of project and degree of interactivity.

Writing a web site can require many different types of writing, such as writing proposals, outlines, flowcharts, on-screen text, and site maintenance manuals. The web writer may also have to write the site in such a way that it will show up well in search engines and directories. This includes writing page titles, page text, meta tags, and alt tags. (See Chapter 10.)

Mechanics of Writing (Part I)

There are many organizational devices that help in the planning of informational presentation, such as flowcharting and card sorting (see Chapter 3). You also have to keep in mind the basic techniques of the print, radio, and script writer, such as keeping sentences short, using the active voice, and writing visually (see Chapter 2).

Writing Interactive Narrative

Figure III-1 *The psychedelic introduction for the Magic Circles Challenge in the computer game* Amped 3. *Copyright Indie Built, Inc.*

Interactive Multimedia Narrative and Linear Narrative

Portions of this chapter originally appeared in the *Journal of Film and Video*.

Chapter Overview

A narrative is what we commonly refer to as a story. An interactive, multimedia narrative allows the user to explore several variations of a story or stories. Interactive narratives are produced for game consoles, PCs, mobile devices, the web and interactive TV. Interactive narratives share many elements with linear film and video narrative. Because of this, it is useful to understand the basic elements of linear narrative before exploring the intricacies of interactive narrative.

Narrative and Interactive Narrative Defined

A narrative is what we commonly refer to as a story. A "story" is one of those terms that we intuitively understand but are hard pressed to define. Critics have written many books defining narrative, but for our purposes we will define a narrative as a series of events that are linked together in a number of ways, including cause and effect, time, and place. Something that happens in the first event causes the action in the second event, and so on, usually moving forward in time.

Narrative interactive multimedia involves telling a story using all the multimedia elements we've discussed in previous chapters, including the use of many media and interactivity. In narrative multimedia, the player explores or discovers a story in the same way the user explored information in the programs discussed in the previous part of the book. Often the player is one of the characters in the story and sees action from that character's point of view. But even if he or she is not a character, the player still has some control over what the characters will do and how the story will turn out. Interactive narratives can be used for pure entertainment or to present information in an experiential way (see Chapter 24).

Interactive Narratives Versus Simulations and Worlds

A narrative or story is an ancient form of communication, but multimedia can also utilize newer forms that are sometimes confused with narrative. These new forms are simulations and worlds structures. As game and web designer David Riordan points out, an interactive narrative, a simulation, and a worlds structure are three distinct forms.

In a virtual world program, the player explores an environment. Examples include the classic *Myst* and the more recent online multiplayer games, such as *World of Warcraft*. The designers of a virtual world create a physical space, such as a mysterious island or an entire war-ravaged mythical world, where the player has the freedom to move about and interact with various elements, opening doors, examining objects, talking to other characters, and even completing noble quests against mighty enemies and monsters. Worlds programs are not narratives, even though some of the characters and locations may have background information presented about them.

In a simulation, such as *The Nauticus Shipbuilding Company* (Chapter 14) or *Amped 3* (Chapter 21) a player explores all the different possibilities in an activity, such as building a ship or going snowboarding. Simulations are not narratives. Even if they have a script attached to them, if the elements in the program come up in a random pattern, they do not comprise a narrative.

In an interactive narrative, a player explores a story. Interactive narratives have beginnings, middles, and ends, even though each user may experience these elements differently. There is nothing unplanned in an interactive narrative. Someone who plays the program long enough will eventually see all the material the writer created. An interactive narrative essentially allows each player to discover the story in a different way. The *Nancy Drew* mystery games (Chapter 20) are excellent examples of interactive narratives.

Simulations, worlds, and narratives can, of course, be combined and that is the most common way they are currently presented. *Dust: A Tale of the Wired West*, profiled in Chapter 23, integrates a narrative into the virtual world of a desert town in the old West. *Just Cause* takes the same worlds approach by making the player a secret agent whose goal is to overthrow the government of the island of San Esperito. The island is a fully developed world that the player can explore and interact with. *Amped 3* takes a different approach and combines simulations and narrative by adding story segment to the snowboarding simulation. Although the original *Sims* game was closer to a pure simulation of building a house and creating a family, *Sims 2* creates a more elaborate world for the characters to inhabit and becomes a combination of a simulation and a worlds structure. Many shooter games such as *Shadow of the Colossus* will also add a little story to help set up the action. In the beginning of this game, you are told that the only way you can save your true love is to hunt down and destroy sixteen colossal beasts. Once the setup is in place, the vast majority of the rest of the game is shooting the monsters. All these combinations are valid entertainment, but in this book our focus will be on games where the narrative is the primary or at least major component.

Computer Games and Video Games: Defining Terms

One of the indications of the young age of the interactive media industry is that even some of the most common terms are not clearly defined. For example, some writers use the phrase "computer game" to mean any game played with a computer involved. This would include all consoles (PlayStation, Xbox, etc.), PC computers, mobile devices, interactive TV, and arcade games. Clearly the web site "Computer Games Online" uses the phrase this way, because their content deals with all types of games. Other writers, however, think "computer game" just refers to games played on PC computers and not consoles.

The phrase "video game" has similar conflicting definitions. Some writers think of a video game as any kind of game using a video display. This would include all consoles (PlayStation, Xbox, etc.), PC computers, mobile devices, interactive TV, and arcade games. Electronic Arts, one of the biggest publishers of electronic games, is using the phrase this way when they title their site, "EA—Action, Fantasy, Sports, and Strategy Videogames." However, other writers think of "video game" as just applying to console games that are played on the TV and do not include games played on personal computers or a mobile devices.

There is even a third phrase, "electronic games," that also applies to all types of video and computer games. But this term is being used less than the other two terms so will not be used in this book.

In this book, I will use "computer games" and "video games" synonymously to mean all types of electronic, computer powered games, including those played on consoles (PlayStation, Xbox, etc.), PC computers, mobile devices (phones, PSP, Game Boy, etc.), interactive TV, and arcades games. I think this makes good sense because many games can be played both on a console and on a PC. Having two different names for the same game makes no sense. If I wish to distinguish that a game is played on a personal computer, I will call it a "PC game." If I want to point out a console game specifically, I will use "video game console" or just "console." For games on mobile devices, such as phones, PDAs, PSP, etc., I will use "mobile game." Just keep in mind that this is the usage in this book, but the final definitions of all these terms are still in flux and may be slightly different elsewhere. So be sure you know how the terms are being defined in a specific context.

Interactive Multimedia Narratives

Interactive Multimedia Narratives Genres

Although, there have been some interesting interactive narrative experiments both online and with interactive TV (*CSI* Interactive, *Homicide: Second Shift*, etc.), currently the most sophisticated commercial interactive multimedia narratives are found in video games. But a distinction needs to be made between games that simply have story elements and those that have fully fleshed out narratives. Marc Laidlaw, the writer of the action-adventure games *Half-Life* and *Half-Life 2*, explains it this way:

> If we distinguish stories from storytelling, I'd say that lots of games have stories, but not many games do a good job of storytelling. A story can be very simple, summed up in a screen or even a single line of text. You read it, forget it, and wade into the game. But storytelling is the deliberate crafting of a narrative, with attention to rhythm and pacing, revelation and detail.

The major types of games that include story elements are action games, role-playing games, and adventure games, with adventure games being the only genre primarily devoted to storytelling. The main focus of action games, such as the *Doom*, *Quake*, and *Halo* franchises, is speed and action that usually takes the form of shooting other characters or blowing things up. These games are also sometimes called shooters or FPS (first person shooters). Role playing games (RPG), such as the *Baldur's Gate* franchise, involve a character taking on a role and exploring a world, usually as part of a mini quest with limited story interaction and development of other characters. A subgenre of this game is the Massively Multiplayer Online Role Playing Game (MMORPG), such as *World of Warcraft*, that can involve hundreds of thousands of people at one time via the web.

As Aaron Conners, the writer of the games *Amped 3* and *The Pandora Directive* explains, in an adventure game, telling the story is the primary focus. There are strong characters and sophisticated story development. Characters overcome obstacles to achieve a final quest. Puzzles are also an important element. *Nancy Drew: Secret of the Old Clock* (Chapter 20), *The Pandora Directive* (Chapter 22), and *Dust: A Tale of the Wired West* (Chapter 23) are all adventure games, with *Nancy Drew* being in the mystery subgenre. The appeal of the mystery and adventure story is clearly that they are strongly goal-oriented. The player has something to aim for, obstacles are easy to establish, and jeopardy is built into the genre.

The Current State of Interactive Narrative and Computer Games

After a golden age of story-based adventure games in the mid-1990s, adventure games fell on hard times. Some interactive narrative adventures were poorly done and perhaps deserved to fail. But a number of adventure games with sophisticated stories, such as *Grim Fandango*, were released to rave reviews and critical acclaim and still did very little business. Because of this, many game publishers turned their backs on interactive narrative to focus on action games. Fortunately for lovers of interactive narrative, one of these action games, *Half-Life*, became a smash hit by including more story elements than a typical action game. Although the *Half-Life* story is fairly linear and the game is more action game than interactive narrative, it did show that there was still a hunger for stories in the audience. *Half-Life*'s success made popular the hybrid genre action-adventure—a game that has extensive action elements and a story. Most action-adventure games of this period did not have the sophisticated stories of the classic adventure games of the mid-90s, but they at least pointed the direction for the creation of commercially successful interactive narratives.

The major elements of this new direction for interactive narrative were the combining of different game genres and including more mature content and story elements. But other factors in the industry have also helped strengthen the resurgence of interactive narrative. A key factor is the introduction of the latest generation of game consoles that are capable of presenting content in a more cinematic and realistic fashion. This new capability has helped improve the success of Hollywood and game tie-ins and increased the convergence of narrative film/TV and the game industry. Another factor in more successful interactive narratives, particularly those tied to specific movie properties has been the involvement in games of major film narrative talents, such as Peter Jackson and Steven Spielberg.

All of these factors have produced a new wave of computer games with extensive stories. Although many of the stories appearing in the current crop of games are fairly linear and allow limited interactivity for the user, there is at least a definite interest in including story in games and a growing willingness to experiment with narrative. A few examples from various game genres follow. *The Chronicles of Narnia*, *Pirates of the Caribbean*, and *The Godfather* are all tie-ins to successful movie stories. The controversial *Grand Theft Auto* franchise combines an elaborate urban world the user can explore with mature themes, violent action, and a narrative. (This author is not endorsing the violent content of the *GTA* games.) *Half-Life 2* and later games in that series followed the direction set by *Half-Life* but with a more complex world and story. *Phoenix Wright: Ace Attorney* successfully brought the point and click adventure game to mobile devices with great writing and humor. *Amped 3* (Chapter 21) integrated story into a snowboarding sports sim. The *Nancy Drew* mysteries (Chapter 20) are based on the successful books of the same name and are aimed at a female audience. *Indigo Prophecy* (also known as *Fahrenheit*) has true multipath scenarios where the story changes depending on user choices.

Matthew Costello, the author of *The 7th Guest*, one of the most successful story-based games ever, agrees that there has been a renewed interest in adding story to games. According to Costello, game companies have realized that story, characters, and dialogue are important components. They are hiring more writers with a grasp of narrative, and they are starting early with the story script, instead of just adding story elements to a game after the fact. His own writing talents have been much in demand with contributions to *Just Cause*, *Pirates of the Caribbean*, *Shellshock*, *Doomed 3*, and *The Italian Job*.

With the game industry in general looking healthy because of long-term growth in console and mobile games, the outlook for the production of more games with story elements and complete interactive narratives looks strong. There is even some hope that weaker areas of the industry will strengthen. PC gaming has been the one game area in decline, but Microsoft's latest operating system is being billed by the company as the most game-friendly operating system ever. Microsoft has also vowed to put its muscle behind the creation of more PC game titles. And there is even hope that the perennial dark horse, interactive TV, will reach its potential. Digital cable, video on demand, and interactive television (ITV) services are now available at some of the largest cable providers. Now we just need ITV programming to match the technological advances.

Larger game budgets; more powerful consoles capable of a realistic, cinematic presentation; Hollywood convergence and story talent; blended game genres; a willingness to experiment with narrative in games; and broadband speeds on mobile devices and the web, allowing presentation of video and animation all point to a promising future for the interactive narrative.

Classical Linear Narrative Elements Defined

Although there are many different types of narrative, such as realist and modernist, successful interactive narratives have largely focused on classical narrative, the same type of narrative that dominates linear film and video. Because of this, interactive narrative shares many of the elements of narrative film and video. As these are forms that most readers are already familiar with, I will first review the basics of classical linear narrative in film and TV before diving into the intricacies of interactive narrative.

Character
Classical linear narrative film and video are character driven. It is the character who grabs our attention and whose situation we are drawn into. Most successful film and video today clearly define their characters early in the piece. Who are the characters? Where are they from? What do they want or need, and why do they want it? What the character wants usually provides the action story of the film or

video; why they want it provides the motivation for the actions and the underlying emotional story.

As an example, the modern classic film trilogy *The Lord of the Rings* establishes the lead character Frodo as a sincere, loyal, innocent, and cheerful nephew of his more adventurous Uncle Bilbo. We learn all this information about Frodo through the simple clothes he wears, his interaction with friends, his own actions and statements, and the setting. The first time we see him, he is reading a book under a tree in a peaceful orchard. When he first hears of the power of the One Ring, he immediately wants to give it away to Gandalf. A little later he tells his adventurous uncle, "I'm not like you." But when it seems that no one else is suited to be ring bearer, Frodo does reluctantly take on the role. What Frodo wants in the film (his action need) is to destroy the One Ring, forged by the Dark Lord. Why Frodo wants to do this is to save the Shire but also to prove to himself that he has the internal courage to accomplish the task. If we are going to care about the story, it is important that we identify with this character and his needs. Identification can be achieved in a number of ways, including casting an appealing actor, creating sympathy for an underdog and having the character do positive things. The best way to achieve identification, however, is to develop the character so that the audience clearly understands the character's needs. *The Lord of the Rings* does all of these things to get us onboard with Frodo.

Structure

Once the character's needs are established, then the writer can begin to structure the script. The key elements of classical narrative structure are exposition, conflict, climax, and resolution. Figure 17-1 lays out the basic structure of the vast majority of film and TV shows produced today.

Exposition or Setup

The beginning of the story must set up the lead character, the setting, and what the character wants—the goal to be achieved or the problem to be solved. Current films and videos tend to limit pure expositional sequences at the beginning and

Figure 17–1 *Classical linear structure.*

jump right into the story, integrating the story with the exposition. Some pieces open with an action scene and then slow down the pace in the next scene for exposition. However it is done, near the beginning of a script, the audience must learn who the character is, where he or she is, and what he or she wants.

Conflict

Once the writer knows the lead character and his or her goal, then he or she can start the character on the way to achieving that goal. Of course, if the character achieves the goal in the first scene, it will be a very short story. To avoid this happening, the writer introduces conflicts or obstacles. There are three basic types of conflict:

- Person versus person.
- Person versus the environment.
- Person versus self.

In *The Lord of the Rings* example, there are many "persons" who oppose Frodo, particularly Gollum, the orcs, Ring Wraiths, Lord Sauron, and all their minions. The environmental obstacles include mysterious forests, snowy mountains, labyrinthine mines, and much more. The last type of conflict, person versus self, is a way of adding considerable depth to a piece. In the case of Frodo, he has serious self-doubts about his ability to carry the task to completion. These doubts are exacerbated by the evil power or the ring itself.

A number of writing critics, particularly Syd Field in *Screenplay*, point to a key plot point or event in the exposition that shoves the character out of the exposition and into the conflict. In Frodo's case, it occurs at the secret council in the elf land of Rivendell when he takes on the task of carrying the ring to Mordor to destroy it. Once the conflicts begin, then each conflict or obstacle should be more challenging than the last obstacle so that the story rises in intensity.

Climax

Finally, the story nears the peak of intensity, and a final event jacks it up to the climax, which is where the character either achieves the goal or not. In Frodo's case, the final event is at the fires of Mordor when Frodo finally reaches his destination. However, because of the power of the Ring, Frodo has been corrupted and is unable to throw the ring into the fire. It is only by chance that another character, Gollum, tries to seize the ring for himself and ends up accidentally plummeting into the fire with the ring. With a little help from Gollum, Frodo has accomplished his physical goal of destroying the ring, but ultimately failed to accomplish his emotional goal of proving he has the strength to withstand the seductive power of the ring. This conflicted climax is one of the elements that adds power to this story. Typically in a Hollywood film, the hero accomplishes both his physical and emotional goal.

Resolution

The resolution wraps up the story after the climax. The resolution of *The Lord of the Rings* involves the return to the Shire and ultimately Frodo's departure with the Elves to a land of peace.

In most stories, the character changes or travels a character arc, a character may start cowardly and by the end prove he is brave, or start the story unsure and by the end be full of confidence. Because Frodo never achieves his emotional goals and because he is so wounded by the evil power of the Ring, he also follows an arc. He travels from a point of carefree, innocence at the beginning to a point of being somber and restrained. Some critics see the journey of Frodo is one from innocence to experience or from childhood to adulthood.

Scenes and Sequences

A narrative is comprised of individual scenes and sequences. A scene is an action that takes place in one location. A sequence is a series of scenes built around one concept or event. In a tightly structured script, each scene has a mini-goal or plot point that sets up and leads us into the next scene, eventually building the sequence. Some scenes and most sequences have a beginning, middle, and end, much like the overall story.

Jeopardy

The characters' success or failure in achieving their goals has to have serious consequences for them. It is easy for the writer to set up jeopardy if it is a life-and-death situation, such as being butchered by orcs in *The Lord of the Rings*. It is harder to create this sense of importance with more mundane events. This is accomplished by properly developing the character. In a well written script, if something is important to the character, it will be important to the audience even if it is not a life and death situation.

Point of View

Point of view defines from whose perspective the story is told. The most common point of view (or POV) is third person or omniscient (all knowing). In this case the audience is a fly on the wall and can flit from one location to another, seeing events from many characters' points of view or from the point of view of the writer of the script. This is the point of view of *The Lord of the Rings*.

The other major type of point of view is first person or subjective point of view. In this case, the entire story is told from one character's perspective. The audience sees everything through his or her eyes. The audience can experience only what the character experiences. Used exclusively, this type of point of view has numerous practical problems. The primary one is that we never get to see the lead character's expressions except in the mirror. Because of this, stories that are told in subjective point-of-view narrative are sometimes told in third-person point of view in terms of the camera. This allows us to see the lead character. Voice-over narration is often used with subjective point of view.

Pace

Pace is the audience's experience of how quickly the events of the narrative seem to move. Many short sequences, scenes, and bits of dialogue tend to make the pace move quickly; longer elements slow it down. Numerous fast-moving events in a scene also quicken pace. Writers tend to accelerate pace near a climax and slow it down for expositional and romantic scenes. A built-in time limit accelerates pace and increases jeopardy by requiring the protagonist to accomplish his or her task in a certain time frame. In *The Lord of the Rings*, Frodo had to destroy the Ring before Lord Sauron and his armies amassed the power to destroy all the good folks of Middle Earth.

Conclusion

The above has only scratched the surface of a complex topic, but it should be an adequate foundation for the multimedia narrative discussion that follows. A key issue we will be looking at is how the writing of multimedia narrative differs from writing linear narrative.

References

Bunn, Austin, and Herz, J.C. "The Frontiers of Game Design." CNET Gamecenter. May 12, 1999. http://www.gamecenter.com/Features/Exclusives/Frontiers/ss03. html

Conners, Aaron. Telephone interviews with the author, December 1995, October 1999, January 2006.

Costello, Matthew. Phone interview with the author, July 1999, February 2006.

Field, Syd. *Screenplay*. New York: Dell Publishing, 1982.

Fitch, Stephan. "Cinema Server = s/t (story over time)." Master's thesis, Massachusetts Institute of Technology, 1993.

Gilligan, Shannon. Telephone interview with the author, July 1994.

Halliday, Mark. "Digital Cinema an Environment for Multi-threaded Stories." Master's thesis, Massachusetts Institute of Technology, 1993.

Jensen, Jane. Telephone interview with the author, July 1994.

Maloney, Janice. "Perlmania." *WIRED Magazine*. 7.07. (July 1999): 102–109.

O'Meara, Maria. Letter to the author, June 1994.

O'Meara, Maria. Interviews with the author, July 1994, October 1995, December 1995, February 2006.

Platt, Charles. "Interactive Entertainment: Who Writes It? Who Reads It? Who Needs It?" *WIRED Magazine 3* (September 1995): 145–197.

Pousette, Lena Marie. Telephone interview with the author, December 1995.

Riordan, David. Telephone interviews with the author, June 1994, October 1995, December 1995, January 2006.

Sherman, Tony. Telephone interviews with the author, July 1994, September 1995.

Stalter, Katharine. "*Voyeur*. A Look into the Creative Process Behind the CD-I Game from POV Entertainment Group." *Film and Video* (April 1994): 64–120.

18

The Elements of Interactive Multimedia Narrative

Portions of this chapter originally appeared in the *Journal of Film and Video*.

Chapter Overview

Major elements of interactive narrative that must be understood by the writer include:

- The Role of the Player
- Character Development
- Structure
- Exposition
- Plot Points
- Scenes
- Pace and Time
- Dialogue and Other Sound

Linear Versus Interactive Narrative

Writer Matthew Costello, who has written successful films, novels, and computer games, points out a key difference between linear and interactive narrative. A film starts from characters. A novel can start with an idea and have characters gather around it. A game starts from the genre and expectations. The story world comes first. A designer comes up with a game story world for a project. Then the writer has to ask, what is the world going to have in it? What are the possible interactions, the environments? What type of story does this suggest?

According to Costello, the story worlds of games are gravitating towards genres. Genres are categories of stories, such as horror, mystery, fantasy, science fiction, and crime genres. Using a genre story world makes it easier to develop a narrative because the user already understands the basic conventions of character and plot lines. The writer does not have to establish everything from scratch as in a nongenre story.

Of course, the key difference between linear narrative and interactive narrative is interactivity. Amy Bruckman of the MIT Media Lab writes, "In making a story nonlinear, the story teller relinquishes the power to control the flow of information to the viewer ... A balance must be struck between giving the viewer freedom and maintaining narrative coherence" (12). Finding this balance—giving the player some control over the narrative, while allowing the writer to perform the necessary functions of the classical storyteller, including establishing characters and an engaging story structure—is a key challenge for the writer of interactive narrative.

Character and the Role of the Player

Characterization in an interactive narrative is vastly more complex than in a linear narrative because of the role of the player. Lena Maria Pousette, the writer of *Voyeur*, identified the key questions the writer must begin with: "What is the [game's] objective? Who is the player? And what does the player get to do?" (Willis, 9). In an interactive piece, the player expects to be one of the characters in the story, or at least to have significant control over the characters.

Player Control

The degree of the player's control over the characters is one of the first decisions in writing a program. If you are writing for an existing story engine, these choices may be already determined. So be sure to learn the capabilities of the program you are working with. The basic types of control the player is allowed are choice of scenes, the character's actions, or all the character's behavior.

Scenes

In this approach, the player can decide which path of the story the characters will choose, but once launched on that path, the characters function independently until the next branching point. *Boy Scout Patrol Theater*, an interactive narrative at the National Boy Scout museum, is a good example. The Boy Scouts in the story must decide whether to search the farm, the neighborhood, or the school. Once the player makes the choice to search the school, the characters function on their own without player interaction until the next interactive point. The characters are usually seen in third person.

See the Boy Scout Patrol Theater *area in the Chapters section of this book's CD-ROM.*

Many games that allow significant interactivity in most of the game will have sections where players can only choose complete scenes. These are often in the form of cut scenes—linear movie-like scenes in the middle of a game.

Actions

In some programs, the player will see the main character on the screen and can control the actions of the character, but not the dialogue. *Grand Theft Auto—San Andreas* works this way. We can see CJ, the lead character, on screen, and we can direct him to steal cars or create other mayhem. This is a third person POV as described in the previous chapter. We do not directly control what the character says or what other characters say to them. The primary place CJ talks is in the cinematic cut scenes where we have no control. Often in games with this type of control, the playable action tends to be seen in long or medium shots so that the player can direct the action.

All Behavior

This is the highest degree of interactivity. In this mode, the player chooses what the character does and what they say. In the *Nancy Drew* mystery games (Chapter 20), the player takes on the role of Nancy Drew in the first person POV. We do not see the character of Nancy Drew, but instead see everything through the character's eyes. This approach allows the player to essentially become the character. In the screenshot from *Nancy Drew: Curse of Blackmoor Manor*, shown in Figure 18-1, the player/Nancy Drew is talking to the rather scary aunt who is in charge of the manor. The aunt's dialogue is spoken and also appears in text in the darker color at the top of the window. In this screenshot, the player is clicking the

Figure 18-1 *Interactive dialogue Player controlling all behavior. Copyright Her Interactive, Inc.*

question, "Is anyone else staying here?" which the aunt will reply to in audio and onscreen text.

Many games with interactive dialogue only show the player's choices in text (*Dust*, Chapter 23) and not the dialogue of the other characters as in the example above. In other games, such as *The Pandora Directive* (Chapter 22), the player does not click the actual line of dialogue but instead clicks an attitude, which indicates the type of dialogue the on screen character will speak. This way the actual dialogue becomes a surprise. Interactive dialogue works great for certain types of games, such as mysteries, but some designers feel that it overly slows the pace of some games, such as action games. In *Half-Life 2*, for example, the lead character never speaks at all.

Player Control Combinations

Few programs function purely in just one of the approaches above. Many programs, such as *Amped 3* (Chapter 21), combine different amounts of player control. During most of the snowboarding game play, you have complete control over the player's actions, but you can choose to take a break from snowboarding and view one of the story challenges. The story scenes are basically linear and there is no interactivity until the scene has finished. Other games, such as *The Chronicles of Narnia: The Lion, the Witch and the Wardrobe*, allow you to change player perspective. In this case, you can choose which of the four main characters to play.

Variable Control

In some programs, players can decide on how much control they want. In *Voyeur*, the player watches the events in the mansion across the street, sees the news on television, and receives telephone calls. If the player just sits and watches, the corrupt politician is the protagonist of the story. If the player decides to try to stop the corrupt politician, the player can have a major effect on the plot.

Impact of Player Options

The degree of player control, player point of view, and the type of character played in a first-person point of view story all have significant impact on the story.

Player as Protagonist

To maximize player interactivity and immersion in the story, one of the best options is to allow the player to become the protagonist of the story by controlling all the character's behavior and seeing the action in first-person point of view. There are, however, drawbacks to this approach. One is that it is difficult to portray certain types of action in first-person point of view. For example, how do you show someone kissing the protagonist? The player also never gets to see the protagonist's expressions and actions, which are the main ways that character is revealed. Because of this, first-person point-of-view interactive stories often rely on dialogue. Gender issues are also raised with first-person point-of-view interactive. Is the character male or female? If the character is assigned one gender, as in the *Nancy Drew* mysteries or *Dust*, are there character identification problems for the player? If no gender is assigned, how do the other characters address the player/protagonist?

If the player is the protagonist, it is also difficult for the writer to develop him or her as a complex character. If the writer does develop the protagonist in detail, as in the case of Tex Murphy in *The Pandora Directive*, you/the player are left with "a fictitious version of yourself who isn't like you at all and who does things you have never done in a world you have never visited" (Platt, 147). The writer will also have to hope that the goal of the protagonist is something the player can identify with.

The alternative approach for the protagonist, as practiced in *Dust*, is to have a very general character, in this case, the Stranger. The player knows nothing about him, and so can perhaps more comfortably become him. But will the player be able to understand and empathize with the action and emotional needs of this sketchily drawn character?

Player Determining the Character

A way around the quandary of either defining a character that the player cannot fit into or leaving the character vague is to give the player a role in determining the character. In *Amped 3*, at the beginning of the program, the player can choose the character's outfits, gender, voices (male or female) and attitude (cheeky or chill). *Grand Theft Auto—San Andreas* takes player definition of character one step further by having the lead character CJ change depending on what type of activities he does. Lots of exercise, he is buff. Lots of food and riding around in cars, he gets fat. He can also shop for clothes at any number of stores. The nonplaying characters (NPC) in the game will also respond to CJ differently based on his appearance. Even though the basic storyline does not alter from one game play to the next, having a different CJ character can change the experience of the storyline.

Player as Minor Character

A more unusual role for the player is that instead of being a major character, the player can be a minor character, as in *Voyeur*. The player may not seem so central to the action, but the advantage is that the portrayal of the minor character is not as crucial. If the minor character is only sketchily drawn, it will not have as much of an impact on the story as a poorly developed main character. It is also much easier to show the main action of the story in third person. For certain types of training and education programs, this type of third-person portrayal is essential. *A la rencontre de Philippe* is an interactive language program in which the player takes on the role of helping Parisian friends find an apartment. This allows the player to watch the native speakers interact in French, which was one of the goals of the program and which would have been more difficult if the player was a first-person protagonist.

Character Setup and Relationships

The player is only one of the characters in a program. Many others must be set up, but the demands of the interactive narrative do not make it easy to bring them to life. Space is always at a premium, scenes tend to be short, and character setup tends not to be interactive and thus is kept to a minimum.

An interactive writer needs to be able to introduce the characters quickly and simply. And once the characters are established, the writer also has to keep track of the different relationships of all the characters in all the possible versions of the story.

 See the Voyeur *area of the "Chapters" section of the* Writing for Multimedia and the Web CD-ROM *for examples of character charts and matrices.*

Architecture: Structure and Navigation

Just as in a linear piece, in an interactive narrative, once the character and his or her goal are established, then the basic structure of the story needs to be developed. In interactive writing, however, this is far more complex than the simple linear structure illustrated in Figure 17-1 in the previous chapter, because in an interactive narrative, the writer must also consider navigation between all the elements of the structure.

Will Wright, the designer of the popular *Sims* series of games, explains the difference between linear and interactive narrative well:

> When I watch Indiana Jones escaping from the Temple of Doom (in the movie of the same name), it's not what happens to him that I find interesting; it's what might have happened had he slipped in front of the boulder. Dozens of potential failure states are compressed into a few seconds of action and transmitted to my brain with amazing efficiency.
>
> Game players are given the ability to explore a space of possibilities—the phase space—and this is the real strength of the medium. It's sort of like the difference between a roller coaster and a car. The coaster is on a fixed track. It's a very exciting track, but it's always the same. I can add branches to the track, but it can still be viewed as a finite amount of track. If I put someone in a car, however, they can go almost anywhere. Since I can't simulate the whole world in my games, I have to put up barriers and limit where they can go in the car. (Bunn and Herz)

These barriers and the road he describes are essentially the structure of interactive narrative. How the user can move between roads is the navigation. The most common interactive narrative structures are described below.

Linear Structure

Defined: Strictly speaking, this is not an interactive structure but it is often used in interactive projects. Linear structure has no branching choices for the user.

Use: Linear structure is frequently used in narrative multimedia to set up the story. All of the narratives profiled in this book open with linear sequences before user interaction is possible. Linear video is also played during an interactive piece for additional background and to tie interactive segments together. The *New England Economic Adventure* (Chapter 24) uses linear video to present information that the audience will later use interactively in exercises and games.

Linear Structure with Scene Branching

Defined: This structure allows the user to choose alternative scenes, but after these alternative scenes are played out, the user is always routed back to the same main story line.

Use: This is a common structure in training and educational narratives. In *Boy Scout Patrol Theater* the basic structure is a linear story about trying to find a lost girl. At various decision points, however, the players get to make a choice, such as choosing to search the farm, the school, or the neighborhood. If they choose the farm, then they detour momentarily from the main story and search the farm, but eventually return to the main story. (See Figure 18-2.) A similar structure if used in role-playing, narrative corporate training programs where the user takes on a role and tries to accomplish a task. They can choose alternate scenes for helping to accomplish the task, but are always routed back to the main task scenario.

A variation on this approach is the structure that Chris Crawford aptly calls "Kill 'Em If They Stray" (130). In this approach, there is only one critical story path through the game. The user can explore different scenes off the critical path, but they usually cannot get very far on any alternate path before they are killed. *Half-Life 2* can be put in this category. It is basically a linear story that sometimes appears to present alternate scenes. But if the players venture down one of those alternate scenes and stay too long, they can expect to be destroyed.

Valve CEO Gabe Newell describes the *Half-Life 2* approach, in the foreword to *Half-Life 2: Raising the Bar*: "A single-player game is really a movie that you create in cooperation with the player, where the lead actor [i.e., the player] doesn't have a copy of the script." (Hodgson foreword)

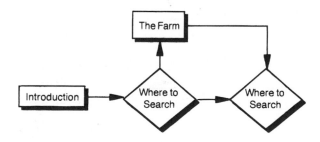

Figure 18-2 *Linear structure with scene branching in* Patrol Theater.

Hierarchical Branching

Defined: This architecture involves taking the story in a completely different direction based on the viewer's choice at a preset decision point. This is a common informational architecture but presents problems in interactive narrative.

Used in a Complete Story: Using hierarchical branching to take the complete story into different directions has limited options. For example, as illustrated in Figure 18-3, the character comes to a point where she can choose one of three options: marry Alan, marry Bob, or marry Carl. After that choice is played out, then the character can choose to be faithful, have an affair, or get divorced. The problem here is obvious: The number of choices increases exponentially. Adding one more set of choices to this chart would mean an additional 27 scenes, the next level would be 81 additional scenes, and the one after that 243 scenes! This is called combinatorial explosion. This is clearly too much material for a writer to present or a viewer to access.

Used with Endings: Although it is rare for an entire story to be completed with hierarchical branching, it is commonly used for the ending of programs. This device gives the viewer a feeling of greater control over the narrative, and branching explosion is obviously limited because the story ends. The end of *The 11th Hour*, where the viewer must choose to save one of three women, is a good example. Each woman equals a different ending to the story. The wrong choice is oblivion; the right choice is bliss.

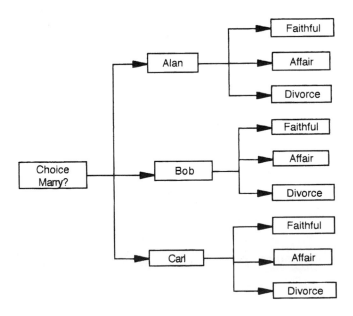

Figure 18-3 *Hierarchical branching explosion.*

Used with Dialogue: This type of branching is also used in interactive dialogue. See the flowchart in Figure 22-1 from Chapter 22.

Parallel Path Stories

Defined: With parallel structure, several versions of the same story play parallel to each other. Depending on choices that the player makes in the story, he or she can move from one path to another. This is a way to give the player an option of multiple paths in a story without the branching explosion of hierarchical branching.

Use: *The Pandora Directive* (Figure 18-4) uses parallel path stories. After a linear introduction, the player enters an interactive scene. Depending on the choices that he or she makes, the player can move up to the A path, which is a Hollywood-type version of the story where the hero wins true love; the C path, a bleak, film noir experience of the story where everything goes wrong; or the B path, which is a middle ground. Each new interactive scene gives the player options to move back and forth between paths depending on the choices they make. And depending on the choices they have made, they have one of several possible endings. Although this can be an effective structure, it is not widely used in complete games mainly because of the difficulty of tracking and creating multiple story paths and the changing relationships of the characters.

It is, however, a little more common to see parallel path structure as part of an otherwise linear game, such as *Metal Gear Solid*.

This sequence, in which the player is tortured repeatedly but has an opportunity to escape between the torture sessions, has three paths through it: the player can escape in a couple of different ways from the cell between torture scenes, they may admit defeat to the torturer, or if all else fails, they are eventually rescued from the cell by a deus ex machina. This parallel path segment also governs a split in the game's ending: if the player does not give up in the

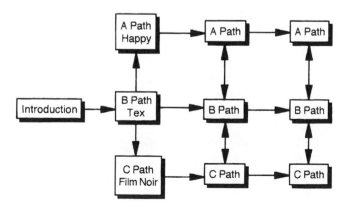

Figure 18-4 *Parallel path stories in* The Pandora Directive *lead to one of several possible endings.*

torture scenes, they will end up rescuing the romantic interest—but if they do, she is killed and the player ends up escaping with a buddy character instead. (IGDA)

Linked Worlds—String of Pearls Architecture

Defined: This approach moves away from simple branching. A string of pearls architecture is a linked series of worlds structures connected by plot points or tasks that the player must accomplish to move forward in the narrative. As defined at the beginning of Chapter 17, the worlds approach lets the user explore a location. By itself, a worlds structure cannot form a coherent narrative, but combined with other forms it can.

Use: *Dust: A Tale of the Wired West* (Chapter 23) uses the string of pearls approach. When the player/Stranger first comes to town in the middle of the night, he is free to roam the town of Diamondback for as long as he wants. There are poker games to be played, hookers to talk to, and mysterious buildings to explore. This is a clear worlds structure—interesting, but by itself there is no story.

To move to the next day and advance the narrative, the player/Stranger must find a place to sleep. He can either stay at the hotel or get one of the town's citizens to take him in. There are a number of ways to accomplish this goal. To stay at the hotel, he needs money. He can get cash at the saloon if he is lucky at blackjack, poker, or the slot machine. If he is nosy, he might also find the four bucks that somebody lost in the hotel couch. But when he does get the money, the hotel owner says there are no vacancies. To get a room, it helps to meet Raddison, another character who lives there and who will introduce the Stranger (the player) to the owner. An alternative to the hotel is to get a citizen to take the player/ Stranger home. To accomplish this, the player needs to sweet-talk the abrasive Mrs. Macintosh.

The player can perform all of these actions in any order desired, but eventually he or she has to find the right combination of actions to get a place to sleep and thus exit from the first night of the story and begin the next day or pearl on the string. In the second pearl, the next day's action, the player must get boots, guns, and bullets before moving on to the third pearl. (See Figure 18-5.) All of the player's accomplishments move the story forward to the final shootout and to solving the mystery in one of six possible endings.

In addition to being used in the classic *Dust*, this worlds structure linked by a narrative thread has become a popular architecture in many other games. *Grand Theft Auto—San Andreas* uses this structure. A series of missions form the critical path of the game. These missions must eventually be taken on to move to all the locations (worlds) of the game, but you can decide when you want to take on the mission. You are free to explore GTA's huge virtual world as long as you want. *Just Cause* is set up in a somewhat similar fashion. In this case, a secret agent has the overall goal of overthrowing the government of an island nation. The agent can explore the island, but as in the case of GTA must complete a series of missions to

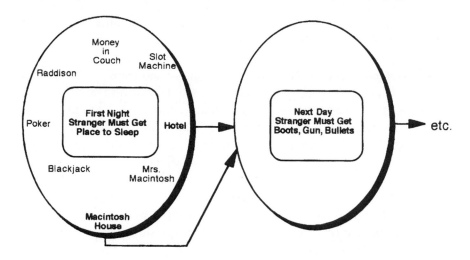

Figure 18-5 *String of pearls architecture in* Dust: A Tale of the Wired West.

move the story forward. Both of these examples though primarily worlds structures also have simulation elements with the ability to drive cars, boats etc. *Amped 3* (Chapter 21) is a game that is mostly a snowboard simulation but also provides the opportunity to explore the locations of top boarding resorts. Similar to *GTA* and *Just Cause*, *Amped 3* has a series of story challenges that link together the simulation sections and form the core narrative of the story.

In some ways, the ideal story for a string of pearls structure is a mystery story. This is the structure used in the *Nancy Drew* mysteries (Chapter 20). Nancy Drew and any detective's goal in a mystery story is to discover what happened—the narrative of the crime. Initially the detective is in the top or outer world of the crime, but as she gets clues and solves puzzles, she gradually gains access to the inner worlds of the narrative, finally concluding with the mystery's solution. See Figure 20-1 for a diagram of the mystery version of the string of pearls structure as used in the *Nancy Drew* games.

Variable State Environment and Types of Links

Defined: The most sophisticated interactive narratives, many of which have been discussed previously in this chapter, have moved beyond direct links and simple branching to something that Dave Riordan, the designer of *Voyeur*, calls a variable state environment. With the help of software and sophisticated design that responds in a sensitive way to the player's actions, there are multiple outcomes to scenes, depending on where the player has been and to whom he or she has talked. In short, the environment responds to the player, much as it does in real life.

A variable state environment can take into account hundreds of actions as opposed to just the A or B choices in branching. And as each interaction is played differently, it will yield different responses. Different combinations of different interactions will also yield different responses.

Use: In *Indigo Prophecy (Fahrenheit)*, how and what Lucas cleans up after the murder and how he escapes, affect what clues can be used against him and the testimony of witnesses. *Deus Ex*'s narrative is also affected by player decisions in subtle ways. If you ignore the rules and kill all the terrorists in a blood bath, your fellow trigger-happy officers will applaud your actions and help you with the case, but your "by the book" officers will be appalled. Either choice affects how the story plays out. In *The Pandora Directive*, if you as the player are tactless with your girlfriend, you will get into a fight. This causes you to get drunk, and because you are drunk, you are unable to save a nightclub singer's life. These types of convoluted reactions to the player's actions are far more like real life than the direct reaction to a player's choices in many video games.

Future or Experimental Structures

The primary focus of this book is to document techniques and processes used to create commercial interactive media. It should, however, be mentioned that game theorist, research labs, and academics are working on innovative, experimental game engines and structures that they hope will be far more responsive to user needs than anything now in existence. Some of the purists in this group of researchers do not consider any of the structures described in this chapter as successful interactive narratives architectures. For a detailed discussion of the theoretical basis of interactive storytelling and some of the experimental solutions being developed, Chris Crawford's book, *On Interactive Storytelling*, is worth a read.

Exposition or Setup

Exposition is another issue that presents special challenges for the interactive writer. Exposition involves introducing characters, setting, and story situation to the player. Exposition is particularly important in games because the player will need that information to make choices and take actions later in the game. Some designers feel that the key is to make the exposition entertaining and brief. Get the story setup and get on with the game. *Nancy Drew: The Secret of the Old Clock* presents the exposition efficiently and entertainingly. The game opens with Nancy driving her roadster to the Lilac Inn, the location of the mystery. As she is driving, we hear in voice-over what sounds like a 1930s radio show (the era of the game). The radio show/voice-over gives us the key background in audio illustrated with cuts to game scenes illustrating the narrator's description. When Nancy's car pulls into the driveway of the inn, the radio show/exposition is complete.

You can view this introductory video in the Nancy Drew *area of the Chapters section of this book's CD-ROM.*

Amped 3 also chooses a brief introductory scene to introduce the characters and setting. In this case, the characters are riding up the chairlift at a ski resort and the lead character/player is wearing a head to toe pink bunny suit. He is fulfilling a dare, which is to ski the mountain in the bunny suit. Through the banter about the dare and the suit, we get to know the characters and the basic situation.

Other designers, such as David Riordan, try to avoid introductory scenes. "If you spend time introducing the characters, the viewer is not being asked to do anything. In interactive that is death. Instead you need to discover the back story more as you go." In his game *Voyeur*, he accomplishes this partially through the user of sets and props to give exposition. They can be subtle props, such as a gun in a suitcase, or more overt props, such as a letter the player is allowed to read, or even active props, such as a television set that gives background information on the characters. The use of props in interactive multimedia differs from their use in linear video because in multimedia, the player gets to choose which props to examine, has far more props to choose from, and can do things that would be impossible in linear, such as move closer to a letter to read it or choose to turn on a television set or PDA.

Another key way for a player to learn exposition is through what other characters say to the player as scenes unfold. Early in *Half-Life 2*, the player is pulled into an interrogation room by a cop who turns out to be a friend. He quickly gives the player key background before he rushes him on his way. A variation on this approach is for the game's writer to introduce a stranger character to the location/story. The stranger shares the expositional needs of the player. They both need to be told the situation and introduced to the characters.

Designing a game around an established story genre also helps with exposition. *Just Cause* is a secret agent thriller. Because we know this genre from endless secret agent movies, such as the James Bond series, we understand a lot of the conventions of the genre. Because of this, these elements do not have to be explained again in the game. For example, we know that the secret agent character will have access to extraordinary gadgets, will be sexy, and must operate primarily on his own or with the help of a beautiful lady.

Guaranteeing that Essential Exposition Is Seen

Because this is interactive media, depending on the game, the player may have a choice to not view certain scenes, including exposition. One solution is to make the exciting linear exposition scenes, such as those discussed above, mandatory. As soon as the game starts, the exposition plays. Most games will allow the introduction to be skipped on later plays of the game. A somewhat dated approach is to include the backstory in a separate document or book that goes along with the game. A better solution is to design the game to lure the player into choosing the essential exposition, often with engaging interactive devices, such as televisions that can be viewed, mini-games of missions that reveal background, and interesting characters who we want to talk to.

Demonstrating How the Program Works

A type of exposition unique to games is that players need an explanation of how the game works. What can the player do? How do they move? Can they pick things up? How does the interactive dialogue work? The best programs integrate this information into the exposition and do not make the users read vast amounts of instructions before they can play.

One way to do this is to set up a simple situation at the beginning of the program that shows how the game works. For example, in *Dust*, the player is confronted with a nasty dog as soon as he or she enters the town. To get by this dog, the player must pick up objects, talk to characters, access help, and move about. A less integrated approach is to have a tutorial that plays a scene for the user and shows what to do.

Plot Points

Plot points or beats are story information that moves the plot forward. For example, in *Grand Theft Auto—San Andreas*, a key plot point we learn in the first cut scene is that a rival gang has pretty much taken over in CJ's absence. In an interactive story, making essential plot points is as difficult as presenting exposition. Because the user can choose which scenes to view, there is no guarantee that the user will choose a specific scene with a certain key plot point.

One solution is to place essential plot points in a required sequence. With this option, the player cannot learn later plot points and progress in the game until they have seen earlier ones. In the example from *GTA* in the previous paragraph, the player must choose the first cut scene/mission before they can progress in the story to additional major missions and complete the game's story. The first cut scene is not actually forced on the player. They have the option of not choosing it, but if they do not choose it, they are limited to the initial location and basic crime activities of stealing cars and having fights.

Another solution to the problem of guaranteeing key plot points are seen is "to put two or three beats (plot points) in a scene" (Pousette). This way if the user selects a scene, multiple plot points will be established. Another approach is to have the same information appear in a number of different scenes. The difficulty here is that the information can't be presented in exactly the same way or players will get bored if they select several of these scenes. The solution is to feed the essential information into multiple scenes but to do it differently each time.

In a narrative that includes multiple story variations, such as *Voyeur*, establishing plot points is even more complex than setting up exposition. Often much of the exposition will be the same for all possible stories. For example, in *Voyeur*, the back-story on the corrupt politician and his desire to be president does not change from story to story. Plot points are, however, usually different in each story variation. This means that essential plot points have to be established for each story. It also means that scenes that are common to all variations cannot include plot points that contradict the plot in a specific story variation. Some writers use charts of plot points or beats to keep all of these elements clear.

 See the Voyeur *area of the Chapters section of this book's CD-ROM for examples of character charts.*

Scenes

As the examples above suggest, strong scene writing is important to the interactive writer. Writer Maria O'Meara believes that "crafting a scene well is the most valuable technique of the interactive writer. Every experience in an interactive ought to be a tiny story or scene. Even if it's short, it still needs to have a beginning, middle, and end." Pam Beason of Microsoft agrees: "Every scene must contain a complete thought. An idea cannot be split over two scenes." Writer-designer Jane Jensen says other characteristics of the interactive scene are that "scenes are smaller and there are vastly greater amounts of them. You have to think nonlinearly. As you approach a given location, think what will occur there."

The interactive writer, in other words, must write vertically as well as horizontally. He or she cannot be concerned only with what scene follows another. The writer also has to be aware of what other scenes in other possible stories might be connected to this one. Some interactive writers script ten or fifteen related scenes at the same time in order to keep tabs on all the connections. And rewriting can be ghastly. Change one element in one of fifteen connected scenes, and all the other scenes need to be rewritten.

Stephan Fitch sums it up: "Interactive writing is more like 3-D writing. The writer has to see the layers and move through the layers of the script, keeping track of parallel actions in a scene" (Willis, 8).

Pace and Time

Interactive multimedia has no set running time. It depends on how the player plays the game. The challenge here for the writer is to create a consistent sense of time in the piece when a player might spend twenty minutes in a scene or might skip it altogether. Because time is also an important factor in pace, how does the writer deal with the way this variability of time affects pacing?

Player Creates the Pace

Jane Jensen says that there is no way to have the kind of pacing in interactive narrative that there is in a linear movie, in which a writer can carefully create and sequence a number of scenes to create a faster or slower pace. In interactive narrative, the player creates the pace. For example, a player goes into a haunted house and has to find a way out. The writer's job is to make sure that the scenes are dramatic in themselves and that the player is surprised when things happen. The player may think a certain room is safe from the last time he or she played, but this time it might contain a monster.

How the player interacts with this environment creates the pace of the sequence, but that interaction is affected by the kinds of elements the writer-designer gives the player to interact with. Another way to heighten the feeling of pace is to create a sense of urgency. Both *Half-Life 2* and *Grand Theft Auto—San Andreas* feel fast paced because if you dawdle too long in any one location, you have a good chance of being killed. You have to keep moving.

Multimedia Pace = Miniseries Pace

The combined running times of multiple plays of an interactive movie is much longer than the running time of a two-hour feature film. An interactive movie can be thought of more like a miniseries or a serial. For example, the writer can deal with much of the exposition the first time the game is played, which allows the pace to be increased in later plays.

Manipulating Time to Affect Pace

Other writers and designers have actively manipulated time to affect the pace of the story. In Tony Sherman's *Dracula Unleashed* (DVD version), the player has four days to solve the crime. A clock in the game keeps track of the time. In the real time of playing the game, going to a library and talking to someone may only take thirty seconds, but in game time the player may be deducted an hour. And while he or she is at one location, other scenes happen whether the player sees them or not, just as they would in real life. If the player is knocked out, he or she will miss several scenes and be docked eighty minutes on the clock. Sherman feels that although this time manipulation can add a sense of urgency to the game, the players do set pace. The story material stays the same; it is how it is played that affects the overall pacing.

Nancy Drew: The Secret of the Old Clock uses a similar device but it is worked more into the characters. The owner of the inn is a young girl who is getting progressively more upset by all the weird events. Nancy has to solve the crime before the girl gives up and sells the inn—the goal of the crooks.

An even more interesting use of time is in Riordan's *Thunder in Paradise*. In this program, the time spent in one scene affects what happens in later scenes. For example, in one scene the heroes have to battle the villains surrounding an island to save the heroine who is held there. If the heroes take a long time to defeat these villains, the other villains on the island itself have more time to prepare for them, and the heroes' difficulties are increased when they finally land. This use of time is an important step in making games reflect how time is experienced in real life. It can also give the designer more control over pacing. For example, if the player spends a long time on one scene, the next scene could automatically be altered to increase the pace of the sequence.

Of course, games don't have to be about real life. *F.E.A.R.*, a first person shooter, allows the player to put the game into a slow time mode to change the pace of the action. In this mode all the action is slowed down.

Dialogue and Other Sound

One of the difficulties of characterization in interactive media is the limited dialogue that is allowed because many scenes are very short, and it usually takes longer to develop a strong dialogue scene. Writer Shannon Gilligan compares dialogue writing in interactive media to "writing a symphony of snippets." She claims that it is how the writer relates these snippets together through the design that makes a successful sequence.

The potential use of other sounds, particularly nonsynchronous sounds, is also important. *Under a Killing Moon* uses the tradition of the ironic voice-over in the detective story and includes over five hours of voice-over that gives the player information about characters, objects, and situations. *F.E.A.R.* presents a lot of its plot points and backstory through voice-mails. Ambient sounds are also essential for setting mood. The echoing industrial sounds of *Half-Life 2* are nearly as important to creating the eerie, futuristic feel of the game as the visuals.

Conclusion

This chapter provides an overview of some of the common elements and structures of interactive narrative, particularly the computer game. The next chapters will examine specific interactive narratives in detail to explore exactly how these structure and elements were utilized in specific situations. In an interview, writer Matthew Costello said that every project is unique. Sometimes storytelling is fairly linear and structured. Other times there is great randomness and more freedom in how the player participates in the story. There is no one right way to create interactive narrative as the case studies in the following chapters will demonstrate.

References

Beason, Pam. Telephone interview with the author, July 1994.
Bruckman, Amy. "The Combinatorics of Storytelling: Mystery Train Interactive." MIT Media Lab, April 1990.

Bunn, Austin, and Herz, J.C. "The Frontiers of Game Design." CNET Gamecenter. http://www.gamecenter.com/Features/Exclusives/Frontiers/?st.gc.fd.bb5

Conners, Aaron. Telephone interviews with the author, August 1995, September 2005.

Costello, Matthew. Telephone interviews with the author, August 2005.

Crawford, Chris. *On Interactive Storytelling.* Berkeley, CA: New Riders, 2005.

Fitch, Stephan. "Cinema Server = s/t (story over time)." Master's thesis, Massachusetts Institute of Technology, 1993.

Gilligan, Shannon. Telephone interview with the author, July 1994.

Hodgson, David. *Half-Life 2: Raising the Bar.* Roseville, CA: Prima Games, 2004.

IGDA (International Game Developers Association) web site http://www.igda.org/writing/InteractiveStorytelling.htm

Jensen, Jane. Telephone interview with the author, July 1994.

Miller, Carolyn Handler. *Digital Storytelling.* Boston: Focal Press, 2004.

Mystery.net web site. http://www.mysterynet.com

O'Meara, Maria. Interviews with the author, December 1995, July 2005.

O'Meara, Maria. Letter to the author, June 1994.

Platt, Charles. "Interactive Entertainment: Who Writes It? Who Reads It? Who Needs It?" *WIRED Magazine* 3 (September 1995): 145–195.

Pousette, Lena Marie. Telephone interview with the author, December 1995.

Riordan, David. Telephone interviews with the author, October 1995, August 2005.

Sherman, Tony. Telephone interviews with the author, July 1994, September 1995.

Willis, Holly. "Let the Games Begin." *Hollywood Reporter* (October 1993): S-1–S-32.

Introduction to the Narrative Multimedia Case Studies

Description of Case Studies

The last golden age of the interactive narrative adventure game was in the mid- to late-1990s. For several years after that, the video game industry was dominated by action games, with relatively few sophisticated interactive narratives being produced. In recent years, however, there has been a resurgence in interactive narrative. For these reasons, I have used a combination of newer games and classic interactive narratives for the case studies in this book. These games and other narrative programs demonstrate a wide variety of different narrative techniques.

These programs are examined in the following chapters:

- *Nancy Drew: Secret of the Old Clock*: a puzzle based mystery computer game.
- *Amped 3*: a snowboarding simulation with integrated story sequences.
- *Dust: A Tale of the Wired West*: a Western game with a worlds narrative structure.
- *The Pandora Directive*: a multiple story path narrative and the sequel to the sci-fi, detective mystery game, *Under a Killing Moon*.
- *The New England Economic Adventure*: an immersive museum exhibit that uses interactive narrative, games, exhibits, and live performers to present information. Also an example of using narrative in an informational program.

 Narrative case studies from previous edition chapters, Boy Scout Patrol Theater, Voyeur, *and* The 11th Hour *are now located in the Chapters section of this book's CD-ROM.*

Approach to Case Studies

An understanding of how these writers dealt with narrative issues will provide the insight to deal with similar issues when they arise in your work. Each case study answers the following questions:

- Program Description and Background. Is the program a typical example of its genre or is it unusual? Who commissioned, developed, and wrote the program? What was the preproduction process?
- Goals. What were the writers and designers' goals in creating this project? What information or experience were they trying to communicate?
- Challenges. Which goals were particularly difficult to achieve? What approaches were successful in achieving these goals and which were discarded?
- Response to the Project. Did the program achieve its goals? Was it a critical and/or commercial success?

The case studies are documented with script examples, screen shots, and flowcharts.

 Additional script samples and other material, including color screen shots and working demos, are available for many of the programs in the Chapters section of the Writing for Multimedia and the Web *CD-ROM.*

How to Get Copies of the Games

Computer games are often released to major stores for only a short period of time. To obtain some of the games discussed in this section of the book, you can go online to Amazon.com and search by the games title in the Video Games section. For the *New England Economic Adventure,* you will have to travel to the Federal Reserve Bank of Boston, where it is one of their exhibits.

Case Study—Adapting Classic Books to a Computer Game for the Female Audience: *Nancy Drew: The Secret of the Old Clock*

Summary

Name of production: *Nancy Drew: The Secret of the Old Clock*
Writer: Anne Collins-Ludwick
Lead Designer: Mari Tokuda
Developer: Her Interactive, Inc.
Audience: 10 and up; rated E for "Everyone" by the ESRB
Medium: Windows CD-ROM
Presentation location: Home, or wherever entertainment games are played
Subject: *Nancy Drew* Mystery Adventure
Goal: Entertain
Architecture: Parallel Paths, linear, dialogue branching

Program Description and Background

Program Description

Nancy Drew: The Secret of the Old Clock is the 12th in the series of *Nancy Drew* mystery computer games produced by Her Interactive. In these games, the player takes on the role of Nancy Drew and sees and hears the events of the game from her perspective. This is a first person game; we never actually see Nancy Drew. The *Nancy Drew: The Secret of the Old Clock* game was inspired by the first *Nancy Drew* mystery book ever published. The game is set in 1930, the same year as the original book's publication.

In this game, Nancy drives her blue roadster to the Lilac Inn to help seventeen year-old Emily Crandall, who has just inherited the inn from her mother. At the inn, an anxious Emily explains to Nancy that she was surprised when her rich uncle left most of his wealth to Richard Topham, an expert on paranormal activities. Emily believes there is a second will that leaves her uncle's money to her.

This sets Nancy off on her investigation. Nancy talks to the paranormal expert Richard Topham, the town banker Jim Archer, and Emily's flakey new guardian Marian Aborn. Nancy soon learns that Emily's uncle was a paranoid eccentric who devised elaborate puzzles and games to protect his privacy and wealth. In order to find out more about the uncle and his will, Nancy has to solve these puzzles and games. The solutions to puzzles gradually point the way to secret tunnels, hidden rooms full of gadgets, and finally the solution to the mystery. The game has two levels of game play: Junior and Senior Detective.

Production Background

Nancy Drew: The Secret of the Old Clock was developed and produced by Her Interactive, Inc. of Bellevue, Washington. Her Interactive was founded in 1995 to create interactive games for the female audience. This is an audience that is largely underserved in the gaming industry, which tends to focus on action and sports games aimed towards young males.

To ensure success, Her Interactive licensed the game rights to an established name with female audiences—the *Nancy Drew* mystery books. The *Nancy Drew* mysteries have been a success with girls of all ages for more than seventy-five years, with two hundred million copies in print worldwide.

Her Interactive also knew it was important to produce a high quality product at a reasonable price. To do this, they set a firm six-month production schedule for each *Nancy Drew* game, producing two games a year. Each game uses the same basic game engine but has different characters, locations, puzzles, and game engine innovations. For example, in *The Secret of the Old Clock*, players can drive around in Nancy's car for the first time and they can spend and earn money.

This strategy has proved successful, with twelve *Nancy Drew* mysteries produced to date and two more in production. There are also other projects in the works including a Nancy Drew and the Hardy Boys collaboration.

The Her Interactive formula for success could be summarized as:

1. Find an underserved segment of the audience.
2. License a known brand.

3. Produce a good quality product at a reasonable price through careful production scheduling and quality control.

An aspiring game writer or designer might consider this formula and think of other underserved audiences to write for, instead of attempting to duplicate current hits.

Anne Collins-Ludwick was the writer and producer of *The Secret of the Old Clock*. Before being involved in writing for games, Collins-Ludwick wrote for television. She was the Story Editor on *Vegas* and *Fantasy Island*, wrote scripts for *The New Twilight Zone*, and wrote and edited scripts for the entire eight year run of the detective show, *Matlock*.

When *Matlock* ended, Anne worked in web development and online games before joining Her Interactive. She has an M.A. in Radio/Television/Film Production from the University of Texas at Austin.

Comparing TV and game writing, Collins-Ludwick says:

> *Computer games, especially the* Nancy Drew *games, are a lot like TV shows, in that you have a main character who meets and talks to other characters in the course of solving some big problem. Although technically the two media are quite different, the principles that guide the writing and production of their content are amazingly similar.*

Collins-Ludwick stresses that writing the *Nancy Drew* games is very collaborative. She is part of a team with the designers and other creative team member who all contribute to the final game story and design.

The lead designer on *The Secret of the Old Clock* was Mari Tokuda, who worked closely with executive producer Robert Riedl. Tokuda holds degrees in Zoology and Creative Writing from the University of Washington.

Goals and Challenges of Writing *Nancy Drew: The Secret of the Old Clock*

Goals

Many of the goals in creating *The Secret of the Old Clock* are shared with other games in the *Nancy Drew* series. The writer and designers wanted to create a game that would appeal to their target female audience in a broad age range from ten to adult. They wanted the game to be an effective mystery, while still allowing significant interactivity, puzzles, and game play. Lastly, they wanted to add some new elements to this version of the game engine to make the game play fresh for repeat players of the *Nancy Drew* series.

Unique to this game is the goal of celebrating the 75th anniversary of the *Nancy Drew* books by setting the game in the 1930s and basing it on the first *Nancy Drew* book, *The Secret of the Old Clock*.

All of the above had to be accomplished within the same budget and aggressive six-month schedule as the previous games.

Challenges

There were several challenges to achieving the above goals:

- Adapting a 1930s book to a 21st century computer game
- Developing a single game that would be challenging and interesting both to a preteen and a late teens female, plus still have some nostalgia interest for older women.
- Accomplishing all of the above, particularly the period elements within budget and schedule.

Meeting the Challenge of Adapting a 1930s Book to a 21st Century Computer Game: The Process of Writing *The Secret of the Old Clock*

Criteria for Choosing a Book for a Nancy Drew Game

Adapting a book to a computer game has many of the same issues as adapting a book to film or television. A book's action must be visualized. Viewers and players do not want to listen to lengthy narration, dialogue, and particularly internal dialogue, which can be an important part of a book. Dialogue in games (and film/TV) needs to be shorter than what is often in a book, more conversational in tone because it is actually being spoken, and a back and forth interaction between two or more characters with limited long speeches.

In addition to the issues above that are shared with film and TV, there are issues unique to writing for a game. A major issue is that, as in the case of the *Nancy Drew* games, the book may have to be adapted to an existing game engine, which has specific requirements. The *Nancy Drew* engine is based on the user finding clues and solving mysteries. Because of this, the story on which a *Nancy Drew* game is based needs:

- intriguing locations for the user to explore to find clues, but the number of locations must be limited because of cost and user orientation.
- interesting characters for the player (Nancy Drew) to talk to.
- potential for puzzles and activities to be integrated into the story.
- objects as clues in the story that can be created in a game and viewed or manipulated by a player.

Besides the needs of the game engine, the Her Interactive team added another restriction on themselves as explained by Anne Collins-Ludwick, the writer of

The Secret of the Old Clock:

> *To never show Nancy, her family or her friends in our games is a stipulation that we*
> *imposed on ourselves. This was not because of game engine limitations, but because we'd*
> *rather leave what Nancy and associates look like up to the imagination of our Players,*
> *which affords them the pleasure of believing that Nancy looks just like they do, that Bess*
> *and George look just like their best friends, that Carson looks just like their dad, etc.*

Lastly, the head of Her Interactive and the Vice President of Marketing added one more criteria for this 12th game in the series—it had to pay tribute to the 75th anniversary of the first publication of *Nancy Drew* in 1930.

Choosing the Book and Product Concept

With the above criteria in mind and no book yet chosen, the task to develop the concept fell to the Creative Director at that time, Max Holechek, and later to lead designer Mari Tokuda. The first task was to choose the *Nancy Drew* book(s) the game would be based on. This choice is explained in the Initial Design Outline. This document is the first stage of story development and includes the product concept, characters, and narratives.

Initial Design Outline (Product Concept Section)

Product concept:

As Creative Director, acting as Lead Designer for ND12, I requested permission to use Nancy's first adventure, *The Secret of the Old Clock*, as the basis for the game. In order to differentiate the game's visual style from the eleven *Nancy Drew* games that precede it as well as showcase the specific elements that have contributed to Nancy Drew's unending popularity, I also requested that *The Secret of the Old Clock* game storyline take place in 1930, the year in which the first four *Nancy Drew* mysteries were published. These requests were approved by the Her Interactive President, the V.P. of Marketing and Sales, and by Simon and Schuster.

Concept challenges:

The Secret of the Old Clock was a difficult book to adapt to the Her Interactive *Nancy Drew* game format. The main challenges were that Nancy, her family, and her recurring friends can never be viewed in the HI games, yet most of the action of the book takes place in or around River Heights and greatly involves Nancy's home and family. Secondly, *The Secret of the Old Clock* is much less of a mystery story as it is an adventure tale. Because of this, the crime or mystery aspects of the book are, at best, flimsy.

Challenge solutions:

I studied the first four *Nancy Drew* books as they were originally written in 1930 (*The Secret of the Old Clock*, *The Hidden Staircase*, *The Bungalow Mystery*, and *The Mystery at Lilac Inn*). Though I found the storylines of all the books too weak to base a game upon individually, I took some of the strongest and most identifiable aspects of each book and wove them together to create a new, cohesive story. The new story not only stands solidly on its own, but it equally represents the spirit and basic conflict of all four books. In the end, *The Secret of the Old Clock* game will be a tribute to all of Nancy's original 1930 adventures.

Note that his description of the book's stories as flimsy means in terms of what would work in the *Nancy Drew* mystery game engine. As books, the stories hold up just fine.

Defining Characters and Narrative: Initial Design Outline

Once the books are chosen and basic concept is approved, the next step in the development of a *Nancy Drew* game is describing the key characters and the basic story narrative. The *Nancy Drew* engine allows four main characters or suspects besides Nancy Drew. The narrative at this point does not include interactivity, but just lays out the main beats of a story, similar to a film treatment. The narrative and characters are also included in the Initial Design Outline referenced above. Below are samples from this same document describing characters and narrative.

Initial Design Outline (Character and Narrative Section Excerpts)

The Secret of the Old Clock
Game Characters:

Emily Crandall
A seventeen year-old, casual school chum of Nancy's. Up until recently, Emily and her mother ran a popular roadside restaurant, the Lilac Inn, but the untimely death of the mother has closed the restaurant for a few weeks until matters are settled. It's Emily wish to continue the family business, and is looking forward to officially owning the property when she turns eighteen.

Marian Aborn
Thirty-seven year-old Marian is an old, close friend of Emily's mother. It was their agreement that Marian would become Emily's legal guardian should anything happen to Emily's mother, and Marian has come to care for Emily and assist in running the inn

for a year or more. Marian has a reputation for being a skilled aviator and amateur archeologist.

(Book Author's Note: The rest of the characters are described in a similar manner in the full Initial Design Outline.)

Game Narrative:

The story opens with Nancy arriving at the Lilac Inn in her blue roadster. Nancy wishes to check in on and support Emily, as Nancy can relate to her recent tragedy. The inn has been closed for a time, but is rescheduled to reopen within the week.

After meeting Emily and having a brief introduction to Emily's new guardian, the friendly and outgoing Marian, the inn shakes with a stove explosion in the kitchen. Amid shouts, the women take action to put out the fire and keep it from spreading.

After the fire has successfully been extinguished and the fire marshal has assessed the damage, Marian tells Nancy that the kitchen was mostly spared, but the large stove is too badly damaged to use. Money is very tight and Marian is not sure how it will be replaced. The inn may have to be sold. Marian says that she is concerned about Emily and how she'll react to this additional tragedy in her life. She says that Emily has been behaving in an increasingly curious manner and Marian fears for the poor girl's nerves.

Emily has indeed taken the news very badly and she confides her woes to Nancy. Emily loves the inn and feels akin to its many regulars. She knows that her mother would have wanted her to do whatever she could to save the inn and Emily says that she's ready to do so, even though the prospects seem grim.

Emily also relates the story of her uncle, Josiah Crowley, who died just before her mother did. Emily and her mother had been assisted financially from time to time by her eccentric, gregarious uncle, and he promised that they would be taken care of upon his death. However, to their surprise, Crowley's will only left them worthless stocks (that had been worth several thousands of dollars before the Wall Street crash) and his remaining assets were bequeathed to Richard Topham's Physic Science Organization, of which Crowley had been a sponsor.

Emily feels that there has been an error and that Josiah must have left a second will somewhere. If it could be found, the inn would be saved! Nancy promises to take the case.

Josiah Crowley used to live roughly a quarter mile away from the inn, and Nancy figures that his house would be a good place

to start the search. When she gets to the house, it is revealed
that Richard Topham, the new property owner, is now living there.
After allowing Nancy a brief tour and an explanation of his work,
Topham cuts the visit short when he realizes that Nancy is looking
for a second will. Nancy gets all but the bum's rush out the door.

The quest also takes Nancy to the local bank, where she meets
Jim Archer. Nancy is curious if Crowley has left any unclaimed
assets at the bank (safety deposit boxes, etc.) and Jim seems very
eager to help her. So eager, in fact, that Nancy senses that he's
quite taken with her. Unfortunately, nothing is found at the bank.
Jim promises to visit Nancy and Emily at the inn soon.

Nancy's investigation reveals that Josiah was a kooky guy and
was rather obsessed with the safety of his valuables. Finding
records of his assets proves difficult, as he has hidden them
behind layers of codes, riddles, and puzzles. Her first lead is a
journal she finds in an old clock that he left with Emily's mother.

Though Carson Drew and Nancy's old chum, Helen Corning, are
quite busy (Carson with a big case, Helen a counselor at a girl's
summer camp), they assist Nancy with the case via phone calls and
written letters when they can.

In the full Initial Design Outline, the complete concept, all the characters
and the full narrative is described. The above is just a sample for purposes of
illustration.

Collins-Ludwick said that the designer works closely with the writer. The
designer primarily does the puzzles, broad story line, and interactions. The writer
is in charge of writing all dialogue, voice-overs, and getting them recorded. The
process is very collaborative between designer and writer.

Structuring the Interactivity: The Project Flowchart

After the narrative and characters are laid out in the Initial Design Outline, the
next step is designing the interactivity. This is done primarily by the designer in the
project flowchart but with the writer's collaboration.

The actual chart is very complex. Before viewing a sample of the actual chart, it
will be helpful to understand the basic game structure. Please refer to Figure 20-1.
This flowchart is simplified for the sake of illustration. In the actual game, there
are many more locations, puzzles, activities, etc. The structure of the *Nancy Drew*
games is a string of pearls structure, which was discussed in Chapter 18. The game
presents a series of locations or worlds that Nancy can search. As she uncovers
more clues additional worlds are available to her, and she moves forward in the
narrative.

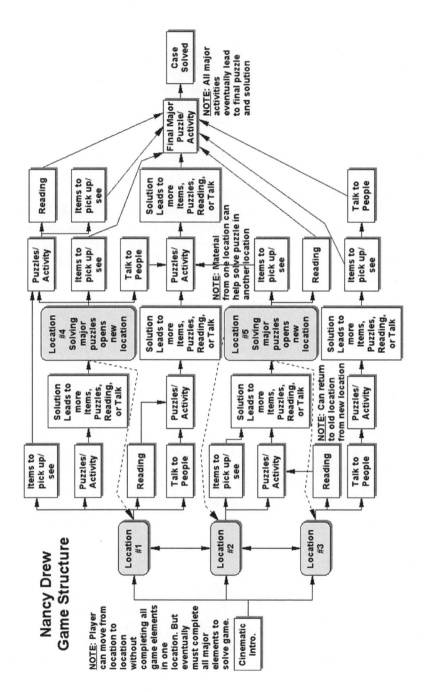

Figure 20-1 *Diagram of Nancy Drew Game Structure.*

Looking at the chart in Figure 20-1, notice that after the introduction, the player can

- choose to go to several locations.
- move from location to location without completing all game elements in one location, but eventually must complete all major elements to solve the game.
- move back and sideways on paths to various locations and even redo some of the puzzles, but to move forward new puzzles have to be solved.
- use material from one location to solve puzzles in another location.

All major elements eventually lead to the final puzzle, which must be solved by the player to unravel the mystery.

One of the challenges of this type of structure is to integrate puzzles and activities so they do not slow story pace but do help move the mystery forward. The puzzles and activities in this game were integrated primarily by establishing the character of Josiah Crowley as an eccentric who created all sorts of puzzles and games to provide security for his possessions and ideas. Once this basic premise is accepted, then the existence of many of the puzzles make sense. Puzzles and activities not directly related to Josiah Crowley were sometimes harder to justify.

The other major challenge with the structure as illustrated in Figure 20-1 is to give players the impression of significant interactivity, while still maintaining control of the unfolding of the basically linear mystery. The player is allowed interactivity through dialogue choices, activities, puzzles, and freedom to move from location to location by walking or driving. But the game's writer and designer are constantly nudging the player into the right direction to solve the mystery. Nudging techniques include:

- comments in the conversations, such as Emily's guardian telling Nancy Drew that she has to talk to Emily.
- voice-overs by others and Nancy Drew herself that indicate the importance of an item or a possible follow-up activity.
- written assets, such as books, newspapers, etc. that Nancy can read.
- hints delivered via the telephone from Nancy's dad or friends.
- Nancy's Journal and Task List, which are combined in her notebook. These are available at any time from buttons on the main interface. (See Figure 20-2.) The journal recaps key information discovered so far. The Task List for Junior Detectives lists the things Nancy has to do to solve the mystery. The game writer has to write both the Journal and Task List.

All of these tools work together to help the player get to the successful conclusion of the game while still maintaining the impression of interactivity.

Keeping the structure in Figure 20-1 in mind, now look at Figure 20-3, which is a section of the actual flowchart used to structure *The Secret of the Old Clock.*

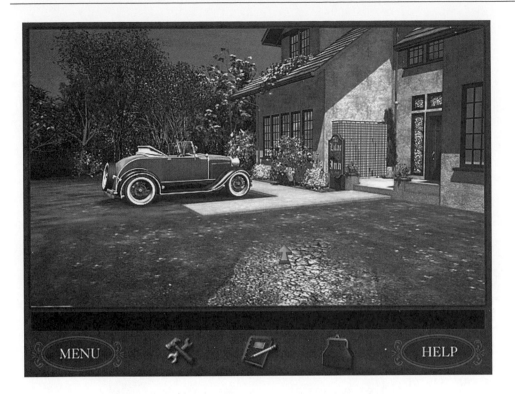

Figure 20-2 *Main Interface showing buttons for Tools, Journal, and Money.*

Note that this chart follows the same structure as the simple chart shown earlier, but is more complex and each symbol has specific labels. This is only a small section of the complete game chart, but it does illustrate many of the actual chart conventions. These include: coding of symbols to indicate type of game element, indicating where money is spent, and use of dashed lines to indicate nonessential action. A player can perform a nonessential action, but it is not absolutely necessary in order to win the game. The number coding on the symbols are currently not used in production.

The production flowchart is a key tool in planning the interactivity of the *Nancy Drew* games. The first iteration (version) of the flowchart is basically the story line as described in the initial outline. As the design and writing process progresses, puzzles, games, conversations, and other interactions are added to move the story forward and develop the mystery.

The game is usually designed so that all options are not open to the user at the beginning. Otherwise it would be overwhelming to have too many initial choices. Instead, several locations are available to explore and a few individuals are willing to talk. As the player solves puzzles, finds items, and completes activities, more options open up to the user. These additional options can be new locations or additional people to talk to.

Nancy Drew: The Secret of the Old Clock
Flowchart Excerpt

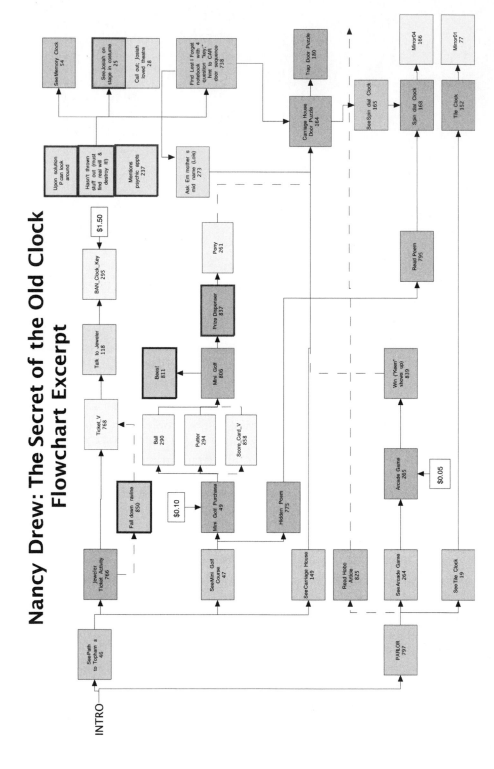

Figure 20-3 *Section of* The Secret of the Old Clock *production flowchart.*

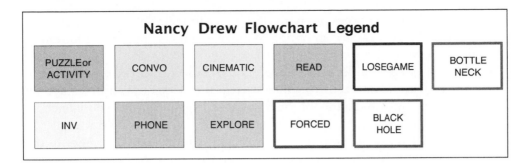

Figure 20-4 *Symbol Legend for* The Secret of the Old Clock *production flowchart.*

For example, when the player/Nancy Drew first tries to talk to Richard Topham, the paranormal expert, Topham will not talk with the player until she first solves a logic puzzle and proves her intelligence. Topham does not want to waste time with a dullard. Another example is that the door to the carriage house behind Josiah Crowley's old house has an elaborate word combination that must be solved before getting access to the building.

In addition to helping plan the story and basic interactions, the flowchart is a valuable tool for planning the production and avoiding design pitfalls in the game. Key to this use of the chart is the flowchart symbol legend as shown in Figure 20-4.

Every type of element that is added to the flowchart has a specific symbol so that the designers, writer, and other team members can easily see how the structure and interactions are developing. Following are descriptions of what the various symbols stand for. This description also gives a better understanding of the various elements in this game and in this type of game in general.

 The chart and symbols are color-coded. If you refer to this book's CD-ROM in the Chapters/Nancy Drew section you will find a color version of the flowchart and key.

- PUZZLE OR ACTIVITY (tan): a puzzle the player solves or something they can do, such as playing a record on a phonograph.
- CONVO (light green): a conversation. The player can talk to another character at this point.
- CINEMATIC (light blue): a linear movie scene, such as the opening with Nancy driving to the Inn. There are no options for interactivity in a movie scene.
- READ (purple): a book, notebook, newspaper, etc. that the player can read and get clues.
- INV (yellow): an item that can be picked up by the player and added to their toolbox (inventory) as if the player physically had the item. The item can later be used to solve puzzles and get information.

- PHONE (gray): an opportunity for the player to make or receive phone calls.
- EXPLORE (dark green): an option to move around or look into a location, such as a room, a drawer, or a tunnel.
- FORCED (green border around one of other boxes described above): a game element with no interactivity. Once started, the element must be completed. The cinematic introduction of the game is an example. Once you launch the game, the cinematic introduction plays and you cannot stop it until it finishes. An example on the chart in Figure 20-3 is Prize Dispenser in the middle of the chart. Once you make Par on the golf game, you automatically are taken to the prize dispenser where a prize pony toy is given. This toy is important later in the game.
- BLACK HOLE (red border around one of other boxes): Collins-Ludwick explained in an e-mail that "a black hole is an event which, although it may enhance a Player's enjoyment of the game, goes nowhere in terms of the central plot. Conversations which don't impart critical information—a name, a code, directions, etc.—could all be correctly termed black holes, which is why usually only plot critical convos are indicated on the flowchart. We mark them on the flowchart to remind ourselves that those elements are 'unnecessary' in terms of the critical path."
- LOSE GAME (blue border around one of other boxes): some action that causes you to lose the game. There are two examples on the Figure 20-3 chart sample near the top of the chart: Bees! and Fall Down Ravine. If you do lose a game, you do have the option of clicking the Second Chance button and restarting from right before you lost.
- BOTTLENECK (magenta border around one of other boxes).

Collins-Ludwick explained this last item in an e-mail:

A bottleneck is a place where "sub-paths" converge, and which therefore has the potential to produce some awkward game play. For instance, if the design of a particular game dictates that a new environment will not open until the Player has gotten two different pieces of information from the same phone character, it's possible—maybe not likely but still possible—that the Player, because of previous choices he/she has made during the game, will have to get those two pieces of info with two phone calls that follow one right after another. We mark bottlenecks to remind ourselves that they are places where the Player could get confused and/or frustrated because they cannot advance until they do one certain thing, or until something happens over which they seemingly have no control (they must enter a certain environment to trigger the needed phone call). When we can't avoid bottlenecks in design, we at least make sure that the Player, at that point in the game, has some indication of what needs to be done, through hints, the journal or the task list.

Once the interactivity is sufficiently laid out in the flowchart, then the next stage is writing the dialogue.

Writing the Dialogue: Animated Characters and off Camera Scripts

As details are filled in on flowchart, the writer can start writing the script. The flowchart summarizes roughly what Nancy says and what other characters say to her; the script has the actual dialogue. The script starts off as two scripts. One is for animated characters who we see talking on screen to Nancy, and the other is for off-camera characters who we don't see. These off-camera characters can be on the phone, actually off-camera, or Nancy musing to herself. See Figures 20-5 and 20-6 for examples of the two types of conversations. When both scripts are done, they are combined into one huge script.

Anne Collins-Ludwick said that the major difference in writing dialogue for a game as opposed to for film or TV is in having to write multiple dialogue responses for interactivity. There are dialogue choices for the player to make for many of the conversations. These are indicated by the lines of light blue text on the bottom of the interface. Unlike some of the games that are discussed later in the book, the dialogue choices made by the player don't change the direction of the story. As explained earlier in this chapter in the section on structure, this game is structured

Figure 20-5 *On-camera conversations with an animated character.*

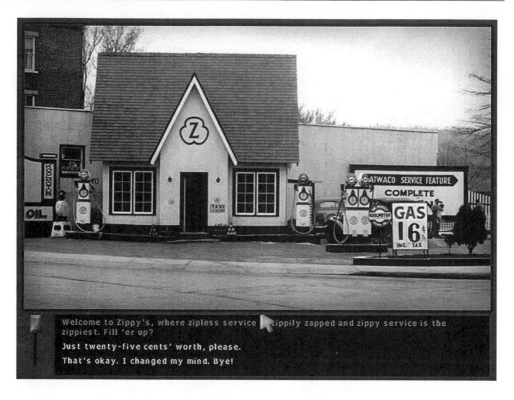

Figure 20-6 *Off-camera conversations.*

along multiple location paths that all eventually lead to the same linear story no matter what choices you make in the dialogue or what information you discover. However, asking the right questions in the dialogue does make you get to the end of the story and solve the mystery sooner. Also in some cases, by asking the wrong questions, you may miss information and lose the game.

There is extensive use of voice-over dialogue in this game. When you are traveling around the town and "park" at one of the buildings, you are greeted by a picture of the building in a photo or on the drive "map," and you hear the building's residents in voice-over but do not see them. There are also voice-overs of Nancy musing to herself as she explores. These function as hints, making sure the players understand what they are seeing and possibly nudging them in a new direction. The games formal Help or Hint system is also delivered in voice-over on the pay phone just outside the inn. Nancy can call her father or friends and get advice on how to solve specific aspects of the mystery.

Both on-camera and off-camera dialogue is also listed in text at the bottom of the screen so that the game can be played without sound or by the hearing impaired.

Script Sample #1: Jane's Introduction

All on camera dialogue (conversation) is written in a Word document script that follows a proprietary format required by the game engine. All journal and checklist entries (see Figure 20-2), as well as the text for most of the voice-overs, in the game are contained in a customized Excel spread sheet. The writer found it initially hard to work with these specialized formats but over time has gotten used to it. The conversation script has to not only indicate what the dialogue will be but also branching dialogue possibilities based on previous things the player has heard and seen. The conversation script was more than three hundred pages long, so the samples below are just a fraction of the complete script.

The first sample below is a fairly simple interaction that takes place near the beginning of the game. Because the player has not experienced much else in the game, the branching possibilities are fairly straightforward. The conversation in straight brackets, [ ], indicates the speech by the animated character Jane. In Figure 20-5, this appears at the top of the dialogue block in the darker blue. The dialogue in arrow brackets, <>, indicates the dialogue choices for the player/Nancy Drew. The words "Go to" followed by a number, indicates which scene a dialogue choice will lead to. Note that often the dialogue choices do not actually make a difference in the evolution of the story or in the responses the player gets, but they do give the player a feeling of additional interactivity. Follow further down the script to see each dialogue choice. Note also that each piece of dialogue has its own unique code for tracking purposes, such as [JWP82].

Scene 1082

[Emily didn't say anything about you coming until just this morning.][JWP82]

<{uncertainly} Is it okay that I'm here?><NJP82b> **Go to 1004**

<She didn't?><NJP82a> **Go to 1004**

Flag Set: None
Info Check: No
Bye: No

===========

Scene 1003 Moved

===========

Scene 1004

[Don't get me wrong. She can invite anybody here she wants. It's just that she's gotten so darn forgetful lately.][JWP04]

<Is she all right?><NJP03a> **Go to 1005**

<Maybe she's just ... you know, still thinking about her mom.>

<NJP03b> **Go to 1006**

Flag Set: None
Info Check: No
Bye: No

==========

Scene 1005
[{with a sigh} Well, now, that's hard to say.][JWP05]

Go to 1006
Flag Set: None
Info Check: No
Bye: No

==========

Scene 1006
[She misses her mom, that's for sure. So do I. Gloria and me, we
were best friends, ya know. The two of us ran this swell little
dress shop over in Capital City.][JWP06]

Go to 1007
Flag Set: None
Info Check: No
Bye: No

==========

Scene 1007
[But then, she got hitched, and I didn't, and the next thing I
know, she's writing me saying it would sure take a load off her
mind if I could take care of her little girl should something ever
happen to her.][JWP07]

<Emily's father ...?><NJP07a> **Go to 1008**

<It was nice of you to say yes.><NJP07b> **Go to 1009**

Flag Set: None
Info Check: No
Bye: No

==========

Scene 1008
[Died in the War. Cantigny, I think. Anyway ...][JWP08]

Go to 1009
Flag Set: EV_JW_Said_Cantigny = True

Info Check: No
Bye: No

===========

Scene 1009
[I couldn't say no. I mean, what're best friends for?
{troubled}I just wish I knew how to help Emily.][JWP09]

<You make it sound like she's in some kind of trouble.><NJP09a>
Go to 1010

<Help her do what?><NJP09b> **Go to 1010**

Flag Set: None
Info Check: No
Bye: No

===========

Scene 1010
[She's been acting so...{then} Look, go talk to her. She probably
just needs to spend some time with a bearcat like you instead of
some dumb Dora like me.][JWP10]

Script Sample #2: Nudging the Player to Talk to Emily

Another function of the interactive dialogue is to nudge the player in the right
direction so they can proceed forward and solve the mystery. If at the end of the
previous discussion, the player clicks on Jane again, they are told to talk to Emily
in Scene 1012 below. If player clicks on Jane a 3rd time without talking to Emily,
they are told even more tersely what to do in Scene 1013 below.

Scene 1012
[Go on up. She's in her room. Just make like a Boy Scout and be
prepared.][JWP12]

Go to Node
Flag Set: None
Info Check: No
Bye: No

===========

Scene 1013
[Talk to Emily, then talk to me.][JWP00c]

```
Go to Node
Flag Set: None
Info Check: No
Bye: No
```

===========

Script Sample #3: More Complex Conditions

In order to solve the carriage house door puzzle, the player needs to discover Emily's mother's middle name. But the player will only know that they need to ask this if they have seen several other clues previously in the game. These conditions are laid out in the first line of the script sample below in the "If ... then" string of conditions. In the example below, the player asks Jane, Emily's guardian who comes up blank. The writer Collins-Ludwick explains the "If ... then" logic in the script below.

> As the writer, I'm responsible for the logic—that is, for indicating what conditions have to be true (or false) in order for something to happen, or for certain dialogue to be available (and oh, can the logic get complicated!). Every time something significant happens in the game—the Player sees or hears something important, gets a piece of info from someone, encounters something new, etc.—we set a flag (i.e., EV_Saw_Questions = True), which the engine keeps track of.
>
> When you played the game you probably noticed that when you clicked on a character, he/she would look up at you and greet you. That greeting will vary depending on what flags have been set at that point in the game. Likewise, in the course of your conversation with a character, there will usually be a point at which you can either ask the character a question (usually there will be several to choose from) or say goodbye. We refer to those questions as "Information Checks." It's a structure, which tells the engine that when certain conditions are met (certain flags have been set), make this question available to the Player. Once the Player asks that question, we (usually) set a flag, which will prevent Player from being able to ask that question again.
>
> It's important to note, too, that while convo.doc (the script) is one of two documents that provide the engine with the text that will be displayed on-screen during the game, the script also serves as a road map for the person who is building the scenes that comprise the convo sequences. So, in the example you cited, "If EV_Saw_Questions = True and EV_EC_Said_Lois = False and EV_JW_Said_Mid_Name = False" means when those three flags have been set as indicated, then Player will be able to click on (ask) the question that follows the conditions (it will be tagged with <>), and the character will respond with the line that's in square brackets ([ ]).
>
> The three lines, "Flag Set: None, Info Check: No, Bye: No," just tell the scene-builder whether a flag should be set when that particular info check plays, whether the scene should go to another info check, and whether Player can say goodbye at that point. Sometimes an info check scene will be hard-coded to go directly to another scene (Info Check: No); sometimes an info check will go to another info check, which the engine will make available (Info Check: Yes). If all info checks have been exhausted at that point, Player can click on the goodbye response.

The sample writer explained on the previous page follows.

Scene 1047 Information Check

```
If EV_Saw_Questions = True and EV_EC_Said_Lois = False and
EV_JW_Said_Mid_Name = False
```

<What was Emily's mom's middle name, do you remember?><NJP47>

['Course I do. It was ...{frustrated} Oh, piffle! It's right on the
tip of my tongue. It was ... it was ...][JWP47]

Go to 1048

```
Flag Set: EV_JW_Said_Mid_Name = True
Info Check: No
Bye: No
```

============

Scene 1048

[{with an exasperated sigh} It'll pop into this feeble brain of
mine one of these days. Why don't you just go ask Emily.][JWP48]

```
Flag Set: None
Info Check: Yes
Bye: Yes
```

============

Script Sample #4: Voice Over Telegram Delivery

Delivering telegrams is the main way that Nancy Drew can make money in the game. Nancy picks up telegrams from the telegraph office then drives to the delivery. Nancy gets a different response each time she delivers the telegram. Below is just a small fraction of the telegram deliveries to Lowood Academy. Note the event conditions at the beginning of each scene beginning with "If."

Scene 5026 Lowood Academy

```
If EV_Tel_Temple_Academy = True and EV_Said_Tel_Temple_Academy =
False and EV_First_Time = False
```

[<c0>Hello. I've got a telegram for Miss Temple?<c1>{NTA26a}

I am she.][TET26aX]

Go to 5140

```
Flag Set: EV_Delivered = True and EV_Said_Tel_Temple_Academy = True
Info Check: No
Bye: No
```

- - - - - - - - -

```
If EV_Tel_Temple_Academy = True and EV_Said_Tel_Temple_Academy =
False and EV_First_Time = True

[<c0>Hello, Miss Temple. I've got another telegram for you.<c1>
{NTA26bx}

Thank you.][TET26bX]
```

Go to 5141
```
Flag Set: EV_Delivered = True and EV_Said_Tel_Temple_Academy = True
Info Check: No
Bye: No
```

```
- - - - - - - - -
```

```
If EV_Tel_Brock_Academy = True and EV_Said_Tel_Brock_Academy =
False and EV_First_Time = False

[<c0>Hello, Miss Temple. I've got a telegram for Mr. Brockelhurst?
<c1> {NTA26c}

He's in class. I'll give it to him.][TET26cX]
```

Go to 5142
```
Flag Set: EV_Delivered = True and EV_Said_Tel_Brock_Academy = True
Info Check: No
Bye: No
```

```
- - - - - - - - -
```

```
If EV_Tel_Brock_Academy = True and EV_Said_Tel_Brock_Academy =
False and EV_First_Time = True

[<c0>Hello, Miss Temple. May I leave this telegram for
Mr. Brockelhurst with you?<c1>{NTA26d}

You may indeed.][TET26dX]
```

Script Sample #5: Hints

The Hints in this game are delivered by the pay phone just outside the Lilac Inn, usually by Nancy's father Carson. See the first two scenes below (5117 and 5118) to get an idea of the kinds of information Nancy can get through the hints. Notice the fairly long "If ... then" conditions in the first line. This allows the programmers to deliver the correct hint based on the player's previous action in the game. Sometimes, there are no hints available and the player has to solve the puzzles on their own. Look at Scene 1901 below. If the long list of conditions at the beginning of the dialogue is met, there is no more help for Nancy, and she is told the line is busy.

Scene 5117 Information Check

If EV_Carson_Said_Hints = True and EV_Solved_Mirrors = True and
EV_Solved_Trap_Door = True and EV_Tried_Attic_Lock = True and
EV_Solved_Attic_Lock = False and EV_Attic_Lock_Hint = False

<I got the window in the carriage house open, but I'm not sure
what to do next. Any hints?><NCD117>

[Try moving the mirrors and see what happens to that beam of light
from the window. I suspect that having everything properly aligned
will put a brand new spin on things.][CDP117]

Flag Set: EV_Attic_Lock_Hint = True
Info Check: Yes
Bye: Yes

==================
Scene 5118 Information Check

If EV_Carson_Said_Hints = True and EV_Saw_Crystal_Note = True and
EV_RT_Said_Zener_First = False and EV_Quartz_Hint = False

<I have a feeling that getting Josiah's ham radio to work could be
pretty important. But it's missing piece of quartz. Any hint as to
where I might find it?><NCD118>

[Richard Topham may've taken delivery of it after Josiah passed
away. Why don't you check with him?][CDP118]

Flag Set: EV_Quartz_Hint = True
Info Check: Yes
Bye: Yes

Scene 1901

If EV_Carson_Said_Stole = True and EV_Carson_Said_Telegrams = True
and EV_JA_Said_Real_Will = True and EV_Carson_Said_JA = True and
EV_Carson_Said_Car = True and EV_JA_Said_Apologize = True and
EV_Carson_Said_Guardian = True and EV_Said_Behind_Wall = True
and EV_Heard_Topham1 = True and EV_Carson_Said_Topham = True and
EV_Solved_Zener = True and EV_Solved_Bertha_Lock = True and
EV_Logic_Test_Hint = True and EV_Memory_Clock_Hint = True
and EV_Carriage_Lock_Hint = True and EV_Par_Golf_Hint = True and
EV_Poem_Puzzle_Hint = True and EV_Tile_Clock_Hint = True
and EV_Spin_Dial_Clock_Hint = True and EV_Gear_Clock_Hint = True
and EV_Bounce_Hint = True and EV_Mirror_Hint = True and
EV_Trap_Door_Hint = True and EV_Attic_Lock_Hint = True and
EV_Quartz_Hint = True and EV_Zener_Hint = True and EV_Pie_Hint =
True and EV_Dress_Hint = True and EV_Fish_Hint = True and
EV_Journal_Hint = True and EV_Bertha_Hint = True and

```
EV_Bottom_Hint = True and EV_Mother_Hint = True
and EV_Special_Golf_Hint = True and EV_Trivet_Hint = True and
EV_Secret_Passage_Hint = True and EV_Snoop_Hint = True

[Hang on a minute.][OPP01]
```

Add appropriate SFX, then
Go to 1762

Scene 1762
```
[Sorry. The line's busy. Here's your nickel back.
<c0>Thank you.<c1>{NOP06}][OPP06X]
```

Script Sample #6: Voice-Over Gas Station

In addition to the telegrams and the phones, another kind of voice-over occurs when Nancy parks at various building in town. Below is what happens at the gas station. This scene is pictured in Figure 20-6. We never see the attendant, just a photograph of a 1930s gas station.

Gas Station Owner
```
===========
```

Scene 5000 Greetings
```
If EV_Tel_Zippy = True and EV_Said_Tel_Zippy = False and
EV_First_Time = False
[Welcome to Zippy's, where zipless service is zippily zapped and
zippy service is the zippiest.
<c0>{a beat} No offense, but that's kind of a silly slogan.<c1>
{NZP00b}
{dejected} I know. My mother made it up. {then} Want some gas?]
[ZIP00bX]
```

Go to 5001
```
Flag Set: EV_Delivered = True and EV_Said_Tel_Zippy = True
Info Check: No
Bye: No
```

The Critical Path: Step-by-Step Outline

When design and dialogue are nailed down, then a document is prepared called the critical path. This is a step-by-step outline describing the ideal, fastest path to get to the end of the game and solve the mystery. This describes the most efficient way to play the game by asking all the right questions and solving the puzzles in the proper order. The critical path also provides the puzzle solutions. The critical path is usually written by the game writer, but sometimes the Lead Designer will write the critical path first as an aid to designing the game. It's largely a guide to understanding game flow, and in its final form is used mainly by the game testers, as well as reviewers. It allows reviewers to quickly play the game to the end. A sample of the critical path follows.

CLK Critical Path (Excerpt)

Italics refer to optional steps

1. OPENING NARRATIVE/CINEMATIC. Radio announcer establishes that it's 1930 and sets the stage. ND has been invited to Lilac Inn by Emily Crandall (EC), a casual friend who lost her mom (Gloria Crandall) the previous month to illness. CROSSFADE TO ND turns onto drive to Inn in roadster, passes car parked at side of drive, pulls up in front of Inn.

2. P sees coin phone on porch and calls father, who asks her to pick something up for him from the telegraph office when she has a chance.

3. P talks to Jane Willoughby (JW) at desk area just outside kitchen/dining area. JW is EC's legal guardian according to the wishes of EC's mom, one of Jane's oldest and dearest friends. JW is worried about EC's mental condition.

4. P meets EC in her room. She seems nervous, distracted, a bit paranoid. She and mom ran the Inn; now it's just EC and Jane (who, compared to her mom, knows very little), and it's been hard. Without going into detail as to why, she retrieves the jewels she inherited from her mother and presents them to P, saying she wants ND to take them home and put them in Carson's safe.

5. Suddenly there's an explosion. From the other room we hear footsteps, and JW yelling "Fire!" EC reacts and we CROSSFADE TO:

6. Aftermath of explosion. P talks to JW; we learn that fire department just left. Stove exploded. Looks like someone (EC maybe) left the gas on. Much damage to kitchen. Line to phone on desk was destroyed. EC is in room, understandably upset. JW goes to answer the pay phone which is ringing. P hears an O.S. scream from EC and we cut to EC's room.

7. P reacts as EC says her jewels are gone! Someone must've stolen them in all the excitement. Now EC and the Inn are really in trouble. P asks whether jewels were insured; EC says their banker, Jim Archer (JA) would know for sure. If only Josiah Crowley, an eccentric old man who died six

months ago, had left money for EC and her mom like he always said he would ("Time will tell," he'd always say). Instead, he left them nothing. Everything went to Richard Topham (RT) instead.

8. *P may play Emily's phonograph on the phonograph player in her room.*

9. P walks over to see RT, who lives in the nearby house that used to be Josiah's and runs a school for the development of paranormal powers.

10. On the way to RT's P catches the receipt for the appraisal of a key that someone has dropped on the path back to the Inn (don't catch it when on the bridge).

11. At RT's house, his cat won't stop meowing until P finds the cat's favorite toy and gives it to him (it's under the table to the left of the front door when facing the fireplace).

12. Topham refuses to waste his time talking further to P unless she can "prove" herself worthy.

13. P solves the logic test he gives her and returns it to Topham. Answers: 1.) All Wet 2.) Doll Up 3.) Double Cross 4.) Dry Up 5.) Big Cheese

14. P is given permission to poke around Josiah's stuff. RT hasn't thrown anything out so the small rooms are very cluttered with mementos (i.e., interesting junk).

15. P will need to ask RT's permission to look around whenever she enters his house

16. *P sees a picture of Josiah in costume on stage; call out reveals that Josiah loved theater.*

17. P finds old clock, learns that it belonged to Josiah.

18. P solves clock puzzle (matching tiles) and finds a mirror inside it, which she takes.

19. P finds Josiah's "Lest I forget ..." pad (in the elephant compartment on the secretary next to the robot) which includes four questions in with verbal reference to carriage house (What are you when you win Bard Bounce? What poet is the cat's meow? What will par on my miniature golf course get you? What's Gloria's middle name?) It also refers to the "tick tock on top," with four names Flute, Thisby, Pyramus, and Bottom. Stuffed into the "Lest I Forget ..." is a carbon copy of a letter with the name smudged out.

20. P exits and locates the carriage house out back and sees that it is locked with four four-letter word spin locks (hence the four questions) (to the right before the bridge when exiting RT's house).

21. P discovers Josiah's private mini-golf course on path back to Inn (on the left just after the bridge when exiting RT's house).

22. P rents a golf ball, putter, and score card.

23. P plays golf and pars all six holes (tricks for the golf holes—3rd hole "Hole Lot of Lava"—to the right is a small hole in the volcano that is a shortcut for the ball—4th hole "Sky Rail Inc."—get it into the middle hole for a shortcut—).

24. P is rewarded with a small, cheaply made toy pony, dispensed by a crudely made machine.

25. P notices a mini-game/puzzle next to the golf course (in a giant golf ball).

26. P solves the puzzle (The answer is random and the different colors can only be used once) and a poem is revealed.

27. P goes back to the Inn, discovers a "Bard Bounce" machine in parlor.

28. P solves Bard Bounce, a sign reveals the word "keen."

Junior
Move yellow left
Move green left
Move green down
Move blue left
Move blue down
Move blue right
Move red down
Move red right
Move red up
Move yellow down

Senior
Move blue left
Move yellow left
Move yellow up
Move yellow right
Move blue up
Move green up

```
Move green left
Move green down
Move blue down
Move yellow left
Move blue up
Move blue right
Move yellow right
Move red up
Move red right
Move green right
Move red down
Move red left
Move green left
```

Adapting a 1930s Novel to a Computer Game Conclusion

The process Her Interactive followed adapting the first *Nancy Drew* novels to a computer game serves as a good example of this type of adaptation. As discussed above, their process included the following steps:

- Careful selection of original source material with a clear focus on the elements needed to make a strong game of this type—intriguing environments, interesting characters, and a complex mystery with potential for integrating puzzles and activities.
- Clear initial definition of characters and basic narrative in a written document.
- Systematic mapping out of the interactive options using a flowchart.
- Writing strong dialogue with multiple options for the users and in a format that can easily be integrated into the game engine.
- Create a step-by-step critical path walkthrough for clear view of the game particularly for testing and reviewers.

By following these steps, Her Interactive created an effective, modern computer game from a seventy-five year old book.

Meeting the Challenge of Developing a Computer Game for a Broad Female Audience

Her Interactive's mission is "to transport girls and women into the fun, interactive world of classic adventure games." The company writes that their games are "ideal for players ages 10 to adult." There are a number of techniques and content considerations used by Her Interactive to reach their target audience.

Considerations for a Female Audience

A key and somewhat obvious consideration is to avoid elements that are repellent to most females. This includes limiting violence and gender stereotypes. There are no blood baths in the Her Interactive games, and you will never see Nancy or any female character act or look like the dumb bimbos popular in many of the hit games today. Even violent scenes, such as the car crash at the end of *The Old Clock* and the kitchen blowing up at the beginning, are portrayed with great discretion. The kitchen explosion is just an off-camera noise and a cross fade to a boarded up charred door.

Besides avoiding elements negative to women, these games also, of course, include material women like. The game's writer points out that most women enjoy social interactions. So the game's designer and writer make sure that the player has lots of opportunities to talk to people, just like in real life even if they are not telling you something important about solving the mysteries. There are a lot of phone conversations between Nancy and her friends that serve no other purpose than fun, like any teenager chatting on the phone with her girlfriends.

Collins-Ludwick writes that most of the time, the designers and writers do not have to consciously worry about creating games that appeal to a female audience because much of that appeal is built into the *Nancy Drew* source material.

When we design a game, we frankly don't worry much about our audience. We simply try to create the most interesting, exciting game we can using the character of Nancy Drew to drive the story. If we make sure the story line showcases her defining qualities—her curiosity, determination, courage, compassion, sense of humor, and sense of justice—our games will naturally appeal to females, just as Nancy has appealed to females for seventy-five years. True, we're well aware that most females seem to enjoy social interaction more than most men, and so we make sure there're lots of opportunities in our games for the Player to talk to people, but questioning suspects and pumping witnesses for information is totally in keeping with the Nancy Drew character. Snooping and talking and breaking codes were everyday activities for Nancy, and happily they lend themselves very well to the engine we've developed for our games. The fact that there is no mayhem, sadism, gore or profanity in our games has more to do with the fact that these elements are absent from the books than with the fact that most women don't seem to buy computer games which feature them. In short, creating games based on Nancy Drew *books has made our lives relatively easy when it comes to appealing to a female audience because if we do our job right, it's Nancy who's doing the appealing, not us.*

Reaching a Broad Audience Age Range

Avoiding violence, profanity, gender stereotypes, and gore while including social interactions and courageous compassionate female characters helps to create games that attract females, but Her Interactive still has to achieve their stated goal of appealing to the broad age range of ten to adult.

One of the major ways they achieve this is that the game has two difficulty levels Junior and Senior detective. As you may have noticed at the end of the critical path example shown previously on page 327, the Senior detective puzzles are much harder. Availability of hints is another major factor as Collins-Ludwick explains:

> *Telephone hints (which are usually given by Bess and George, although in some games Ned Nickerson, Nancy's boyfriend, or Carson Drew provide them) are only available to Junior Detectives, as are many of the more pointed VOs. And while all Players have access to Nancy's Journal, in which we can and quite often do clarify or emphasize pieces of information that Players come upon during the game, only Junior Detectives can look at the Task List, which reminds Players of what they've done and, based on that, what they still need to do.*

Different difficulty levels may be the major reason that the *Nancy Drew* games can be enjoyed by a wide age range, but Her Interactive also tries other techniques to include the older audience. *The Secret of the Old Clock* game provides a good example of this in its use of the 1930s *Nancy Drew* books as source material and in setting the game in 1930. The game makes good use of the 1930 setting with period music, slang, photographs, and clothing styles. This is a clear attempt to appeal to older gamers who may have been introduced to the original *Nancy Drew* books. This is not to say that they read the books in the 1930s, but that the books they read twenty or thirty years ago were the original books set in the 1930s.

Perhaps the last major item that helps with broad audience appeal is that even though each *Nancy Drew* game uses the same basic game engine, each new game includes some enhancement to the engine so there is something new for the player to experience. In *The Secret of the Old Clock* game, the major innovation was that Nancy could drive her car around town. Adding to the interest and complexity of driving the car is that gas gets used up and tires get worn out, especially if you drive over potholes. Gas and new tires both cost money, another new issue for Nancy to face.

Meeting the Challenge of Completing All of the Tasks Described Above and Still Staying on Budget and Schedule

When writing a book or a short story, a writer can create elaborate actions, scenes, and multitudes of characters without affecting the budget of the final book. Unfortunately in film, TV, and computer games, these same elements can quickly inflate a budget so the product is no longer profitable.

In addition to building great games, Her Interactive's key to success is building these games on schedule and on budget. Each game has a six month schedule, and in most cases, the same budget as the previous game. This has allowed Her Interactive to price their games correctly for their market and still turn a profit.

Keeping within budget while writing a game is an important skill for the writer. A writer will often be asked for an alternative way to accomplish a game goal that is less expensive but equally effective. In *The Secret of the Old Clock*, this was a particular challenge because this was the first game that was set in the 1930s period and the first to allow the character to drive a car and thus visit more locations.

Some of the solutions to staying on budget are built into the game specifications to begin with. The same basic engine is used for each game, but something new is added each time to keep it fresh. All of the *Nancy Drew* games are also limited to four speaking, on-screen characters besides Nancy Drew. This means that other interactions have to be handled in different ways. As discussed previously, *The Secret of the Old Clock* makes very effective us of voice-over to solve this problem. For example, in the scene pictured in Figure 20-6, Nancy has "parked" at the gas station but instead of seeing the attendant, we see a photo of a 1930s gas station and hear the interaction with Nancy in voice-over. This use of old photos is also a very effective way to set the 1930s setting without great expense. When Nancy delivers her telegrams throughout the town, many locations are pictured with photos and a lively voice-over. Other locations are pictured on the animated map (Figure 20-7) of

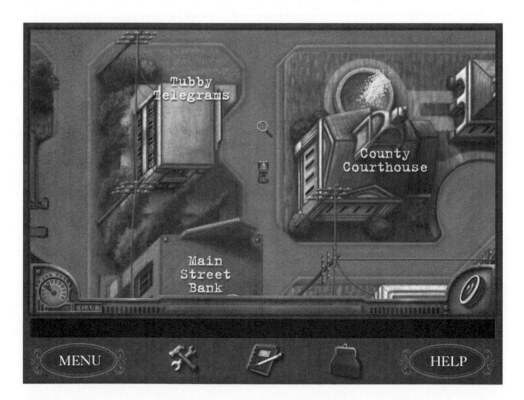

Figure 20-7 *Driving map of town. The cursor drags car through streets.*

the town that allows the player/Nancy to drive to various locations. In these cases, the images on the map are all we see of the locations, but these are supplemented with amusing voice-overs, often coupled with effective sound effects. To keep things fresh, the writer wrote more than sixty interactions around telegram delivery.

The 1930s settings was further enhanced through opening narration in the style of a 1930s radio play, 1930s music, songs, radio shows, print material, and conversational slang, particularly by Emily and Marian. Here's an example from Marian's dialogue: "She probably just needs to spend some time with a bearcat like you instead of some dumb Dora like me."

Other things that help keep costs down include puzzles and games that have potential for repeated game play, such as the mini-golf game. In general, good games and puzzles were emphasized over elaborate special effects and unlimited characters. Lastly, sometimes nonessentials just have to be cut if they can't be done on time. For example, one idea that was discarded was to allow the player to watch 1930s movies when they clicked on the movie theater in town.

The end result of all these efforts is an effective game sold at a very reasonable price.

Conclusion: Response to the Project

The Nancy Drew games from HerInteractive have won numerous awards including: Children's Software Revue—All Star Award, iParenting Media—Great Holiday Award, Parents Choice—Gold Award, Best Software, ages 10–18, Amazon.com Best Children's Software, Family Life Magazine—Favorite Software, SuperKids Software Review—Best Software for Girls, and many other awards.

Commercial acceptance of these games has matched the critical acceptance as each game has sold better than the previous as the word spreads and the audience grows for *Nancy Drew* games.

References

Collins-Ludwick, Anne. Telephone interviews with the author, August 2005.
Collins-Ludwick, Anne. E-mails to the author, August 2005.
Corporate Backgrounder, Her Interactive, Inc., August 2004.
Nancy Drew Games, Awards and Accolades, Her Interactive, Inc.
"Women in the Game—Interviews," *Games4Women*,
    http://www.games4women.com/women.html#Drew

21

Case Study—Adding Story to a Simulation: *Amped 3*

Summary

Name of production: *Amped 3*
Writer: Aaron Conners
Developer: Indie Built, Inc.
Audience: Rated E-10, Main audience is 18–25 year olds
Media: Xbox 360 and PlayStation 3
Presentation location: Home, wherever entertainment games are played
Subject: Snowboarding simulation, stories about snowboarding and boarders
Goal: Entertain
Structures: String of Pearls, Linear

The script samples and images used in this chapter are copyright Indie Built, Inc.

Program Description and Background

Program Description

Amped 3 is the third edition of the popular snowboarding game created by Indie Built, Inc. The *Amped* games are known for their realism and the sophisticated AI behind the snowboarding action, as opposed to many other snowboarding games, such as SSX, which tend to introduce more fantasy elements and unrealistic courses.

The producers of *Amped 3* wanted to stick with the realistic snowboarding game play that had been successful in the previous releases of the games, but they wanted to add something "different." That difference eventually evolved into character customization and several off-the-wall story segments.

The player of this game takes on the role of one of the snowboarders in a rowdy crew. The player's character is customized at the beginning of the game in gender, appearance, and attitude. The attitude can be either "cheeky" or "chill." For this reason there are four player voice options: Male/Cheeky, Male/Chill, Female/Cheeky, and Female/Chill. In most instances, four different lines of dialogue represent each personality. This customization can change considerably the player's experience of the game.

The game features snowboarding in seven different resorts: Northstar (California), Snowbird (Utah), Valle Nevado (Chile), Laax (Switzerland), Avoriaz (France), Zugspitze (Germany), and DC Mountain Lab (Utah). In order to move from one resort to another, the player most solve a series of story challenges. The story challenges in each resort are presented by one of the player's snowboarding crew. Each challenge requires snowboarding and other skills by the player to solve.

Each challenge is told from the point of view of one of the crew members. Because of this, each challenge/story varies widely in tone and presentation, including anime (Japanese style animation), stop motion, animated hand drawings, Jib-Jab (collage style) animation, and several other techniques. This diversity of styles and the stories themselves make the story challenges a fantastic counterpoint to the more realistic snowboarding action (Figure 21-1).

In addition to the story challenges, the game also has a backstory that runs throughout the piece. Part way through the game, the player is accused of taking money belonging to the crew for a trip to South America. The player has to clear

Figure 21-1 *Main snowboarding interface for* Amped 3 *showing realistic mountain action.*

his name to be reunited with his friends and complete the game. The player is helped in his quest by a mysterious snow goddess.

Production Background

Amped 3 was produced by Indie Built, Inc. Indie Built was founded in 1983 under the name Access Software. Access created both adventure games and sports titles. Its *Tex Murphy* futuristic detective games won numerous awards including the Software Publishers Association (SPA) Adventure Game of the Year award. The most successful Access sports game was the *Links* golf game released through Microsoft.

Microsoft bought Access in 1999 and changed the name to Indie, which participated in the launch of Xbox with the successful *Amped* snowboarding title. In 2004, Indie Built was purchased by Take Two Interactive Software (TTWO) as part of the 2KGames brand. In 2006, Indie Built was closed by Take Two.

Indie Built, as a subsidiary of Take Two Interactive Software, focused primarily on sports titles. Indie Built's most recent product line included the latest offering in the long running *Links* golf series; *TopSpin*, a tennis game; and the next generation of their popular snowboarding title, *Amped 3*, which is profiled in this chapter.

Nate Larsen, the Art Lead at Indie Built, is an avid snowboarder and the driving force behind *Amped 1* and *2*. Larsen believed that *Amped 2* lacked "soul" and brought writer Aaron Conners onto the *Amped 3* project to create a story to reenergize the franchise. Matthew Seymour, the Executive Producer of *Amped 3*, supported Conners' story development and gave him as much free rein as possible to explore a wide range of ideas.

The *Amped 3* writer Aaron Conners has been a pioneer in interactive storytelling. He wrote and codesigned the games *Under a Killing Moon*, *The Pandora Directive*, and *Tex Murphy: Overseer*, the first two winning the Software Publishers Association's Adventure Game of Year award. Aaron has also published two original novels and one nonfiction title. At Indie Built, Inc., he worked as a game producer in charge of story content and design.

Goals and Challenges Writing *Amped 3*

Goals

Writer Conners' goal on *Amped 3* was to add story elements to a snowboarding simulation. These story elements had to appeal to its core audience and add to the fun of the game without restricting the snowboarding sim activities.

Challenges

Conners summed up the main challenge of this project: "How to tell a story in an environment (sim) not conducive to story and to people who don't necessarily want a story." This general statement can be broken down into the following specific challenges:

- Coming up with the right type of story and humor that will appeal to this game's 18–25 year old audience and gain consensus from the *Amped 3* production team.
- Structuring the integration of the story in a simulation in a way that does not negatively impact the snowboarding sim part of the game, while adding to the enjoyment of the overall experience.

Writing *Amped 3:* Meeting the Challenges

Meeting the Challenge of Determining the Right Story for This Game

Presenting Story Options

Unlike the *Nancy Drew* game in the previous chapter, in the case of *Amped 3*, there was no existing story material to draw upon. All options were open. At the beginning of the story development process, there were a wide variety of opinions on the team as to how the story should be presented, or if there should be a story at all. Before starting serious discussions on the narrative, writer Conners immersed himself in the material that is a hit with the intended audience of 18–25 year olds.

Based on his research, Conners came up with an initial story discussion document for the team. His document laid out six different types of stories on a scale from very realistic to very fantastic. Conners said that the writer should always come in with set number of defined options for initial story meetings. This works better than having a wide-open discussion with no defined options on the table.

Conners said that having defined options considerably speeds up the discussion process and keeps it focused. Another benefit of a structured discussion is that it is easier to get consensus by the production team. On this project, according to Conners, gaining consensus was a key issue. "Maybe the biggest challenge I faced was coming up with a story that everyone could (mostly) agree on."

As you read his Initial Story Discussion Document, notice the following sections:

- Story Golden Rules: These rules lay out the core assumptions about the story that have already been determined. It is important to include these core assumptions to set a starting point and limit for discussions.
- Story Tone: Tone is the style of the story telling (e.g., realistic, fantastic, dark) and is frequently overlooked or minimized by inexperienced writers. Conners knows that tone is essential for the development of the story and makes this one of the main points of discussion early in story development. Under Tone, he also included discussion of genre. Most stories fall into

categories or genres, such as adventure or science fiction. The conventions of these genres are well known by the audience.

- Story Concept: This section builds on the Story Tone section, providing examples of each type. He also provides discussion points for each type both pros and cons to guide the discussion in relationship to *Amped 3*.

Initial Story Discussion Document

NOTE: *Pyro* was the working title for *Amped 3*.

Story "Golden Rules"

1. The story shalt incorporate players' customized characters.
2. The story shalt be tied to players' escalating experience/gear/skills/access.
3. The story shalt work within integrated gameplay modes.
4. The story shalt be entertaining.

Story Tone

In my opinion, the central story line should have a **relatively consistent tone** (though story "tangents" can certainly have widely varied tones). Everyone agrees that the story should be humorous and entertaining, however there are at least <u>six</u> potential, fundamentally different approaches:

(A) High Adventure: A rollicking tale involving a mystery and/or quest, colorful characters, good humor; player is swept into the action and, by accomplishing tasks and overcoming obstacles, goes through a variety of twists and turns and gradually reveals the existing backstory, leading to a big payoff (or several, with pathing).

(B) Faux Fantasy: A story set in the real world, with the focus completely on the player, who may interpret reality in a fantastic way, have a double (fantasy) life, display his thoughts in a unique way, etc.; For this concept, the backstory is less important than the player's reaction to what's happening around him.

(C) Sci-Fi (Lite):   This encompasses lighter sci-fi elements,
                     such as time travel, alternate history,
                     urban legends, aliens, etc. Levels of humor,
                     technicality, and weirdness vary a lot from
                     story to story.

(D) Parody: A tongue-in-cheek approach to storytelling
                     that pokes fun at clichés, pop culture,
                     movies, books, people, genres, etc.

(E) Pythonic: A unique style of humor that walks a fine
                     line between wildly zany and ridiculously
                     stupid; In Monty Python's full-length
                     features, the story is structured on a
                     well-known quest and utilizes elements of
                     parody.

(F) Fantasy: The broadest category of all, this can be
                     anything from sci-fi to anime, limited only
                     by the creators' imaginations; humor isn't
                     precluded, but can be more difficult to
                     pull off without the standard perception of
                     reality to play against.

STORY CONCEPT "A": HIGH ADVENTURE
  [EXAMPLES]

- Indiana Jones movies
- *XXX*
- Robert Ludlum/John Grisham novels

[PROS]

- Most reality-based
- Most natural transition from gameplay in *Amped 1* and
  Amped 2
- Easily integrated with career and/or players' escalating
  experience/gear/skills/access

[THE BIG QUESTION(S)]

- Will the game be built around a substantial story line
  (which, in my opinion, this story concept requires)?
  Do fantasy elements have a place in this type of story?
  How well will this story concept gibe with the
  Pyro Soul?

STORY CONCEPT "B": FAUX FANTASY

[EXAMPLES]

- *Big Fish* (story/flashbacks)
- *Scrubs*, Andy Richter (protagonist POV fantasy sequences)
- *The Fisher King* (protagonist-only perception of reality)
- Calvin and Hobbes (protagonist-only fantasy life)

[PROS]

- Reality-based, but with lots of creative leeway
- Good opportunity to use a wide variety of graphic styles
- Possibly best fit with the Pyro Soul

[THE BIG QUESTION(S)]

- Can the story content be customized? (This is the most player-centric story concept, so each player's experience should be at least slightly different.)

STORY CONCEPT "C": SCI-FI (LITE)

[EXAMPLES]

- *Back to the Future*
- *X-Files*
- *The Butterfly Effect*
- *Sky Captain and the World of Tomorrow*

[PROS]

- Unique story concept for a sports title
- Freedom to create our own "rules"
- Appease Brenner's Chupacabra obsession

[THE BIG QUESTION(S)]

- Can a sci-fi story be hilarious? Should it be? Should we consider sacrificing some of the humor for an extra helping of weirdness? Will the sci-fi lean toward reality or fantasy? What does our target audience think about sci-fi?

STORY CONCEPT "D": PARODY

[EXAMPLES]

- Austin Powers movies
- Beastie Boys videos (Sabotage, Intergalactic, etc.)
- *Kill Bill*

[PROS]

- Hip, intelligent humor style (if executed properly)
- Opportunity to poke fun at ourselves, gaming conventions, snowboarding culture
- Good counterpoint to *THUG 2*'s "in your face" jackassness

[THE BIG QUESTION(S)]

- Can this concept be hip, smart, and entertaining without crossing the line into *stinky* cheese? Can fantasy elements be added without disrupting the tone?

STORY CONCEPT "E": PYTHONIC
[EXAMPLES]

- *Holy Grail*
- *Baron Von Munchausen*
- Roger Rabbit

[PROS]

- No restrictions on humor or realism
- Greatest potential to achieve cult status
- Good fit for Snow God, Snow Sharks, Snow Weasels

[THE BIG QUESTION(S)]

- Is it just too much? Are we going for cult status or broader appeal?

STORY CONCEPT "F": FANTASY
[EXAMPLES]

- *Wizard of Oz*
- *Yellow Submarine*
- Heavy Metal

[PROS]

- Anything goes
- Opportunity to create unique Pyro Universe
- Most differentiation from *Amped 1* and *2*

THE BIGGEST QUESTION OF ALL: *REALITY VERSUS FANTASY*
Amped 1 and *Amped 2* provided an essentially realistic snowboarding experience with little zaniness and no fantastical (i.e., unrealistic) elements. Currently, *Pyro* is headed in a very different direction with proposed elements such as Snow Gods, Snow Weasels, Awesomeness Displays, etc., and this raises some fundamental questions:

1. Is a realistic snowboarding experience still a vital element of *Pyro*?
2. If so, will the game be based in reality with forays into fantasy? Or will this be a fantasy world that features realistic snowboarding?
3. If we're offering a *non*realistic snowboarding experience (i.e., a unique Pyro universe), do we need to explain this to the player? Should we use the story to transport the player from the realistic world of *Amped 1* and *Amped 2* to this new universe (*a la* Wizard of Oz)?
4. Could *Pyro's* new direction alienate fans of *Amped 1* and *Amped 2*?

The previous sample is a good model of an initial story document, which might include discussion of:

- tone
- genre
- well known examples of works using a certain tone and genre to reference the discussion to something concrete
- pros and cons of each option including questions to consider for this particular project

Focusing Story Discussion: Tone, Scope, Storytelling Devices

The well-defined options in the document above made it much easier for the production team to quickly eliminate options that won't work and begin discussing the type of story that they want. The next step is to focus in more detail on the approach to the story that was determined in the first step.

The agreements from the first meeting and continued points of discussion are outlined in the document that follows, which includes some of the elements from the previous document but eliminates others. For example, science fiction, adventure, and total fantasy genres were eliminated as options in the first discussion. The basic tone has now been defined as fun, good-hearted parody with fantasy elements. The author adds more examples of the agreed upon tone and expands the "Golden Rules" from the first document into Story Scope, which lays out the specific rules for story implementation as it pertains to *Amped 3*. The new material introduced is a discussion of specific story characters (Snow God) and story elements.

Tone, Scope, and Storytelling Devices Discussion Document
NOTE: *Pyro* was the working title for *Amped 3*.

STORY TONE:

"PARODY":	A tongue-in-cheek approach to storytelling that pokes fun at clichés, pop culture, movies, books, people, genres, etc.
Reality/Fantasy:	Alternate, exaggerated, or distorted pseudo-reality (aka *fantasy lite*—mostly realistic foundation with fantastic elements of varying degrees).
Theme/Moral:	Story elements will be fun, funky, and good-hearted, rather than dark, cynical, or bitter; the focus will be on the positive side of snowboarding (and youth) culture with an underlying message of "What's so funny 'bout peace, love, and understanding?"

[EXAMPLES]

* Austin Powers movies
* *Airplane*
* Beastie Boys videos (*Sabotage*, *Intergalactic*, etc.)
* *South Park*

[PROS]

* Hip, intelligent humor style (if executed properly)
* Opportunity to poke fun at ourselves, gaming conventions, snowboarding culture
* Good counterpoint to *THUG 2*'s "in your face" jackassness

[THE BIG QUESTION]

* Can this concept be hip, smart, and entertaining without crossing the line into *stinky* cheese? Can fantasy elements be added without disrupting the tone?

STORY SCOPE:

* Will incorporate players' customized characters;
* Will be tied to players' escalating experience/gear/ skills/access;

❖ Will work within integrated gameplay modes;

❖ Will be entertaining;

❖ Will offer customized content (for different types of player characters), but to what degree is TBD;

❖ Will not conflict with "real world" boarding mechanics;

❖ Will motivate players to complete the game with a strong narrative thread;

❖ Will have levels of content so players can (partially) control story intensity;

❖ Will integrate real-world locations, pros, etc.;

❖ May have some pathing and/or multiple resolutions (TBD).

POSSIBLE STORY INSPIRATIONS AND STORYTELLING DEVICES:

- *It's a Wonderful Life* (Clarence the Angel, changing the future [save snowboarding, et al.])
- *Star Wars* (Obi Wan, the Force)
- *Big Fish* (story/flashbacks, act out tall tales, legends [chupacabra], etc.)
- *Scrubs*, *Alley McBeal* (protagonist POV fantasy sequences)
- *The Fisher King* (protagonist-only perception of reality, hero/quest elements)
- Monty Python (myth parody, animation blended with live action)
- Calvin and Hobbes (protagonist POV-only fantasy life, animation)

POSSIBLE STORY INSPIRATIONS AND STORYTELLING DEVICES:
Snow God

- Could be a guardian angel;
- May be a loveable loser trying to earn his wings (think *It's a Wonderful Life*);
- There may be an entire pantheon of Snow Gods (of which ours is the most junior or misfit member);
- Some Snow Gods may be evil and be in conflict with good Snow Gods (think the Council of Wizards in *Lord of the Rings*);
- Snow Gods could provide story direction, help, incentives, task intros, etc.;
- Snow Gods could appear in different guises;

- Snow Gods may appear only to the player (and maybe a few other NPCs) and be invisible to most other boarders (think *Harvey*).

Bruce Lee, Che Guevara, etc. We've discussed the idea of seeing someone fall off a cliff (to his death, presumably), and then reappear later in advancing states of decomposition (think *American Werewolf in London*). If we tie the player's ability to see a dead person to his/her association with the snow god, then maybe we could justify the appearance of other dead people, such as Bruce Lee or Che Guevara? The snow god could even introduce them as his buddies ...?

Snowboarding Lifestyle/Xen

- The "Moral of the Story" will be along the lines of *South Park* episodes ("... You know, I learned an important lesson today ...");
- Keep the message very positive and life-affirming;
- Use themes of acceptance, diversity, and goodwill.

Defining the Objective and Plot Discussion Document

NOTE: *Pyro* was the working title for *Amped 3*.

The previous discussions determined the type of story, basic approach, and introduced some of the possible elements and storytelling devices. The next document begins getting into more specifics on the story for this game particularly the theme and the "backstory." A backstory in a novel or a screenplay is usually the underlying story that provides the background for the main story we are viewing. One of the most famous backstories is from the film *Casablanca*. The aborted romance in Paris happened years earlier and provides the context for the two lovers when they meet again in Casablanca.

The way the *Amped 3* writer is using the term "backstory," he is referring to the main story of the game. But because the main focus of the game is snowboarding, in this context the main story is more of a backstory that provides context for the snowboarding and the other story challenges.

STORY OBJECTIVES

- Strong Single Player Experience
- Limited Multiplayer Experience
- Crew Interaction
- Complement (not Obstruct) Gameplay
- Male AND Female Player

- Reality/Alternate Reality Blending
- Clever Premise
- Humor (smart and/or silly); Allegory; Irony
- Snow God
- Strong Payoff
- Theme: "Freedom"
- Theme: "Selling Out Snowboarding"
- Theme: "Gaminess/Gaming Conventions"
- Theme: "The Magic of Snowboarding"
- Fight the Power
- Beat the Game
- Freedom
- Take the Long, Strange Trip
- Freedom tastes nothing like chicken. Hang with your crew ... trick to shock and awe ... chase the Yeti ... maybe even save the world as you know it. Do what you want to do.

PYRO BACKSTORY IDEAS

1. **The Haunted Mountain**. Mysterious happenings, ghost sightings, etc., are scaring the boarders off the mountain. You and your posse decide to investigate. One by one, your buddies disappear and it's up to you to find out what's happened to them. Eventually, you discover that it's a nefarious ploy concocted by Old Man Withers from the Amusement Park.

2. **The Snow Job**. Someone on the mountain is on a crime spree. What starts out as petty vandalism and tagging soon escalates to putting sugar in the ski patrols' snowmobiles' gas tanks, and then cutting the lift cables. Worst of all, it seems that someone is trying to pin the crimes on you and your posse. Can you identify the villain(s), catch them in the act, and clear your name before you get busted and/or someone really gets hurt?

3. **The Treasure of Monte Bordo**. Rumors of a lost silver mine are confirmed when you and your crew discover the frozen corpse of an ancient telemark skier while carving up the back country. An oilskin pouch found in the dead skier's jacket contains a yellowed map and a number of clues. You must locate both natural and manmade markers scattered around the mountain in order to find the secret mine entrance.

4. **The Unbearable Lightness of Boarding**. After a near-death
   fall, you are revived by a strange, *Obi Wan*-type character
   who then mysteriously vanishes—or was it only a dream?
   His whispered words lead you to investigate and you find
   out about the legend of the Mountain Man. Many have
   attempted to find and ride the paths (or *chutes*) of
   enlightenment hidden around the mountain, but only the
   truly pure of heart will commune with the Mountain Man and
   reach snowboarding nirvana. But beware! There are those of
   the dark side who would reveal the Mountain Man's secrets.

This story discussion process continued until the final story was determined. It involves a mysterious snow goddess and a backstory dealing with the supposed theft of the crew's funds by the player. With the basic story defined, the large problem still remained of how to integrate this story into a simulation.

Meeting the Challenge of Integrating Story into a Sports Simulation

Problems with Story in a Sim

When the producers brought the writer Aaron Conners onto the project, they told him that they wanted to add something different, some new life to their snowboarding game. They had not settled on this new life necessarily being a story.

In an interview for this book, Conners explained that the producers' initial hesitancy about adding story elements was because in the past, story in games of this type has been often handled badly. "Problems with story in past games were, that they were an interruption or intrusion into the main action. This is something that gamers hate." In a simulation, whether it is driving a car, flying a plane, or snowboarding, the main appeal is doing the activity not the story. If there was going to be story in this simulation, it had to be integrated in a way that did not interfere with snowboarding game play.

Story Structure

Given the story limitations imposed by the type of game (sim) and the audience expectations, Conners realized that in this project, story would be a subsidiary element. The game will still primarily be a snowboarding simulation with the story elements as extra bits of fun thrown in. As Conners put it, "The story in this game is like chocolate chips in ice cream."

As noted earlier, the problem with story elements in many computer games is that they interrupt the activity. The player is having a good time solving puzzles, shooting aliens, or snowboarding when suddenly the interactivity is interrupted and they are forced into a situation where they have to go through a series of story related interactions.

Instead, Conners suggests that for a game of this type, the story elements be set up at a natural break in the action. One story element can be an introductory piece setting up information needed to get the next scene going. After viewing this introductory story segment, the player then enjoys the main action of the game, such as winning a snowboard challenge. Once they achieve the challenge, then they have the back bookend story—payoff to the setup. This lets players know they have accomplished something and can move forward in the game without interrupting the main action of snowboarding.

The overall structure of this game is the string of pearls approach discussed in Chapter 18 and also used in *Dust*, which is profiled in Chapter 23. In a string of pearls structure, a player can perform all sorts of activities in one location (the pearl), such as a snowboarding resort, but to move on to the next location (pearl) she has to accomplish some tasks or meet some challenge.

This approach applied to *Amped 3* resulted in a bit of introductory story to set up a scene at a snowboard resort. The user can then play at the resort for as long as they want. They can board various slopes, play in terrain parks etc. The story elements are not imposed on them. But when they are finished with one resort and want to move on, they can choose to enter a story challenge. Once they solve all the story challenges in that resort, they can go to the next resort. The story elements are indicated on the mountain slope by a rainbow image and one of the characters yelling to the player. Usually the character that is calling to the player becomes the teller of this particular story segment.

Below is an example of a story challenge from the first act of the game. This challenge is introduced by the character Hunter. This story is told from her point of view. An unusual element in *Amped 3* is that the character telling the story also controls the style of the presentation. Hunter sees the interaction with the bullies as being similar to a Japanese samurai tale. Because of this, the story challenge is presented in anime style, a type of Japanese animation (see Figure 21-2).

Figure 21-2 *Anime-style scene in* Hunter's story.

As noted earlier, story challenges presented by other characters are presented in completely different styles, such as anime, stop motion, animated hand drawings, collage animation, etc. Conners hopes this stylistic device will help create the narrative randomness important to this game's audience. This segment below also introduces the main backstory of the game, which is that the player stole the crew's money.

Script Sample from Act 1

Notes on script format and terms:

- [GAMEPLAY] indicates an interactive section where players can ride their snowboards. All scene types must be clearly labeled in the script for the production team.
- [GROVER] indicates a noninteractive scene rendered within the game with player character customization.
- [PRESENTATION] is a linear, noninteractive sequence usually from a specific character's point of view.
- SANDBOX or SNOWBOX refers to boarding on the mountain.

```
1.4: ANIME
[GAMEPLAY] SCENE 1.4.a
EXT. - NORTHSTAR RESORT - AFTERNOON
PLAYER rides into the STORY ZONE, where BULLY BOARDERS are hassling
WIENER BOY.
[10 SECONDS OF HASSLING WIENER BOY IN GROVER].
```

```
                                                            CUT TO:
```

```
[GROVER]   SCENE 1.4.1
PLAYER:    (1) Hey, you dill-holes! Knock it off!
           (2) Hey, how 'bout everybody just chill ...
           (3) I just LOVE guys that pick on helpless kids.
           (4) I just LOVE guys that pick on helpless kids.
```

BOOK AUTHOR'S NOTE: The numbered lines of dialogue above refer to choices that the player made in customization at beginning of game. Only one line of dialogue will be played.

```
The Bullies toss the Player dismissive looks and ride off. After the
Bullies ride away, HUNTER rides up to Player and Wiener Boy—she has seen
what happened and is super pissed.

HUNTER:   Hey, you [FUDGE BROWNIE]!
```

BOOK AUTHOR'S NOTE: "FUDGE BROWNIE" replaces a curse word. It is a more humorous alternative to bleeping text. It is also said by a different actor.

| WIENER BOY: | Don't worry about it. Those guys are just jerks. |
| HUNTER: | Hey, Franklin, NO ONE screws with me ... or my friends— |

CUT TO:

[PRESENTATION] SCENE 1.4.2

CLOSE ON HUNTER'S EYES IN ANIME STYLE:

HUNTER:	(anime) —We must defend our honor!
JAPANARRATOR:	And so it was that three of the *yuki taishou* vowed vengeance upon the [FUDGE BROWNIE].
HUNTER:	(anime) —We meet tonight! At the great tower! A price will be paid!
JAPANARRATOR:	Hunter's words echoed through the hero's mind—
HUNTER:	(anime, echoed) —We meet tonight! At the great tower! A price will be paid!
JAPANARRATOR:	But first, a quest lay ahead, for only by earning the *Night Pass of Seiyuu* could one return to mountain and fulfill destiny in legendary Battle of *Kitaboshi* ... which happens that very night ... around eleven o'clock ...
[IN-GAME]	**SCENE 1.4.b**

The Player returns to the SANDBOX, earns a NIGHT PASS, and then goes to the STORY HOT ZONE at the Lift to the NorthStar Tower.

[IN-GAME]   SCENE 1.4.3

EXT. - THE TOP OF NORTHSTAR RESORT, NEAR THE TOWER - NIGHT

FADE IN: "NIGHT" ... "Around 11:00" (w/accompanying Japanese characters)...

In Anime style, the Player, Hunter, Sebastian, and Wiener Boy are shown gathered near the Tower.

JAPANARRATOR:	Snow fell like delicate plum blossoms as *Seiyuu* returns to mountain with Mighty Night Pass. At the Tower of *Kitaboshi*, *Seiyuu* learns Fate has dealt lethal blow to vacation plans of *Yuki Taishou*!
SEBASTIAN:	(anime) Someone broke into Hunter's locker and purloined all our vacation cash!
WIENER BOY:	(anime) If it was those jerk guys, they will feel the wooden wrath of my real numchucks!

JAPANARRATOR: To search mountain for jerk guys, splitting up four
                 Yuki Taishou: *Bishoujo*! Beautiful danger girl with
                 courage of *hitokiri* assassin and fighting hotness!
                 Oukii Nikuma! Big Pork Buns, with triple strength
                 of delicious super-size! *Gaki*! Upstart punk, super
                 fast verocity of foot and mouth! And set of real
                 numchucks! *Seiyuu*! Man or woman—who can know?
                 Chameleon power of customization!
                 It is *Seiyuu* who comes upon, the—let's call them
                 Colonatrons—who appear from darkness, reveling in
                 their evilness:

COLONATRON: (robot voice) So then the Pleasure Droid turns to
                 me and says: "Now I see why they call it a half
                 pipe!"

JAPANARRATOR: *Seiyuu* sets off in heavy pursuit, oblivious to
                 almost certain peril that is awaiting.

[IN-GAME]   SCENE 1.4.c1

The Player rides after the Bullies, keeping them in sight but not
getting too close.

[GROVER]   SCENE 1.4.4

EXT. – HALFWAY DOWN THE RUN – MINUTES LATER

Midway through the run, the Bullies suddenly stop in the center of
an open area and wait until a SNOWMOBILE RIDER rides up to them.

CLOSE ON: J-DAWG is the Snowmobile Rider [Cue MYSTERIOUS WIND
CHIMES]. After a brief exchange, J-DAWG rides off and the Bullies
continue their run.

[IN-GAME]   SCENE 1.4.c2

The Player resumes shadowing the Bullies.

[GROVER]   SCENE 1.4.5

EXT. – BOTTOM OF THE RUN – MINUTES LATER

At the end of the run, the Bullies ride up to a STORAGE BUILDING
and around to the other (blind) side of the building (out of the
Player's view). Moments later, they come roaring out on snowmobiles
and take off.

                                                           CUT TO:

INT. – STORAGE BUILDING

There is ONE REMAINING SNOWMOBILE. The Player climbs on and takes
off after the Bullies.

[IN-GAME]   SCENE 1.4.d

The Player follows the Bullies on snowmobile. Eventually, the Bullies ride over a crest and disappear from view. When the Player rides over the crest, CUT TO-

[PRESENTATION]   SCENE 1.4.6

In ANIME: PLAYER is surrounded by the Bullies; J-Dawg appears and pulls up alongside the Player; they ride beside each other and talk:

JAPANARRATOR:	And so it was, *Seiyuu* surrounded by evil Colonatrons. And then appears J-Dawg, who rides up to *Seiyuu* and makes starting crazy talk of stealing crew money:
J-DAWG:	(anime) You stole our crew money!
JAPANARRATOR:	Also, there is video, it seems, of *Seiyuu* breaking into locker and stealing money!
J-DAWG:	(anime) There's video of you breaking into the locker and stealing the money!
JAPANARRATOR:	And what about Colonatrons? Why was J-Dawg riding with them? The answer, it seems, all are now working for mysterious new sponsor!
J-DAWG:	(anime) You're out of the crew, dude! [beat] Quit staring at my hair!
JAPANARRATOR:	And so began legendary Battle of *Kitaboshi*— falsely accused, honorable *Seiyuu*, escaping evil Colonatrons down treacherous Cat Tracks of Doom!

[IN-GAME]   SCENE 1.4.e

The Player races down cat tracks, pursued by the Bullies on snowmobiles. Eventually, the Player reaches a snow bridge, which disintegrates as s/he rides over it, allowing the Player to escape into the darkness.

The Player escapes from the Bullies on snowmobiles by going off a JUMP.

                                                          CUT TO:

[GROVER]   SCENE 1.4.7

FREEZE THE SNOWMOBILE IN MID-AIR! Dandelion voices-over the frozen image:

DANDELION:	Looks like that player's gotten into a little bit of trouble.

```
[PRESENTATION] SCENE 1.5
CLOSE ON Dandelion's Scrapbook and a series of scrapbooked pages:

DANDELION:    Oh, I knew my friend didn't steal the money, but
              it sure did look bad. J-Dawg's mysterious sponsor
              flew the rest of the crew down to Chile the next
              day. And that's how my friend ended up all alone.
              Well, not TOTALLY alone. I had plenty of room in my
              van and, before you knew it, we were on the road to
              Salt Lake City! While I was at the scrapbooking
              expo, my friend would be looking for work at
              Snowbird to try and earn back the money that had
              been stolen. What a super special person. OUCH!
              But how d'ya earn 5,500 bucks in just a few days?
              Well, if I'd just quit ramblin' on, maybe we'd
              find out ...!

END OF ACT I
```

Adding Interactivity and Randomness to Linear Story
Narrative Interactivity and Character Customization

As discussed in the previous section, the decision was made not to have interactivity in the story elements. Conners decided that the player would find that intrusive in a snowboarding simulation, where the basic goal is boarding challenging trails and terrain parks. Because of this, the story elements are linear, setting up action scenes and offered as fun rewards after the player achieves a boarding challenge.

Conners did want to add some interactivity to the story elements. He achieved this through allowing the player to customize his character at the beginning of the game. The game opens with an introduction of the player with his crew. The player is completely dressed in a pink bunny suit so the player's character cannot be seen at all.

After the crazy first scene introducing the characters, the player is taken to a customization area, where he can customize the character. The player can choose gender, appearance, and attitude. The attitude is determined primarily by choosing the player character's voice. Choices include male, female, cheeky, and chill.

In the example from the script that follows, Sebastian offers to show the player his "special place." The chill male response follows (1) below; the cheeky male response (2) has more attitude. The female lines show similar attitude changes with the chill (3) and cheeky (4). The customization of the player's character, particularly the voice, affect the player experience of each scene, even though they do not affect the actual direction of the story.

```
SEBASTIAN:   Yeah. Either way, it'd be cool to win another 500
             bucks. That's why I brought you up here. I'm gonna
             show you my special place.
PLAYER:      (1) You hittin' on me, big man?
             (2) Uh ... your special place?
             (3) I don't think I wanna go there.
             (4) That sounds nasty.
```

Adding Randomness

When Conners researched what was successful with the game's target audience, he discovered that one of the major appeals in humor and story is randomness. Look at films and TV, such as *South Park*, *Napoleon Dynamite*, and *Big Fish*. Much of the humor is generated by odd, random elements that are completely unexpected and sometimes seem to come out of nowhere in terms of the story. Conners decided to try to capture the same feeling of randomness in the story elements of *Amped 3*.

The main way this randomness is achieved is that the story elements are each controlled by one of the characters' point of view. Their point of view not only controls the content of the story but the actual style. As noted previously, Hunter's story in the long script sample earlier in this chapter is in Japanese anime style. Each of the other characters' story is also told in a widely different style. See Figure 21-3 for an example of one of the other styles—Sebastian's animated sketches. Conners explains that the story gets even crazier towards the end. Like Monty Python,

Figure 21-3 *Animated sketches shown as part of Sebastian's story.*

Figure 21-4 *The psychedelic introduction for the Magic Circles Challenge in the computer game* Amped 3.

it combines animation with live action and puppets. The narrative becomes wild and off the wall.

Of course this crazy approach to the narrative is mirrored by the story elements themselves, such as a wiener mobile that looks like a giant hot dog and a snow goddess who eventually comes to the player's aid.

In addition to making the story elements a bit wild, the writer also made minor changes to the snowboarding sections of the film. These changes don't affect the mechanics of the boarding but are window dressing that add to the fun. For example, one of challenges is to run an obstacle course. It is tracked by passing through big rings on the slope. The player has to complete all the rings to win the challenge. The writer named the challenges after old rock albums and songs, such as *Magical Mystery Tour* and *White Rabbit*, with images to match, such as a ring composed of psychedelic images (Figure 21-4). On other challenges and resorts, a similar technique is used by parodying RPG (Role Playing Game) elements, such as alchemy challenge, wizard challenge, etc.

Conclusion: Response to the Project

The off-the-wall story segments of *Amped 3* received a positive response from most of the critics. With quotes like, "With a story mode that demands to be finished and pacing so good that it'll steal big chunks of your life, *Amped 3*'s one of the best extreme sports titles since the original *SSX*" (Computer & Video Games). "The story and presentation for *Amped 3* is the funniest, most tripped out, wacky and bizarre thing you have ever seen!" (Ace Gamez). In general, critics felt the story elements were a big plus for the third generation of this snowboarding simulation. The game won awards and award nominations for Most Outrageous Game, Best Story, Best New Character, Funniest Game, and others.

References

Ace Gamez. http://www.acegamez.co.uk/reviews_x360/Amped_3_X360.htm
Computer & Video Games. http://www.computerandvideogames.com
Conners, Aaron. Telephone interviews with the author, September 2005.
Conners, Aaron. E-mails to the author, September 2005.
Indie Built, Inc. web site, http://mgsindiegames.com

Case Study—Parallel Stories Narrative: *The Pandora Directive*

Summary

Name of production: *The Pandora Directive*
Writer: Aaron Conners
Developer: Access Software Inc.
Audience: General audience
Medium: CD-ROM
Presentation location: Home
Subject: Tex Murphy detective mystery
Goal: Entertain
Architecture: Parallel story paths, linear, hierarchical dialogue branching

---

The script samples and images used in this chapter are copyright Access Software Inc.

Program Description and Background

Program Description

The Pandora Directive is the fourth adventure game in the *Tex Murphy* science-fiction mystery series. The program is released on CD-ROM and intended for home use. It is played by one person and is highly interactive. Much of the game is played in first person. Users can choose where Tex goes, what he does, and even what he says.

At the beginning of *The Pandora Directive*, Tex is hired to find Dr. Thomas Malloy. Tex soon learns that Malloy has secret information that the National Security Agency (NSA) and others are willing to kill for. To safeguard his secrets, Malloy sent out five puzzle boxes, each carrying a component of *The Pandora Directive*, which will explain his project. Tex's search for Malloy quickly turns into a quest

357

for those boxes, which seem to have a bad habit of getting their owners killed. Romantic complication ensues between Tex and Malloy's daughter, Regan, which doesn't exactly thrill Tex's girlfriend, Chelsee. The climactic ending takes place in a Mayan labyrinth where Malloy's project is hidden. The plot has three basic story paths with seven possible endings, so Tex's success in love and war depends on how you play the game.

This game has a couple of elements that are unique in terms of the other case studies in this book. It is the only game examined in this book that has true parallel path story structure. (See Figure 18-4 in Chapter 18 for a diagram of this structure.) This structure involves having multiple distinct story lines in the narrative. In this case, there are three different story paths that the user can travel down, depending on choices made in the game. Parallel path stories are relatively uncommon primarily because of the extra cost and effort to prepare three distinct stories and to plan the intricate navigation. These challenges are discussed later in this chapter.

The other elements that this game does not share with any other of the narratives in the book is the use of live, full motion video shot against a blue screen. This process allows live actors to be shot in the main roles of the game. Separate computer generated backgrounds are then created, and these backgrounds are then keyed in behind the actors. These computer-generated backgrounds replace the blue background, thus placing the actors in a computer generated setting. This process was heavily used at one time in games. But because of the cost and the reduced flexibility compared with a project with computer generated actors and settings, it is now fairly rare.

 See the Voyeur *area in the Chapters section of this book's CD-ROM for a more detailed explanation of the blue screen process.*

Production Background

The Pandora Directive was developed and produced by Access Software Inc. of Salt Lake City. Chris Jones, the cofounder of the company, produces and stars in the Tex Murphy series, which includes *Mean Streets, Martian Memorandum, Under a Killing Moon* (the first collaboration with Aaron Conners), *The Pandora Directive*, and *Tex Murphy Overseer*. Conners wrote and codesigned *The Pandora Directive* based on his novel of the same name, which was published by Prima Publishing. Chris Jones codesigned the game. The video sequences were directed by Adrian Carr.

Since the production of *The Pandora Directive*, Access has been purchased by Microsoft and then sold to Take Two Interactive Software (TTWO) as part of the 2KGames brand. For Take Two, access operated under the name of Indie Built and primarily produced sports games. Indie Built was closed by Take Two Interactive in 2006, but it still holds the rights to the Tex Murphy series and has not ruled out the possibility of a sequel.

Goals and Challenges Writing *The Pandora Directive*

Goals

One of writer Aaron Conners' goals was to present a complex story that combined the best elements of the detective genre with off-beat science-fiction material reminiscent of the classic television shows *The Twilight Zone* and *The Outer Limits*. Some critics have compared the Tex Murphy series with *The X Files*. Conners also wanted to present well-developed characters, particularly in Tex, but also in his love interests, Chelsee and Regan.

So far this sounds like any good movie. But we are talking an interactive story here, and Conners also wanted to allow for maximum interactivity on the part of the user. His goal was interactive choices integrated in a way that disturbs the flow of the narrative as little as possible. He hoped to achieve this by having the choices affect the story in the same way that such choices affect us in real life.

Although not strictly a writing goal, Conners, as writer-designer, and his codesigner, Chris Jones, also wanted this video game to capture the feeling of a theatrical movie. They achieved this through heavy use of close-ups, video, and action sequences.

Challenges

The key elements of these goals and the major challenges are:

- Developing a complex interactive story and characters.
- Creating smooth and realistic interactivity at the shot and dialogue level and the scene and sequence level.
- Making the complex story and interactivity work together in an engaging and coherent fashion.

Writing *The Pandora Directive*: Meeting the Challenges

Although this case study will be focused primarily on *The Pandora Directive*, comparisons will occasionally be drawn with the previous Tex Murphy mystery, *Under a Killing Moon*.

Developing a Complex Interactive Story and Characters
The Novel

Writing *The Pandora Directive* novel first, said Conners, gave him a chance to develop the story and characters thoroughly. He started the novel writing freehand in a smoky Salt Lake City bar with red vinyl seats and sparkly countertops, the kind of place Tex Murphy might hang out in. Conners first roughly outlined the story, listening to snatches of conversation and sometimes jotting down lines of dialogue.

He also developed the basic characters at this stage. He decided what he wanted them to be like and what their signature character quirks would be, such as using faulty grammar. Finally, he laid out how he wanted the characters to progress and develop in the story. He generated a lot of pages in this preparatory stage.

Once this preliminary work was done, he sat at the computer and developed an extended hierarchical outline broken down by acts and scenes. He determined what would happen in each scene and gradually laid out the story. He wrote the novel based on this outline.

The Script

This is one of the more complex interactive narrative programs produced, and the writing process reflects this complexity. After Conners completed the novel, his codesigner, Chris Jones, cut key story elements out of the novel to make a rough script, which was just one path of the story and conversation (the B path, the same as the novel). Screenwriter Scott Yeagamn polished this script, and Conners completed it.

The script serves primarily as a reference for people outside of Access Software, such as actors, so they can understand what the program is about. The script includes few interactive elements and comprises only 20% of all the material written for the project. A script sample follows.

INT. BREW AND STEW—DAY (Interactive Scene #22)

...Tex sidles up to the bar.

> LOUIE
> Hey, Murph. How goes the battle?

> TEX
> (a forced grin)
> Louie, you wouldn't believe it if I told you.
> (Louie doesn't ask)
> Say, did Chelsee leave some things of mine...

> LOUIE
> (retrieves a couple items from under the bar)
> You bet...
> (lays them on bar top)

> LOUIE (Cont'd)
> Amongst the items...Looks like someone's business
> card...and your lucky Pez dispenser.

>   TEX
>   (Picks things up. Inspects Pez dispenser)
>   Wondered where that went to. Thanks.

>   TEX
>   (on a more serious note)
>   So how's she doing?

>   LOUIE
>   Yuh mean Chelsee?
>   (weighs it)
>   She just turned 30. She thinks it's the end of
>   the world.

>   TEX
>   I don't understand it.

>   LOUIE
>   You're not supposed to. Just accept that she's
>   having a hard go of it and leave it at that.
>   She's looking for something more in her life,
>   that's all.
>   (beat)
>   Tell me somethin', Murph? You ever been in love?
>   I'm talking about "True Love."

Tex twists his neck nervously, plays with his Pez
dispenser.

>   TEX
>   I dunno, Louie. What the hell's that mean anyway,
>   true love?

>   LOUIE
>   Nothin'. It's all just chemicals. Endorphins or
>   whatever. Fallin' in love's simple as one, two,
>   three. Any idiot can do it. What's hard is gettin'
>   ta know someone, and after all that,
>   still likin' 'em.

>   TEX
>   No kidding.

<pre>
                        LOUIE
     But that's not even the hardest thing. Hardest
     thing is what makes all the difference.

                         TEX
     What's that?

                        LOUIE
     ...Finding someone you can trust.

  Tex thinks about it.

                     LOUIE (Cont'd)
     Chelsee's givin' you a shot,...but she's
     not gonna wait forever. There's a whole load
     of guys who'd give their right arm for one
     minute of Chelsee's attention. You know it.

  CLOSER ON TEX...

  ...as he continues to reflect on what LOUIE has said.
</pre>

The Walkthrough

After the script, Conners developed the walkthrough (part of which is included at the end of this chapter). This is a description of the story line and the key interactive elements. A walkthrough of a computer game is similar to a linear film/TV treatment, which gives the basic story line without extensive dialogue or calling shots. The *Pandora* walkthrough primarily explains how to get through the B path, but it also refers to key interactions with the other paths.

Conners divided the walkthrough story into days. This device not only makes the transitions between the program's multiple discs easier, but the writer also feels that this structure makes good sense for an adventure game. Because an adventure game can include as much as sixty hours of game play, it should be thought of not as a feature film but rather as a miniseries with a number of small conflicts and cliffhangers at the end of each day that gradually lead to the major climax at the end.

Puzzles

After developing the basic walkthrough story line, Conners came up with puzzles that the player must solve to advance in the game. Integrating puzzles into interactive narrative is one of the challenges that faces writers of adventure games. Many of the users of a program such as *The Pandora Directive* are primarily interested in following the interactive story. For dedicated gamers, however, the challenge of solving difficult puzzles and racking up high scores is a prime appeal.

Conners and his codesigner solved this problem by coming up with two levels of play: a game player level and an entertainment level. On the game player level, there is no access to hints, there are additional puzzles, and the solutions to the puzzles are more difficult. For their extra effort, the game players can earn twice as many points as the entertainment-level players, who in addition to having hints and easier puzzles can skip the puzzles altogether by simply typing, "I am a cheater," on their keyboard. Both categories of user earn points by solving puzzles and making the right choices to advance the story. A running tally of points scored is constantly on the screen.

Interactive Conversations

For Conners, the last phase of writing an adventure game is coming up with the characters' interactive conversation. To do this, Conners makes a list of the characters and develops the interactive dialogue, flowcharts, and "Ask Abouts" (key information that the player/Tex can ask other characters about). Each of these elements is explained in detail later in this chapter under "Making a Complex Story and Interactivity Work Together" and "Creating Smooth and Realistic Interactivity."

Game Play Addendum

Another document that the writer created during development of this project is the addendum, which consists of five hundred pages explaining all the rules of interaction and game play. These clarifying inserts are sometimes referred to in the walkthrough or other production material to make it clear to the people putting the program together how the game is supposed to work.

There is no unified document that unites all of these written elements on which the game is based. That is the job of Conners and his codesigner, Chris Jones.

Creating Smooth and Realistic Interactivity
Interactive Dialogue

One of the more innovative elements of *Under a Killing Moon* and *The Pandora Directive* is the degree of interactivity that is allowed at the dialogue level. In an interactive dialogue scene, the viewer is given a list of three "Response Attitudes" for Tex's dialogue. Clicking one of these attitudes causes Tex to respond in a certain way. If the player does nothing, there is a default path, a middle ground between the bad Tex and the good Tex.

Under a Killing Moon **Interactive Dialogue Examples**   In the following examples from *Under a Killing Moon*, the dialogue in parentheses is Tex's girl, Chelsee, speaking. The empty brackets indicate that Chelsee's dialogue at the top of the list can initiate each of Tex's responses. The Response Attitudes are in all capitals. Clicking on one of those Response Attitudes causes Tex to respond with that line of dialogue to Chelsee. This is the list of all the Response Attitudes for a scene. Of course, the player would see only one list of three Response Attitudes in the menu at a time, and would not see all the dialogue written out. Tex would speak it in response to the attitude choice (see Figure 22-3 later in this chapter).

Conners decided to use this approach as opposed to having all the dialogue options written out because it would slow the story too much if players had to read three lines of dialogue before making a choice, and the Response Attitudes maintain the element of surprise. Players don't know what line they will get when they click an attitude. Surprise is essential for humor and shock.

(See the flowchart in Figure 22-1, for a sense of how the scene below would play out interactively.)

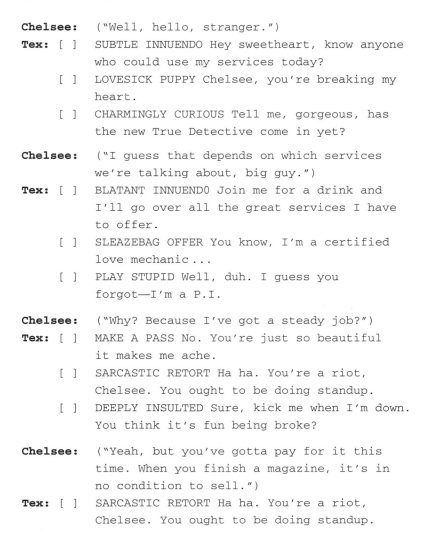

```
(Tex/Chelsee)

Chelsee:   ("Well, hello, stranger.")
Tex:   [ ]   SUBTLE INNUENDO Hey sweetheart, know anyone
             who could use my services today?
       [ ]   LOVESICK PUPPY Chelsee, you're breaking my
             heart.
       [ ]   CHARMINGLY CURIOUS Tell me, gorgeous, has
             the new True Detective come in yet?

Chelsee:   ("I guess that depends on which services
           we're talking about, big guy.")
Tex:   [ ]   BLATANT INNUEND0 Join me for a drink and
             I'll go over all the great services I have
             to offer.
       [ ]   SLEAZEBAG OFFER You know, I'm a certified
             love mechanic...
       [ ]   PLAY STUPID Well, duh. I guess you
             forgot—I'm a P.I.

Chelsee:   ("Why? Because I've got a steady job?")
Tex:   [ ]   MAKE A PASS No. You're just so beautiful
             it makes me ache.
       [ ]   SARCASTIC RETORT Ha ha. You're a riot,
             Chelsee. You ought to be doing standup.
       [ ]   DEEPLY INSULTED Sure, kick me when I'm down.
             You think it's fun being broke?

Chelsee:   ("Yeah, but you've gotta pay for it this
           time. When you finish a magazine, it's in
           no condition to sell.")
Tex:   [ ]   SARCASTIC RETORT Ha ha. You're a riot,
             Chelsee. You ought to be doing standup.
```

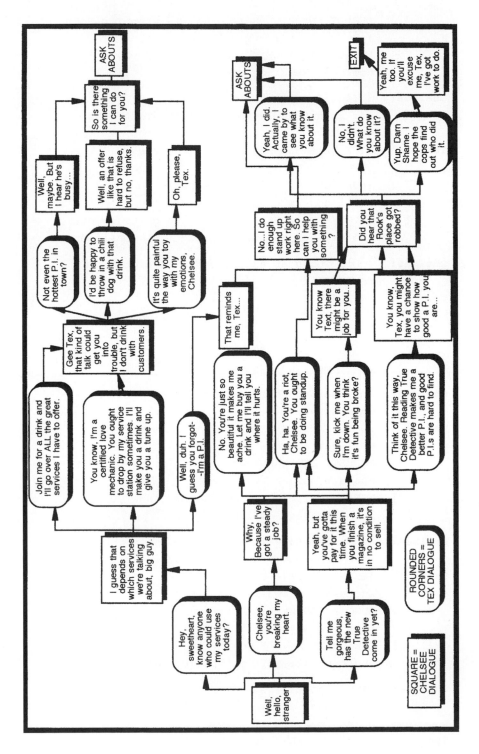

Figure 22·1 *Dialogue flowchart for* Under a Killing Moon.

[ ] DEEPLY INSULTED Sure, kick me when I'm down.
     You think it's fun being broke?

[ ] MACHO P.I. TALK Think of it this way,
     Chelsee. Reading *True Detective* ...

Chelsee: ("Gee, Tex, that kind of talk could get
             you into trouble, but I don't drink with
             customers.")

Tex: [ ] STUD RESPONSE Not even the hottest P.I. in
             town?

     [ ] BLUE COLLAR OFFER I'd be happy to throw in a
          chili dog with that drink.

     [ ] PRICKED BY CUPID'S ARROW It's quite painful,
          the way you toy with my emotions, Chelsee.

Chelsee: ("Did you hear that Rook's place got
             robbed?")

Tex: [ ] ON THE CASE I...
             [ ] NO, BUT EAGER FOR INFORMATION No,
             I didn't. What do you know about it?

     [ ] YES, BUT UNCONCERNED Yup. Darn shame. I hope
          the cops find out who did it.

Chelsee: ("I hear you took care of Rook. Pretty
             impressive.")

Tex: [ ] MODEST AND UNEMPLOYED Thanks. Maybe word
             will get around...

     [ ] MODEST, BUT MANLY Oh, it was nothing. Just
          another day at the office.

     [ ] WINK WINK, NUDGE NUDGE Let me show you my
          investigative abilities...

Chelsee: ("Oh, I'm sure it will. Maybe then you'll
             have some money and quit mooching off me.")

Tex: [ ] TENDER HEARTED C'mon, Chelsee. Let me savor
             success for awhile.

     [ ] RUGGED BANTER Admit it, doll, you love me
          just the way I am.

     [ ] INDIGNANT Hey, I don't like being broke. Why
          don't you lay off the insults and help me.

Chelsee: ("You know, Tex, it must take quite an
             effort to be lonely and broke and still
             be so smug.")

Tex: [ ] RUGGED BANTER Admit it, doll, you love me
             just the way I am.

```
[ ]    INDIGNANT Hey, I don't like being broke. Why
       don't you lay off the insults and help me...
[ ]    REEKING OF CONFIDENCE I have talents that
       money just can't buy. And some I charge for.
```

Chelsee: ("I'm sure I would, but I just don't date my
            customers. Especially ones with no money.")

```
Tex: [ ]   INDIGNANT Hey, I don't like being broke. Why
           don't you lay off the insults and help me...
     [ ]   REEKING OF CONFIDENCE I have talents that
           money just can't buy. And some I charge for.
     [ ]   GOING FOR THE HARD SELL Did I ever tell you
           that I'm a gourmet chef...
```

The flowchart for the above dialogue is in Figure 22–1.

***The Pandora Directive* Interactive Dialogue Example**   *The Pandora Directive* dialogue is more complex than that of *Under a Killing Moon* just discussed. The flowchart in Figure 22-2 and the dialogue examples that follow are from a *Pandora*

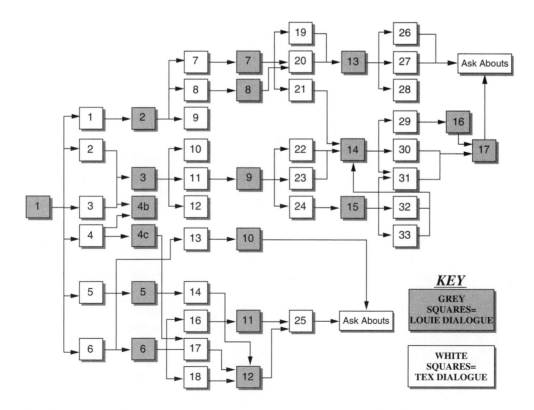

Figure 22-2 The Pandora Directive: *Louie Scene 7, interactive dialogue flowchart.*

Interactive Dialogue and Response Attitudes in *The Pandora Directive*

LOUIE
1. You just missed Chelsee. She stopped in to say goodbye. Apparently, she's off to Arizona. Everything OK with you two.

TEX
1. Definitely maybe
1. (A1) Let's see...Chelsee came by my office and redefined the word "frustration" and now she's headed off to Phoenix. I'd say things are going pretty darn well.

2. Dumb male response
2. (A2-B2) It's kind of hard to tell...Chelsee being a woman and all.

3. Look to Louie for illumination
3. (A3-B2) I have absolutely no idea. What did Chelsee have to say?

4. Nuptial worries
4. (C1-B-3) We had a bit of a tiff at the Fuchsia Flamingo. Felt just like we were married.

5. Condensed explanation
5. (C2) No. We decided to go with the *Readers' Digest* relationship and break up on our first date.

6. Hard-boiled attitude
6. (C3) I don't want to talk about it. I'm so sick of dames I could puke.

LOUIE (Response to Tex #1)
2. That's kinda what I figured. She looked happier than I've seen her in quite a while.

TEX
7. Pessimistic viewpoint
7. Well, she should. She's got a leash on most of my vital organs. That always makes women happy.

8. Play it down
8. Well then, my work is done. It's always been my mission in life to make anyone I can just a little happier.

9. Express total confusion.
9. So, of course, she leaves town, just when things are picking up steam. I don't get it.

LOUIE (Response to Tex: #2 or 3)
3. Well, she and I talked for a bit. She's havin' a rough go of it.

TEX
10. Be moderately offended
10. Should I take that personally? I think I'm...

11. Trivialize Chelsee's plight
11. Oh, you mean the unbearable trauma of turning thirty?

12. Manly incomprehension
12. Maybe I'm just not in touch with my feminine side. What exactly is so rough?

scene for the character Louie Lamintz, the owner of the greasy spoon Brew & Stew. In order to make the example clearer, I combined the Response Attitudes and dialogue lists into one. Find a number on the flowchart and then look for the corresponding number in the dialogue table, "Interactive Dialogue and Response Attitudes for *The Pandora Directive,*" to understand the flow of the conversation. On the flowchart, gray blocks are Louie's dialogue, and white blocks are Tex's dialogue.

Interactive dialogue in *The Pandora Directive* follows the same general structure as that in *Under a Killing Moon*. The screen shot from *The Pandora Directive* in Figure 22-3 shows the dialogue on the bottom left and the response attitudes on the right.

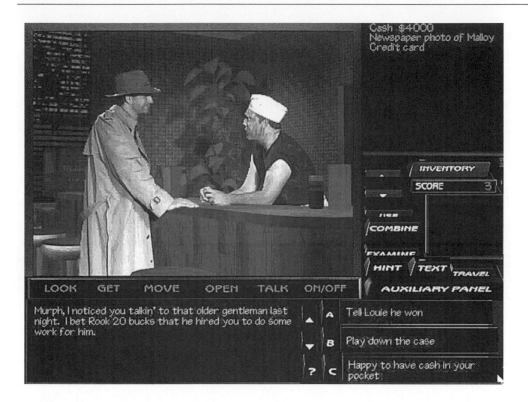

Figure 22-3 *Interactive dialogue and response attitudes in* The Pandora Directive.

Because the interactive dialogue in *The Pandora Directive* is more complex than that in *Under a Killing Moon*, it is broken down by character and written in three separate documents:

- A flowchart with the boxes numbered and shaded
- A numbered list of the other characters' and Tex's dialogue
- A numbered list of Tex's Response Attitudes

There are several possible responses to certain lines of dialogue, depending on which story path (A, B, or C) the player/Tex is on. In the "Interactive Dialogue and Response Attitudes in *The Pandora Directive*" table, the Response Attitudes are in italics. The dialogue they elicit follows immediately after.

The complete list of dialogue and response attitudes is available in the Pandora Directive *area of the Chapters section of this book's* CD-ROM.

Interactive Dialogue and Story Paths

The A1 before the first line of Tex's dialogue in the table "Interactive Dialogue and Response Attitudes for *The Pandora Directive*" refers to which story path Tex is on. Lines 1, 2, and 3 are the three possible lines of dialogue for a player on the A path. Lines 2, 3, and 4 are the three possible lines for a player on the B path, and lines 4, 5, and 6 are for the C path. There is some reuse of lines in different paths. (The different paths will be explained later in this chapter.) This is only the interactive dialogue for one scene for one character. This has to be done for every scene for every character.

Effect of Interactive Dialogue

The Response Attitude chosen and the resulting dialogue spoken mold Tex into the kind of character the player wants him to be. He can be a jerk or a hero, depending on which attitudes are clicked. The dialogue choices also have far-reaching effects on the story. These choices at the micro-level ultimately affect Tex's life (and the flow of the plot) at the macro-level. This is a more natural type of branching than that seen in many other interactive games, where the user simply chooses major actions, such as shooting the sheriff or the outlaw.

In *Pandora*, such larger action choices often become inevitable because of smaller choices made earlier in dialogue. This is one way that this game embraces the fatalistic viewpoint of its hard-boiled detective genre. In this genre, characters rarely make clear choices for their future. Instead they make a series of small choices that set off major consequences that shove them in one direction or another.

Emily's murder sequence is a good example of the effect of interactive dialogue. The steps that lead up to the death actually occur well before the actual event, and when the death does happen, it affects the rest of the story.

Tex stumbles onto the dark path that leads to Emily's death long before he ever sets foot in her nightclub, the Fuchsia Flamingo. The trouble starts in the linear introduction to the program. Tex and Chelsee are sitting in Louie's diner. Chelsee, about to turn thirty years old, is feeling stuck and confused. She tries to get a response from Tex that would let her know that he really cares about her. But being an unsubtle male, Tex misses the point; she gets angry and leaves. Louie and Rook, who are also in the diner, however, understand her completely and lay into Tex after she has left: "Tex, you idiot, what she meant was . . ."

Once the game goes into the interactive mode, the player can go back and talk to her at her newsstand. Tex knows that she is upset, and really wants to go out with her. He has wanted to go out with her for years. What the player/Tex chooses to say to Chelsee at this point can send Tex down the dark path to Emily's death or to the light path and Emily's rescue.

The response attitude choices are: "ATTEMPT AN APOLOGY," "PRETEND NOTHING IS WRONG," or "LIGHTEN THE MOOD." If Tex pretends nothing is wrong and just asks, "Any new detective magazines?" he has stumbled onto the dark path because this waffle makes Chelsee angry, and she'll respond with, "Sure, I've got Butthead Detective, you ought to like that one." Continuing this pattern of dialogue choices sets off an argument, which plants a seed of mistrust in Chelsee. Tex does, however, eventually calm her down enough to set a dinner date.

The player/Tex can take another step on the dark path when talking to Leach, Emily's boss. If Tex is rude to him, Leach gets mad and later will block Tex's entrance when he tries to rescue Emily.

After talking to Leach, Tex searches a room and gets knocked out, causing him to miss his dinner date with Chelsee. She, of course, is angry: "I can't believe you stood me up." At this point, Tex can try to explain and move up to the light path, or he can stay on the dark path by saying, "Look, that's the way it is. I'm a PI," causing another argument between them.

When they finally do get to the nightclub, he tells Chelsee he wants to see if he can get backstage to see the singer, Emily. Chelsee snaps, "You're here with me, and you're watching another woman." She says this because she is still angry about the argument they had before they went to the club. They have a huge fight. She leaves. Tex stays and gets drunk.

When he finally does see Emily at the club, he is in a totally different frame of mind than he would have been if not for the fight with Chelsee and being drunk. Because of this, and because Leach (mad from their earlier interaction) blocks him from Emily's room, he is unable to save her life.

After failing to save her, his whole perspective changes. He says, "I've got to get out of this business; it's killing me." He's now in for the kill, trying to get money so he can quit the PI business. He also loses Chelsee and later hooks up with the dark woman, Regan. If he continues on this path, he is killed at the end of the story.

Dialogue Explosion and Reusability

Although interactive dialogue is an excellent way to give the viewer a high degree of control and create realistic interactivity, it is not without its drawbacks. This degree of interactivity demands that a vast amount of dialogue be scripted. Pandora has six to twelve totally unique paths of conversation, depending on the scene. This doesn't mean there are twelve different choices per line of dialogue, but it does mean that there are twelve possible dialogue sequences or paths that could be charted through a scene. (Take some colored highlighters and chart a few paths through the *Pandora* flowchart in Figure 22-2 to see what I mean.)

A writer who isn't careful can be buried in a dialogue explosion of hundreds of lines for just one scene. The conversation grows vertically and requires massive amounts of dialogue writing. On the *Pandora* flowchart (Figure 22-2), notice the towering vertical stack of boxes 7 to 18, a total of eleven different lines of dialogue. *Pandora*'s writer, Aaron Conners, said that the extra work of writing all these dialogue options doesn't actually pay off with viewer satisfaction. It is rare for the viewer to access all lines of dialogue, and because of the number of lines of dialogue in a scene, the lines had to be quite short.

Because of this limitation, Conners tried to make the *Pandora* dialogue branching more horizontal by reusing the same lines in different situations. Notice on *The Pandora Directive* flowchart (Figure 22-2) the number of places where multiple arrows go into one box. This means that the same line is being reused several times, such as Louie's shaded box #14, which is a possible response to three of Tex's dialogue lines.

The Mechanics of Flowcharting

Conners uses the software ABC Flowcharter to draw his charts. In *Under a Killing Moon*, he used flowcharts with dialogue typed in and indicated different characters by different-shaped boxes. Because the *Pandora* charts are more complex, he used numbers in the chart that refer to numbered lines of dialogue in a list. He indicated different characters by shading boxes. This technique makes it easier than the different-shaped boxes to distinguish the characters.

First Person Point of View and Control of Character Movements

The Pandora Directive also gives the viewer a high degree of control over Tex's actions. Most of the interactive scenes are shot in first person. The player becomes Tex. He or she sees what Tex sees, and as Tex, the player can move all around the room and examine objects. The player can also click on items, such as a painting, to get Tex's sarcastic voice-over about art. Or the player can click on a picture of Tex's ex-wife, which might trigger a flashback video sequence. See the list of player options just above the dialogue in Figure 22-3.

Interactivity at the Scene and Sequence Level: Multiple Story Paths

These interactive choices at the dialogue and movement level launch the Tex character on one of three main story paths with seven possible endings. There are three main paths:

- **A—Light Path:** This is the basic Hollywood ending in which Tex saves the world and wins the good woman, Chelsee.
- **B—Middle Path:** This is middle ground. He doesn't lose Chelsee, but he doesn't win her either.
- **C—Dark Path:** This is film noir—a chance to explore the negative possibilities. Tex fails to save Emily. He loses the good woman, Chelsee, takes up with the bad woman, Regan, and dies at the end.

As Tex continues to make choices in dialogue and movement, he will hit key dialogue lines or flags that will shift him back and forth between paths. And redemption is hard won. Once entrenched in the dark C path, the best he can hope for is to move up to B. The saintly A path is out of reach.

The player molds Tex into what he wants him to be: good, middle, or bad. Sometimes one choice can mean the difference between life and death. For example, which of the seven endings the player gets depends to a large degree on whether Tex sleeps with the bad woman, Regan. If the player has been on the A or B path and says no to Regan, then Tex solves the final puzzle on the spaceship before escaping safely. If the player follows the C path throughout the game, but says no to Regan, the player gets the B ending: Tex is wounded and sent limping off the ship by Fitzpatrick. If the player follows the C path throughout the game and Tex says yes to Regan, depending on the player's choices in the last scene, Tex could end up dead.

Making a Complex Story and Interactivity Work Together in an Engaging and Coherent Fashion

A detective story is very information-based. It requires readers or viewers to keep track of many characters, clues, and locations. This problem is exaggerated when the story has a high degree of interactivity, as in *The Pandora Directive*. Aaron Conners does a number of things to keep the audience well oriented, such as voice-over for exposition and character background, a hints file, a travel list and map, and Ask Abouts.

Ask Abouts

As a detective, Tex is constantly asking people questions. If Tex/the player chooses the right questions and goes to the right places, he gets key information. Where a real detective might scribble something in a notebook, Tex's key information automatically appears in his Ask Abouts list, which the player can access from the main interface at any time. See the top right in Figure 22-4.

The following example from *The Pandora Directive* walkthrough explains how the Ask Abouts work. All the Ask Abouts are in bold. They appear on the on-screen Ask Abouts list (Figure 22-4), when someone tells Tex about them. He can then ask others about these Ask Abouts.

When Tex finds a scarf, he takes it to the Brew & Stew and shows it to LOUIE, who tells him about a **young blonde woman. Young blonde woman** is automatically placed in your Ask About list. When Tex asks him more about the young blonde woman, he responds with, "She was real pretty, though a little heavy on the makeup. I think she said her name was Emily." This puts **Emily** in your Ask About list. You can now ask anyone about Emily including Louie, but all he has to say is, "I don't know anythin' else about her."

However, when you ask another character, Clint, about Emily, he'll tell you she works for **Gus Leach**. Gus Leach is now placed in your Ask About list. Ask Clint about Gus Leach and he'll give you the **Leach's Key** Ask About. Ask Clint about Leach's key to get

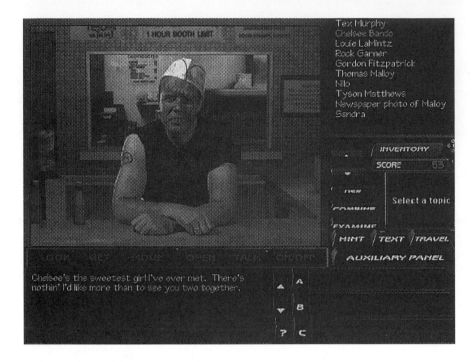

Figure 22-4 *Ask Abouts in* The Pandora Directive.

```
the key. You now know that the scarf belongs to the girl who sings
at the Fuchsia Flamingo and that her name is Emily. You also know
that the Flamingo is run by Gus Leach.
```

The Ask Abouts not only help the player keep track of key clues, they also limit the player to questions that the characters might have answers for. Otherwise, the viewer would be faced with the irritation of characters' constantly saying, "I don't know," or the writers would have to write Ask Abouts for everything mentioned in the game. The Ask Abouts also give a convenient way to ask questions. Simply click on the item on the list.

Louie's Ask Abouts Example   Following are some of the responses that the Louie Lamintz character can make if questioned on various Ask Abouts. Note that in some cases, as in the Chelsee Ask About, his responses depend on what path Tex is on (A, B, or C). Refer back to the Pandora flowchart (Figure 22-2) and you'll see that all the interactive conversations eventually end up in Ask Abouts.

```
If Tex Murphy asks about:

   1. Tex: (Louie answers) You're OK in my book, Murph ... no
      matter what anyone else says.
```

2. Chelsee: (1) Chelsee's the sweetest girl I've ever met.
There's nothin' I'd like more than to see you two together.

     (2a) Just between you and me, I get the feelin' she's
          sweet on ya.
     (2b) I don't know what to tell ya, Murph. The mind of
          a woman can be a great mystery.
     (2c) She called a while ago. I guess she's gonna make
          her visit to Phoenix permanent. Sorry.
  (3a/b) Yeah, I've heard from her. She wanted me to say hi.

3. Louie: What are ya askin' 'bout me for? I ain't nothin'
special.

4. Rook: Rook's just an ornery son-of-a-gun, but, believe it or
not, he's pretty soft underneath.

The complete Ask Abouts list is available in the Pandora Directive *area of the Chapters section of this book's CD-ROM.*

Sometimes Ask Abouts involve more than just asking about a name. They can involve showing things. What is shown and in what sequence affects Louie's response:

Offer photo of Malloy: Yeah. I've seen this guy. Lemme think ... He
came in here a week or two ago. Had a young blonde girl with him.
Ordered liver and onions if I remember correctly.
Offer untranslated letter: Well Murph, if I had to guess, I'd say
this is written in Yucatec. It's a Mayan language, spoken in
southern Mexico. I can't help ya with the translation, though.
You know who might be able to help ya is Clint. I heard he's quite
a world traveler. Might give it a try.

Offer scarf:
   If Tex offers Photo of Malloy first: Yeah, I remember this guy.
Came in here to eat a couple times. Probably a month ago.
   Then Scarf: Oh, yeah. I remember this scarf ... and the perfume
on it. Young, blonde girl ... In fact, she came in here with the guy
in the photograph.
   If offer Scarf first: Oh, yeah. I remember this scarf ...
and the perfume on it. Young, blonde girl. Came in here a
while ago.
   Then Photo of Malloy: This guy was with that young blonde girl
who wore the nice-smelling scarf.

Ask About Lead-Ins   You as the player can't just walk up to and start quizzing a character about Ask Abouts. Like a real detective, it usually requires a bit of chatter to warm up the source and get to an Ask About. In the example that follows, the numbers refer to the *Pandora* flowchart (Figure 22-2).

```
Louie:
   17. My point is, fallin' in love don't mean a lot. What's
       hard is knowin' someone real well and still likin' 'em. But
       that ain't even the hardest thing. The hardest thing is
       findin' someone you can trust. Remember that. [beat] Now
       I'll get off my soapbox ... What can I do for you?

Tex:
   25. Yeah, I'll keep that in mind. Not to be rude, but can I
       ask you a few questions before I go?
```

Sometimes, getting to the Ask Abouts requires quite a bit of smooth talking. Refer to the *Pandora Directive* flowchart (Figure 22-2) to see the twisted path it takes to get to the Ask Abouts in that scene. Other times, Ask About lead-ins are fairly short, such as when Tex dials a telephone number and the person appears on the videophone ready for questions. But even these brief lead-ins can have relevance to the plot or character development.

The Pandora Directive *Narrative Walkthrough*

To get a sense of how all of the elements discussed (complex story, interactivity, and Ask Abouts) work together, read the walkthrough sample that follows. The walkthrough is a rough description of the story and key interactive elements. It is an attempt to provide an overview of how the program is going to work. This is essential, because much of the other written material for an interactive program can be simply lists of dialogue, flowcharts, and phrases.

The walkthrough is broken down by days, as is *The Pandora Directive*. This makes it easier to use multiple CDs and to get the miniseries type of pacing that the writers and designers were looking for. Following is Day One of the walkthrough.

 The complete walkthrough has ten days and is available in the Pandora Directive *area of the Chapters section of this book's CD-ROM.*

Options are frequently listed for the character in the walkthrough, such as, "Your options at the outset (in likely order of importance) are (1) find out about Malloy staying at the Ritz, (2) pay the rent to Nilo, (3) pay Rook and/or Louie, (4) go to the newsstand and talk to Chelsee, or (5) go to the Electronics Shop." In the actual game, these options are clear because of the situation or are explained through

Tex's voice-overs (VO). There are different versions of voice-overs for the different paths. Voice-overs are enclosed by brackets.

THE PANDORA DIRECTIVE WALKTHROUGH

Day One

After the Introduction is finished, we have met Louie, Rook, Glenda, Chelsee, and Fitzpatrick. You have also seen Sandra Collins (dead) and the Black Arrow Killer (Dag Horton).

In the introductory conversation with Chelsee, you learn that she is about to turn thirty years old and is in an emotional quandary about it. After she leaves, Louie and Rook lead us to believe that Chelsee is romantically susceptible.

In the introductory conversation with Gordon Fitzpatrick, you learn that he is looking for a Dr. Thomas Malloy, who recently stayed at the Ritz Hotel. Fitzpatrick and Malloy used to work together (where, unspecified). Fitzpatrick then says he saw a photograph of Malloy in the Bay City Mirror and found out that the photograph had been taken at a local university (San Francisco Tech). Fitzpatrick gives Tex a copy of the photo. The only person at SFT able or willing to recognize Malloy was a grad student named Sandra (Collins). She said she had worked with the man Fitzpatrick knew as Malloy, but that she knew him as Tyson Matthews. Fitzpatrick arranged to meet Sandra later to discuss what she knew, but she didn't keep the appointment and Fitzpatrick was unable to locate her again. Fitzpatrick then saw another reference to Malloy in the Cosmic Connection, an underground paranormal journal, which mentioned an upcoming interview with Dr. Thomas Malloy. The interview never appeared in the magazine and no explanation has been given. Finally, Fitzpatrick says he was able to pay 500 dollars to get Malloy's address at the Ritz, but Malloy had already moved on.

Tex accepts the case and Fitzpatrick leaves. This initiates the first interactive portion of the game. [Play TEX VO—Tex owes $ to Rook, Louie, Nilo.] Your inventory consists of the newspaper photo of Malloy, $4000 cash, and Tex's Electronics Shop credit card (from UKM). Your options at the outset, in likely order of importance, are: (1) find out about Malloy staying at the Ritz, (2) pay the rent to Nilo, (3) pay Rook and/or Louie, (4) go to the newsstand and talk to Chelsee, or (5) go to the Electronics Shop.

Going to Rook, Louie, Chelsee, or the Electronics Shop can be done in any order at any time. In order to talk to Nilo, however, you must make a date with Chelsee (Path: A/A/A/A/C). Until this is done, Nilo isn't at the front desk of the Ritz.

Note: In order to initiate the A path, you must use Path C/B/B/... In order to initiate the C path, you must use Path A/C/C/... When returning to Chelsee (after initiating one of the alternate paths), you must use Path C/A/C to make the date.

Once the date with Chelsee has been set, she is still available at the newsstand for Ask Abouts until Tex gets jumped at the Ritz. After that, she's no longer at the newsstand at any point in the game. Also, once you've set the date, Nilo becomes available at the front desk in the Ritz lobby.

If you go to the Brew & Stew and talk to LOUIE, you can choose A, in which case, you lose $20 from inventory; otherwise, you don't lose any money. Once the Ask Abouts start, you can also offer $200 to pay your tab to Louie. This is totally optional, though it will earn you points. At the pawnshop, you must pay Rook $300 in order to get him to answer Ask Abouts. At the Electronics Shop, you must pay Zack $1220 in order to make a purchase.

Once you've made a date with Chelsee, you're free to talk to Nilo. You must pay Nilo $2100 for rent before doing anything else. After paying the rent, Nilo will ask for more money in order to get to the Ask Abouts. You must pay either $300 (choice A or B after "no comprende") or $100 (choice C after "no comprende"). Offering the photo of Malloy will get Nilo to tell you that Malloy stayed in Apartment A, but is no longer there. [TEX VO—Probably no one else has been there since Malloy left.]

When you go to Apartment A, you'll find the door locked. There is a security panel on the wall by the door, which requires a number code in order to enter. [TEX VO—Nilo keeps notebook on desk.] You now have two ways to get into the apartment: (1) Go back to Nilo and ask for the code, or (2) set off the fire alarm, getting Nilo to leave the front desk and allowing you to get his notebook. If you ask Nilo for the code, he'll ask for another $500. Using Path C/C will get you the code for free. Any other path will cost you $500. In order to find the fire alarm, locate the painting on the wall in the second floor hallway of the Ritz and move it. Get the screwdriver from Tex's office, and use it on the face of the fire alarm. This will initiate the fire alarm puzzle. Click the top left nodule, then the top right nodule. Next, click the second nodule from the top on the left; then click the bottom nodule on the right. Next, click the second nodule from the bottom on the left; then click the second nodule

```
from the top on the right. Finally, click the bottom nodule on the
left; then the second nodule from the bottom on the right. This
will start the fire alarm. Go to the front desk in the lobby and
get Nil's notebook. Examine the notebook and find the code to
Apartment A (4827). Go to the apartment and enter the code on the
security panel ... then enter the apartment.
     A movie sequence is initiated. Tex is jumped and knocked
unconscious.
```

Conclusion: Response to the Project

The Pandora Directive was a major success. *Computer Gaming World* and *PC Games Magazine* named it adventure game of the year, and *PC Gamer Magazine* named it an Editor's Choice. It frequently appears on lists of the top adventure games of all time.

References

Conners, Aaron. Telephone interviews with the author, December 1995, October 1999, May 2005.

Dickens, Evan. Top 20 Adventure Games of All-Time. Adventure Gamers Web Site. http://www.adventuregamers.com/article/id,186/p,7

Case Study—Worlds Narrative: *Dust: A Tale of the Wired West*

Summary

Name of production: *Dust: A Tale of the Wired West*
Writer: Andrew Nelson
Developers: CyberFlix Inc.
Audience: Rated for teenagers (13 and up)
Medium: CD-ROM
Presentation location: Home
Subject: Western
Goal: Entertain
Architecture: String of pearls, linear, hierarchical

The script samples and images used in this chapter are copyright CyberFlix, Inc. Parts of this chapter originally appeared in *Creative Screenwriting*.

Program Description and Background

Program Description

Dust: A Tale of the Wired West is an adventure game Western set in 1882 in Diamondback, New Mexico. In the pre-credit linear video scene, the Stranger catches a gunslinger, the Kid, playing foul at cards and nails his cheating hand to the table with a knife. Before the Kid can recover, the Stranger flees.

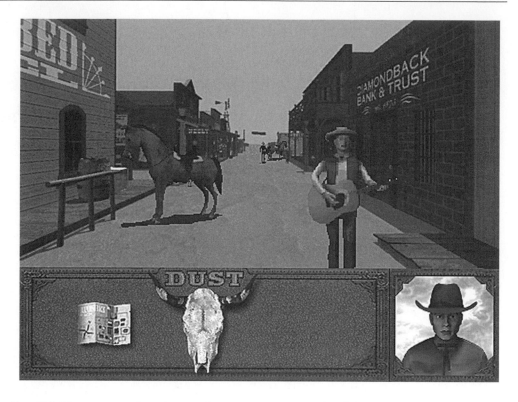

Figure 23-1 *The main interface showing the town in* Dust: A Tale of the Wired West.

In the next scene, the player becomes the Stranger as the rest of the game is played through first-person point of view. What the Stranger sees, the player sees. When people talk to the Stranger, they are talking to the player.

Running from the Kid, the Stranger stumbles into the town of Diamondback (see Figure 23-1) in the middle of the night with no gun, little money, and a hole in his size-twelve boots. The goal is first to get cash, gun, and boots, and then to defend himself from the Kid, who is gunning for revenge. If the Stranger survives the high noon shootout, he may get appointed sheriff and lured into helping a Native American schoolteacher recover her tribe's lost treasure.

The town of Diamondback is a three-dimensional world populated with forty animated characters. Dust's writer, Andrew Nelson, calls it "*Myst* with people in it." The Stranger can move through the town, exploring most of its buildings and talking to its citizens. They will sometimes help and sometimes mislead; a big part of the game is judging the character of the people the Stranger meets and deciding whose advice to follow.

In addition to the story, this program also has games to play, such as blackjack, poker, slot machines, checkers, and a shooting range. These games are well integrated into the story, and success at them helps the player advance the narrative.

For example, on the Stranger's first night in town, he must win enough money gambling to stay at the hotel.

Dust: A Tale of the Wired West *and the Adventure Game*

Dust's writer Nelson says that sophisticated navigability and interactivity is a major feature of this game. The user in *Dust* enters a world populated by cyber-puppets who have lives and personalities of their own. They do their shopping, gambling, or drinking in real time, whether the player interacts with them or not. If the player does interact, they will address him or her directly, and they will remember how the player treats them. This can cause a chain of events that radically changes the progress of the narrative.

All the buildings in town can be entered whenever they are "open," and objects can be looked at and picked up. Sounds that are heard in the distance will get louder as the player approaches their source. This complex navigability and interactivity is made possible by CyberFlix's DreamFactory authoring program, described in detail later in this chapter under "Creating an Inhabitable, Believable World." *Dust* is the first program to be completely developed in this process.

Production Background

Andrew Nelson wrote and produced *Dust: A Tale of the Wired West*. Michael Gilmore and Jamie Wicks were the art directors in charge of the design. The program was developed by CyberFlix Inc. of Knoxville, Tennessee. After producing several more successful games, including the best selling *Titanic: Adventure Out of Time*, the CyberFlix president, Bill Appleton, decided to cease producing computer games. Appleton is currently Chief Technical Officer at the company DreamFactory, where he has redesigned the DreamFactory authoring software as a suite of browser-based tools for developing rich client user interfaces for enterprise web applications.

Goals and Challenges Writing Dust: A Tale of the Wired West

Goals

A primary goal for the developers of *Dust* was to create an inhabitable, believable world with its own constants and laws. They also wanted to give the user the maximum possible freedom to explore this world and interact with its citizens as part of a complex, interactive story. They hoped this program would have broad appeal and reach a wider audience than the typical video game.

Challenges

The key elements of these goals and the major challenges are the following:

- Creating an inhabitable, believable world.
- Giving the user the opportunity to explore this world and interact with its citizens.

- Developing a story within this highly interactive world through establishing plot points, characterization, and other story functions.

Writing *Dust: A Tale of the Wired West*: Meeting the Challenges

Creating an Inhabitable, Believable World

The key to *Dust*'s success in creating an inhabitable, believable world is CyberFlix's proprietary multimedia authoring tool, DreamFactory. This technology allowed writer Andrew Nelson to "write" *Dust* in a radically different way than most other multimedia programs are written today.

Preliminary Writing

The writing of *Dust* started off with words on paper, as do most other multimedia titles. First Nelson developed the backstory on the town of Diamondback, giving the history of the town and the characters. When creating a world such as this town, the designers need to know background on every individual and building, so that they can create a consistent, realistic environment that has a life of its own.

The writer next wrote the walkthrough, outlining the basic story line and key interactions. Then came the game design, which is basically a blown-up storyboard showing the interactive puzzles. Finally came the table of events, which became the basis for the hint book. This book has suggestions that help the player solve key problems and move forward in the game. Up to this point, the writing process on *Dust* is similar to that of other worlds games. But from this point forward, the writer used DreamFactory, and the similarities quickly fade.

DreamFactory® Defined

DreamFactory is a set of multimedia authoring tools designed by CyberFlix's president, Bill Appleton, and used to create *Dust*. DreamFactory is designed so that nontechnical people, such as writers and designers, can develop an interactive multimedia piece without programming.

DreamFactory develops 3-D interactive environments that are peopled by "cyber-actors" who interact with the user. The cyber-actors are not videos of real people, nor are they traditional, drawn animations. Instead they are created from photographs of real people that are developed into computer-generated animations. The final results are cyber-actors who walk around town and talk to the user. (See Figure 23-2 later in this chapter.)

These synthetic actors allow for greater realism than cartoon-style animation, and they allow much higher levels of interactivity than video, because these computer-generated characters, like the letters on a word processor, are simply bits of code that can be instantly assembled and reassembled. This advantage has made 3-D animation similar to that used in *Dust* the most popular approach for video games.

In *Dust* the characters respond smoothly to the user, remember interactions, and change future behavior based on these interactions. Most of the characters develop significantly during the four days of the story. The characters also move about on their own in real time, whether the user interacts with them or not.

DreamFactory has these specialized tools:

- **SetConstruction:** Builds 3-D digital sets that the player can move through in real time.
- **PropDepartment:** Creates accurately scaled props that increase or decrease in size as they get closer to or farther from the user.
- **CentralCasting:** Creates and animates the cyber-actors who move through the 3-D sets, speak, and react to the user.
- **HeadShot:** Animates the close-ups of the talking characters based on photographs of actual actors.
- **MovieEditor:** Edits animation sequences and can add special effects, camera movement, and transitions.
- **SoundTrack:** Builds and controls the audio.
- **FlatPainter:** Creates backgrounds, interfaces, and interactive buttons.

DreamFactory and the Writer

After the writer develops the basic characters, story line, and some of the dialogue on paper, he or she stops writing a plan for a world and instead uses DreamFactory to build the world itself. Once the characters are defined, artists use the HeadShot and CentralCasting tools to create the characters. Other designers use the SetConstruction and PropDepartment tools to create the environment or world of the story (in the case of *Dust*, the town of Diamondback). The newly created cyber-actors are placed in this world, and from this point forward, the writer doesn't put words on paper again.

The writer thus functions more like a writer-director. When the writer types lines for a certain character, the appropriate cyber-actor on the computer screen will speak the lines. When the writer types in screen directions, the cyber-actor will do what he or she is told to do. The writer thus gets to see the world being created come immediately to life.

Editing is just as easy. The writer can click on a cyber-actor to get his or her dialogue and reaction to changes in the script. *Dust*'s writer, Andrew Nelson, said that there was no other effective way to test all the variables in a program as complex as *Dust*. DreamFactory allows the writer constantly to test game play and interaction all the way up to the alpha stage and beyond. (Alpha stage is the earliest full working version of a multimedia program.)

Nelson estimates that half of the original dialogue and most of the dialogue and story editing occurred in DreamFactory. Once he started working with

DreamFactory, he did not work with paper again until the end of the project, when a hard copy of the script was printed out. The final script does not look like a screenplay. It is more like a treatment of the characters and character interactions, off of which hangs huge amounts of dialogue. Nelson estimates that there are about 5,000 individual lines of dialogue in *Dust*.

Writing in DreamFactory requires using a special scripting language, but Nelson says that it was not much more difficult than learning to write in linear screenplay style, which has its own specific formatting and technical vocabulary. Like writing in linear screenplay format, writing in DreamFactory is cumbersome at first, but eventually it becomes second nature. What is difficult (and this is shared by any other highly interactive script) is the need to write mosaically. When a writer is using Dream-Factory to develop a worlds program such as *Dust*, there is no linear structure outside of the central story line. The linear progression is built by the user out of the snippets of dialogue and bits of interaction the writer creates.

Giving the User the Opportunity to Explore This World

Perhaps the best way to explain the extensive navigability the user has in *Dust* is to describe some of the options available the first night of the story. After the introductory material, *Dust* starts with the Stranger coming into town in the middle of the night. After a few preliminary interactions to orient the viewer to the game, the user/Stranger is free to explore the town. He can wander the streets and talk to people he meets, or he can enter the buildings that are open. Because it is the middle of the night, the open buildings are limited to the saloon, the hotel, and the curiosities shop.

The curiosities shop is owned by a character named Help, who is always there if the player gets stuck. The hotel has no rooms available when the Stranger arrives, but the saloon is hopping with gambling, music, and women upstairs.

Players can visit each of these sites as often as they want and talk to anyone they meet. Because the characters all move in real time and have lives of their own, different characters appear as the evening progresses. However, in order to advance in the story and move on to the next day, the Stranger needs to find a place to sleep.

This can be done in a couple of ways. The Stranger needs money to stay at the hotel. He can get this by gambling or by searching the couch in the hotel, which has four dollars under the cushions. If he loses all his money gambling, he can ask Help for a loan. The other way to get a bed for the night is to be nice to the mayor's wife, who will then ask him home. But this works only if the Stranger sees her on the street and says just the right things. In *Dust*, there is usually an easy way and a hard way to achieve goals.

There are myriad story paths that the user/Stranger could travel the first night, depending on where he decides to go and whom he decides to talk to, but all the story paths will eventually lead to the Stranger's going to bed that night. Nelson describes this structure as a circular experience with several doors that will shoot the player out to the next level of the story. Depending on what the player does on one level of the story, he or she will be better or less prepared to meet the challenges in the next level. Eventually, all of these story paths on all of the levels lead to a common destination, which is a branching of six different endings.

The overall structure can be compared to a string of pearls (see Figure 18-5 in Chapter 18), with each pearl being a set time period and location that the character is free to explore. To leave the pearl and advance the story, the player must achieve certain things, such as get a place to sleep, get a gun, get bullets, and so on.

This type of structure means that the writer and other developers must prepare vast amounts of dialogue, interactions, and places for the user to explore. It also means that it is difficult to create many emotions common to linear video that require a tight sequencing of action, such as suspense. However, Nelson explains that *Dust* offers something different from the linear experience. He compares *Dust* to Disneyland. Whatever players would like to do, they can find it in *Dust*. They can play cards, shoot in an arcade, and if they are lonely, there are lots of folks willing to talk. The experience of *Dust* essentially revolves around getting things, doing things, and having fun.

See the demo in the Dust *area of the Chapters section of this book's* CD-ROM.

Interactive Dialogue
Dust's Approach to Interactive Dialogue

A major way to get information and have fun in *Dust* is through talking to the characters. Like the creators of *The Pandora Directive*, the developers of *Dust* decided that interactive dialogue provided the best opportunity for detailed and fluid interaction. The two games, however, take different approaches to dialogue interactivity. In *The Pandora Directive*, the primary dialogue interaction is through the main character, Tex, who has a series of response attitudes that the user can click to elicit different lines of dialogue. The user cannot choose Tex's actual dialogue. The other characters do not have attitudes to click on; their responses are dictated by Tex's lines. They also have considerably less variation in their dialogue than Tex does.

Dust takes the opposite approach. The Stranger's lines are presented in a menu of written choices. We never hear him speak. The other characters speak in response to the Stranger's questions, which the user picks from the menu. For example, when the player first encounters the character Marie Macintosh, she will be in the form of what CyberFlix calls an "actor," which is an animation of Marie going about her daily business in the streets of Diamondback (see Figure 23-2). When the player clicks on her, she will walk toward the player, and then dissolve to a more lifelike close-up. At this point she will speak her opening lines: "Why, if it isn't the stranger in our midst! I was out for a stroll."

Once she completes her opening lines, the player will have the option of responding by clicking text questions and comments from a menu at the bottom

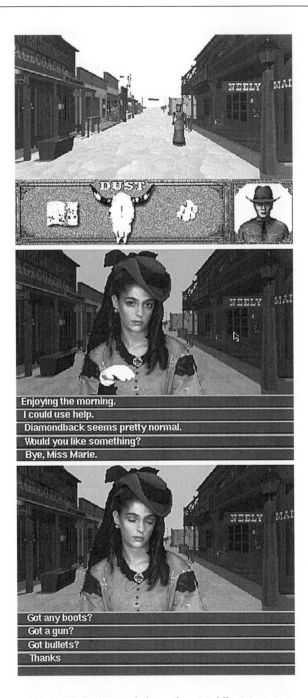

Figure 23-2 *Top: Marie as "actor" before user clicks on her. Middle: Marie in interactive conversation after the user clicks on her (menu items are the user's questions/comments. In this example, the user clicks, "I could use help"). Bottom: Marie continues interactive conversation (the menu is narrowed to the things the user needs help with).*

of the screen. If the player chooses "I could use help" from the menu, in Figure 23-2, Marie will say: "However can I be of assistance?" Now the menu will change to these options:

```
Got any boots?
Got a gun?
Got bullets?
Thanks.
```

The user can choose one of the above menu items, and Marie verbally responds. The conversation continues until the user cuts it off with a menu item such as "Thanks" or "Bye." But the user/Stranger never speaks. (This approach is similar to the interactive dialogue approach used in the *Nancy Drew* mysteries described in Chapter 20, except that the *Nancy Drew* mysteries also show the other character's dialogue in text.)

Andrew Nelson chose this approach to interactive dialogue because he thought that the written lines were more neutral than choosing attitudes and hearing the main character speak. He said that with the written text, it is easier to infer that the dialogue would be delivered in the way the player imagines. He also said that he wanted to give the user more choices by: (1) giving the user the option of choosing the specific lines to speak, and (2) giving a number of possible user responses for each line of the other character, as opposed to a limited number of Response Attitudes. Nelson does not, however, rule out all use of Response Attitudes in projects where they are effective. (See Chapter 22 for a discussion of the Response Attitudes approach.)

Effect of the Interactive Dialogue in *Dust*

The characters in *Dust* remember and react to what the player/Stranger says to them. If the Stranger is rude, they may not give him the information he needs or help when he needs them. For example, when he first meets the mayor's wife, if he flatters her, she'll invite him home to spend the night. If he insults her, she'll run off in a huff.

How the Stranger treats one character may also affect how a character who is connected to that character will treat him. Marie Macintosh hates her father. If the Stranger is rude to her father, she'll like the Stranger. This type of complex reaction to the user's dialogue choices can change the progress of the story.

Possible Dialogue Scene: Marie Macintosh— Day One—Morning

Following is an example of a more complex dialogue scene, but it is only one possibility. (The sequence is from the morning of Day One.) The actual dialogue sequence depends on which questions the user chooses to ask. This conversation is not written out in order like this in the actual script. It was reconstructed here to explain how the interactive conversation works. The complete list of dialogue options as they appear in the actual script follows this example (the Stranger/user's questions and comments in boldface type are answered by Marie Macintosh's comments that have the same number as his questions):

```
MARIE MACINTOSH

MORNING—DAY ONE

                    MARIE: A1. Cheerful greeting
          Why, if it isn't the stranger in our midst!

                    MARIE: B. Question to user
          (She's suspicious) However do you do?

               STRANGER: C1. I'm doing fine.

                    MARIE: C1. Teasing you
          I'm delighted to hear that Diamondback provides all
          that you need, but aren't you curious about us?

               STRANGER: C1a. Should I be?

                    MARIE: C1a. Being mysterious
          (tinkling laugh) Diamondback is a town of secrets.
          Some are useful. Others aren't. But I don't mean
          to imply mystery. You have, no doubt, more pressing
          questions ...
```

[This is an example of the writer nudging the user to ask more questions to advance the story.]

```
          STRANGER: C1b. Why is the school deserted?

          MARIE: C1b. Explaining simple facts of life
          The mission school? Well, once the Yunni left,
          there really was no need for it. Diamondback's
          youngsters go to the Hildago School five miles
          from here. And there are no more Indians ...

               STRANGER: C1b-1. Why was that?
```

[Her answers to some of the questions depend on whether she likes the Stranger, which is based on the types of questions asked earlier. For example, for C1b-1, if she doesn't like the Stranger, she will answer:]

```
MARIE: C1b-1. Impatient. Not answering him,
              but speaking from the heart
       Really. That's all in the past.
```

[If she does like the Stranger, however, she will say:]

```
C1b-1a. Confiding in you.
"You know, since you came here I have felt a
(looks for word) kinship with you. I feel you
have known great tragedy, and because of that,
you understand me.
```

Dialogue Transcript Marie Macintosh—Day One—Morning

This is a list of the Morning Day One dialogue for Marie Macintosh and the Stranger as it appears in the actual script. This is a first draft; the final draft as seen on screen deals with the mission, not the school. Using DreamFactory, most of the editing and revisions are done on screen, and there is no second draft on paper.

In the dialogue that follows, the Stranger's questions are in boldface type, Marie's attitudes are in italics, and her response matches his question of the same number. "Home base" refers to the location where the cyber-actor is usually stationed. For Marie, it is outside Bolivar's store, but like the other characters, she can wander about on her day's activities.

```
Marie Macintosh

(Marie is a petulant, spoiled girl who, at 17, is thoroughly bored
with this backwater she finds herself in. She's very intelligent
and wants to appear older than she is, which makes her very young
indeed. With her alliance with Raddison, Marie can become
suspicious of your motives, guessing you may know about their
pyrite mine scheme. She can also shift her allegiance, if you
choose the right questions to ask her. We meet her usually in the
street where she whiles away the day fingering the fabrics at
Bolivar's or teasing the cowboys who wander into the Hard Drive
Saloon.)

Morning—Day One

A1. Cheerful greeting
"Why, if it isn't the stranger in our midst!"
```

A2. If unknown from previous night
(offering hand) "I'm the mayor's daughter, Marie."
A1a. if outside home base
"I was out for a stroll ..."
A1b. if outside first destination
"I was out for a stroll ..."
A1c. if inside first destination
"I often come here. To think"
A1d. if outside second destination
"Picking up a few items at Watsons."
A1e. if inside second destination
"I was fetching something." ·
A1f. if outside third destination
"I'm returning home from shopping."

B. Question to user
(She's suspicious) "However do you do?"
C1. I'm doing fine.
C2. I could use help.
C3. Play, if possible
C4. Thanks. Bye.

C1. Teasing you
"I'm delighted to hear that Diamondback provides all that you need,
  but aren't you curious about us?"
C2. Amused
"However can I be of assistance?"
C3. Giving you her hankie, speaking softly "There's sweat on your
  brow. Here ... Take my hankie. A token of a friendship?" (She
  ends this on a provocative note.)
C4. End conversation comment
"Goodbye. I am so very glad you've come to stay in Diamondback.
  If we are lucky, perhaps you'll stay for a long, long time."

C1a. Should I be?
C1b. Why is the school deserted?
C1b-1. Why is that?
If Marie likes Stranger
C1b-1a.
C1c. Who is the school teacher?

C2a. You got boots, size 12?
C2b. You got a gun?

C1a. Being mysterious

(tinkling laugh) "Diamondback is a town of secrets. Some are
  useful. Others aren't. But I don't mean to imply mystery. You
  have, no doubt, more pressing questions ..."

C1b. Explaining simple facts of life

"The mission school? Well, once the Yunni left, there really was
  no need for it. Diamondback's youngsters go to the Hildago
    School five miles from here. And there are no more ..."

C1b-1. Impatient. Not answering him, but speaking from the heart

"Really. That's all in the past."

If Marie likes Stranger

C1b-1a. Confiding in you

"You know, since you came here I have felt a (looks for word)
  kinship with you. I feel you have known great tragedy, and
  because of that, you understand me."

C1c. A little irritated to be back on the subject of Indians

"A Yunni called Sonoma, who lived with the Grangers until they
  died. Now I wouldn't know where she was. She is, after all,
  an Indian."

C2a. She is amused

(tinkling laugh) "Oh, I do not mean to make light of your
  situation, but your feet [giggles], they are simply enormous.
  The only ones bigger belong to the
  Nevans boy, Jay, who has a terrible crush on me"
  [giggles]

C2b. Lying sweetly through her teeth

"Oh, no! I don't even know how to shoot a gun! Guns scare me"

If Marie is suspicious

C2c. She responds

"Now, if I don't know a Colt from a Remington what would I know
  about bullets? [laughs] Maybe you could borrow a few from some
  cowpoke!"

 Additional dialogue transcripts are available in the Dust *area of the*
Chapters section of this book's CD-ROM.

Developing a Story Within This Highly Interactive World

This level of dialogue interactivity, coupled with the nearly unlimited opportunity
to explore Diamondback, creates a highly interactive world in the control of the
user. In order to create a story within such a world, the writer must develop a
series of devices that nudge the user in the right direction, while still leaving the
impression that the user is making the ultimate choice. These nudges establish key

plot points, introduce characters, engineer confrontations, guide the user where the writer wants him or her to go, and generally keep the story moving forward.

Help

One of the ways the writer guides the reader in this program is through the Help option. Unlike some programs where help is a text-hints window that clearly disrupts the story, help in *Dust* is a Chinese gentleman named Help who runs a curiosities shop. He always knows where the player is in the game and gives just the assistance needed. For example, if the Stranger runs out of cash, he'll give him a five dollar loan but also chase him out of the store, calling him a "hopeless case."

Other Characters' Dialogue

It is not only Help who knows where the player is in the story. The other characters are also aware of the Stranger's situation and can prompt him in the right direction. For example, when the Stranger gets a note at the hotel to meet a character outside, the hotel Clerk says, "So you going out again?" The Stranger can ignore the note and the prompt and go to bed, but if he does, he will miss the fun of a fistfight with a local bully and some key information. Even if dialogue in this piece is not prompting the user in a certain direction, it is usually giving key plot points or setting up character. There is not much room for idle chatter in an interactive program. The same information must be included in a variety of ways in different pieces of dialogue, because there is no guarantee that any one piece of dialogue will be accessed by the user.

Written Material

The note mentioned above is only one example of written material used to prod the character. *Dust* also includes a book on Diamondback in the curiosities shop that gives key information about the town. The town's newspaper also provides updates.

At one point, the user can read in the paper that Congress has passed anti-Asian legislation. A smart user realizes that the Chinese gentleman Help might be endangered and rushes to his store, saving it from being burned. This was also a way to bring in historical events as a context for the story.

The Narrator

The narrator allows the writer to compress and deliver instructions. In *Dust*, the narrator is triggered automatically at key times, particularly at the beginning of each day, telling the user what he or she has to accomplish. This is one way to ensure that the user will get key plot points without intruding significantly on the interactive experience.

Short Linear Movies

Short linear movies also occasionally appear to give important information, such as the opening card game that shows the Stranger's fight with the Kid.

Film Language and Genre

Film has spent a hundred years teaching the audience its visual language. Smart interactive writers can take advantage of this language to communicate meaning. *Dust* makes particularly good use of the icons associated with the Western genre. For example, when the town of Diamondback rises up from the desert, it creates a whole range of associations that users bring from their experience of other Westerns.

Conclusion: Response to the Program

Dust: A Tale of the Wired West was named Best Multimedia Game of the year by *MacWorld*. It has also received critical acclaim in such publications as *Newsweek*, *People*, *Next Generation*, and *CD-ROM Today*, and was a best seller for CyberFlix.

References

DreamFactory web site. http://www.dreamfactory.com

Garrand, Timothy. "Writing Interactive Narrative." Creative Screenwriting. Spring 1997.

Nelson, Andrew. Telephone interview with the author, December 1995, September 1999.

Production Notes. *Dust: A Tale of the Wired West*. Knoxville, TN: CyberFlix Inc., 1995, p. 5.

Case Study—Immersive Exhibit: *The New England Economic Adventure*

Summary

Name of production: *The New England Economic Adventure*
Writer: Maria O'Meara
Developers: Jeff Kennedy Associates, Inc., Northern Light Productions
Audience: Primarily students and teachers of economics and history
Medium: Theater with live presenter, large video screen, and touch pads for audience
Presentation location: The Federal Reserve Bank of Boston
Subject: Economic History of New England
Goal: Teach
Structures: Linear with scene branching for audience input

The script samples and images used in this chapter are copyright Federal Reserve Bank of Boston.

Program Description and Background

Program Description

The New England Economic Adventure (NEEA) is an immersive exhibit that is part of the education program of the Federal Reserve Bank of Boston. The exhibit is at their headquarters in Boston, Massachusetts, serving the economic education needs of students and teachers in the New England area. An immersive exhibit involves some combination of live presenters or actors, video, animations, physical objects,

Figure 24-1 The New England Economic Adventure *(NEEA) with live host, screen for video and animation, related objects in front of video screen, and audience interaction with the electronic program through PDA touch pads (inset picture).*

and audience interaction with the program through an input device such as a PDA. See Figure 24-1 for the setup of *The New England Economic Adventure.*

The New England Economic Adventure is part of a larger program delivered by the Federal Reserve Bank of Boston educators in an adjacent gallery. In addition to visiting the NEEA and the gallery, most groups will also participate in workshops in the Fed's economic labs. The NEEA also has a companion web site with additional information and activities. The link to that site is at the end of this chapter.

The NEEA explores three important events in New England's economic history: the founding of the textile industry, the mass production of bicycles with inter-changeable parts, and the successful introduction of one of the first mini-computers for a mass audience. The program takes users back in time and uses a game show format to test their economic knowledge and skills at making investment decisions.

NEEA writer Maria O'Meara explained that there are three types of interactivity for each of the three economic stories in this program. The activities occur in this order:

- The lightning round—players answer multiple choice and other questions presented on the video screen and their PDAs to build up their bank accounts

- The investment round—players view video on each economic event, invest money, or make similar business decision
- Round of risk and reward—an audience member is invited to spin a wheel of chance, which selects a random event, such as a natural disaster, that affects players' holdings

The narrative video material presented in the large center screen (see Figure 24-1) involves two young, energetic, time travelers who journey to the past and visit the three New England economic events: textile industry, bicycle manufacturing, and the mini-computer (see Figure 24-2). The time travelers take on

Figure 24-2 The New England Economic Adventure *time travelers who appear on the video screen in various historical periods.*

contemporary roles in each period, such as one of the investors in the textile industry. They also present background information, questions for the audience, and the correct answers to the questions using video, animations, graphics, and audio.

At the end of the game, each audience member's total dollars earned from investments and correct answers in the lighting round are displayed on their PDA screen. The person with the highest dollar amount wins the game!

Use of Stories to Present Information

The New England Economic Adventure (NEEA) could have presented its information as a set of well-organized facts that the user could assimilate. This is the way that the case study in Chapter 11 presents economic information. The NEEA, however, chose to present the bulk of its information in the narrative video of the two time travelers described above. The time travelers essentially take on our role as people of the 21st century, and take us back in time to participate in the great economic stories of New England.

Users' minds are particularly open to information presented through storytelling. Before the printing press and extensive access to written works, much of human knowledge was conveyed through the oral tradition of storytelling. Where nonnarratives deliver information through argument and description, narratives allows the user to become part of the information by becoming or identifying with a character in the story. Information embedded in a story is also linked by time and events and thus large bodies of information and the connection between different elements can be easier to remember through narrative. Because a user can identify with characters in a story and a story can carry emotional content, "these narratives also direct persons' judgments, decisions, conduct, actions, and behaviors. Stories are universal and powerful guides for living and understanding of our own and others' conduct" (Cole). Lastly, curiosity is a crucial component in learning. The user has to want to know what happens next in a sequence. This is hard to accomplish in a logical presentation of information, but is a key element in any good story.

For the reasons discussed above and others too complex to discuss here, story has always been and will continue to be an effective way to present information, particularly information related to human behavior and actions. Using narrative to present information is a common technique in many types of interactive media, including: edutainment programs, such as *The Oregon Trail* where we follow a family by wagon train across the untamed American West; training programs that allow users to role play key characters in performing essential tasks, such as selling or marketing a product; and immersive exhibits, such as *The New England Economic Adventure*, discussed in this chapter.

Popularity of Immersive Exhibits/Experiences

Presentations such as *The New England Economic Adventure* that include large screens, live presenters, theatrical lighting and sound effects, audience interaction, and other elements to bring the audience fully into the experience are called immersive exhibits or experiences. These types of exhibits are growing in popularity in museums because, as the writer of NEEA, Maria O'Meara, points out.

> *Video games and the web do so much more interactively now, the museums are turning more to immersive experiences that involve live presenters, big screens and theatrical experiences that you can't get sitting in front of your TV or computer.*

Even when standard computer screen kiosks are used in museums, there is often an attempt to make them more immersive by creating a set, such as a car sticking out of a wall, an ATM machine, or any kind of structure that will attract users. Immersive exhibits/experiences are also popular in theme parks, casinos, major conferences/conventions, and even the wired classroom. Many schools now have classrooms set up similarly to *The New England Economic Adventure* with audience touch pads, big screens, and accompanying software/media programs. With all these markets, developing immersive exhibits/experiences is a big business and the writing skills studied in this case study can apply to most of the situations described above.

Production Background

The Federal Reserve System is the central banking system of the United States. The Federal Reserve System is headquartered in Washington, D.C. with twelve regional Federal Reserve Banks located in major cities, including Boston. The Federal Reserve regulates banks, implements monetary policy, maintains the financial payments system, performs economic research, and presents economic education to the public.

To fulfill its mission of presenting economic education, the Federal Reserve Bank of Boston, one of the twelve regional banks, engaged Jeff Kennedy Associates to develop *The New England Economic Adventure*. Jeff Kennedy Associates is a Boston-based museum planning and exhibit design firm. Their work for history museums, science centers, and children's museums often involves the development and production of highly interactive role-playing games and immersion environments.

To help the exhibit designer, Jeff Kennedy Associates, develop the content for this project, the Federal Reserve Bank of Boston (sometimes referred to as the "Boston Fed") assembled an academic advisory board of economic historians. This advisory board, led by economic historian Peter Temin, Elisha Gray II Professor of Economics at MIT, made significant contributions to the treatment over the many months the project was in development. Once the exhibit designer, the client, and the advisory board had identified the three case studies for *The New England Economic Adventure* (NEEA), Jeff Kennedy Associates commissioned short papers by historians on the events to be presented in the show. Based on all this research, the treatment for *The NEEA* was developed and written by Jeff Kennedy, principal, and Marjorie Prager, exhibit developer for Jeff Kennedy Associates.

Jeff Kennedy Associates hired Northern Light Productions to develop the video and programming for *The NEEA*. Northern Light Productions is a Boston-based film and video production company. They create motion picture and video installations for museums and visitor centers, plus work for broadcast and independent projects.

Northern Light Productions hired Maria O'Meara as the writer on the project because of her extensive experience with interactive museum exhibits. Working with the Federal Reserve and the production team, O'Meara developed the script treatment and the final script from the initial treatment originally created by Jeff Kennedy Associates.

Maria O'Meara, has written for interactive media for more than twenty years. She writes extensively for family audiences, developing interactive scripts for museums, publishing companies, and the web. She especially enjoys working on museum projects that blend video, interactivity, and theater to create a unique visitor experience. She has worked on a wide variety of museum projects, including the Atlanta Federal Reserve, the Newark Children's Museum, The Franklin Institute, California Science Center, North Carolina State Museum of Natural Sciences, and many more. While at D.C. Heath, a textbook publisher, Maria was the head writer for a series of immersive multimedia programs focused on natural history including the Everglades and the Sonoran Desert. Maria holds a B.A. in English from the University of Notre Dame and a M.S. in Broadcasting from Boston University.

Goals and Challenges Writing *The New England Economic Adventure*

Goals
The writer had the following goals for this project:

- To teach the audience the history of the economic engine of New England and how key technologies built upon each other.
- To make the content fun and engaging for a student audience.
- To bring historical figures to life.

Challenges
The challenges the writer faced were with both content and presentation technique.

- A substantial amount of historical content was needed to understand the contexts of the economic choices.
- This dense content worked against creating an exciting narrative.
- The target student audience often considers economic issues dry.
- Because this immersive experience has a live host, video, objects, and audience interaction through a PDA, the writer is required to have the skills of a writer of video, multimedia, and theater.

Writing *The New England Economic Adventure*: Meeting the Challenges

Defining Presentation, Basic Content, and Narrative: The Initial Treatment

After considerable research and discussions with the economic advisory board and the client, the first major written document was a treatment created by Jeff Kennedy and Marjorie Prager of Jeff Kennedy Associates, the museum design firm on the project.

A treatment is a preliminary written document used on many types of multimedia and film/video projects. The major part of the treatment is a narrative prose description of what will occur in the proposed project. Technical information is usually fairly limited in this type of document; the goal is a clear description of the proposed projects sequence of events and activities. There are no set rules for treatments, however, and they can include other elements important to explain (and sometime sell) the project. The initial treatment for *The New England Economic Adventure* included the following components:

- An introduction explaining the rationale and setting for the project
- An overview of the game elements
- Economic themes
- A detailed description of all three stories in the NEEA
- A presentation walkthrough
- A presentation outline

Following is only one segment of the full treatment—the presentation outline. This outline gives an overview of the complete program.

To read the complete treatment and other script samples in this chapter, please refer to The New England Economic Adventure *area in the Chapters section of this book's CD-ROM.*

The Presentation Outline, Part of the Initial Treatment

Presenter welcomes group, takes audience photo	Presenter
1st time travel effect, spotlight lands on textiles 1. SCENARIO #1 WHO WILL JOIN ME?	Lighting/fx Story Video/
a. Story video #1, sets up life in 1820 (post Waltham, pre Lowell) & intros Boston Associates	meet Mr. Lowell
b. Advisors jump in with rules, tell you how much $ you have, argue pros and cons of investment (shipping vs. mills)	Advisors on Video

c. Presenter takes it back to audience for choice	Presenter
d. PDA input of investment (all, half, none)	PDAs
e. Presenter introduces wheel of risks/rewards, volunteer spins	Presenter, volunteers
f. Results come up on PDAs and screen	Data
g. Advisors debrief, recap impact of mills on standard of living	Advisors on Video
2nd time travel effect, spotlight lands on bicycles	Lighting/fx
2. SCENARIO #2, IS BIGGER BETTER?	Intro Video
a. Story video #2a, sets up life in 1890	
b. Advisors jump in with Standard of Living quiz; last questions re bike (how many, what cost)	Advisors on video
c. PDA quiz (possibly with on stage volunteers?)	Data
d. Story video #2b, intro bicycles, Col. Pope	Story Video/ meet Col. Pope
e. Advisors set up investment decision, argue pros and cons of banking money or making investment or borrowing/investing	Advisors on video
f. PDA decision (bank your $, invest, borrow/invest)	Data
g. Wheel determines year (1890, 1893, 1896)	Presenter, volunteer
h. Results come up on PDAs and screen	Data
i. Advisors show what would have happened for each of the years; sum up standard of living benefits of mass production	Advisors on Video
3rd time travel effect, spotlight lands on PDP8	Lighting/fx
3. SCENARIO #3 NEW PRICES, NEW USES?	Presenter
a. Presenter asks "what is this?" (PDP8)	
b. Advisors jump in with quiz (re computers in 1962: how many, how big, how much they cost)	Advisors on Video
c. PDA quiz, results on screen	Data

d. Story video #3, sets up life in 1960s, rise of early computers through Ken Olsen and DEC	Story Video
e. Advisors explain that our $ is now DEC stock, intro the pricing/marketing decision to be made, argue pros and cons	Advisors on Video
f. PDA decision re market to invest your R&D $ in	Data
g. Presenter asks volunteer to spin wheel for economic conditions	Presenter Volunteer
h. Results come up on PDAs and screen	Data, Advisors on Video
4th time travel effect	Lighting/fx
4. FINAL RESULTS/WRAP UP/PHOTO	Data, Presenter
a. Presenter leads into grand totals, asks those who made the most to stand and be applauded	
b. Advisors jump in to liven up ending and summarize teaching points; segue into showing surprise audience photo, those who will reinvent the New England economy in the future	Advisors on Video
c. Presenter has last word, turns the Advisors off with remote control	Presenter
Lights up, walk-out music, audience exits	Lighting/fx/Music

The outline gives a good overview of the project, but an important part of an historical content-based program such as this is a clear narrative of how the content will be presented. This is handled in the next sample, the Presentation Walkthrough, which is also from the treatment. Later in this chapter, the script for this story will be presented for comparison to see the changes the writer made.

Presentation Walkthrough from Initial Treatment

Welcoming the Audience

The presenter, an FRBB staff educator, welcomes the visiting group to *The New England Economic Adventure*, has them settle into their seats and says that we always like to take a photograph to add to the Adventure visitor book (the flash of a strobe accompanies picture-taking).

Suddenly, the room comes alive with an environmental "time travel" effect, a combination of sound and light. As it ends, a spotlight illuminates the part of the stage that presents a loom and bolts and hanging samples of textiles.

Now the large video screen at the center of the stage comes into play. The title of Scenario #1, WHO WILL JOIN ME?, fades up and holds as we plunge directly into the first 'story video,' finding ourselves in 1816. We get a sense for what life was like at that time for average folks, then meet Francis Cabot Lowell, who addresses us directly from the screen as if we are the highly successful group of men known as the Boston Associates, investors who, having taken a flyer with him to start a prototype mill at Waltham, he believes he can now convince to invest in a much larger scale operation in a location he tells us our colleagues Nathan Appleton and Patrick Johnson are excited about—a little town with plenty of water power and a great location for attracting the right kind of mill girls (God-fearing young farm girls who will work hard for low wages).

As on-screen images illustrate his pitch, Lowell outlines the basic idea of large-scale textile manufacturing, reminding us that we trusted him before to take what he observed in the mills of England and manufacture good, cheap cloth. Waltham, while it has its drawbacks, is enough of a success to make him sure that, by pooling our money—something we can now, for the first time, do with a new innovation in financing called a joint stock company, which lets you buy shares in a venture and sell your shares when you want to get your investment out—we can build on a scale that will make us all part of the most exciting experiment in industrial history: the creation of a profitable textile industry here in New England. Summing up, he asks if we are ready to join him in an enterprise so daring and revolutionary that it just might change the American way of life.

Suddenly, footage of our two contemporary Advisors interrupts Lowell's entreaty. They jump right in with the basics of our game, telling us that we each, as wealthy mercantile shippers of spotless reputation, have a healthy bank account of X. That bank account is kept in the funny little device we find at our seats (our PDAs). With those PDAs, we will make choices and make investments.

The Advisors plunge into an entertaining argument (one which reveals their characters of conservative and liberal spenders, with wit and energy) of the pros and cons of keeping one's money in shipping or joining with Lowell and others to back the new enterprise, the mills. They summarize the key points on each side in a spirited way. Briefly, Advisor 1 might challenge the idea of investing in the mills by asking why someone would want to own just a little part of something big instead of being the top guy in control (as in shipping); why should we assume the world will want to buy cheap cloth; how we will be able to avoid the horror of the "dark Satanic mills" that fester in England; and why not stick with a sure thing, shipping, something you know how to do and how to get a quick return on investment. Advisor 2 would respond, point for point, making the case for an investment offering freedom from the stress and anxiety inherent in the shipping business; describing the huge and new markets for cheap cloth that will make the venture successful; pointing out the dangers and risks of putting all one's money in shipping; and being part of the next big thing.

The presenter interrupts the Advisors' back and forth repartee and says it is time for the audience to make its first decision. He or she reminds us we have X amount in our accounts and asks us to now choose how to invest our money, using the PDAs at our seats. Our options are presented, first for shipping and then for textiles: invest it all, invest half, or invest none.

The audience now inputs its choices using the PDAs, and the data collected goes to a central computer.

The presenter asks for a drum roll (and gets one) as a large "wheel of risks and rewards" is spot lit on stage. The presenter asks for two volunteers to come up to pull the lever that controls the on-screen spin of the wheel (the lever is mechanical and the wheel is electronic; sound effects of a ratcheting wheel of fortune augment the effect). The first wheel that appears is marked for the shipping investors and includes a range of possible natural disasters and catastrophes (shipwrecks, piracy, storms at sea); the second wheel that appears is filled with events that would have an impact on investments in textile manufacturing (protective tariffs, production problems, scarcity of supplies, customers who cannot pay their bills on time, unavailability of skilled laborers, etc.). Each sector of the wheel has a monetary impact attributed to it (i.e., lose everything, double your money, etc.). The two volunteers pull the lever in turn, first for shipping, then for textiles.

When the computer tabulates results of the wheel spins, the large screen shows the impact of chance on the audience's aggregate investments, and audience members also see changes to their own results on their individual PDAs.

The Advisors immediately reappear on screen to debrief, their comments are general enough to relate to the way this audience chose to invest. They show us the success of Lowell through illustrations that appear on screen as they speak, and making a direct connection between the impact of joint stock companies, large scale textile manufacturing and average peoples' rising

```
standards of living; the availability of affordable cloth has
ramifications on many fronts, including health and hygiene as well
as comfort, style, and practicality.
     Now, for the second time, our environmental "time travel" effect
fills the room with light and sound. At its end, a spotlight
illuminates the part of the stage on which bicycles are displayed.
```

Refining the Content and Presentation: The Script Treatment and Script

When the writer came onto the project, she was handed the complete treatment described in the previous section. Writer O'Meara said that compared to other projects, the presentation and content was well developed by the museum designers in this treatment. The stage that a writer joins a project like this varies widely. Sometimes, writers are given no more than a single paragraph and have to write the initial treatment themselves.

On this project, the writer's primary task was transforming the initial treatment into a script treatment, do research, and create a final production script.

Making Content More Interactive—the Script Treatment and the Lightning Round

O'Meara explains the process from initial treatment to production treatment:

We (writer and Northern Light Production team) got the initial treatment from Kennedy (museum designer), read it and then had a kick off meeting with them to discuss their content, messages, audience, the exhibit space and set up, how audiences would use this space, review floor plans, and discuss results of their focus group testing.

After these meetings, we then wrote a script treatment. In this treatment, we came up with the lightning round as a way to break down some of the background information you would need in order to make an informed investment decision. We were really trying to get away from having the kids sit there with all these buttons, but not get to push one until they had watched about twenty minutes of video. The lightning round idea was readily accepted by everyone because they could see its benefits to the game.

The lightning round concept presented the background information in an interactive game show format. The writer suggested presenting a series of questions that the audience members could answer individually. So instead of having a solid stretch of video, this content was broken down like this:

1. Brief video, animation, graphics, and audio background appears on the main screen introducing the question.
2. The question appears on the main screen and the student's individual PDA.
3. The student answers the question, and a light blinks on the chairs of the students who choose the correct answer. The students with correct answers

also get additional game dollars added to their bank account that they can use later in the investment section of the game.

4. Brief video, animation, graphics, and audio appear on the main screen explaining the correct answer.

O'Meara said that the above issue with the background content and the lightning round is an example of one of the main problems that faces a writer on a content intensive project like this. The client is concerned that the desired content is included in the project. Because of this, the client will often want to add more content than can be easily digested by the target audience.

When this happens, it is part of the writer's job to come up with better ways to deliver the content and present these options to the client. One technique that O'Meara likes to use is to stage readings of the material with the client. She said that a simple out loud read-through of the script with the client will often demonstrate that a particular segment is too content dense and needs to be shortened or presented in a different way. In general, read-throughs are a good tool for the author to hear how her work will play to an audience. O'Meara said she is not adverse to gathering friends or family to be a mock audience for one of her scripts. On this project, there were also formal read-throughs with the target audience. A group of high school students was gathered in a classroom and the script was read by the writer and members of the team. Lots of valuable feedback was gained this way to fine-tune the script.

Based on the read-through experience and the writer's suggestions, the team adopted the lightning round game show approach and thinned the amount of linear content presented. With this major change in place, Maria created a script treatment. This is somewhat similar to the walkthrough shown above, but has more production detail and far less background material.

An excerpt of the Script Treatment follows including the introduction of the lightning round. Notice how it is different from the previous sample of the initial treatment. The script treatment:

- has more detail, such as actual examples of questions, details of scoring, and the role of the host.
- is broken down into clear sections with headers all in caps.
- includes approximate timing information to get a sense of project flow and run time.

Excerpt of Script Treatment

```
GROUP PHOTO
   Prior to the game, the audience lines up for a group photo.
   The photo could be taken in a designated area that would be set
up so they could stand close to one another, possibly on a grid
painted on the floor. This area would be pre-lit and could
```

possibly have backdrops of the mills, a bicycle scene, and an early DEC office setting that could be placed behind the students. Taking group shots in a designated area allows for better lighting and composition.

HOST 1:00
The Host opens the show with a welcoming speech and general description of the game.

LOG-IN :15
In some way to be determined, the visitors log-in. This activates the station and allows the host to see on the computer screen which seats are occupied.

The players are immediately given a predetermined amount of money in their account. The host explains this is only the beginning. In this game, as in real life, they will soon have opportunities to increase, or decrease, that amount through work, investment, and luck (good or bad.)

SCORE A
A predetermined amount is given to each player. Depending on how difficult such calculations are, we could designate the amount in 1816 dollars. The host could explain the approximate value in today's dollars. At the end of each story, the amount would be recalculated to reflect its worth in today's dollars.

LIGHTNING ROUND 2:00-3:00
(This a different name for the pop quiz referred to in the treatment.)
The lightning round allows visitors to earn money and add to their initial amount by answering questions about the time period they are entering. Although the questions are knowledge based, with a little thought some of them can be deduced. The question appears as an attractive graphic on the main screen. The PDA's allow the visitors to select the correct answer. Once the selections have been made, video highlighting the correct answer plays. The video answers should be short—:10-:30 at the most in order to keep the pacing quick. Each video should focus on only one piece of information.

General or background information required to set up the investment story can effectively be communicated through these questions.

For example:
QUESTION
It's 1816. What war ended just two years ago?

- The American Revolution

```
- The Civil War
- The War of 1812
- World War II
```

```
A very brief video about the War of 1812 focuses on the dilemma
of our investors, who made their money as merchants, are facing.
While great fortunes were made in shipping, embargos during the
war showed how risky the business was. When the war ended, wealthy
men who made their fortunes in shipping looked to invest their
money in something that would be profitable, more secure, and
long-lasting.
```

Writing the Script: Using All the Available Tools

After the treatment was approved, the writer started working on the script. A lot of research went into writing the script, and the client, the Federal Reserve Bank of Boston, was a great resource. According to O'Meara,

> *The key to the success of this project or any project is the involvement of the client. In this case, the Boston Fed was extremely helpful. They themselves are very knowledgeable about the time periods that we were writing about and provided good leads on research. They gave us helpful feedback and listened to our suggestions.*

When the research was completed, the writer could execute the script. For an immersive script, the writer has many of the same concerns as a typical multimedia project, such as interactivity, structure, pacing, and strong dialogue. However, a script for an immersive exhibit has special challenges because, as mentioned previously, the writer is not just creating an experience that will happen on a computer or video screen, but also has to write for a live audience, host, and physical objects in the room. Some understanding of theatrical writing has to be added to multimedia writing skills.

One key issue is how to integrate the host. The writer O'Meara wrote that:

> *The host's role would be subject of many discussions as we went through script development. We (writer and production team) were nervous because a live host is something that is out of our control. You are afraid that if they get someone awful, the whole program will stink. At a certain point though you have to say, well this is what the client wants, so these are the things you need to do in order to make it work (i.e., pick people who have stand-up experience, make sure they are trained to use the program and make sure you have enough of them in case someone gets sick or goes on vacation!). In the end, I think the program benefits from having a live host who is involved at key points in the game.*

The initial concept for the host was to have him or her introduce the presentation, and then the rest of the program would be self-running. But this did not make full use of the advantages of having a live host who could fine tune the presentation and answer questions for this specific audience. So the decision was made to give the host some control over the pacing of the show through controls at their podium. By clicking a "Next" button, the host could move the program on to the next segment when the group was ready. This allows the host to ad lib and deal with any unresolved issues or questions before continuing.

The challenge was determining just how often the live host should come into the program. Too much could feel like an interruption; too little could lose the advantages described above. The correct solution, as always, is to test and retest. The team did a number of paper tests with live audiences. A paper test uses sketches, text, and verbal description to give the audience a feel for how a program will unfold. This allows the writer and the rest of the team to get feedback on issues, such as the role of the host. The client's commitment to training live hosts also needs to be considered before including this in a program. In this case, the Boston Fed already had educators on staff that led groups and were quite capable of playing hosts for *The New England Economic Adventure*.

Another "theatrical" issue was how to use objects in the room and lighting. The decision had been made to include a large object for each of the three stories. These objects included a loom, a bicycle, and a 1965 mini-computer. The writer had to decide how these objects could be highlighted in the script. She did this by suggesting the use of a gobo lighting effect, which is a shaped light and shadow effect that can also use color. This lighting technique is used to highlight objects, the host, and even members of the audience. O'Meara said that on some immersive projects she has worked on, lighting effects are used extensively, for example an ocean related exhibit has a blue shimmering ocean gobo to emphasize key moments in the presentation.

Even when the major elements are in place, such as the host and the lighting, seemingly small issues can have a substantial impact on the overall experience. The writer will sometimes have to fight for such elements. For example, O'Meara thought it was important that the audience member who got a correct answer in the lightning round should have the light on their chair turned on. In testing this turned out to be a hit. Students liked having their light come on and looked around to see how many other people got the correct answers.

Another "small" issue was adding more variety and interactivity in the types of responses possible in the lighting round and investment decisions. At the investment stage in the Lowell story as illustrated in the script below, the audience member has to decide what percentage of their wealth they will invest in trading or in the textile mills. It would have been easier to have a simple multiple choice for this item, but the writer argued for a slider tool that would appear on the PDA and allow the student to move it back and forth and get a wider range of investment combinations.

In general the writer has to be an advocate for what technology and effects will be engaging for the audience and get the message across.

Segment of Script for Game 1: Will You Join Me?

After an opening section of the program where the host welcomes the audience and the program introduces the basic premise of the game and how to use the equipment, game 1 begins. This is the section that explores the founding of the U.S. textile industry by Lowell in 1813.

Compare the script on the next page with the initial treatment that was included earlier in this chapter. It covers the same material. Notice how the treatment is executed into script form. Also notice the changes made to the script from the treatment. This is the writer's contribution. The notable addition was the Lightning Round as a way to break up and make more interactive the background material. Also note all the elements that a writer of an immersive script is responsible for including:

- host action and dialogue
- items that appear on audience PDA
- video images
- lighting in room on objects and people
- screen dialogue
- screen narration
- sound effects

The sample on the following pages is only a section of the script.

 See the Chapters section of the CD-ROM for the complete scripts of this project.

Development: The Prototype

After the script is completed, the next step is the prototype. A prototype is a portion of a product that is completed, usually for testing. Although not strictly a writing issue, the prototype is worth mentioning.

This project required the creation of three different stories that were going to use the same technique and approach to content. In situations like this, it makes the most sense in terms of time and budget to focus on one of the three stories first. In this case the Lowell story was the focus. This story was refined and tested until all major issues were solved before additional development was done on the other two stories. A prototype saves a lot of time in the long run because once all the issues are resolved in the prototype, then the rest of the production goes much more smoothly. Even if a project does not have multiple identical segments as this one does, sometimes a prototype is developed out of a section of the program.

HOST	VOTE; PDA	VIDEO & LIGHTING	AUDIO, NARRATION & SFX	EFX	CUES
In our first game, we'll be visiting the year 1813 and exploring the beginnings of the textile industry here in New England. Look down at your screen to see how much you have to start with.		Graphic or animation Bank account icon from PDA.		1813 Gobo effect on queue with movie	Host—next at the word screen activates PDA info
HOST As you see, you each have $10,000 in your accounts. Remember, that's $10,000 in 1813 dollars. But in that time, just as today, you could earn money ... so let's earn a little more money right now in our Lightning Round.	PDA GRAPHIC on system shows each person how much they have.	MAIN SCREEN Graphic Bank account shows amount of money each person has.			
HOST You'll have a chance to answer 3 questions. For each one you answer correctly, you'll earn $1,000! You'll have 10 seconds after the question to enter your answer. Anyone have any questions? ... Let's start the lightning round.		GRAPHIC Lightning Round graphic or animation flashes on main screen. Possible lighting effects flash throughout room.	SFX Lightning round theme song plays.	Host spot and blue wash fade out. Gobo Lightning effects timed to main screen.	Host—Next on the words Lightning Round. Movie starts 30 frames after lights fade out.

VISITORS have a preset amount of time to answer the questions	GRAPHIC & MAIN SCREEN TEXT BUILD, with graphics What was the relationship between Britain and the United States in 1813? a. They were at war. b. They were allies. c. The U.S. was a British colony. d. Europeans had not yet come to North America.	CHRIS (VO) First question. What was the relationship between Britain and the United States in 1813? a. They were at war. b. They were allies. c. The U.S. was a British colony. d. Europeans had not yet come to North America.	
	ROOM EFFECTS Lights dim a bit; gaming music counts down preset time for voting to be done. Onscreen countdown with SFx indicating that time is up.		Possible gobo effect over seats during countdown. Lighting Effect ends at 3,2,1...
PDA Correct answers add to score. Lights of people who answered correctly go on.	MAIN SCREEN Graphic The correct answer, "a." is highlighted with corresponding sound effect.	CHRIS The correct answer is, a. They were at war. If you got that right, you just added $1,000 to your bank account, which is displayed at the top of your screen.	Correct score PDA lights go on and stay on until the show segue's to the on-screen response. Possible gobo effect?
		SFX Sounds of war, cannons, as if all around visitors.	

(Continued)

415

HOST	VOTE; PDA	VIDEO & LIGHTING	AUDIO, NARRATION & SFX	EFX	CUES
		MAIN SCREEN VIDEO ADVISOR 2 In simple t-shirt, possibly with life jacket or other nautical prop. Behind him, we see images a graphic: **"War of 1812"** images of naval battles, illustrations, cannons firing and other exciting shots. Animate a little merchant ship sinking. FLASH of cannon ends clip,	CHRIS In 1813, the United States was at war with Britain . . . and the two world superpowers of the time, Britain and France, were at war with each other! The Atlantic ocean was a *dangerous place!* British warships seized American merchant ships, confiscated cargo, and kidnapped crew members, forcing them to serve in the British navy. The war was literally sinking the trading business! SFX Naval battles Penny whistle as ship sinks.		

BOOK AUTHOR'S NOTE: There are several more questions similar to the one above as a way to establish context for the economic story to be told in the next section.

HOST	VOTE; PDA	VIDEO & LIGHTING	AUDIO, NARRATION & SFX	EFX	CUES
HOST Now let's begin the Decision Round. In this round, you'll have a chance to go back in time ... to the year 1813,... where you'll decide how to invest your money ... and you'll see if you make a profit. Ready to make some money? Let's begin our trip.		LOGO Decision Round	SFX Decision Round SFX	1813 gobo effect timed to movie Lights fade out.	Host—Next at the words Decision Round activates movie Host—Next on the words our trip, starts the movie

416

VIDEO	AUDIO
CHRIS and SARA on screen in modern-dress against plain background. They matrix out of the scene.	CHRIS Ready? SARA Ready.
TRANSITION TO PAST Lights dim as sound effects fill room. We enter a door, and then a dark, private office.	EFFECTS *:5-:10 seconds* Lighting and sound effects in room take visitors back to 1813 Boston.
MAIN SCREEN VIDEO ADVISORS matrix into an area outside of LOWELL'S office. CHRIS and SARA materialize in costumes of the day that would make them fit in with Lowell and his friends. The sounds of "aheming" and murmuring from inside the office. They open the door and enter the office.	CHRIS (looking at his outfit, brushing himself off, maybe little flecks of electronic time transport material fly off) (to audience) Well, it looks like we all got here in one piece! SARA (brushing herself off) Let's fill you in quickly. We are all prosperous associates of a man named Francis Cabot Lowell. CHRIS We've made our money in trading, but Lowell has called us together to hear a startling new proposal. SARA C'mon. Let's go in.
LOWELL is presiding over a meeting. He sits at a functional office, or desk with ledgers, papers. There are two or three other men in the room. CHRIS and SARA	LOWELL (to the advisors/audience) Welcome, welcome. Come in. Sit down. Meet my associates. This is Patrick Jackson and Nathan Appleton. Sit down.

(Continued)

HOST	VOTE; PDA	VIDEO & LIGHTING	AUDIO, NARRATION & SFX	EFX	CUES
		enter the room, the camera following as if they are leading us to our seats. They slip into a couple of seats.			
		Props may hint at China trade, a porcelain tea service, a silk pillow or wall hanging of a Chinese scroll.	LOWELL I've called you here with a business proposition ... After long hours of planning, I have devised a way by which we may avoid the catastrophic risks of the trading business ... a new way to invest our money.		

BOOK AUTHOR'S NOTE: The scene continues as Lowell lays out his plans for setting up a textile factory. He asks Sara, Chris, and the others to invest in his plan. They discuss the pros and cons and then it is time to decide.

HOST	VOTE; PDA	VIDEO & LIGHTING	AUDIO, NARRATION & SFX	EFX	CUES
			SARA (sipping) Thank you. I'm keeping most of my money in trading like Mr. Appleton here (aside to audience) and so should you. Trust me. CHRIS Like Mr. Jackson, I intend to invest heavily in your plan, Mr. Lowell. (aside) I'm telling you, this guy has it all figured out. Go for it!		
			LOWELL (to audience) And what about the rest of you. Will you join me? It's time to decide.		

418

Visual / Screen	Audio	Effects	Technical Notes
MAIN SCREEN Illustrate slider system rolling all the way to one side for trading; All the way to other side for Lowell.	SARA (VO) So Lowell has asked you to decide how to invest your money. Use the slider on your screen to make your decision. Right now, the slider shows that your money is equally invested in trading and Lowell's mills. To invest more of your money in trading, move the slider towards the left. CHRIS (VO) To invest more of your money in Lowell's mills, move the slider towards the right.	Host spot fades up on the word right	At the word right **screen fades** generic background?
		Gobo effect during countdown	Host—Next at the word Choices starts the (movie) countdown. After countdown movie goes to generic background.
	HOST (Host reactivates the countdown.) It's time to make your decision. You now have 10 seconds to make your choices. Enter your final choices ... Time's up.		
	HOST Now let's see how the money you invested with Lowell did. We'll wait until the Risk Round to see what happens to your trading investments! If you invested in Lowell's mills, the right side of your screen will show your investment and how much profit you earned.		Host—Next at the word investments – activates the DVD graphic.

(Continued)

419

HOST	VOTE; PDA	VIDEO & LIGHTING	AUDIO, NARRATION & SFX	EFX	CUES
HOST As you can see, money invested with Lowell tripled in value over the first 10 years. That's a good investment. Let's find out more from our time travelers.	PDA Calculates all Lowell dollars	GRAPHIC Show chart with return on investment of Lowell over 10 year period 1813–1823 $1,000–$3,000		At next blue wash and host spot fade out	Host—Next at the word Travelers. Movie starts
		CHRIS matrixes back into "today." The image of a mill appears first. He brushes himself off, perhaps bits of cotton are in his hair. He looks around for Sara. She's a bit late and arrives with all things her tea cup.	CHRIS Well, we're back. (Does double take to see if Sara is coming.) Those of us who joined Lowell were well rewarded. Though Lowell himself lived only a few more years, the group stayed together for many years making many excellent investments		

BOOK AUTHOR'S NOTE: Chris and Sara discuss the outcome of their investments and then it is time for the risk round. This mostly affects the students who decided to keep their money in trading. In the risk round, a member of the audience spins the wheel of chance.

HOST Can I get a volunteer from the audience to come up and help me with the Risk Round? (After someone comes up.) Just pull the lever and let's see what happens.	RISK ROUND LOGO appears on main screen.	Gobo whirling effect changes and lands on lever. The lighting effect continues until lever contact is made. On contact lights fly off and away.	Host—Next at the words see what happens. Movie Graphic begins.
	MAIN SCREEN Wheel/Grid/Board/Barrel comes up. Some choices may not affect everyone.		
HOST: *(during the spin ...)* Will your ships be attacked by pirates ... or sunk in a storm? Or will you be successful trading in lumber ... or exotic spices?	*Pirates* *Lumber* *Storm* *Spices*	*SFX* *Accompanying sfx of spinning* *Then any item chosen has its own sfx*	

At this point in the script, one of the members of the audience spins the wheel and the results affect the investments of the traders in the audience. The winner is identified with a flashing light. The host introduces the next story in the program. The final tally of each player's investments is made and displayed on the PDA.

Conclusion: Response to the Project

The New England Economic Adventure has hosted hundreds of students and educators at the immersive exhibit described in this chapter and in related exhibits and workshops at The Federal Reserve Bank of Boston. The exhibit continues to enthusiastic response.

References

Cole, H.P., McKnight, R.H., and Piercy, L.R. "Preventing Injuries Through Interactive Stories." http://www.cdc.gov/nasd/docs/d001401-d001500/d001414/d001414.html

Jeff Kennedy Associates, Inc. web site. http://www.jkainc.com

New England Economic Adventure web site. http://www.economicadventure.org

Northern Light Productions web site. http://www.nlprod.com/

O'Meara, Maria. Telephone interviews with the author, September 2005.

O'Meara, Maria. E-mails to the author, September 2005.

Prager, Marjorie, Jeff Kennedy Associates, Inc. E-mails to the author, September 2005.

Key Points from Part III: How to Write Interactive Narrative

A Story with Interactive Potential

There are no hard and fast rules about what makes a good interactive narrative, but some things that have worked in the past include the following:

- A clearly defined goal to lead the player through the story. Example: Solving the mystery at the inn (Chapter 20, *Nancy Drew: The Secret of the Old Clock*).
- An interesting role for the player that allows some control over the narrative flow. Example: In *Dust* (Chapter 23), the player becomes an Old West drifter named the Stranger. The player controls what this character says and does.
- Various plot possibilities and choice points. Scenes can be played out in a number of ways, and the player's choices in these scenes can lead to a number of possible endings. Example: In *The Pandora Directive* (Chapter 22), the player/Tex Murphy can choose to have a fight with his girlfriend and can decide to sleep with the evil woman, but these choices lead to his death at the end.
- A story line into which puzzles and games can be easily integrated. Examples: *Amped 3* (Chapter 21) justifies its games by making them part of the snowboarding action. Other programs, such as *The Pandora Directive* (Chapter 23), integrate the puzzles into the obstacles facing the player, such as deciphering a secret code to disarm an alarm.
- An intriguing, unusual world to explore. Examples: Part of the fun of immersing ourselves in the multimedia experience is a chance to explore unusual locations, such as a desert town in the Old West (*Dust*, Chapter 23), great snowboard resorts (*Amped 3*, Chapter 21), and the past at a time when

great economic decisions were made (*The New England Economic Adventure*, Chapter 24).

Strong Linear Narrative (Chapter 17)

Most of the writers in the programs featured in the case studies first wrote a linear story, which they later developed into an interactive narrative. The main reason for this approach is to make sure that the idea can be developed into a strong story. All the interactivity in the world won't make a bad idea interesting. It is also sometimes hard to determine the full interactive potential of a story idea until it has been fully developed.

Classical Structure (Chapter 17)

Many successful interactive narrative programs are based on classical narrative structure. Classical narratives usually have a lead character who has a need or goal that he or she wants to accomplish. When the lead character tries to achieve that need, he or she meets obstacles that create conflict. Obstacles can be another person, the environment, or inner conflicts. The conflicts build until the climax, where the character achieves the goal or not.

Characters

The Player (Chapter 18)

At the same time as the writer lays out the basic story, he or she needs to define the role of the player(s) clearly. Who are they in the story? The lead character? A minor character? What will they get to do? How much control will they have over the characters' behavior? What is the player's goal? What are the key obstacles to achieving that goal? Will these obstacles be personalized in the form of an opponent?

Character Interactivity (Chapters 22, 23)

It's necessary for the writer to devise a way for the lead character/player to interact with his or her environment. If it is limited interactivity, the writer might merely need a menu or map of options. However, if there is to be complex interactivity, the writer has to come up with a more sophisticated approach, such as interactive dialogue. One approach to interactive dialogue, as used in *The Pandora Directive*, is to allow the other characters to speak and give the player/main character a series of Response Attitudes to choose from. What Response Attitude the player chooses determines what line the character will speak.

Another approach, as used in *Dust: A Tale of the Wired West*, is to have dialogue menus for the main character that show the complete dialogue that the user can choose. In addition to dialogue, most programs also give the user other options, such as moving, picking up objects, and clicking on objects and characters to get information or initiate interactions.

Architecture: Structure and Navigation (Chapter 18)

Once the writer has a clear idea of the plot, characters, goals, and conflicts, he or she can decide which interactive structure might work best. The types of structure available depend to a large degree on the authoring system—the story engine that will be used to produce the program.

Linear with Scene Branching (Chapter 18)

If the story will be primarily linear with occasional branching choices for the users that eventually loop back to the main plot, consider a scene-branching structure.

 This approach is used in Boy Scout Patrol Theater, which is described in the Chapters section of this book's CD-ROM.

In this piece, a Boy Scout patrol searches for a little girl. The player assumes the role of one of the scouts and can decide which locations to search, such as the school or a farm. Once launched on the search of a location, the scene is primarily linear until the next branching point. Although interactivity is limited in this approach, it does allow the writer more control over story elements. In this case, the writer thought that limited interactivity was the best way to maintain the suspense of the search for the girl.

Puzzle-Based Narrative (Chapter 20)

A writer whose major interest is presenting puzzles and games might want to use a puzzle-based narrative. This is the basic approach used in *Nancy Drew: The Secret of the Old Clock*. The lead character (player) is trying to determine who is doing evil things to drive the current owners from the inn. To solve the mystery, many puzzles of all types have to be solved. Much of the interactivity is in the puzzles, not in the narrative itself.

Hierarchical Branching (Chapter 18)

If a story has a number of major choices that take it in a completely different direction, then the writer is involved in hierarchical structure. The problem with this structure is branching explosion. Five options with five choices each equals 25 scenes; five choices for each of those scenes equals 125 scenes. This quickly becomes too much to write or produce. This is why hierarchical branching is primarily limited to the endings of stories, as in *The Pandora Directive* and *Dust: A Tale of the Wired West*.

Parallel Structure (Chapters 18, 22)

A way to have multiple story paths and avoid the branching explosion of hierarchical structure is to have parallel story paths. In this case, there are multiple story paths that the user can explore, but the paths are limited, usually to three or four. Choices the user makes send him or her back and forth between these paths instead of onto completely new story paths as in hierarchical structure.

Parallel structure is useful for showing multiple perspectives on a story or various ways a story could unfold based on user choices. *The Pandora Directive* uses this structure. Its "A" path is a basic Hollywood story where everything turns out all right and the hero gets the woman. The "C" path is bleak film noir, ending in death for the hero. The "B" path is a more realistic, middle ground compromise story. This approach allows a high degree of interactivity for the user but still allows the writer some control over the story.

String of Pearls (Chapters 18, 23)

The string of pearls structure combines a worlds approach with a narrative. In this structure, the character is allowed to explore a certain world or portion of a world, but to move on in the story, he or she has to achieve certain plot points. In *Dust: A Tale of the Wired West*, the first pearl of the story allows the player/lead character to explore a desert town at night. But to advance in the story to the next pearl, the player must find a place to sleep. The next morning is the next pearl of the story. The player/Stranger can continue to explore the town, but now he (or she) must find guns, bullets, and boots. This approach allows maximum interactivity for the player and the least writer control over the narrative.

Immersive Exhibit/Experiences (Chapter 24)

Not strictly a narrative structure, but another way to present a narrative is to make it part of an immersive experience or exhibit. This type of program includes large screens, live presenters, theatrical lighting and sound effects, audience interaction, and other elements to bring the audience fully into the experience. The narrative and interactivity is created by the combination and interaction of all these elements. In addition to the techniques of interactive media, the writer for such a program also needs to understand how to write for live theater. These programs are popular in museums, theme parks, casinos, major conferences/conventions, and even the wired classroom.

Information Based Narratives (Chapter 24)

If you are planning an educational program, consider structuring the content as a narrative for the following reasons:

- User's minds are particularly open to information presented through storytelling.

- Where nonnarratives deliver information through argument and description, narratives allows the user to become part of the information by becoming or identifying with a character in the story.
- Because a user can identify with characters in a story and a story can carry emotional content.
- Information embedded in a story is also linked by time and events and thus large bodies of information and the connection between different elements can be easier to remember through narrative.
- Lastly, curiosity is a crucial component in learning. The user has to want to know what happens next in a sequence. This is hard to accomplish in a nonnarrative presentation of information, but is a key element in any good story.

Storytelling Devices (Chapters 18, 20, 23)

Structure gives the overall approach to the story, but to develop narrative within that structure, the writer needs to use a number of storytelling devices. It helps the players to have some sort of map of the story and/or location so that they know where they are at any give time. Often this is an actual map, such as the maps of the towns in *Dust* and *Nancy Drew: The Secret of the Old Clock*.

Interactive devices help make the user aware of interactive possibilities. These devices can be as simple as text menus or icons that indicate what action is allowed in a certain situation. The Help feature, on-screen text, the narrator, and linear movies are other useful tools for telling an interactive tale.

Mechanics of Scriptwriting (Part 1)

There are a number of organizational devices that help in the plotting of narrative, such as flowcharting (Chapter 3) and character charts (*Voyeur* area in the Chapters section of the CD-ROM). The writer has to keep in mind the basic techniques of the scriptwriter (Chapter 2), such as showing the audience the story with dramatic action instead of simply telling the story with words, as in a novel. Finally, the writer must come up with a proposal and script format suitable to the project (Chapter 5).

Interactive Writing Careers

PART IV

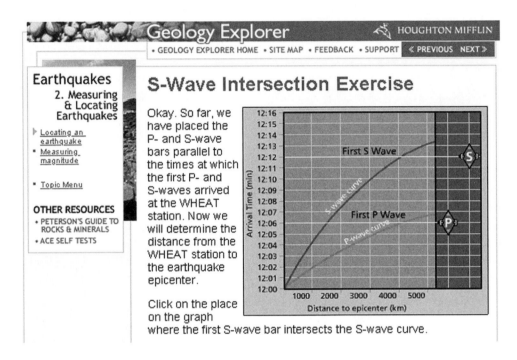

Figure IV-1 *An interactive Flash animation exercise from the Houghton Mifflin Geology Explorer web site and CD-ROM. Users can move the slider bar and get feedback. Copyright Houghton Mifflin Company.*

Conclusion: Becoming a Professional Interactive Writer

Types of Jobs

Don't be too narrow in the types of writing jobs you are willing to consider. One of the basic premises of this book is that a strong writer should be able to write for all types of interactive media (with the proper training, of course). Don't just focus on the most obvious types of writing, such as computer games or web sites. There are many other types of programs being created in interactive media, such as e-learning, training, and museum and theme park exhibits. Each of these categories represents multibillion dollar industries that do exciting work.

That said, you should be aware of some common flavors of writing jobs in the interactive media field.

- **Writer Versus Editor.** Do you want to write original copy or do you want to be in charge of all or much of the content for a web site, intranet, etc. and have writers work for you? An editor is usually a good writer first, but also has the skills to improve other writers' work by careful editing and applying sound online writing style guidelines. This is usually not an entry-level position.
- **Contract Versus Permanent.** Contract, sometimes called freelance, positions involve working as a contractor for a specific company for a set period of time or on a specific project. Contractors have freedom to work for a variety of clients, flexible schedules, and often can work from home. The downside is that you need to keep finding new jobs as contracts end and usually you do not have benefits, such as health insurance.

  Permanent jobs are full-time positions for a specific company. For these jobs, you usually work on-site at the company's location, have a set schedule with limited annual vacations, and usually work on one type of content. The pluses are a consistent paycheck, health insurance, and the camaraderie of working with a team.

- **Agency Versus Single Company.** Agency and consulting firms help a variety of different companies with their web sites, training, and other interactive media needs. If you work for an agency, you will work on a wide variety of projects, but have the consistency of a regular paycheck. Usually you can expect long hours and a frantic pace working with an agency.

  A single company usually sells one type of product or service, such as software or cars. If you work for a single company your writing will be focused on that company's business. Unless it is a very large company, you might also expect to be more of a generalist writer. You might do work on the web site as well as print material. Usually the pace working for a single company is a little slower than that for an agency.

- **Entertainment Versus Information.** Some types of programs, such as action video games, are clearly for entertainment, while other programs, such as corporate marketing web sites, are primarily informational. But there is a fair amount of crossover with games being common elements in training programs and some highly entertaining programs, such as edutainment titles and museum exhibits requiring significant information. So as mentioned earlier, don't be too narrow in your career goals, particularly for that first job.

The Challenges

No matter what type of job you are interested in, before you can be ready for that first interactive position, you need to master a number of challenges. These challenges have been discussed in this book. They include:

- Creative challenges
- Technical challenges
- Productivity and organizational challenges

 See the careers area in the Chapters section of this book's CD-ROM for links to web sites for the resources discussed below.

Creative Challenges

The interactive writer has to be able to write for many media, such as video, print, and audio. He or she also has to understand how the elements of interactive media affect communicating information or telling a story. These elements include interactivity, the role of the player, interactive structure, and interactive approaches to material, such as simulations and worlds.

Technical Challenges

In addition to meeting creative challenges, the interactive writer needs a certain amount of technical knowledge. The writer does not have to be a programmer or have any formal technical training, but he or she does need to have a general understanding of interactive technology to effectively use these tools to communicate. For example, an understanding of the expressive power of Flash animation made possible writing the effective exercise pictured on the opening page of Part IV of this book.

Productivity and Organizational Challenges

Whether it is a huge web site or a video game with an eight hundred-page script, the sheer volume of work that must be produced for an interactive media project can be overwhelming. In addition, an interactive writer has to write quickly to meet production deadlines. Strong word processing skills are assumed. Knowledge of information management software, such as flowcharters and databases, can also help organize a large project.

Meeting the Challenges

Meeting the challenges described above to become a successful interactive writer will require you to:

- Get new skills
- Network with industry professionals
- Present your portfolio as effectively as possible to clients and potential employers

Getting the Skills

Whether you are a beginner or an experienced professional, the first thing you have to do is get the needed skills in this field. Studying web sites, games, and books (such as this one) is a good first step. This may be adequate for some of you who are good at learning on your own. But for many people who are learning a new skill, formal study can significantly accelerate the learning process. Keep in mind that for a writer, having a broad liberal arts background and training in a wide variety of writing, such as journalism and creative writing, are as important as an understanding of the web and multimedia.

College Degree

If you have the resources and the time, there are excellent degree programs at universities and colleges around the country. Check out the computer department or communication department of an institution near you and chances are they will have offerings in multimedia or the web. Some of the major schools in this field include:

- MIT Media Lab (http://www.media.mit.edu)
- California Institute of the Arts (http://www.calarts.edu)
- University of Southern California (http://interactive.usc.edu)
- International List of Schools. The International Game Developers Association (IGDA) maintains a list of schools in their resource section. (http://www.igda.org/breakingin/resources.htm)

Certificate Programs

If you already have a college degree, a good alternative to a degree program is a certificate program. Certificate programs are packages of courses in a certain subject areas. These certificates are usually offered by the continuing education departments of colleges and universities. A certificate program may only be a half dozen courses and could be completed by taking classes part-time. An added plus of continuing education courses is that many of the people teaching these courses are working professionals who can provide you with contacts in the industry. The following are examples of schools that have good certificate programs, but also check your local college or university.

- New York University (ttp://www.scps.nyu.edu/degcert/index.jsp)
- San Francisco State University (http://msp.sfsu.edu)

CyberEd (Online Courses)

If you are busy with family and work, or you simply do not live near a college or university, consider online education. Many colleges offer courses on multimedia and the Internet via the web. As long as you have a web connection, you can take these courses sitting in front of your computer at home. There are many sites that offer online education. You can view an example of an online program at the University of Massachusetts at Lowell (http://continuinged.uml.edu/online). This author occasionally teaches a course for their program.

Conferences and Professional Seminars

Conferences and professional seminars offered by professional and educational organizations are another resource. Find out more about professional organizations under "Networking" later in this chapter.

Internships

Internships are a great way to get professional experience and build up your portfolio. In many cases, internships are not paid, but often they are. You can learn while you earn, and if you are good, get hired by the company where you are interning. If at all possible, do your internship full-time for as long a time as you can afford to. If you are a full-time intern, you get full-time responsibilities. If you are a part-time intern, you may end up answering phones and getting coffee. It is usually more difficult to get an internship if you are not at least a part-time student, but if there is a specific company you are excited about, it doesn't hurt to offer your services. Many of the job resources at the end of this chapter also include leads for internships.

Creating Your Portfolio

It is usually better to have samples of several shorter pieces of different types rather than one long piece in your portfolio. This way you have a better chance of having a type of work that will interest the client. You should break your work down into clearly defined categories, such as book review, web feature story, scene for game, etc. It is also fine to include noninteractive work if it is a professional piece and/or if it relates to the position you are applying for. For example, if you want to be a writer on a medical web site, and you have published in print medical journals by all means include this material. Many top writer-designers have gotten into writing for games and the web from linear media backgrounds, including journalist, novelist, and film scriptwriter.

Even though you might be selling yourself as a writer, it will catch potential employers' eyes if you can demonstrate your writing and understanding of interactive structure in some way other than just prose text. At least try to develop some impressive flowcharts or storyboards to accompany your text.

Even better than charts and graphics is to get at least part of your interactive writing produced as an effective web site or multimedia program. If you have friends with a business, volunteer to write and produce their web site for little or no payment. If you don't have production skills, team up with a classmate or colleague who does. Once completed, your first web site is now a professional piece of work, and your friends with the business are clients. If you are currently employed, use your multimedia and writing skills on the job to develop portfolio pieces. You can also donate your multimedia or web services to a nonprofit organization. Obviously, you can't keep working for peanuts forever, but when you are starting out, it helps to get a few produced professional pieces in your portfolio.

Presenting Your Portfolio

Once you have a few pieces to put in a portfolio, the most effective way to actually present your material is to create a portfolio web site. This site should have a page describing your skills with links to work samples. A portfolio web site is a good way to go because almost every potential employer or client that you are dealing with will have a browser and access to the web. If your work is high bandwidth multimedia that will not work well on the web, try to include some trimmed samples on your portfolio web site, but also have your material on a CD-ROM or other disk to show clients if your web site material catches their interest.

A few technical considerations:

- Make all your samples easily accessible through a single interface. This can be as simple as an HTML page with text links. Don't make your potential client have to dig around and open various directories just to see your material.
- Try to present your material in one format. Don't force a potential client or employer to download all sorts of browser plugins or have special software to view your work.
- Be sure to view your samples in a variety of browsers and operating systems, including Macintosh and Windows. Sometimes something that looks great on one operating system and browser will totally fall apart on another.

If you are lucky to get an interview, it is a good idea to bring print copies of your work as a backup and easy reference to your online samples. Spend a few dollars for a nice looking portfolio that will make your paper presentation look well organized and professional.

Networking

In addition to getting strong skills and a good portfolio, you need to meet people in the industry, because so many jobs are made through personal contact. One way to do this is to join professional organizations and attend their meetings, conferences, and seminars. Most of these organizations have inexpensive student memberships. They also often have print journals, newsletters, and web sites that list jobs. If you are a student, look for "student" or "beginner" links on their web sites that offer special benefits for students such as mentoring, conference scholarships, and advice on breaking into the business.

- Association for Applied Interactive Multimedia (AAIM), http://www.aaim.org. AAIM is for multimedia users at any level who are looking for information, support, training, and techniques to apply interactive multimedia and educational technology to enhance their education, training, business, and skills.
- The Association for Computing Machinery (ACM), http://www.acm.org. The first and still the largest international scientific and educational computer society in the world. They have a special interest group (SIG) for multimedia and for graphics. The graphics SIG sponsors a major annual conference, SIGGRAPH.
- Association for Educational Communications Technology (AECT), http://www.aect.org. An organization of professionals interested in the use of educational technology and its application to the learning process.
- CMP Game Group, http://www.gdconf.com. Offers market-defining content on computer games. Sponsors the extensive Game Developers Conference (GDC).

- Computer Game Developers' Association (CGDA), http://www.cgda.org. The Computer Game Developers' Association is a professional society for interactive entertainment, educational software, and multimedia.
- The International Game Developers Association, http://www.igda.org. A nonprofit professional membership organization that advocates globally on issues related to digital game creation. It has an excellent section for students on their web site.
- Society for Technical Communication (STC), http://www.stc-va.org. STC's members include technical writers, editors, graphic designers, multimedia artists, web and intranet page information designers, translators, and others whose work involves making technical information understandable and available to those who need it.

Getting the Job

When you have the skills, a slick portfolio, and a few contacts in the industry, it's time to go after that job or sell that project. As discussed throughout the book, there are a wide range of companies involved with interactive media including game publishers, game developers, museums, ad agencies, consulting firms, major companies, government departments, web site businesses, and even Hollywood studios and production companies. Many useful tools for finding a job exist on the web. I've outlined some key ones below. Some of these links also provide internship information, but usually the best way to find an internship is to go directly to the web site of a company that you are interested in and look for internship links.

Employment Web Sites

In addition to the job sites listed below, most of the organizations listed in the previous section have job sections on their site. Major company sites also have career sections.

The following links are for some of the largest job sites on the web. They all allow the creation of software job agents. You create your agent on the site by entering criteria for the type of job you are interested in. Then after you save your agent, you will get a daily list of jobs via e-mail that match your criteria.

Job Site Name	Type	URL
Monster.com	General job site	http://www.monster.com/
HotJobs.com	General job site	http://hotjobs.yahoo.com/
America's Job Bank	General job site (government)	http://www.ajb.dni.us/
Dice.com	Technology careers	http://dice.com
MediaBistro.com	Media professionals	http://mediabistro.com/

New Media Job Recruiters

These companies find jobs and charge the employer (not you) a fee. They are not very useful if you are a beginner, but if you have some skills and professional experience, they can be a good resource for finding employment. Search the web with the terms "professional staffing recruiting" and you will get a long list of firms. Go on their sites to see if they are local to you and they handle the types of positions you are interested in. A few examples are listed below.

- CDI, http://www.cdicorp.com. This is one of the largest placement firms in the United States, with offices across the country. CDI offers a wide range of career opportunities through its three distinct job banks.
- Clear Point Consultants, Inc., http://www.clearpnt.com. A Massachusetts professional staffing firm that specializes in placing contract and permanent Information Design and Delivery professionals. Job categories include: Online Information Designers, Web Designers, Technical Writers, and Instructional Designers.
- Information Technology Partners, http://www.itp-inc.com. A staffing firm serving the IT organization market in the Silicon Valley area.
- Aquent, http://www.aquent.com. Their Creative Staffing division often has writing jobs.

Marketing Original Articles and Projects

An alternative to getting a writing job and writing the copy defined by your employer or client is to sell your own written articles, educational projects, or game ideas. Keep in mind that the further you can develop your idea, the better chance you will have of selling it. Before you put a lot of time into a project, it is a good idea to explore the market you are interested in and learn what the opportunities are and exactly how they want you to submit your work. A few of the main markets for original writing and projects are described below.

Articles for Web Sites and Online Magazines

Although many of the content-based sites have been struggling and rely heavily on staff written articles, there are still markets for submitting original article ideas to web sites and e-zines (online magazines). As stated before in our discussion of informational writing, if you bring special expertise to your articles, you will have a better chance of making the sale. Also if you are a beginning writer, don't focus on the top sites and e-zines. Almost every industry or trade group has a web site. These are often good places to start. Search "Trade and Professional Associations" on the web or try the Internet Public Library's list at: http://www.ipl.org/div/aon/. If you are new, you may have to do the first couple articles for free to build up your portfolio. Other types of articles are also regularly purchased by all types of online sources. Check out some of the links below to get a better idea of the market for freelance articles online.

- Writers Weekly, http://www.writersweekly.com. Click the "Search" link and then enter the words "web" and "online." You will get a listing of web sites and online magazines that will accept original articles.
- Writers Digest, http://www.writersdigest.com/101sites. The venerable print magazine for writers has an annual review of the top 101 sites for writers. Once on "The 101 Best Websites for Writers" page, click the menu link for jobs.
- Online Markets for Writers, http://www.marketsforwriters.com. This is the web site for the book *Online Markets for Writers* by Anthony and Paul Tedesco. The book is a good resource if you are serious about freelancing your articles online.

Educational Projects for Publishers

Although the edutainment market that produced entertaining educational programs, such as *The Oregon Trail* or *Where in the World Is Carmen Sandiego?* is tight and has limited interest in hearing original pitches, the classroom textbook and electronic educational materials market remains huge. Most major textbook publishers are always looking for the next great book or product for the classroom. At this point, the emphasis is still on books, but the interest in electronic products is rapidly growing. So if you have a great idea for a better way to teach primary school math or college chemistry, this is the place to try.

In most cases, the publishers will require that their authors are certified experts in the field. Most textbook/educational material authors are professors or teachers. If you have a great idea, and you are not a teacher yourself, you can always partner with an experienced teacher at your local school or college.

The web sites of the major publishers all have links for authors or new submissions that outline the process for submitting a potential project to them. It is a good idea to review the publisher's product line first to make sure that they publish the type of product that you are proposing. Don't submit an English grammar product to a company that focuses on science. The four largest textbook publishers are currently Pearson, McGraw-Hill, Reed Elsevier, and Houghton Mifflin.

For a directory of all textbook publishers, go to the Association of American Publishers web site (http://www.publishers.org) and click on the "School" or "Higher Education" links for a list of publishers for K-12 and colleges.

Computer Games

With major games now costing tens of millions of dollars to produce, selling an original concept to a game publisher or developer has become as difficult as selling a story to a movie studio. Your chances increase considerably if you can develop at least a portion of your game. Even a simple prototype in something like Macromedia Flash or a series of eye catching graphics, are better than coming in with just a design document or script. Another alternative is to consider developing your game yourself in a lower cost technology for online presentation.

The International Game Developers Association has a whole series of articles about breaking in to the industry and submitting games. Look at the "Project" heading in the Breaking In/Resources/Web Links section of their site, at http://www.igda.org/breakingin/resource_links.htm. They also offer a game submission guide with many useful tips on how to submit your idea. That document can be found at http://www.igda.org/biz/submission_guide.php, or just search their site for "Game Submission Guide." You will need to be a member to get the guide, but the association offers low cost student memberships and limited free memberships that give you access to content.

Good Luck

Good luck with your interactive writing career. Feel free to e-mail me (tpg@interwrite.com), and I will look forward to meeting you some day on a project or at a conference. Happy cyber trails.

Appendix

Writer and Designer Biographies and Company Descriptions

The following individuals or companies either contributed script material or gave interviews for this book. They are listed alphabetically by company or individual name. The name of their program or web site discussed in the book is next to their name. For detailed descriptions of the companies and biographies of the individuals, see the References Section of the CD-ROM.

Access Software (*Under a Killing Moon, The Pandora Directive*)
See Indie Built.

Peter Adams (T. Rowe Price Web Site)
At the time the first version of the T. Rowe Price site was created, Peter Adams was Director of Interactive and Creative Services at poppe.com/New York, advertising agency Poppe Tyson's interactive division. Adams is also one of the pioneers in the Internet arena, setting up one of the first web sites on the Internet in 1993.

Fred Bauer (*Vital Signs*)
Fred Bauer has written over 200 scripts for linear video, interactive video disk, and interactive multimedia since opening his Marblehead, Massachusetts-based business, "Fred Bauer, the writer."

Butler, Raila & Company (*Boy Scout Patrol Theater*)
Butler, Raila & Company has specialized exclusively in the development of high quality custom interactive media presentations since 1985. Markets and application areas served include publishing, sales and marketing, public information, museum exhibition, and learning (medical, technical, consumer).

441

Chedd-Angier Production Company (*The Nauticus Shipbuilding Company*)

Chedd-Angier is a Boston-based media production company.

Anne Collins-Ludwick (*Nancy Drew Mystery Games*)

Anne Collins-Ludwick was the writer and producer of *The Secret of the Old Clock*. Before being involved in writing for games, Collins-Ludwick wrote for television. She has an M.A. in Radio/Television/Film Production from the University of Texas at Austin.

Aaron Conners (*Under a Killing Moon, The Pandora Directive, Amped 3*)

Aaron Conners joined Access Software in 1991 as its first full-time writer. In addition to writing the *Tex Murphy* CD-ROMs *Under a Killing Moon*, *The Pandora Directive*, and *Tex Murphy: Overseer*, he is the writer of *Amped 3* and the author of *Tex Murphy* science-fiction novels.

John Cosner (*Vital Signs*)

John Cosner is an instructional designer and multimedia producer for Consultec, a training and consulting company.

Mathew J. Costello (*The 7th Guest, The 11th Hour*)

Mathew J. Costello is the author of 14 novels and numerous nonfiction books. He wrote the script for *The 7th Guest*, an interactive drama that has become a best-selling CD-ROM (nearly 2,000,000 copies). The sequel, *The 11th Hour*, was released in 1995 and also became an immediate best seller. He is also the writer of the Zoogdisney web site and many other computer programs, such as *Just Cause* and *Pirates of the Caribbean*.

CyberFlix Incorporated (*Dust: A Tale of the Wired West*)

An interactive storytelling company and CD-ROM publisher, CyberFlix was founded in 1993 and is based in Knoxville, Tennessee. Titles include *Titanic*, *SkullCracker*, and *Red Jack's Revenge*. CyberFlix has ceased game development to concentrate on licensing its story engine software.

D.C. Heath and Company (*Sky High*)

D.C. Heath and Company has as its basic mission the development, publication, and marketing of materials of instruction to schools and colleges. These include textbooks, computer software, videos, and CD-ROMs. D.C. Heath is an imprint of Houghton Mifflin Company.

Encyclopaedia Britannica (Britannica.com and the *Harlem Renaissance*)

Encyclopaedia Britannica produces web sites and disk-based media version of its print encyclopedias and other publications. Its web site, Encyclopaedia Britannica Online, also serves as a research portal.

The Federal Reserve Bank of Boston (*The New England Economic Adventure*)

The Federal Reserve System is the central banking system of the United States. The Federal Reserve System is headquartered in Washington, D.C. with twelve regional Federal Reserve Banks located in major cities, including Boston. The Federal Reserve regulates banks, implements monetary policy, maintains the financial payments system, performs economic research, and presents economic education to the public.

Shannon Gilligan (*Who Killed Sam Rupert?*)

Shannon Gilligan is an author of children's and mystery books, founder of the Santa Fe, New Mexico-based Spark Interactive, and writer of numerous successful multimedia titles including: *Who Killed Sam Rupert?*, *Who Killed Elspeth Haskard?*, and *The Magic Death*.

Shawn Hackshaw (*Interactive Math Lessons*)

Shawn has taught high school pre-algebra and algebra and currently teaches developmental math at New England College and Hesser College in New Hampshire. He has a master's degree in math education at the secondary level and is a certified math teacher in the State of New Hampshire.

John Hargrave (ZDU (Smart Planet) Online Ad Campaign)

ZDNet Editorial Projects Director and principal of interactive media development company, Media Shower, Inc.

Her Interactive (*Nancy Drew* Mystery Games)

Her Interactive, Inc. of Bellevue, Washington was founded in 1995 to create interactive games for the female audience. This is an audience that was and is today largely underserved in the gaming industry, which tends to focus on action and sports games aimed towards young males.

Houghton Mifflin Company (*Sky High, Geology Explorer, Interactive Math Lessons*)

HMCO is one of the largest producers of textbooks and educational materials including CD-ROMs, web sites, and e-learning programs.

Indie Built (*Amped 3*)

Indie Built was founded in 1983 under the name Access Software. Access created both adventure games and sports titles. Its *Tex Murphy* futuristic detective games won numerous awards. Microsoft bought Access in 1999 and changed the name to Indie, which participated in the launch of Xbox with the successful *Amped* snowboarding title. In 2004, Indie Built, Inc. was purchased by Take Two Interactive Software (TTWO) as part of the 2KGames brand.

InterWrite (Prudential Verani Realty web site, Geology Explorer web site, *Interactive Math Lessons*)

InterWrite of Londonderry, New Hampshire, specialized in the writing, developing, and information architecture of high content web sites and multimedia. InterWrite has been serving the greater Boston area since 1996.

Jane Jensen (*Gabriel Knight*)

Jensen is a writer-designer who has worked on *Police Quest 3*, *Ecoquest*, *King's Quest VI*, and *Pepper's Adventures* for Sierra On-Line. She is also the designer of the award winning *Gabriel Knight 1—Sins of the Fathers* and *Gabriel Knight 2—The Beast Within*.

Jeff Kennedy Associates

The Federal Reserve Bank of Boston hired Jeff Kennedy Associates to develop *The New England Economic Adventure*. Jeff Kennedy Associates is a Boston-based museum planning and exhibit design firm. Their work for history museums, science centers, and children's museums often involves the development and production of highly interactive role-playing games and immersion environments.

Ron McAdow (*Sky High*)

Ron McAdow has written books, CD-ROMs, and the award-winning films *Hank the Cave Peanut* and *Captain Silas*. He is currently a multimedia developer for CAST Inc. of Peabody, Massachusetts.

National Scouting Museum (*Patrol Theater*)

The National Scouting Museum, in Irving, Texas, is a place where history, theater, and technology combine to give visitors an engaging interactive experience with the history of the Boy Scouts of America.

Andrew Nelson (*Dust: A Tale of the Wired West*)

Andrew Nelson was producer and writer for *Dust* and writer for *Jump Raven* and *RMS Titanic*. He was also a producer at Britannica.com. He currently works as a journalist for publications such as *National Geographic*.

Maria O'Meara (*Sky High, Patrol Theater, The New England Economic Adventure*)

Maria O'Meara has written for interactive media for more than twenty years. She writes extensively for family audiences, developing interactive scripts for museums, publishing companies, and the web. She especially enjoys working on museum projects that blend video, interactivity, and theater to create a unique visitor experience. She has worked on a wide variety of museum projects, including the Atlanta Federal Reserve, the Newark Children's Museum, The Franklin Institute, California Science Center, North Carolina State Museum of Natural Sciences, and many more. While at D.C. Heath, a textbook publisher, Maria was the head writer for a series of immersive multimedia programs focused on natural history including the Everglades and the Sonoran Desert. Maria holds a B.A. in English from the University of Notre Dame and a M.S. in Broadcasting from Boston University.

poppe.com (T. Rowe Price web site)

poppe.com is Poppe Tyson's online development unit dedicated to strategic web planning, content design, and data capture systems. Web sites poppe.com has created include the White House, AT&T, Chrysler, IBM, Jeep, LensCrafters, Merrill Lynch, Netscape, T. Rowe Price, and Valvoline. Poppe Tyson has merged with Modem Media to form Modem Media.Poppe Tyson. Modem Media is now a Digitas company.

Lena Marie Pousette (*Voyeur*)

Lena Marie Pousette is a writer, producer, and designer. Some of the other multimedia titles she has been involved which include *Caesar's World of Boxing*, *Droid Wackers*, and *Endorfun*.

David Riordan (*Voyeur*)

David Riordan has been a creative executive for Disney Interactive, Time Warner Interactive, and Phillip POV's. He is the designer of *Voyeur*, *Thunder in Paradise*, and many other titles. He is currently producing games and television, including the Bravo series *Random1*.

Anthony Sherman (*Dracula Unleashed, Club Dead*)

Anthony Sherman was the game designer for Viacom New Media's *Dracula Unleashed* and *Club Dead*.

T. Rowe Price Associates (T. Rowe Price web site)

T. Rowe Price Associates is a Baltimore-based investment management firm that serves as investment adviser to the T. Rowe Price family of no-load mutual funds and to individual and institutional clients, including pension, profit sharing, and other employee benefit plans, endowments, and foundations. T. Rowe Price Internet Services is the in-house group that developed the site profiled in this book.

ZD Net (*ZDU* Online Ad Campaign)

ZD Net is the online branch of Ziff Davis Publishing, a major publisher of computer magazines and books.

 See the References Section of the attached CD-ROM for additional appendices and other information. The CD-ROM table of contents is at the beginning of the book.

Glossary

This glossary defines multimedia, web, and writing terms used in the book and CD-ROM.

 For links to additional glossaries, please see the reference section of this book's CD-ROM.

A

ADOBE PHOTOSHOP—See Image Manipulation Software.

AGENTS—See Guides and Agents.

ANALOG VERSUS DIGITAL—The elements of an analog image, such as a photograph, are analogous or resemble the elements of the original. In a photograph, the different lights and darks of the original that make up a person's face in the real world are transformed into various lights and darks on the photographic image by exposing flecks of silver to different intensities of light. The elements of the scanned image of the same photograph, however, have no resemblance to the image. To put it simply, a digital photograph is a series of 1s and 0s and number codes, which represent certain colors and values that the computer can read and transform into an image with the help of the monitor. The text typed into this word processor is also digital information (1s and 0s), as opposed to the inked analogous letters of a typewriter. Because a digital image is nothing but 1s and 0s and number codes, it is infinitely variable. The color, shape, size, contrast, etc. of a digital photograph can be instantly changed with just a few clicks of the mouse button.

ARCHETYPE—A model upon which later examples of the same type are based. Humphrey Bogart as Sam Spade is the archetypical hard-boiled detective.

ART DIRECTOR—The art director creates the look of the production and creates or oversees the creation of all visuals: backgrounds, interface screens, graphics, and animations.

ATTRACT ROUTINES—These sounds and/or visuals play when no one is using a kiosk program. The routine functions like bait luring in or attracting the players. Without a strong attract routine, a kiosk program is ineffective because no one will play it.

AUDIO SOFTWARE—Software that records, edits, and manipulates sound.

AUTHORING PROGRAM—Software that determines how the programmer and designers will be able to organize, combine, and sequence the multimedia elements produced by the production software. The authoring program also determines how the viewers will be allowed to interact with the production through the user interface and navigation flow. For example, will they be able to walk through 3-D landscapes, will they click on images on a 2-D map, or will they be limited to choosing items on a text menu? The authoring system also affects the degree of interactivity. Can the viewer interact at the shot level or just jump to new chapters? Lastly, the authoring tool determines how the user can input information into the program. For example, can they enter text information that the program can read and understand?

B

BACKSTORY—Events in a narrative that happened before the beginning of the current story. See also Setup.

BANKS—Collections of media elements that can be reused in various places in a production. For example, a bank of negative sound effects can be created for use in a training program as feedback when the user chooses the wrong answer. The same sound effect can be reused many times.

BANNER—A small image and text composition that looks like a billboard or a banner that is used in online advertising. This banner is placed on a popular web site whose users have some connection to the product or service being advertised.

BIDIRECTIONAL COMMUNICATION OR TWO-WAY COMMUNICATION—A well designed learning program gives the user ample opportunity to communicate with the program as well as for the program to communicate with the user.

BITS—See Bytes.

BLOG OR WEBLOG—A web site or portion of a web site that is set up to allow easy creation of additional content by one or more individuals. Entries are posted on a regular basis, usually with the newest coming first. Some blogs are restricted to one person or a set number of individuals, but many blogs are public so that anyone can add information and respond to earlier comments. Blogs are often used for non-commercial expression about a wide range of topics with current events, politics, and business among the most popular, but some commercial sites are starting to use blogs as a way to present news, PR information, and customer service.

BLUE SCREEN—One approach for video in multimedia is to film live actors in front of a blue screen. This blue screen is later keyed out (erased) and replaced with computer-generated background. Green screen is also sometimes used.

BROWSER—Software used in a computer to find and view pages on the World Wide Web. The browser's two main functions are (1) to locate a specific web page when it is given an address or URL and (2) to interpret the code on the distant web page and display it on your computer as images, text, sound, and video. Popular browsers include Safari, Firefox, and Internet Explorer.

BYTES—1 Bit = A single number, a 1 or 0 used to record computer information.
   1 Byte = 8 bits; a single byte, such as "10100100," might signify a certain letter
            or number to the computer.
   1 Kilobyte (KB) = 1,000 bytes
   1 Megabyte (MB) = 1,000 KB
   1 Gigabyte (GB) = 1,000 MB
   1 Terabyte (TB) = 1,000 GB
The above often refers to the storage capacity of various drives and disks. A 100 Gigabyte hard drive can hold 100 GB of data. Video and audio files can be many Megabytes or Gigabytes. Simple text files may only be a few Kilobytes.

C

CAD/CAM—Process stands for Computer-Aided Design or Drafting/Computer-Aided Manufacture. This is a process by which items, such as ships, are designed on screen and then built with the aid of computers.

CBT—Computer-based training.

CD-I—A digital media player that attaches directly to your television and plays CD-I disks. This player was discontinued in the late 1990s.

CD-ROM (Compact Disk–Read Only Memory)—A disk designed to store digital information, such as software, text, and multimedia programs. A single CD-ROM can hold approximately 650–700MB of data. CD-ROMs are read by a laser in a CD-ROM player. See also Hybrid CD-ROMs.

CD-ROM PLAYER—A Device often connected to or built into a personal computer that reads the digital information on a CD-ROM and displays the information on a monitor or other device.

CENTRAL PROCESSING UNIT—See CPU.

CLIENT COMPUTER—The destination/user's computer in a client-server setup. It is usually served information by another computer in a different location called a server.

CLIENT SERVER—See Server.

CLIMAX—The high point of the story near the end where the character either achieves her goal or not. For example, the murderer is discovered in a mystery story.

COMBINATORIAL EXPLOSION—See Hierarchical Branching Explosion.

COMMERCIAL WEB SITES—A site created by a company for some sort of financial or business goal. Companies create sites for various purposes:

- Transactional site. The primary purpose is to perform transactions, such as ordering merchandise. All the content in the site revolves around setting up that function.
- Consumer site. This type of site is promotional. It's fun and highly visible but does not usually offer much information.
- Marcom (marketing communications) site. This approach has lots of information about the company, including material on the company's products and how to contact the company.
- Content site. A content site offers extensive information on the general type of product or service that the company is involved in, such as investment information or real estate information. The goal of a content site is to draw users to the site because of the strong content and then get them interested in the company's products.

COMPUTER GAME—In this book, I use "Computer Games" and "Video Games" synonymously meaning all types of electronic, computer powered games, including those played on consoles (PlayStation, Xbox, etc.), personal computers, mobile devices (phones, PSPs, Game Boy, etc.), interactive TV, and arcades. Be aware that some writers limit computer games to games placed on a PC, and video games as primarily played on consoles.

CONCEPT MAP—A way to visualize and organize information for the user in a multimedia program. The museum and journey approach are fairly common. The museum approach allows us to enter a virtual museum and enter exhibit rooms in our area of interest and view exhibits about our particular subject. The journey allows us to travel along a certain sequence.

CONFLICT—The opposition of two forces. Most film, video, and narrative multimedia focuses on conflict whether it is a fictional story between man and shark or a documentary on the concerned citizens of India versus their nuclear power industry.

CONSISTENCY—The use of the same or similar elements, organizational schemes, and navigation throughout an interactive media program. For example, one should not use buttons as the main navigational tool on one screen and then suddenly switch to text links on the next screen.

CONTENT EXPERT OR SUBJECT MATTER EXPERT (SME)—A member of the development team in informational or educational multimedia who has considerable knowledge of the subject matter. For example, medical pieces often have doctors as content experts.

CONTENT STRATEGY—An expertise in interactive media development that involves deciding the most effective way to present content for the user while also furthering the brand and business goals of the client. A content strategist must first clearly understand the content to be communicated, the needs and technical skills of the users, the business goals of the client, and budget constraints. Then the strategist can recommend the best approach for presenting the specific content. For example, would an explanation of erosion on a geology web site be best presented as text, text and graphics, video, animation or some combination of the above?

CPU OR CENTRAL PROCESSING UNIT—The brain of the computer or other playback system that processes the information inputted via keyboard, CD-ROM, floppy disk, etc., and presents it on the screen.

CREATIVE PLATFORM—This is the second stage of creating an online ad. This is the creative team's basic strategy session when they decide what they are trying to say, who is the audience, and what are the possible approaches to present the message.

CRITICAL STORY PATH—This is the quickest most efficient plot to follow through an interactive narrative from beginning to end. All of the required plot points are covered in a critical story path, but optional elements are left out. Game reviewers often follow a critical story path to get a quick sense of the game.

CUT SCENES—These are cinematic sequences in a computer game that play like a movie or TV show. There is no user interaction in a cut scene. Cut scenes usually occur between interactive sections to present plots points, character information, exposition, and other story elements that are hard to present interactively.

D

DATABASE—Software program that catalogs and organizes large amounts of data and makes it easily accessible to the user.

DESIGN DOCUMENT—The first detailed description of an interactive project. This preliminary description is sometimes called a design document proposal, a design proposal, or just a proposal.

DESIGNER—On a large project, there may be several types of designers, including instructional designers, graphic designers, and interface designers. These categories are sometimes lumped into one title, multimedia designer or just designer. Because of overlapping duties, these titles frequently become meaningless, but in most cases a head designer or interface designer's responsibilities include the overall visual look of the project including the interface design.

DIALECTICAL STRUCTURE—A content structure used in both interactive and linear media programs. This structure sets up a dialogue between two different points of view. First we hear from the bureaucrat who loves Indian nuclear power, then we hear from the doctor who hates it. This a/b, love/hate pattern is repeated until a conclusion emerges or the viewers are left to draw their own conclusion.

DIGITAL—See Analog versus Digital.

DIRECT LINKS—See Links.

DIRECTOR—The video or film director is in charge of the creating live action video. The director may also be in charge of developing the original audio for stock footage.

DISSOLVE—A video transition in which one image gradually fades away and is gradually replaced by another image. For a brief period, both images are on screen at the same time.

DVD (DIGITAL VIDEO/VERSATILE DISK)—An optical disk storage media with high capacity that can be used for data and high quality video and audio. A single sided, single layer DVD can hold 4.7 GB, but a double sided, double layer disk can hold up to 17.1 GB.

E

ENTERTAIN—To entertain is to present information in an amusing way that engages the audience. All programs must entertain or engage their audience to some degree. Even if a program had the greatest information, if it was boring, it would have limited communication value.

EPSS (Employee Performance Support System)—See Just-In-Time Training.

EXPLORER—An approach for designing an informational program. This involves letting the user explore a physical space. This can be a complete program or a component of a program.

EXPOSITION—See Setup.

F

FILM DIRECTOR—See Director.

FIRST ROUND CREATIVE—See Rounds Creative.

FLOWCHART SYMBOLS—Different geometric shaped symbols on a flowchart that indicate the type of media and/or user interactions.

FLOWCHARTS—An organizational and planning tool for creating multimedia and web sites. A flowchart is a series of boxes and other symbols labeled with content segments or steps in a process and connected by lines. The lines and/or arrows illustrate graphically how the content or process steps are connected.

G

GAME DESIGNER—He or she structures the game play, the visual look of the project and sometimes also the interface design.

GAMER—Someone who plays computer games. Also an approach for designing an informational program where the user gets to be a player in a game that presents information.

GIGABYTE (GB)—See Bytes.

GRAPHIC DESIGNER—See Art Director.

GREEN SCREEN—See Blue Screen.

GUIDES AND AGENTS—Software programs that help users work with large amounts of loosely related or unrelated information by presenting the information of most value to the user.

Guides are usually software creations that are part of the program or application in use, such as the ubiquitous, animated paper clip in Microsoft Office that helps guide the user through various word processing tasks by offering suggestions related to the exact tasks being attempted.

Agents usually require the user to first enter a set of criteria for the type of information he is interested in. Then the agent will search a database or the entire web and deliver the information the user requested. A common use of software agents on the web are those used on job sites, such as Monster.com. A job seeker enters the criteria for the type of job he/she is interested in on Monster.com. This creates an agent that will e-mail the user a daily list of jobs that match his criteria as the right jobs appear in the database.

H

HIERARCHICAL BRANCHING—An interactive media structure that organizes information according to categories, subcategories, and sub-subcategories. This allows users to work their way to the content they want by clicking down the category and subcategory information tree. For example, a pets category might lead to dog, cat, and fish subcategories; the dog subcategory could then lead to many sub-subcategories of individual dog breeds. With a story, this structure involves providing several distinct branching story options, based on the viewer's choice at a decision point.

HIERARCHICAL BRANCHING EXPLOSION OR COMBINATORIAL EXPLOSION—See Hierarchical Branching, above. This is a problem with hierarchical branching structure that goes too many levels deep and results in a vast number of branches on lower levels, creating navigation and content development problems. For example, if each branch on each level has four branches, the number of branches on a level will quickly jump from 4 to 16 to 64 to 256 to 1,024!

HOME PAGE—The first page of a web site. It usually includes some sort of a menu and introduction to the remainder of the site.

HTML (HYPERTEXT MARKUP LANGUAGE)—A markup language that is used to create web pages that can display a variety of media and contain links to other documents. HTML is text-based.

HYBRID CD-ROMs—A type of disk that has a combination of local material on the disk and links to material in a remote location, such as the web. Another meaning for hybrid CD-ROM is that the same disk can be played cross-platform, usually on both Mac and PC.

HYPERTEXT—Text that is linked interactively with other text in the same document or (more commonly) different documents. When a user clicks a hypertext link, they instantly jump to the new content. Hypertext and linking is a common feature of the web.

I

ICONS—Images that stand for something other than themselves. For example, the small house symbol on a button at the top of my browser stands for my home page. Various types of icons, such as a home page symbol, are used for interactive devices in multimedia and the web.

IF-THEN ACTIONS—Interactive choices made by the user of a multimedia program that elicit certain consequences. *If* you do this, ***then*** that happens. For example, if the user chooses to pick up a woman hitchhiking, then that automatically sets off a whole series of consequences that the user may not control and that may not unfold until later in the script. Nested if-then actions are even more complex. The viewer performs a certain action, which automatically places her in more "if then" situations, where additional choices can have consequences.

ILLUSTRATION SOFTWARE—This software allows the creation and manipulation of original artwork with digital tools that resemble traditional artist tools, including pens, paint, brushes, and pencils. Added to these tools are special effects tools that can alter your image in ways that would be impossible with traditional tools.

INTERMERCIAL—See Online Ads.

IMAGE MANIPULATION SOFTWARE—Software, such as Adobe Photoshop, that allows the artist to edit and alter existing images and create original artwork.

IMAGE MAP—A feature that allows a user to click on different parts of a picture to link to different web pages or other documents.

INDIRECT LINKS—See Links.

INFORM—A writer whose goal is to inform wants to provide users with easy access to a large body of information. This could be an online encyclopedia, a magazine site, or a comprehensive product information site. The viewers need not and usually are not expected to access all of the information. Instead, they simply take what they need. The information is usually presented clearly and is structured into discreet units so users can find precise answers to their questions.

INFORMATION ARCHITECT OR INTERACTIVE ARCHITECT—The team member responsible for the overall structure and navigation of an informational multimedia or web project. The Information Architect, sometimes also called an Interactive Architect, is a close cousin to the Instructional Designer (see following definition). Sometimes the same person has both skill sets, but the overall goal is somewhat different. A project requiring an Information Architect is not necessarily instructing the user, but instead is making a body of information easy to find and use, such as product information on an automaker's web site. As well as dealing with information, an Interactive Architect might also be designing interactions, such as the process flow for an online tool for doing your taxes.

INSTRUCTIONAL DESIGNER—This role occurs most commonly in educational multimedia, training, and e-learning programs where a specific skill or subject is being taught. Drawing from knowledge of the user, content, and instructional design principals, the Instructional Designer carefully structures the information to teach the desired content to the user. Some of the tasks include: breaking information into smaller units, sequencing information units, and determining the need for interactive elements, such as tests, exercises, feedback, etc.

INTELLIGENT LINKS—See Links.

INTERACTIVE—The user has some control over the flow and presentation of information or story material. This control can be exerted in a number of ways, such as clicking on a menu or guiding a character's actions with the mouse. This is the opposite of linear media, such as a traditional video, where the creator controls the flow of information and the viewer is a passive recipient. Interactivity allows users to get the content that they want when they want it, and it allows the users to be active participants in the communication process.

INTERACTIVE DEVICES—These devices include on screen menus, help screens, icons, props, other characters, and cues imbedded in the story itself. The designer and writer must develop interactive devices to make the player aware of the interactive possibilities they've created.

INTERACTIVE MEDIA—This has traditionally been a much broader term than "multimedia." "Interactive media" is used to describe all media with interactivity. It usually refers to computer delivered interactive media, including both multimedia programs and nonmultimedia interactive programs, such as click-and-read web sites that have limited interactivity and no animations, video, or sound. This is how the term interactive media is used in this book.

INTERACTIVE MULTIMEDIA OR MULTIMEDIA—A combination of many media into a single work where media altering interactivity and linking are made possible to the user via the computer. This definition includes all the disk- and cartridge-based (CD, DVD, Xbox, etc.) programs and most of the web sites in this book.

INTERACTIVE NARRATIVE—See Narrative.

INTERACTIVITY—See Interactive

INTERFACE—The interface is simply the "face" or basic on-screen visualization of the information or story material in a program. It determines how the users will be allowed to interact with a multimedia program. For example, will they be able to walk through 3-D landscapes, will they click on images on a 2-D map, or will they be limited to choosing items on a text menu?

INTERFACE DESIGNER—This multimedia development team member creates the layout and the visual look of a project's interface as presented to the user. The interface could be as simple as an information web site with menus and text or as complex as an elaborate computer game world with buildings, people you can talk to, and functional objects like telephones and cars.

INTERNET—A network of computers networks all over the world. This could include computers at the Australian agriculture department, the Chamber of Commerce for the city of Los Angeles, or an elementary school in France. Anyone with a computer and an Internet connection can visit any of the computers on the Internet and view their information. The World Wide Web is one way of accessing the information on the Internet.

INTERRUPTABILITY—The capacity for a student to interrupt a multimedia information program at any point and go in the direction that is useful for them. They should, for example, be able to return to earlier material for review.

INTRANET—An intranet is a network of computers within an organization or association. Usually only members of that organization have access to the information on the organization's intranet. Most large companies have intranets for employee information and communication.

J

JEOPARDY—A narrative element that means that the character's actions will have consequences for the character. It is easy for the writer to setup jeopardy in a life and death situation, such as escaping a murderer or blowing up a Death Star. It is harder to create this sense of importance with more mundane events.

JUST-IN-TIME TRAINING—Instead of presenting entire training programs, Just-In-Time Training presents small snippets of information when they are needed. With this approach, if an employee had a question about a particular process, he could jump on the computer and get immediate help. This is similar to Help programs in some applications, such as Wizards in Microsoft Office. The formal name for Just-In-Time Training is EPSS: Employee Performance Support System.

K

KILOBYTE (KB)—See Bytes.

KIOSK—A kiosk is a computer and monitor installed in a public location, such as a museum. Kiosks are sometimes on stands or walls, but are also often part of an environment that relates to the program's content, such as a mockup of a ship's bridge for a marine navigation program.

L

LINEAR MEDIA—This type of media allows no interactivity by the user. The creator controls the flow of information and the viewer is a passive recipient.

LINEAR STRUCTURE—This structure has no linking or interactivity. Linear structure can be compared to a desert highway with no crossroads. It is the structure of most motion pictures and television programs.

LINEAR STRUCTURE WITH SCENE BRANCHING—This is basically a linear structure with a few limited choices as to how certain scenes will play out. This structure can be compared to the desert highway that has a few detours. The detours, however, always return the traveler to the same highway.

LINGO—A computer programming language used with the authoring software Macromedia Director.

LINKS—The connections from one section of an interactive media program to another section of the same program or (if online) to a totally different program. The simplest link is a text menu choice that is clicked on to bring up new information. There are three basic types of links.

1. In an immediate or direct link, the viewer makes a choice and that choice produces a direct and immediate response that the viewer expects.

2. Indirect links, also called "if-then" links, are more complex. Instead of directly choosing an item, with an indirect link, if you take a certain action, then another action will occur that you did not specifically select. An example of an indirect link in an informational piece is a student who fails a test in a certain subject area and is automatically routed to easier review material, instead of being advanced to the next level. The student didn't make this direct choice. It was a consequence of her actions.

3. Intelligent links remember what choices you have made earlier in the program or on previous plays of the program and alter future responses accordingly. These links can be considered delayed "if-then" links. Intelligent links in a story create a realistic response to the character's action; in a training piece, they provide the most effective presentation of the material based on a student's earlier performance.

LOOP—Short media element repeated, often to create a longer piece. For example, a ten second piece of background sound can be looped or replayed three times, instead of requiring a full thirty seconds of new sound. Can also refer to the constant replaying of a program in a location, such as a trade show kiosk.

M

MAP OR SITEMAP—An element of interactive design that represents the overall structure of an interactive media piece in a concrete manner. It can be as simple as a text menu that lists all the key pages of a web site broken down by categories. The sitemap can even be a literal map, as in *Grand Theft Auto—San Andreas*, in which the player can consult a map of the cities that make up the island of San Andreas to get oriented and decide where to go next.

MEGABYTE (MB)—See Bytes.

METAPHORS—For software developers, metaphors are concrete images or other elements that represents an abstract concept, making it clear and comfortable to the user. Perhaps one of the best-known software metaphors is "the desktop." Windows PCs and Macs present the abstract concepts of computer files, directories, and software as file folders and documents that you can arrange and work with on your desktop.

MIDDLE PAGE—The second page of an online ad. A user reaches a middle page by clicking on a banner ad. The middle page is usually more detailed than the banner.

MMOG OR MASSIVELY MULTIPLAYER ONLINE GAME—An online graphical computer game that allows hundreds of thousands of players to interact in a fantasy online world, usually on the Web. *World of Warcraft* and *Ultima Online* are examples of this type of game.

MODEM (modulator and demodulator)—A computer related device that varies or modulates a carrier signal so that it can carry digital information and also decodes the signal so it can be displayed on a user's device. For example, a telephone modem converts the digital information in a computer to sounds that can be transferred over a standard telephone line. The process for signals incoming to the computer on a phone line is reversed, allowing the information to be displayed by the computer on a monitor. There are several different type of modems, such as telephone modems, optical modems, radio modems, and cable modems.

MOSAIC—The first World Wide Web browser that made it possible to view images and sound via the Internet. It ceased development in 1997.

MUD (Multi-User Dungeon game)—A type of online computer game that is usually text based. It allows distant players to interact and play a game together via an online connection, such as the Internet. The players often start with a premise, such as being a prisoner on an island surrounded by pirates. Each player assumes a character and creates interactions in text based on the premise and the actions of other characters. For example, I could assume the role of the pirate captain. In text I would type in how I was attacking the island. If you played the role of the captain defending the island, you would respond by typing in text how you would repel my attacks. Although still in existence, the text based MUD has been largely eclipsed by the graphical MMOG (massively multiplayer online game).

MULTIMEDIA—See Interactive Multimedia.

THE MULTIMEDIA WRITER—A writer who creates proposals, treatments, walk-throughs, scripts, design documents and all the other written material that describe the content of a multimedia production. This can include developing overall structure, dialogue, characters, on-screen text blocks, narration, and much more.

MULTIMODAL COMMUNICATION—Uses many media—text, graphics, and sound. One medium can support another if a viewer has weak comprehension in a certain area. This is particularly important to people with disabilities. Multimedia is an example of this type of communication.

MULTIPLAYER GAMES—Computer games that are played by more than one player at a time. Most of these games occur online with players on distant computers playing together. The games can also be played in smaller numbers on gaming consoles or PCs. Lastly, some museums and theme parks have multiplayer games with live audiences.

MULTISITE BRANCHING—CD-ROMs, museum kiosks, etc. are all closed systems. The user has access to the program material in that system and nothing more. On the World Wide Web and other networks, however, it is possible to link from a word or picture on one site to related information on other sites all over the world.

MYST (1993)—The first major CD-ROM computer game hit and one of the best-selling games of all time. The basic premise of the game is that you are dropped on a mysterious, apparently abandoned island. You must explore the island to discover what occurred there. An early version of the Worlds type of adventure game.

N

NARRATIVE—A narrative is what we commonly refer to as a story, but "narrative" can be a complex critical term about which entire books have been written. Briefly, a narrative is a series of events that are linked together in a number of ways, including cause and effect, time, and place. Something that happens in the first event, causes the action in the second event, and so on usually moving forward in time.

In an interactive narrative, you explore a story. Interactive narratives have beginnings, middles, and ends, even though each user may experience these elements differently. There is nothing unplanned in an interactive narrative. If you play the program long enough, you'll eventually see all the material the writer created. An interactive narrative essentially allows each player to discover the story in a different way.

NAVIGATION FLOW—How the viewer can travel through the information or story and the order in which the information will be presented. This is often demonstrated through flowcharts and diagrams.

NEEDS MEETING—The beginning of creating an online advertisement in which the creative team meets with the client to determine what the client's needs are.

NETSCAPE NAVIGATOR—A web browser. Once the most popular browser, it has since been supplanted by other competitors, such as Internet Explorer.

O

OCR (OPTICAL CHARACTER RECOGNITION)—This software transforms printed text into digitized text that can be edited in any word processor.

ONLINE ADS—A type of interactive advertising or intermercial usually seen only on the World Wide Web. Many of the techniques used in online advertising are also used in other interactive advertising forms.

ONLINE MAGAZINES AND NEWSPAPERS—Newspapers or magazines that are presented over networks such as the web and America Online.

ONLINE PUBLISHING—The presenting of digital material over networks, such as the World Wide Web, as opposed to printing and distributing information on paper.

OPTICAL CHARACTER RECOGNITION—See OCR.

P

PACE—The audience's experience of how quickly a program seems to move. Pace is affected by speed of screen events, length of scenes and shots, the amount of interaction, and other elements.

PARALLEL STRUCTURE—A type of interactive story structure that has several versions of the same story that play parallel to each other. Depending on choices that the player makes in the story, he can move from one path to another. This is a way to give the player an option of multiple paths in a story without the branching explosion of hierarchical branching. When applied to an informational program, this approach creates two or more distinct paths the user can travel through a specific body of information or process.

PATH—This term has several meanings in the computer and multimedia field. One meaning is the text represenation of a file or directory's location within a file system, such as "hard_drive/documents/book_text/glossary.doc". In interactive multimedia, a path also suggests one possible route that a user can take through the information or story in a multimedia or web program.

PDA (Personal Digital Assistant)—A pocket-sized computer that keeps phone numbers, calendar, e-mail, and other computer programs.

PERIPHERAL HARDWARE—External equipment add-ons to a computer, such as scanners, printers, external hard drives, etc.

PERSISTENCE OF VISION—The tendency of the eye to briefly retain an image on the retina after the image has changed or disappeared. Look at a bright light and close your eyes for an example. This tendency is one of the characteristics that helps make possible the illusion of motion pictures, which are actually a series of still images briefly displayed on the screen at twenty-four images a second.

PERSONAL DIGITAL ASSISTANT—See PDA.

PHOTOSHOP—See Image Manipulation Software.

PLATEN—In computing, a flat plate that is sensitive to pressure. Sometimes combined with a stylus and used as a computer input device for graphics.

PLOT POINT—Key plot information that advances the story. For example learning that Bilbo's ring is the "one ring that rules them all" is a key plot point in *The Lord of the Rings*.

PODCAST—A type of web feed of audio files that a user can download and play on their computer or their mobile device, such as an Apple iPod, PSP, etc. Initially used for music, podcasts are now used for a wide variety of content, including radio programs, education, politics, religion, and much more.

POINT OF VIEW (POV)—Defines from whose perspective the story is told. The most common point of view in film and video is third person or omniscient (all knowing). In this case the audience is a fly on the wall and can flit from one location to another, seeing events from many characters' points of view or from the point of view of the writer of the script.

The other major type of point of view is first person or subjective point of view. In this case, the entire story is told from one character's perspective. The audience sees everything through his or her eyes. The user can only experience what the character experiences. This is a common POV in many computer games.

PRESENTATION PROGRAMS—Software programs primarily designed to create digital slide shows for business and educational presentations. The slides can include graphics, text, audio, video, animations, and more. Microsoft PowerPoint dominates this field.

PROBLEM SOLVER—An approach for designing a multimedia informational program by setting up a problem and then asking the user to solve it interactively with the resources provided in the program. Also called Problem/Solution structure.

PRODUCT MANAGER—The member of a software development team who interfaces directly with the client. If the program is aimed at the mass market, she also deals with marketing issues. You'll usually only see this position on very large projects; otherwise the project manager takes on these tasks.

PRODUCTIVITY PROGRAMS—Software dedicated to specific tasks, such as spreadsheets, databases, and word-processing programs.

PROGRAM FLOW—See Navigation Flow.

PROGRAMMER—The computer expert who actually writes the code and/or uses the authoring program to make the dreams of the writer, designer, and other production members become reality on the computer screen.

PROJECT MANAGER—Manages the budget, the personnel on the project, and the overall design and assembly of all the elements. The project manager is similar to the producer in linear production who sees everything through from the beginning to the end.

PROPS—Small objects, such as guns, canes, etc., that a character in a film or video can actually handle. In multimedia, often not only the on-screen characters can handle the props, but the computer users can use the props as well, such as picking up weapons in a computer game with the mouse. Props are a popular interactive device.

PUFF SWITCH—A straw-like device for people without the physical ability to click a mouse. They can blow into the puff switch to make choices on the computer screen.

Q

QUICKTIME—Digital video format dominant on the Macintosh and popular on Windows.

R

RANDOM ACCESS MEMORY (RAM)—The fastest memory in the computer. It is roughly analogous to a person thinking about something. When you perform operations or enter information into a computer, such as typing text or displaying images, that text is initially held in RAM. Information can be accessed very quickly from RAM, and with sufficient RAM multiple complex operations can occur smoothly at the same time.

REAL TIME VIDEO—Playing video or animation as it is transmitted to your computer over a network, as opposed to waiting for it to download to your hard drive and then playing it. Streaming technologies play a video in real time as it reaches your computer.

REPORTER—An approach for designing an informational program. A number of educational programs, allow users to report on their multimedia experience by using a virtual camera and a word processor to write a journal.

RESOLUTION—The final part of a narrative that wraps up the story after the climax. Sometimes the emotional ending of the piece can be included in the resolution. Another meaning of resolution is the clarity of a graphic image.

RESPONSE ATTITUDES—A technique used in interactive dialogue in multimedia programs. With response attitudes, the user clicks an attitude, such as HAPPY, SAD, GRUMPY, and the on-screen character speaks a line of dialogue in keeping with that attitude.

ROLE-PLAYING GAMES (RPG)—A type of computer game that allow the player to take on the role of one or more characters in the game. Usually these games are from first person POV. The player sees what the character sees, performs the character's action, etc.

ROUNDS CREATIVE—Stages of creating an online advertisement.

- First round creative: The first attempt at creating an ad. The ads are posted for feedback from client and in-house team.
- Second round creative: Based on in-house reaction and client comments on the first round creative, a second series of ads are created.
- Third round creative: This is usually the finished product.

RPG—See Role Playing Games.

S

SALIENT VIDEO STILL—A still picture that incorporate all of the key elements of the scene in a sort of collage.

SCANNER—A piece of computer equipment that transforms an analog image or object, such as a photograph or flower, into a digital image. There are also scanners for 3-D objects that create digital 3-D images.

SCENES AND SEQUENCES—A scene is an action that takes place in one location. A sequence is a series of scenes built around one concept or event. In a tightly structured script, each scene has a mini-goal or plot point that sets up and leads us into the next scene, eventually building the sequence. Some scenes and most sequences have a beginning, middle, and end much like the overall script.

SCREEN READERS—Software or computer equipment that read printed and on-screen text out loud as an aid to the visually impaired.

SEQUENCES—See Scenes and Sequences.

SERVER—A computer system that is dedicated to delivering information and providing services to other computers (clients) on a network. There are several types of servers. One type of server is a web server, which delivers information via an online connection over the Internet. Depending on the arrangement, a server may also have the software that the client uses and store the data that the client produces.

SETUP—Another word for exposition, which is establishing the key elements of a narrative including character, time and place, and backstory. Without proper setup, characters are shallow, themes are undefined, and the setting is unclear.

SFX (SOUND EFFECTS)—Any sound other than music or speech used in a media production.

SIMULATION—In a multimedia simulation, an experience or activity is recreated virtually on screen. The activity can be driving a car, flying a plane, snowboarding, or building an entire city. The structure is dictated by the activity.

SINGLE LEVEL BRANCHING OR LINKING—This multimedia structure has no hierarchy to the information. Usually the user is presented with a problem and given a number of possible resources for solving this problem that can be accessed in any order.

SITEMAP—See Map.

SME—See Content Expert.

SOUND EFFECTS—See SFX.

SPREADSHEET—A software program that computes numbers and presents data in charts and graphs. Excel is a popular spreadsheet program.

STORYBOARD—A storyboard is preliminary text and graphics presentation of a multimedia or film program. In a storyboard, images of the main screens of a program are combined with text explanations of the elements and how they will work together.

STRING OF PEARLS STRUCTURE—This type of multimedia structure is a linked series of worlds structures connected by plot points or tasks that the player must accomplish to move forward in the narrative. A worlds structure lets the user explore a location. By itself, a worlds structure cannot form a coherent narrative, but combined with other forms it can.

SUBJECT MATTER EXPERT (SME)—See Content Expert.

SYNCHRONIZED SOUND—Refers to a sound that appears to be produced by the image on screen, such as a person talking on camera. The sound is synchronized or connected to the movement of the image.

T

TARGET AUDIENCE—The specific audience for which a program is designed.

TEACHING—In a teaching program the information is narrowly defined and the writer has a clear goal of what information he/she want the user to take away from the program.

TERABYTE (TB)—See Bytes.

3-DIMENSIONAL OR 3-D SOFTWARE—Creates objects and environments in 3 dimensions: height, depth, and width.

TREATMENT—A preliminary text document used in both multimedia and film/TV. Although there a several variations, a treatment usually describes the proposed program in prose text in a form similar to an essay or short story. Script details, such as dialogue, shot descriptions, and technical directions are usually not included.

TURNAROUND TIME—In multimedia, this usually applies to the amount of time it takes someone to complete a public multimedia program, such as a kiosk. Long turnaround times could mean long lines and frustrated visitors to the museum or other display location.

U

USABILITY—As applied to multimedia and the web, denotes how easy it is for a person to employ or use a web site or multimedia program to accomplish their goals. The usability of interactive media programs are often tested by usability experts working with groups of typical users. Usability experts often have degrees in human-computer interaction.

USER EXPERIENCE—As applied to multimedia and the web, is related to usability (see above), but is a broader term. User experience is the overall level of satisfaction resulting from person's interaction with a web site or multimedia program. Usability is part of this, but it also includes all other elements connected to the program, such as graphic design, quality of the content, and even offline elements, such as call center support for a web site.

V

VARIABLE STATE ENVIRONMENT—The most sophisticated interactive narratives today have moved beyond direct links and simple branching to something that Dave Riordan, the designer of *Voyeur* calls a variable state environment. With the help of software and sophisticated design that responds in a sensitive way to the player's actions, there are multiple outcomes to scenes, depending on where you've been and whom you talk to. In short, the environment responds to the player, much as it does in real life.

A variable state environment can take into account hundreds of actions as opposed to just the A or B choices in branching. And each interaction played differently will get different responses. Different combinations of different interactions will also get different responses.

VIDEO CAPTURE—The process of transforming video from an analog videotape to digital media that can be used by the computer. Special hardware and software are required to do this effectively.

VIDEO DIRECTOR—See Director.

VIDEO GAMES—See Computer Game.

VIDEO SOFTWARE—Software that allows the user to capture, edit, enhance, and manipulate video and audio.

VIRTUAL WORLD PROGRAM—See Worlds Structure.

VOICE—In media, the voice of a program is the type of person who seems to be talking to you through the writing and general presentation. This can be an actual character or just the tone of the content presentation. For example, a web site aimed towards children might have a lively, playful voice where a banking site would be much more serious.

W

WALKTHROUGH—A walkthrough is a description of the story line and key interactive elements in a computer game. A walkthrough is similar to a linear film/TV treatment, which gives the basic story line without extensive dialogue or calling shots.

WEB PAGE—Individual screens of information that are displayed on the World Wide Web. A single web page can have text, images, video, audio, etc. Web pages are usually accessed via a web browser. In actual practice, many web pages are not actually static pages of information, but instead dynamically assembled screens from bits of content residing in databases and other locations. (See Home Page and Web Site.)

WEB SERVER—See Server.

WEB SITE OR WEBSITE—A collection of web pages often built around a certain subject or theme, such as a commercial web site on mutual fund investing. A web site typically shares the same domain. For example, all the InterWrite company web pages are in the InterWrite domain, i.e., http://www.interwrite.com. There are four basic categories of web sites:

- Personal: created by individuals to provide information about themselves or their interests.
- Educational: created by schools, museums, and other educational institutions to provide information.
- Governmental: created by government agencies or elected officials as a service to their constituents.
- Commercial: created by businesses to promote and/or sell their company's products and/or services. This also includes entertainment sites, such as online games, which sell entertainment.

(See Web Page and Commercial Web Sites.)

WIPE—A video transition in which one image appears to push the other image off the screen.

WORKSTATIONS—Powerful computer systems used to perform demanding computer tasks, such as virtual reality, 3-D games, and digital video effects. These systems are much more powerful with better displays than the typical personal computer.

WORLD WIDE WEB—The World Wide Web is a network of computers (servers and clients) all over the world that can present information graphically via the Internet. With a web browser and an Internet connection, users can access text, pictures, video, and sound from web servers and display them on their home or office computer screen. Much of the information on the web is organized on web pages. These pages are interactive. A simple mouse click on a "hot" spot can link a user to a different section of the same document or to another web page continents away.

WORLDS STRUCTURE—This multimedia structure organizes the options available to the viewer not in a linear fashion or in a hierarchy but in a graphic spatial representation. This approach is most useful if there is a large body of information that can be incorporated in a location. It does not have to be a physical location that we normally visit. The museum interactive piece *Into the Cell* allows viewers to take a fantastic voyage into a living cell.

WRITER—See The Multimedia Writer.

Index

LIMITED WARRANTY AND DISCLAIMER OF LIABILITY

Writing for Multimedia and the Web—The CD-ROM

To Start the CD-ROM

1. Launch a web browser
2. Open the CD-ROM on your computer and double click on the file "index.htm."
3. If the file does not lauch, open it from your browser's File/Open File menu.

Case Study Material Supporting Book Chapters

Genre and Title	Scripts & Charts	Images	Demos & Videos	WWW Links *
Web Site *Prudential Verani Realty*	√	√		√
Web Site *T. Rowe Price Web Site*		√		√
Web Feature Story *The Harlem Renaissance*	√	√		√
Museum Kiosk Simulation *The Nauticus Shipbuilding Co.*		√		√
Multimedia Training *Vital Signs*	√	√		√
E-Learning Lessons *Interactive Math & Statistics*	√	√		√
Puzzle Based Mystery Game *Nancy Drew*	√	√	√	√
Story in a Sports Sim *Amped III*	√	√		√
Parallel Stories Narrative *The Pandora Directive*	√	√		√
Worlds Narrative *Dust*	√	√	√	√
The Immersive Experience *New England Econ. Adventure*	√	√		√
Worlds Narrative *Titanic*		√		√

Case Study on CD-ROM Plus Chapters from Previous Books

Genre and Title	Scripts & Charts	Images	Demos & Videos	WWW Links *
Online Advertising *ZDU & Personal View*		√	√	√
Educational Multimedia *Sky High*	Included in Chapter			√
Multiplayer Narrative *Boy Scout Patrol Theater*	√	√		√
Puzzle-Based Game *The 11th Hour*	√	√	√	√
Cinematic Narrative *Voyeur*	√	√		√

Background / Reference

Background	Reference
Playback/Delivery Systems	Glossaries of Media Terms
Production Systems and Software	Writers & Production Companies
Accessible Multimedia & Web Pages	Info. for the Teacher & Student
Multimedia & Web Legal Primer	Links To Writing Related Software

* Links to sites on the World Wide Web can be accessed if the reader has an Internet connection.